KAMIKAZES, CORSAIRS, AND

PICKET SHIPS

KAMIKAZES, CORSAIRS, AND PICKET SHIPS

Okinawa, 1945

ROBIN L. RIELLY

CASEMATE

Philadelphia & Newbury

Published in the United States of America in 2008 by
CASEMATE
1016 Warrior Road, Drexel Hill, PA 19026

and in the United Kingdom by
CASEMATE
17 Cheap Street, Newbury RG20 5DD

ISBN 978-1-932033-86-1

Cataloging-in-publication data is available from the Library of Congress
and the British Library.

Printed and bound in the United States of America.

For a complete list of Casemate titles please contact:

United States of America
Casemate Publishers
Telephone (610) 853-9131, Fax (610) 853-9146
E-mail: casemate@casematepublishing.com
Website www.casematepublishing.com

or

United Kingdom
Casemate-UK
Telephone (01635) 231091, Fax (01635) 41619
E-mail: casemate-uk@casematepublishing.co.uk
Website www.casematepublishing.co.uk

TABLE OF CONTENTS

To Emma Kaitlyn Rielly

Preface and Acknowledgments

My initial interest in the ordeal of the radar picket ships at Okinawa was aroused during previous research on the LCS(L) gunboats in the Pacific theater. Many had served on the radar picket stations at Okinawa; however, the books about the battle for Okinawa hardly mentioned them. I began to realize that no historian had made a complete study of the radar picket ships' ordeal at Okinawa. In the few works that touched upon the subject, destroyers were the focus of attention. With this in mind, I began a study to look further into the events surrounding the radar picket ships' story.

As the project began, I had preconceived notions that the primary focus would be on the activities of the ships assigned to the radar picket stations. It soon became evident that there was another aspect to the ordeal, the flyers of the combat air patrols. At first the easiest and most obvious sources to find were those covering the activities of the navy and marine squadrons. After much research, occasional references to army air force planes began to show up, leading me down new paths. Within the first year of the study, the project had grown to include several classes of ships as well as the activities of navy, marine and army pilots as they worked in conjunction with the ships below them.

Since the fighting around the picket stations involved the kamikazes, it also seemed necessary to briefly describe their activities as well. Much of the informative material came from interrogations conducted by the United States Strategic Bombing Survey, the Far Eastern Bureau of the British Ministry of Information, the Advanced Allied Translator and Interpreter Section, and the Military Intelligence Section of the General Headquarters Far East Command. The *Japanese Monograph* series was quite useful, providing information about various activities. As a result of the ULTRA program, numerous Japanese communications intercepted during the war were translated by American intelligence and are available as *Magic Far East Summaries*. In addition to supplying information about Japanese preparations and military movements, the summaries also helped to pinpoint the locations of various air units. Through these diffuse sources I have been able to write about the kamikaze's activities as they relate to the picket ships.

Throughout the reports generated by American forces, as well as post-World War II literature, the kamikazes have continually been referred to as suicide pilots and I have used "suicide" throughout the text in order to keep some consistency in the writing. I do not, however, believe that this is an accurate descriptor for the actions of the men who flew special attack missions. When faced with the invasion of their country, these men were convinced by a militaristic government that the only way to save their homes and families was to use their aircraft, boats and other weapons in the most effective way, by crashing them into an American ship. Many did not believe their government to be correct in this assertion, but they did what men frequently do in combat, they followed orders and sacrificed themselves for their family, friends and country. This is quite different from committing suicide. I feel it important to make this distinction at the outset since I have, of necessity, quoted many reports describing their activities as suicidal. The Japanese themselves never considered these missions to be suicidal. They viewed the tactic as a special type of weapon borne of necessity. In spite of my disagreement with the term, it has been necessary to use that term continually as all of the official records contain it. Mixing terms would lead to confusion.

In an interview after the war, Lt. Gen. Masakazu Kawabe, who served as commanding general of the General Air Army noted:

> You call our Kamikaze attacks "suicide" attacks. This is a misnomer and we feel very badly about your calling them "suicide" attacks. They were in no sense "suicide." The pilot did not start

out on his mission with the intention of committing suicide. He looked upon himself as a human bomb which would destroy a certain part of the enemy fleet for his country. They considered it a glorious thing, while suicide may not be so glorious.[1]

To which his interrogator, Col. Ramsay D. Potts, replied, "We call it suicide because we cannot find any other word in our vocabulary to describe those certain tactics."

Throughout the text, I have used the Allied code names for Japanese aircraft. The most famous of them was the Mitsubishi A6M5 Zero. However, all action reports filed by ships and aircraft squadrons use the allied code name of Zeke. To avoid confusion, I have used this code name throughout the text. Other aircraft are best known to Western readers by their code names. Japanese names are given in the western style, that is, surname first and family name last. Although it is not Japanese practice, it is more familiar to American readers. Ranks for individuals mentioned are contemporaneous with the event. Throughout the reports utilized in this work, times of the day have all been given in military time, i.e. 0-24 hours. In addition, all times are "Item," which is Greenwich Mean Time minus 9 hours.

American ships have a class designator and hull number after their name. To make the text more readable, I have only included them in the full list of radar picket ships in the appendix. In a few cases I have included them for lesser known types of civilian ships or auxiliaries.

The overwhelming majority of the text is based on original source material, including unit war diaries, action reports, ship logs, interviews, correspondence, interrogations, and official documents. In many cases I have been able to access private diaries kept by men involved in the action as well as those who personally communicated their stories to me. A number of self-published books by participants have also been written, providing the reader with eye-witness accounts of the action.

I have tried to avoid a journalistic style in my writing; however, in order to understand the extent of the carnage on the radar picket stations it was sometimes necessary. Ship action reports do not describe the grisly aftermath of a kamikaze attack. In contrast there were torn limbs, decapitated bodies and terrible burns suffered by the men who experienced the kamikaze's crash. By comparison, aircraft action reports frequently read as though they were written by journalists. In order to keep some semblance of continuity in writing style, I have attempted to bridge the gap between both writing styles in my own prose. In regard to the many quotes from action reports and other primary sources, I have not made any alterations to their text. In many cases the reports are terse, slang ridden, missing words, and not always grammatically correct, having been produced under conditions that might conservatively be described as difficult. The term for unidentified aircraft, "bogeys," is frequently spelled as "bogies" in many of the official reports and the plural for various ships usually is spelled using an apostrophe "s." In order to maintain accuracy, I have not altered the originals even though many are grammatically incorrect. I have also refrained from constantly inserting [sic] to indicate these errors in order to maintain readability. In a few instances it was necessary to insert a word to enhance clarity.

I have organized the text in chronological order and discussed the activities on each radar picket station in turn. The reader will note that there are no entries for some days or for activity at some of the stations. Although the picket ships were on station at all times, in many cases there was little action to report. Simply listing that ships were present did not seem practical. This does not mean, however, that the ships on station during those times had it easy. They suffered from frequent calls to general quarters whenever unidentified planes approached. In many cases they simply fired on an enemy aircraft and drove it away. The discussion of such incidents did not lend great interest, so they are not included.

Historians whose forte is social, political, or economic history sometimes note that military historians seem inordinately fond of describing the hardware used in battle. In a broad sense, the history of war is also a history of technology, and it is difficult not to include the details of various ships, planes and weapons that are an integral part of the story. Technology, as it relates to war, is an important facet of military history and in many cases determines the outcome of a particular battle. Certainly, in the story of the radar picket stations, technological advances in aircraft, aircraft detection and the comparative performance of various aircraft are important to note.

Historians cannot operate alone. They are continually dependent upon the good will and cooperation of others as they search for numerous materials. Accordingly, it is with great appreciation that I must acknowledge the support and assistance of many individuals. During my frequent trips to the National Archives in College Park, Maryland, I have benefited greatly by the expert help given to me by Barry Zerby of the Textual Reference Branch. In many instances, he has helped to locate records of an obscure nature buried within the vast collection housed there. As the reader will observe, I like to use historic photos and maps to illustrate various events whenever possible. While this is most definitely not a pictorial history of the radar picket ships, I believe that the use of photographs is invaluable in helping the reader to better understand the ordeal. In the Photographic Reference Branch of the National Archives, Sharon Cully and Rutha Beamon have been most generous with their help. There were many instances where I felt that a particular illustration would be impossible to find, but their patience in finding the desired photographs always provided positive results.

The staff of the Navy Historical Center in Washington, D.C. has always been helpful in locating various materials in their collection, both textual and photographic. Edward Finney was able to locate a number of photos not in the collection at the National Archives, thereby completing the illustrations. At one point, toward the end of my research, I came to realize that I had managed to obtain virtually every photo for which I had searched. In the Operational Archives Branch of the Navy Historical Center are the collected papers of the National Association of USS LCS(L) 1-130. Many rare photos and personal documents are in the collection and help to bring added detail to some of the actions described herein. At the United States Army Military History Institute at Carlisle Barracks, Pennsylvania, the staff of Dr. Richard Sommers were helpful in searching through various collections for material relating to my subject. The archives of the Tailhook Association in San Diego proved to be of significant value as well. Lieutenant Commander Doug Seigfried directed me to miscellaneous records for the Navy squadrons that I had not seen elsewhere.

In our modern age, the computer has proven to be an invaluable tool for researchers. In addition to providing contact with various libraries and research facilities, it has also made it possible to quickly find veteran's groups with individual members who served on the radar picket ships. Although I have been able to meet with many individually, the number has been increased through the use of e-mail, giving me access to many veterans who might otherwise have been impossible to contact. Numerous veterans of World War II have willingly shared their personal papers, photographs and recollections with me. Their contributions have helped bring life to the text. For their assistance, I am indebted to Robert Augustad, Dr. Donald Ball, John L. Barkley, Raymond Baumler, Earl Blanton, Otis Wayne Bennett, Robert Blyth, Harold H. Burgess, William R. Christman, Frank M. Davis, Sr., Willis A. "Bud" Dworzak, Melvin Fenoglio, David Gauthier, Paul Glasser, John Huber, Curtis Irwin, Lawrence Katz, Harold Kaup, James W. Kelley, Lee Kendall, Doyle Kennedy, Robert W. Landis, Wendell Larson, Stanley E. Logan, Walter Longhurst, Dr.William Mason, Captain Richard M. McCool, Marvin Pederson, Robert F. Rielly, John Rooney, L.R. Russell, Mark Sellis, Tom Spargo, Robert Sprague, Joseph Staigar, Donald H. Sweet, Harold Tolmas, Douglas Towner, Robert H. Tyldesley, Lieutenant Colonel Harry B. Vaughan, Colonel Durwood B. Williams, Colonel David B. Weisman, Gordon H. Wiram, and Dr. Robert Wisner.

Ronald Mackay, a researcher whose field of expertise is the LSM(R) ships, willingly shared his information about these rocket ships which suffered great losses on radar picket duty. Mike Staton, author of *The Fighting Bob A Wartime History of the USS Robley D. Evans (DD-552)*, shared materials and leads on the *Evans* and also on VMF-441, his current research project.

I must thank my friends John Rooney, Clifford Day and my wife Lucille for their help in proofreading the manuscript and making valuable suggestions. In spite of their diligent efforts, the final responsibility for the quality of the manuscript rests with the author.

Robin L. Rielly – April 2008

Introduction:
The Nature
of Radar Picket Duty

The invasion of the island of Okinawa represented the largest amphibious landing in the Pacific theater of operations.

The assault engaged 1,213 U.S. Navy vessels of all types, with an additional 104 in supportive roles. Committed to the battle were a total of 451,866 navy, marine and army personnel. During the assault phase and in the ensuing weeks, the waters around the invasion beaches were covered with ships of all description landing men and supplies, firing on selected targets on the beaches and screening the area against attack from the land, sea and air.

This huge assembly of ships was an irresistible target for the aircraft of the Imperial Japanese Navy Air Force and the Japanese Army Air Force. As the invasion developed, the men, their equipment, and the ships supporting them were ready targets for Japanese planes bent on their destruction.

Okinawa was considered crucial by both sides and would prove to be extremely costly to the Japanese and Americans alike. Located about 350 miles south of Kyushu, the island was in Japan's back yard. Were the Americans to capture Okinawa, Japan would be subject to increased air attacks and the island would be a perfect staging area for the invasion of the Japanese home islands.

To defend Okinawa, the Japanese had eighty thousand troops ashore and the ability to strike the American forces there from bases in Taiwan, Kyushu and some of the islands just to the south of Kyushu, such as Kikaigashima and Tokuno Shima.

Since the distances were not so great and the missions of the kamikazes one- way, the Japanese could use a variety of plane types that might not normally be used for regular combat missions. Pilots who flew these kamikaze missions were usually not well trained. As the last year of war began the crush of time and fuel shortages precluded extended pilot training.

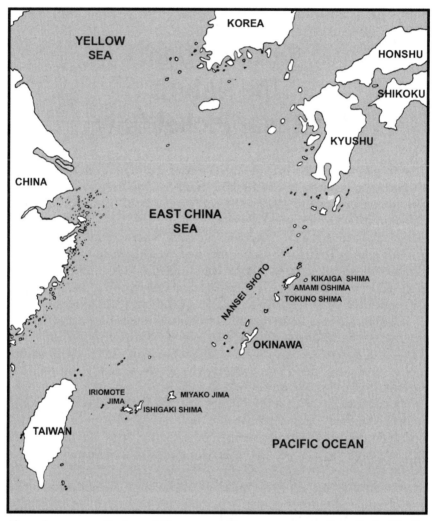

Above is an overall view of the geographic areas surrounding the battle for Okinawa. Japanese aircraft were able to attack American forces from Taiwan and Kyushu as well as a number of islands between them and Okinawa. Adapted from *CINCPAC–CINCPOA Bulletin No. 77-45. Daito Shoto.* 20 March 1945.

The invasion of Okinawa, code named Operation Iceberg, began about 08:32 on 1 April 1945 as American troops landed on the beaches. For several days prior to the landings, the Americans bombarded Okinawa and seized islands of the Kerama Retto group west of the southern coast of Okinawa. On 1 April American forces quickly moved inland and captured the airfields at Kadena and Yontan. Within a few days they were operational and served as bases for marine fighter squadrons. These squadrons were instrumental in defending the ships on the radar picket stations around Okinawa and formed an important part of the combat air patrol.

To protect the troops ashore and their support ships, the planners of Operation Iceberg set up a ring of radar picket stations around Okinawa to give advance notice of air raids headed for the Hagushi beachhead. Low flying planes, in particular, were a serious threat as shipboard radar might not be able to pick them up. Patrolling on each of these stations was a specially equipped destroyer with a fighter director team aboard. Flying overhead was a combat air patrol of American aircraft from the carriers and shore bases which were prepared to intercept the incoming enemy aircraft. As the fighter director team detected aircraft approaching their station, it vectored the combat air patrol toward the Japanese intruders. This coordinated team of ships and planes provided the primary defense for the invasion fleet at Okinawa. If all went according to plan, the enemy aircraft would be shot down before they could inflict damage on the troops and vessels in the landing area. The commander of Task Force 51, Vice Adm. Richmond K. Turner, asserted that "The bulk of the defense of the OKINAWA amphibious operation evolved around the raid reporting and fighter direction exercised by the exposed Fighter Director ships and their supporting elements in the Radar Picket Stations."[1]

A study of any subject must have limits. The author's goal is not to cover the actions of every ship at Okinawa that encountered kamikazes. The ships on the radar picket stations were not the only ships involved in protecting the Okinawa area. Various other screens were set up around the Hagushi anchorage and other critical areas to patrol against submarines and aircraft and to protect various task forces and task groups. They all used radar or sonar to detect the approach of the enemy. While many of these screens suffered from the kamikaze's attacks, they are not included in this work. Of necessity, I have had to limit the ships covered herein to those on the actual designated radar picket stations. These numbered 206 ships and their tale alone takes much telling.

Radar picket ships had been used before, but in a different way. In the earlier stages of the war, single picket ships had been stationed at a distance from the main force. Their primary mission was to detect Japanese surface and air units. After the campaign for the Philippines, it became increasingly evident that the threat from Japanese warships had diminished considerably. However, another peril had arisen; Japan's newly developed Special Attack Corps sent its pilots to crash their planes into American ships. Since the ships on the radar picket stations might be the first that the kamikazes encountered, they were in grave danger. This meant that the picket destroyer needed additional support in the form of other destroyers or gunboats. The commanding officer of the destroyer *Dyson*, Comdr. L.E. Ruff, explained the rationale for using additional ships on the picket station:

> The picket of old – the "lonely sentinel" who frequently took station just within range of high frequency voice communication with the mother force - enjoyed a certain security which the present picket does not enjoy. If this picket ship encountered a strong enemy surface force, he was expected to report and then retire to the shelter of the heavier ships. Any enemy aircraft which he detected was probably more interested in sinking a carrier, battleship, or cruiser than in chalking up "a light naval unit."
>
> The Kamikaze Corps made its entry with much the same thought in mind - to attack the heavy ship. The suicide boys soon discovered that while they might bruise one of the heavies they could, with the same expenditures of material and personnel, sink a light vessel. Destroyers and lighter units became the chief "pieces de resistance."
>
> Under coordinated suicide attack the single picket was a very vulnerable target. Planes attacking simultaneously from different bearings compelled the control officer to divide his battery, shifting some guns to the Mark 51 director with the consequent reduction of accuracy. It was most evident that the radar picket required additional vessels to support his station. Supporting ships were added until the station reached the present strength.[2]

For most of the period that the radar picket stations were patrolled, from one to three additional destroyer types and several smaller support ships covered each station. The majority of the ships consisted of eighty-eight Landing Craft Support (Large) (Mark 3) ships or LCS(L)s and eighty-six Destroyers (DD). Other ships assigned to the duty included nine Light Mine Layers (DM), six High Speed Minesweepers (DMS), eleven Landing Ships Medium (Rockets) (LSM(R)s), four Patrol Motor Gunboats (PGMs) and two Destroyer Escorts (DEs). Some of them were better equipped for the support role than others, and those that were not paid a heavy price. In all, 206 ships and more than 36,000 men served on the designated radar picket stations ringing the island.

Although the original plan called for a total of fifteen radar picket stations, a sixteenth was soon added with additional intermediate stations created as the situation demanded. Thus, Radar Picket Stations 15A and 16A were also included on later maps. Although fifteen stations were shown on early maps, the addition of a sixteenth along with "A" variations on some others meant that by the end of the war there were actually twenty-one locations where the ships might have been assigned to patrol. The radius of the hub was located at Point Bolo (Zampa Misaki). This point of land was just north of the invasion beaches at Hagushi and the airfields at Kadena and Yontan. In his *Operation Order of 16 March 1945*, Vice Admiral Turner indicated that he had originally planned to use Radar Picket Stations # 1, 2, 3, 4, 10, and 14, but by the time of the invasion this had been changed.[3] As the campaign developed and the Japanese became familiar with their locations, some flexibility was needed. Ships frequently occupied day and night stations with the positions of some stations, such as # 3, 5, and 9, shifted at night to confuse the Japanese. As losses began to mount, the actual locations of the day stations were eventually moved as well. During the operation, the locations of RP Stations # 9 and 15 were adjusted for greater safety and efficiency in detecting incoming raids and became 9A and 15A respectively. Radar Picket Stations # 11 and 16 were changed to 11A and 16A. Radar Picket Stations # 6, 8, and 13 were not used at all.

Radar Picket Station # 11, situated twenty-one miles to the west of Point Bolo, was the closest and RP Station # 8, ninety-five and one-half miles to the southwest, was the farthest. The average distance from Point Bolo to a radar picket station was fifty-two and one-half miles. Most crucial were RP Stations 1, 2, 3, and 4 as they were to the north of the island and stood directly in the path of planes coming from Japan. Of these, the most dangerous was RP Station # 1. Eighteen of the sixty ships sunk or damaged on radar picket duty were hit while patrolling this station.

Although the original plans called for the occupation of RP Stations # 1, 2, 3, 4, 10, and 14, as the campaign developed RP Stations # 7 and 12 were filled as well. These were the active posts from 24 March until mid-May 1945. In time, concern was raised over increasing attacks from Taiwan and on 1 May RP Station # 9, which had been used briefly at the end of March, was put back into use.

During the invasion of Iheya Shima, from 3 June to 7 June, a special radar picket station was set up just to the north of the island to protect the invasion forces. On my chart I have designated this as Radar Picket Station "S," since no number was assigned to it.

Radar picket stations surrounding the island were a necessity, since some of the outlying islands that might be good sites for radar installations were in enemy hands. The desirability of having radar installations on shore was great, particularly since the radar picket ships began to take a severe beating from Japanese air attacks. Vice Admiral Turner reported:

> Due to the severity of the radar picket losses CTF 51 requested that the planned radar installations at HEDO-MIS-AKI, on the northern tip of Okinawa, and an installation at BISE on the tip of the MOTOBU Peninsula be established on a high priority basis. Although these points were under Marine control by 13 April, the site at HEDO-MISAKI was not operational until 21 April, and four additional days were required to establish satisfactory communications. The emergency station at BISE was not established. With the capture of IE SHIMA an SCR-527 Radar and an SCR-602 Radar were set up and in operation by 23 April.[4]

By mid-May 1945, some of the eastern islands and Tori Shima had been occupied and new radar installations had been established that relieved the radar picket ships of some of their duties. As a result, the ships no longer had eight stations to patrol, the number was reduced to five. Some of the stations were only patrolled at night.

Radar Picket Stations and Dates of Operation
24 March–13 August 1945

Radar Picket Station	Dates of Operation
1	1 April – 6 May (night station for RP # 15, June – 17 July)
2	1 April – 6 May
3	1 April – 6 May
4	1 April – 4 May
5	24 March, 28 March, 6 May – 23 June
6	*
7	1 April – 21 May
8	*
9	24, 26, 28-31 March – 1 April, 29 April – 1 July
9A	2 -19 July, 21 July – 1 August, 3 – 13 August
10	1 April – 6 May
11	Used as a night station for RP # 11A, 2 –16 June
11A	21 May – 16 June
12	1 April – 6 May
13	*
14	1 April – 6 May
15	1 April, 6 May – 21 May
15A	21 May – 17 July
16	6 – 8 May
16A	9 May – 1 July
S	3 June – 7 June

* These stations were not put into use during the campaign for Okinawa.

One of the controversies surrounding the ordeal of the radar picket ships was the failure on the part of Iceberg's planners to consider the capture of outlying islands first, which could have served as ideal radar posts thus eliminating the need for ships to patrol on the radar picket stations. This would have been a relatively simple matter as some of the most important islands were eventually taken with no opposition. Radar set up on Tori Shima, occupied on 12 May with no opposition, could have covered the area patrolled by ships on RP Station # 10. Radar was eventually installed on Aguni Shima, captured on 9 June and nearby Kume Jima on 26 June. Both were captured without opposition and could have eased the burden of the radar picket ships at RP Stations # 9 and 11A. Iheya Jima, also undefended, was taken on 2 June. Radar there would have significantly eased the plight of the ships at RP Stations # 1, 2, and 3. One can only speculate as to why the capture of these islands was not accomplished earlier.

Some of the stations were close to islands which the Japanese planes used to cover their approach. Lieutenant Comdr. J.F. Miller, commanding officer of the destroyer *Pritchett*, noted: "Radar Picket station #11A is considered by this command to have been very poorly located. The SC-2 radar scope was so thoroughly blocked by land echoes that it was of little use either in fighter direction or in early warning of approaching raids. It was felt that when on that station the safety of the ship and the mission was at a low ebb."[5] A change to RP # 3 was recommended by Comdr. R.D. Fusselman, commanding officer of the destroyer *Wadsworth*. He recommended shifting the station ten miles to the east since nearby land also interfered with radar.

Initially, the plan was to have the destroyer types directly on the station with the support gunboats between stations. This requirement led to some problems as the campaign developed. Support gunboats stationed that far from the fighter director destroyer were at too great a distance to lend their firepower in case of attack. This quickly became evident during the first of the *Kikusui* attacks in early April 1945. Commander Ruff noted that: "A divergent policy of a few OTCs [Officer in Tactical Command] would place the fire support craft 5 miles from the destroyer body at all times, thus relegating the LCS group to the role of medical assistants and fire fighters."[6]

The early stages of the radar picket operation were problematic, with only one to three ships assigned to an RP station. Usually there was one destroyer type (DD, DM, or DMS) with two LCS(L) gunboats acting as support vessels. Ideally, the gunboats were supposed to add their firepower to that of the destroyer in an attempt to intercept incoming aircraft. However, the area to be covered was so great that they might be stationed miles apart and only occasionally be able to support each other. By 10 April 1945, more ships became available and one or two destroyers and two to four of the LCS(L) gunboats were on each station. At times they were also supplemented by LSM(R)s and PGMs. By 19 May 1945, more ships had arrived from the states and other areas of the Pacific theater and on each radar picket station there were usually three of the destroyer types and four of the LCS(L) gunboats.

In order to have the most effective reporting of incoming raids, specially equipped destroyer types were used. At the beginning, nineteen were designated as fighter director ships and had fighter director teams with supporting radio and radar equipment. This enabled them to identify incoming raids and vector combat air patrol fighters to intercept the planes.

Unidentified aircraft approaching the ships were referred to as bogeys. Once a positive identification became possible, the bogey was identified as either a friendly or a bandit. Bandits came under immediate attack and, on occasion, friendly's were fired upon before they were identified as such.

As the operation progressed, and ships were hit by kamikazes and put out of action, their fighter director teams were transferred to other destroyer types. Some of these were also sunk or damaged but by 17 May 1945 the number of manned radar picket stations was reduced from eight to five. By the end of July and the beginning of August 1945, American land forces had captured many outlying islands and established radar installations. Only two of the radar picket stations were in use at that time.

The danger to ships from Japanese aircraft was terrible, but fatigue and frayed nerves took their toll as well. One of the many problems plaguing the picket ships was the lack of rest resulting from constantly being called to general quarters with unidentified planes approaching the station. It was not unusual for tired and jumpy gunners on the ships to open fire on friendly aircraft.

Charles Thomas, a crewman on the *LCS(L) 35*, wrote:

> After the stresses of the invasion and ten days on the picket
> line, our capacity to endure is waning. Our nerves are at a
> breaking point. Close friends snarl at one another. I went below
> this morning to get something from my locker. As I opened my
> locker door, someone working on one of the guns dropped a
> heavy wrench on the steel deck above. I jumped like I had been
> jolted with high voltage electricity.[7]

Pilots assigned to fly combat air patrol missions above the
radar picket stations were well aware of the situation below.
Hellcat pilot James W. Vernon later wrote that the VF-87 planes
"stayed out of range of their hair-trigger gun crews."[8]

The campaign for Okinawa officially ended on 21 June 1945,
however, ships continued to patrol the remaining radar picket stations until 13 August 1945 with resultant casualties. Totals for the
ten *Kikusui* raids between 6 April and 22 June 1945 were 1,465
suicide aircraft, with numerous other planes flying conventional
missions and serving as escorts for the kamikazes. Still other raids
occurred before and after the period 6 April to 22 June 1945. In all,
the United States Strategic Bombing Survey estimated that
"approximately 4,000 Japanese planes were destroyed in combat,
of which 1,900 were suicide planes. . . . of 28 ships sunk by air
attack, 26 were by Kamikaze planes; of 225 damaged by air attack,
164 were by this means."[9] Of the numbers cited above, fifteen of the
ships were sunk on radar picket duty and forty-five damaged.[10]
These figures alone would be indicative of the danger inherent in
the duty, however, when one considers that a total of 206 ships
served on the radar picket stations, it means that radar picket
ships endured a 29 percent casualty rate. Others suffered on the
radar picket stations as well. The pilots who flew combat air patrol
missions and the radar picket patrols whose mission it was to protect the picket ships were also at great risk. Numerous fatalities
and plane losses occurred on this duty as well.

Why were the losses on the radar picket stations so great? A
superficial analysis of the radar pickets' ordeal would seem to indicate that kamikaze aircraft were simply difficult to stop. No matter what happened, the kamikazes were bound to take their toll. To
a certain extent this is true, however, other factors came into play

as well. Among them were the improper use of the support gun-boats, failure to establish land-based radar at the earliest possible time, assignment of ships ill-suited to the task, and crew fatigue.

Kamikaze attacks, rather than being fanatical missions launched by madmen, were actually the only possibility for the Japanese to prevent the invasion of their homeland. They were the only rational means by which it could be demonstrated to the Americans that an invasion of Japan would be too costly. As a result, the Japanese committed a large percentage of their aircraft and available pilots to the one-way missions. Kamikaze numbers far in excess of those encountered in the Philippines' campaign rendered the planning for Operation Iceberg's air defenses insufficient. Support gunboats, conceived as an added protection for the fighter director destroyers were, in many cases, not used to their full advantage. Among the ships assigned to the duty were the LSM(R)s. As specialty ships designed to attack shore targets, they lacked the best armament for fighting aircraft. In addition, they were large and slow. Fatigue also played a role in the losses. Officers and men, worn out by continual calls to general quarters and constantly on alert, were probably not capable of making the best tactical decisions.

What was the experience of men assigned to the ships and how did the action unfold? The following is an attempt to put together the story of the ships and planes of the navy, marines and army air force and the men who drew, what may arguably be described as, one of the most hazardous naval duties of World War II.

CHAPTER 1

Tin Cans and Gunboats

Assigning ships to picket duty was not a new concept in the United States Navy. Such assignments were a regular part of any major operation and usually involved stationing pickets at some distance from the main unit to warn of approaching enemy air or sea forces. This had been a standard practice in the Pacific for some time. The increasing availability of destroyers made their use by fast carrier task groups possible. Destroyers were particularly useful at night for early warning of enemy aircraft and ships. What differed at Okinawa was the close proximity to the home islands of Japan and the magnitude of the forces involved in the invasion. The vast numbers of ships and troops required more than a few single pickets, and the previous experiences in the Philippines' campaign had alerted the Navy leadership to the probability of more intense kamikaze attacks. Special, more extensive, picket coverage was needed for the invasion of Okinawa.

The ships that manned the radar picket stations at Okinawa were under the command of Capt. Frederick Moosbrugger, who served as the commander of Task Group 51.5. At the beginning of Operation Iceberg, Moosbrugger was the Amphibious Force Area Screen Commander (CTU 51.1.13). His unit was assigned to screen the Western Islands Attack Force as it made its way from Leyte to Kerama Retto. On 1 April 1945, as the invasion of Okinawa proper began, his unit became Task Group 51.5 and was responsible for the radar picket destroyers and their support ships, as well as the maintenance and control of the anti-submarine and anti-aircraft screen around Okinawa.

Other tasks that fell under his direction were the screens that intercepted suicide boats and other small craft, local hunter-killer

Captain Frederick Moosbrugger. *NARA 38 MCN 377.*

groups, the escorting of various elements of the seaborne forces, and rescue missions. In this capacity, he reported directly to Vice Adm. Richmond Kelley Turner (CTF 51) who was headquartered on *Eldorado AGC 11.* For most of the campaign, *Eldorado* was anchored in the Hagushi area and had overall control of the fighter direction at Okinawa. Moosbrugger made his headquarters aboard the amphibious assault ship *Biscayne AGC 18*. *Biscayne* would spend much of her time anchored in the Hagushi area near *Eldorado* directing the various screens under Moosbrugger's command. From 29 May through 11 June 1945, Moosbrugger temporarily shifted his command to *Panamint AGC 13*, since Rear Adm. L.F. Reifsnider needed *Biscayne* for the invasions of Iheya Shima and Aguni Shima. On 1 July, Moosbrugger left the ship for a conference in Pearl Harbor and the *Biscayne* departed Okinawa for Leyte.

Coordinating the Combat Air Patrols

Operating over Okinawan waters at any given time were aircraft from the various carriers, as well as those from the fields on Okinawa and Ie Shima. Coordinating their efforts was the task of the combat information center on board the *Eldorado*. As the force fighter director ship at Okinawa, the *Eldorado* controlled all defensive air activity. The Fighter Director Officer in the CIC determined the size of the combat air patrols and assigned them to the various radar picket destroyers which controlled them. Each of these radar picket destroyers had a fighter director team aboard.[1]

The CIC on board the *Eldorado* had to coordinate the activities of various CAPs from Task Force 58, Task Group 52.1 and the shore-based aircraft of the Tenth Army Tactical Air Force. Control of these CAP units could be transferred to local fighter director teams, such as those on board the fighter director ship at a radar picket station. Night fighters on combat air patrol first reported in to *Eldorado* and were then assigned a sector. One was usually retained under the control of *Eldorado* and a second placed under the control of *Panamint, Teton AGC 14,* or one of the fighter director destroyers on the radar picket stations. On nights when additional night fighters were aloft, they would be assigned to the *Estes AGC 12* or to one of the fighter director destroyers. Through this process, the activities of the numerous American aircraft flying combat air patrols over the skies at Okinawa were coordinated.

On 17 May 1945, Vice Adm. Harry W. Hill took over command of Task Force 51, relieving Vice Admiral Turner. As a result, *Ancon AGC 4* became the new amphibious force flagship and assumed control over the skies for the remainder of the operation.

Vice Admiral Richmond K. Turner — January 1945. *NARA 80G 302369.*

An Overview of the Picket Ships

In preparation for the task of covering the radar picket stations, special fighter director teams were trained to identify incoming aircraft and work with the combat air patrols. Nineteen ships were outfitted with special equipment to perform the task, each with a fighter director team assigned to them. The ships were the destroyers *Bennett, Bennion, Brown, Bryant, Bush, Cassin Young, Colhoun, Cowell, Gregory, Halligan, Hudson, Luce, Mannert L. Abele, Pritchett, Stanly, Wickes,* and the light mine layers, *Aaron Ward, Robert H. Smith,* and *Shea.* One of the destroyers, *Halligan,* never served on radar picket duty. She struck a mine and sank on 26 March 1945, several days prior to the invasion. Still others made it through invasion day but were sunk or damaged while on RP duty. *Bush, Colhoun, Luce,* and *Mannert L. Abele* all went to the bottom and *Aaron Ward, Bennett, Bryant, Cassin Young, Gregory, Pritchett, Shea,* and *Stanly* were sidelined by kamikazes. Three other fighter director ships, *Bennion, Hudson,* and *Wickes* were also damaged by kamikaze attacks.

Although many ships were put out of action, the need for their services still existed. The fighter director teams from the damaged or sunk destroyers were transferred to a new group of ships and the *Ammen, Bradford, Daly, Douglas H. Fox, Gainard, Hugh W. Hadley, Laffey, Lowry, Jeffers, Macomb, Morrison, Shubrick, Wadsworth,* and *William D. Porter* became fighter director ships. Of this group, *Morrison* was sunk by kamikazes and *Daly, Hugh W. Hadley, Jeffers, Laffey,* and *Macomb* put out of action. *Lowry* and *Wadsworth* also sustained damage in the kamikaze raids but not to the extent that they were unable to continue on duty.

By 16 May 1945, the reduction in the number of radar picket stations made it possible to reduce the number of fighter director ships. On duty at that time were *Ammen, Bennion, Bradford, Cowell, Douglas H. Fox, Gainard, Lowry, Pritchett, Robert H. Smith, Shubrick, Wadsworth,* and *William D. Porter.* Later, still other ships would be equipped for the duty and would include *Anthony, Aulick, Braine, Brown, Cassin Young, Claxton, Dyson, Frank E. Evans, Ingersoll, Irwin, Massey,* and *Preston.*

In the early days of the campaign, the plan was to have the destroyer types directly on the station with the support gunboats positioned between stations. The support ships patrolled approxi-

Ship Types Assigned to Radar Picket Duty

Destroyer Types	Number of Ships	Appx. Number of Men
Benham	2	368
Sims	2	384
Gleaves	3	624
Fletcher	57	15,561
Sumner	22	7,392
DM	9	3,024
DMS	6	1,248
DE	2	426
Support Types		
LSM(R)	11	891
LCS(L)	88	6,248
PGM	4	256
Total for all Ship Types	**206**	***36,422**

* This number is probably on the conservative side as men rotated off ships and were replaced by others. It is based on the recommended number of the crew and officers for each class of ship. (Based on Commander Task Flotilla 5 *Action Report, Capture of Okinawa Gunto 26 March to 21 June 1945.* 20 July 1945, relevant ship logs, and ship action reports).

mately one-third of the way to the next radar picket station, providing for a broad band of coverage. The position of the support ship would be designated as right or left of the line from Point Bolo. Thus, radar picket station assignments were designated as RP Station # 2R or # 2L. Accordingly, RP Station # 2R was located seven miles from the center line of RP Station # 2 in the direction of RP Station # 3. This widespread positioning led to some problems as the mission developed. Support gunboats stationed that far from the fighter director destroyer were at too great a distance to lend their firepower in case of attack. This quickly became evident during the first of the *Kikusui* attacks in early April 1945.

Ships assigned to radar picket duty at Okinawa were primarily destroyer types and LCS(L) gunboats. For limited periods LSM(R)s and PGMs were also used, but their time on station was only a fraction of that served by the destroyers and LCS(L)s. Notwithstanding, their contribution was significant and the price paid by the LSM(R)s was great. Two destroyer escorts were also briefly assigned to the duty.

Ships assigned to the radar picket stations were limited as far as their anti-aircraft capabilities were concerned. Captain Moosbrugger recognized this, but also knew he had little choice in the assignments. According to him,

> The 2200 ton type destroyer or heavy minelayer and a few 2100 ton type were the only light vessels of the area screen which were so equipped, in regards to armament, as to have a reasonable chance to survive repeated suicide air attacks. Many of the 2100 ton type, all DMS (ex-1630 DD'S) and light DD's (1630) lacked the Mark 12 and 22 fire control radars. The DMS had only three 5 inch single mounts and the light DD's were equipped with four 5 inch single mounts. DE types had no modern AA fire control computers and directors. All types were lacking in adequate heavy automatic weapons.[2]

In order to make up for the inadequacies of the destroyer types, Moosbrugger determined that additional ships of other classes might be helpful in lending fire support against Japanese air attacks. None of the support gunboats were particularly well equipped for the task, however, some were better prepared than others. Supporting the fighter director ships on the radar picket stations were Patrol Motor Gunboats (PGM), Landing Ships Medium (Rocket) (LSM(R)s, and Landing Craft Support (Large) (LCS(L))ships. These vessels had been used to support the landings at Okinawa and were primarily designed to attack shore targets; their ability to defend themselves against attacking aircraft was not a primary consideration in their design. As the campaign developed and the fighter director ships became targets, additional destroyer types were added to the mix in an effort to fight off the kamikazes.

Patrol Motor Gunboat *PGM 9. NARA 80RG
19 LCM PGM9.*

While on the radar picket stations, these ships were supposed to have the support of others in their company. This was crucial during the times that kamikazes attacked shipping at Okinawa. However, the ships were frequently alone when traveling to and from their assigned radar picket station.

Patrol Motor Gunboats

Patrol Motor Gunboats (PGM)s were wartime adaptations of steel hulled Patrol Craft (PC). In all, twenty-four of the PCs underwent this conversion. *PGM 9* (ex *PC 1548*) was the prototype and was converted while under construction at Consolidated Ship Building Corporation in New York, NY. Patrol Craft were originally developed for escort duty and antisubmarine warfare, but the PC conversion into PGMs was for a specific purpose. With their speed of twenty-two knots it was thought that they could work successfully with torpedo boats, but this soon proved impracticable, and they were then given a myriad of tasks. In short order, they were assigned to work with mine sweepers and to assist in amphibious assaults. In April of 1945, they were given a new job as support ships on the radar picket stations. Four of the PGMs, the *9, 10, 17,* and *20* were assigned to the duty and served on various radar picket stations between 18 and 27 April 1945 and again from 5 through 21 May 1945.

The 173' PGMs shared the same disadvantage that the LSM(R)s had in their assignment to radar picket duty. Both were ill suited to combat enemy aircraft because of their armament. The PGM mounted a 3"/50 gun forward, a twin 40mm aft and six 20mm guns. Since the director controlled twin 40mm was considered to be the best weapon against the kamikazes, the PGM simply did not have the fire power necessary to protect itself against enemy aircraft. Had more of the ships served on radar picket duty for a lengthier period of time, they might have suffered the same fate as some of the destroyers, LCS(L)s and LSM(R)s. As it was, the four that did serve escaped damage on the radar picket stations.

The Landing Ship Medium (Rockets)

Experience in the Pacific theater of war had demonstrated the importance of close fire support during amphibious assaults. One of the possibilities that proved expedient was the conversion of the Landing Ship Medium into a fire support vessel. The Bureau of Ships began considering the conversion in mid-1944 and by September had determined to modify some of the vessels. LSMs numbered *188* through *199* were adapted to a new role, supplying fire support for amphibious landings. The forward bow doors were eliminated and the new LSM(R) was fitted with multiple rocket launchers and additional guns. The first of the new rocket ships, *LSM(R) 188,* was launched at Charleston Navy Yard, South Carolina. Commissioned on 15 November 1944, she was soon headed to the Pacific.

With their relatively shallow draft of 6' 6" it was expected that the LSM(R)s would be able to get in close to shore and bombard it with rockets. Additional capabilities against onshore targets were provided by their 5"/38 DP gun, as well as their 20mm and 40mm single guns. Since these vessels were conversions they were con-

LSM(R) 196 on the Chesapeake. *NARA 80G 449942.*

sidered to be interim models to be used until a new LSM(R) could be produced.

Their first assignment came during the invasion of Okinawa when they were used in the pre-landing bombardment of the Kerama Retto Islands on 26 March 1945. Two days later, *LSM(R) 188* was hit by a kamikaze and put out of the war. It was a portend of things to come on the radar picket stations, where the remaining eleven LSM(R)s would face the kamikaze threat again.

Although the LSM(R)s were ideally suited for their role as fire support ships, their ability to defend themselves against kamikaze attacks was limited and they suffered greatly on radar picket duty. They were larger targets than the LCS(L) gunboats which accompanied them on the radar picket stations, having a length of 203' 6" and a beam of 34' 6" as compared to the 159' length and 23' beam of the LCS(L). Although the LCS(L) was no speed boat, at a maximum speed of 15.5 knots, it still was faster than the 13 knots of which the LSM(R) was capable. In short, the LSM(R) was a much easier target for a kamikaze attack as evidenced by the fact that of the eleven that served on radar picket duty, three were sunk and one damaged so severely that she could not be repaired during the war. It is possible that kamikaze pilots might have mistaken them for escort carriers at a distance, since they were large and had a conning tower on the side. Their unsuitability led some to question the reason for their assignment to radar picket duty. According to official reports, the main reason for their appearance on the radar picket stations was to tow damaged ships, since the LCS(L)s were too small for the task.

A major deficiency of the LSM(R) was that she lacked the twin or quad mount director controlled 40mm guns that were considered so valuable by the LCS(L)s and the destroyers. It is possible that the LSM(R)s fell victim to a shortage of ordinance that plagued the Navy at that time. Quad and twin mount 40mm guns seemed to be in short supply. In a letter dated 1 December 1944, the Planning Officer of the Navy Yard in Charleston, South Carolina, expressed concerns that the required ordinance for the LSM(R) conversion might not be available in time for their completion. Proposals by ComInCh and by the Bureau of Ships had been modified. Among the proposals for armament on the LSM(R)s were two director controlled twin 40mm mounts and four twin 20mm mounts.[3] This arrangement would have given the ships a better chance of fighting off kamikaze attacks. As produced, the ships only carried two single 40mm and three 20mm singles in addition to their 5"/38 DP gun and rocket launchers. That this combination of guns did little to protect the rocket ships against suicide attacks was well known. In his *Action Report of 6 May 1945*, Lieutenant Allen M. Hirshberg, the commanding officer of *LSM(R) 194*, wrote:

> Armament aboard the USS LSM(R) 194 proved inadequate to protect the ship from a low flying ramming plane. . . .The 5"38 dual purpose gun was unable to score hits because of the evasive action of the plane and the fact that the Mk 51 Mod 3 director was not in working order. The two single mount 40mm guns scored a few hits but failed to effect sufficient damage to destroy the plane. One 20 mm machine gun and one 50 cal. machine gun fired at the plane but also failed to score a sufficient number of hits to destroy the aircraft.[4]

Hirshberg knew his subject only too well. His ship was sunk by a single kamikaze at RP Station # 1 on 4 May. With an estimated forty to fifty planes attacking the station that day, the rocket ship did not stand a chance. Both destroyers on the station were also hit. *Morrison*, was sunk and *Ingraham* was severely damaged and put out of the war. The LCS(L) ships on station, *21*, *23*, and *31* escaped damage. The destroyers' speed and extra armament did not save them but the LCS(L)s small size and heavy fire power helped the gunboats escape harm. Also, the LCS(L)s were not as prized a target as the larger vessels. Larger, slower, and unsuitably gunned, the *LSM(R) 194* did not stand a chance.

Commander Task Force 51 proposed that the use of the support gunboats should be increased, particularly LCS(L)s, LSM(R)s and LCI(M)s. Why he continued to choose the LSM(R)s is confusing in light of the fact that they were the least suited for the duty of any of the ship types assigned. By the time his report was submitted on 25 July 1945, four of the eleven LSM(R)s assigned to radar picket duty had been hit by kamikazes with *LSM(R)s 190*, *194*, and *195* sunk and the *189* damaged.

The Landing Craft Support (Large) (Mark 3)

It quickly became necessary to add fire power to the destroyers on radar picket duty. In addition to other destroyer types, from one to four LCS(L)s usually accompanied them on patrol. The number depended on their availability and the relative danger of the particular station. As the campaign proceeded into mid-April and May 1945, more of the ships became available for support duties and were given the assignment. The original plan was to have them in close proximity to the destroyers so that they might be able to shoot down planes headed for the fighter director ship or other destroyer type.

The LCS(L)(3)s were the most numerous ships on the radar picket stations, with eighty-eight of the gunboats assigned to the hazardous duty. The development of the LCS(L)(3) had been spurred by the difficulties encountered in landing troops during the many island invasions prior to 1944. Naval observers had noted that the fire support given to marines as they landed was insufficient to prevent the Japanese from regaining the initiative and more close in fire support was needed. Early experiments in adding additional guns and rockets to LCI(L) craft and turning them into amphibious gunboats had been successful. Once these new gunboats had demonstrated their capabilities a new version was desired, one that would be built as a fire support craft from the

LCS(L) 71 with a twin 40mm bow gun. This was considered to be the best armament for the gunboats assigned to radar picket duty. Ships with a single 40mm gun mount on the bow were not as well armed. *Official U.S. Navy Photo courtesy of Richard O. Morsch.*

beginning and not converted from a troop carrier. Fortunately, the George Lawley and Sons Shipyard of Neponset, Massachusetts, had already developed plans for what would come to be known as the Landing Craft Support (Large) Mark 3, a heavily armed 159' gunboat that would be used to lead assaults on the Japanese held islands in the Pacific. Production had begun on these new gunboats early in 1944 and the first of them was launched at the Lawley yard on 15 May 1944. They would serve at Iwo Jima, the Philippines, Okinawa and Borneo.

The LCS(L) ships all had the same armament, with the exception of the bow gun. Original design specifications called for a director controlled twin 40mm mount on the bow, giving the gunboat a total of three twin 40mm guns. Thirty of the ships were produced with a single 3"50 gun as the forward mount. These were used in the Philippines and Borneo. Ships destined for Okinawa were supposed to carry twin 40mm guns as the forward mount, however, the shortage of 40mm twins previously mentioned led to many being fitted with an "interim" single 40mm gun in the number one position. This practice continued until December of 1944 when the Lawley yard launched the first ships fitted with twin 40mm guns. The following month, Albina Engine and Machine Works and Commercial Iron Works, the other producers of the LCS(L)s, followed suit. Most of the ships with the new armament were launched from January through March of 1945. Their late launching date meant that they were not included in the invasion plans for Okinawa and many arrived late on the scene in June and July 1945.

Of the eighty-eight LCS(L)(3) ships assigned to radar picket duty off Okinawa, sixty-three were configured with a single 40mm and twenty-five had a twin 40mm gun at the bow. In the assault on Okinawa, the interim fit single 40mm gun did not present any problems in regard to shore bombardment. Once the initial part of the campaign had ended, the LCS(L) ships found themselves heavily engaged in fighting off air attacks, both on the radar picket stations and during screening duties at the anchorage. The deficiencies of the interim mount soon became apparent, and in numerous action reports, the commanding officers of the LCS(L) ships called for the change over to a director controlled twin 40mm gun on the bow. The conversion would not be a problem, as the ships already had the mount and wiring installed for the director. Given the task of intercepting kamikazes, the third twin 40mm would have been preferred by all. In addition to a bow gun, LCS(L)(3) ships mounted two twin 40mm guns, four 20mm guns, ten Mk. 7 rocket launchers and four .50 caliber machine guns.

The effectiveness of the twin 40mm cannot be denied. In his work, *An Analytical History of Kamikaze Attacks Against Ships of the United States Navy During World War II*, Nicolai Timenes, Jr. stated that "A further result of the limited open-fire range was that numerous smaller weapons accounted for a large proportion of the targets killed. One estimate is that 40mm and 20mm accounted for almost 80 percent of the kamikazes shot down by anti-aircraft, and 5-inch for only about 15 percent."[5] Other studies conducted by the Division of Naval Intelligence in May of 1945 showed similar results. They reported that 40mm gunfire had accounted for 50 percent of the shoot downs and 20mm for 27 percent. Five-inch guns accounted for only 20 percent.[6]

Gunboat crews were justifiably proud of their ships and the fact that they usually led the assault. Vice Adm. Richmond K. Turner, Commander Task Force 51, in a congratulatory message on 29 May 1945, referred to them as the "Mighty Midgets" and the name stuck. In the aftermath of an attack they assisted in putting out fires on the destroyers and in rescuing survivors. When the *Morrison* and *LSM(R) 194* went down on RP Station # 1 on 4 May, the *LCS(L) 21* rescued a total of 236 survivors, cramming every space on the vessel. Since the ships were only 159 feet long with a twenty-three foot beam and carried a normal complement of seventy-one, including officers, this feat is mind-boggling.

In his *Report on the Okinawa Gunto Operation from 17 February to 17 May, 1945*, Vice Adm. Richmond K. Turner wrote "The gunboat types proved valuable additions by their AA armament, and by the fact that they are a difficult target to hit. Of 51 planes destroyed by gunboats, most of them were accounted for while supporting Radar Pickets." Small and heavily gunned, the Mighty Midgets soon proved their worth.

Throughout the time that the ships were on radar picket duty with the destroyers, they shot down many Japanese planes, fought fires on damaged destroyers and rescued numerous survivors. The view of them held by destroyer men, somewhat disdainful at first, quickly turned to admiration.

> Until the attack of 12 April, the writer felt that the LCSs assigned to him were wonderful moral support, especially handy to pick up the pieces after that one suicider got through. After the way they took care of a group of VALS on the 12th, the writer would particularly desire to have them in any kind of engagement."[7]

The effectiveness of the Mighty Midgets was also noted by the enemy. Tokyo Rose called them "miniature destroyers." In the early days of radar picket duty, the destroyer types were the main targets. The LCS(L)s shot down many Japanese planes while suffering only moderate losses. Toward the end of the campaign it became increasingly obvious that the gunboats were being singled out for attack as well.

The Destroyer Types

Destroyer types serving on the radar picket stations played two roles, those which were assigned as fighter director ship and those which were there to support them. At the outset, it might be noted that none of the ships were specially equipped for the assignment as far as their anti-aircraft abilities were concerned. They carried guns and other armament that were designed to allow them maximum flexibility in their various roles during the war. Some of the destroyer types on radar picket duty, such as the *Benham* or *Sims* class destroyers, were not as well equipped to fight off the kamikazes as were those of the *Fletcher* and *Sumner* class. This disparity reflected the rapid changes in destroyers that had taken place in the two decades prior to the war.

At the time of the attack on Pearl Harbor, the United States Navy had a series of destroyers in its fleet, each an improvement over the previous class. Afloat in December 1941 were 423 destroyers representing seventeen classes. The most numerous and latest model of these were the 119 *Fletcher* Type destroyers of 1940. They stood in sharp contrast to *Allen DD 66*, the one 63-68 Type of 1914 destroyer still remaining in service. As the war progressed, newer types were added to the fleet, notably the *Gearing* and *Allen M. Sumner* classes of which there would be a total of 245 by war's end. Eighty-six destroyers served on the radar picket stations at Okinawa. Most of them were *Fletchers*, which totaled fifty-seven. The more modern designs were better equipped for the duty and fared better in difficult situations than their predecessors.

The *Benham* Class

Benham-class destroyers, such as the *Sterrett*, had been designed in the mid-1930s and the twelve ships in the class were commissioned in 1938 and 1939. Test runs of *Benham* had demonstrated her ability to top 40 knots unloaded, and the class was considered an improvement over the preceding designs. Carrying four quad torpedo tubes, the ships were not conceived as anti-aircraft specialists and mounted only two twin 40mm guns. *Sterrett*, aided by two LCS(L)s, was hit while on RP Station # 4 on 9 April 1945 after fighting off several other kamikazes. Although she shot down three

Sterrett DD 407 shown on 13 February 1943. *NARA 80G 276606.*

of her attackers, additional 40mm guns might have saved her. The fourth plane, a Val, crashed her in spite of being hit by 40mm and 20mm fire from the ship. *Sterrett* was refitted with more 40mm guns in July 1945, but never returned to combat.

The *Sims* Class

Sims-class destroyers were very similar to *Benhams*. They were originally designed to mount a fifth 5-inch gun aft, but this was changed in favor of three 40mm single guns. They mounted eight torpedo tubes as compared to the *Benham's* sixteen. With their limited number of twin 40mm guns the *Sims class* destroyers were no better prepared than the *Benhams* for fighting off the massed kamikaze raids. This was noted by the commanding officer of *Mustin*, Lt. Comdr. J.G. Hughes, who reported:

Mustin DD 413 at Pearl Harbor 14 June 1942. *NARA 80G 10124.*

It is believed that the AA gunnery of this vessel is not comparable with that of ships with later installations. This applied particularly to full radar control. Destroyers of this class (SIMS) have had little success in knocking down enemy planes with 5"/38 battery (Mk. 37 director, Mk. I, Mod. O computer, and Mk. 4 radar). With the progress of the war, it becomes apparent that the enemy intends to rely more and more on her aircraft and less and less on her dwindling fleet to oppose our movements. . . .

Removal of the after torpedo mount and installation of a quad 40MM mount would greatly enhance the AA defense of this class destroyer.[8]

The request for additional guns made by commanding officers of this class of destroyers was eventually undertaken. *Mustin* and *Russell* had their torpedo tubes removed and a pair of twin 40mm guns installed. This upgrade took place in August 1945, too late to assist them in the campaign for Okinawa.

The *Livermore* Class

Livermore-class destroyers were the latest design commissioned prior to the American entry into the war. Although their 5-inch

Nicholson DD 442 on 3 December 1943. *NARA 80G 43896.*

dual purpose (DP) guns were occasionally useful in fighting off kamikazes, they were also hindered by having a total of only four 40mm barrels. As Timines has noted, the 40mm guns were the most important piece of armament for shooting down kamikazes and the *Livermores* had only two twin 40mm mounts about a third of the way forward from the aft end of the ship. This proved to be a handicap. In *Shubrick's Action Report* of 16 June 1945 her commanding officer, Lt. Comdr. John C. Jolly, reported that "1630 ton destroyers so far seem to be incapable of effectively firing at two different air targets during a night action."[9]

The *Fletcher* Class

Fletcher-class destroyers were the most numerous of the destroyer types serving on radar picket duty. Their four to five 40mm twin mounts gave them an increased ability to fend off kamikaze attacks, but in spite of that, eight of the ten destroyers sunk on radar picket duty were *Fletchers,* and sixteen of the twenty-five hit were also *Fletchers.* This may also be explained by the fact that so many *Fletchers* were involved in patrolling the stations.

Action reports filed by commanding officers of the *Fletcher* class destroyers almost all contain notations commenting on the

Twiggs DD 591 underway on 23 February 1945. *NARA 80G 311490.*

need for additional guns to be used against kamikazes. Since their torpedo tubes were of no use on the radar picket stations, it was thought that replacing them with 40mm guns was the logical change to make. In their place, varying combinations of 40mm and 20mm guns could be installed to combat the anticipated increase in kamikaze and other air attacks. Fifty caliber machine guns were of no interest to them as their range was too limited and they could not stop an attacking suicide plane.

The effectiveness of the ships' guns was, in large part, dependent on the type of radar used to control them. A number of commanding officers recommended that only ships equipped with the Mark 12/22 fire control radar be assigned to the radar picket stations. Many of the ships still used the older Mark 4 equipment which had proven insufficient for the task.

Communications with the combat air patrol were crucial as incoming raids appeared near the RP stations. On each station, only one ship was equipped with a fighter director team that was skilled in vectoring the planes toward the kamikazes. Some destroyer COs saw this as inadequate and one, Commander Madison Hall of *Little*, recommended that all of the RP destroyers on the station have them.

Defending themselves against one or two aircraft bent on crashing them was considered feasible. However, when faced with five or six, it was felt that the *Fletchers* could easily be overwhelmed and destroyer captains felt more comfortable with another destroyer or two on station with them. Still another concern about the *Fletchers* was their ability to maneuver. As with other earlier classes of destroyer, the *Fletchers* had twin screws and a single rudder. This gave the class an excessive turning radius which made it difficult to keep the guns bearing on their targets at all times. Planes capable of rapid maneuvers could minimize their risk as they approached the *Fletchers*. This deficit was addressed in the newer *Sumner* class destroyers which were equipped with twin rudders and had superior maneuvering ability.

The *Allan M. Sumner* Class

Many of the problems noted by commanding officers of earlier destroyer classes had been rectified in the *Sumners*. With their twin rudders, the *Sumners* could turn in a tighter circle than their predecessors and their 40mm armament was superior. Commander Julian Becton, of the *Laffey*, credited the twin rudders with saving his ship from additional damage.[10] They mounted two quad 40mm mounts, as well as two twin 40mms.

Willard Keith DD 775 underway on 8 March 1945. *NARA 80G 310258.*

Even though the number of 40mm barrels on the *Sumners* exceeded those of the other destroyers, their commanding officers still wanted more and also suggested replacing the aft torpedo mount with a quad 40mm mount. Additionally, they felt that 40mm fire power was desirable against enemy aircraft approaching from ahead.

The Light Minelayers (DM)

The light minelayers (DM) serving on radar picket duty were all converted *Sumner* Class destroyers and, as such, shared their anti-aircraft capabilities. But the commanding officers of these vessels also found themselves desiring more firepower to be used against Japanese aircraft.

Harry F. Bauer DM 26 shown underway. *NARA 80G 285987.*

In almost all cases, the recommended replacements of 40mm guns came at the expense of the torpedo tubes.

The High-Speed Minesweepers (DMS)

The high-speed minesweepers serving on the radar picket stations had been converted from *Benson* class destroyers. As a result, they also suffered from a lack of 40mm guns, mounting a total of only two twin 40mms. This was noted by Lt. Comdr. S.E. Woodard:

Ellyson DMS 19 at Boston, 17 December 1944. *NARA 80G 382791.*

The fire power of this class of vessel is considered woefully inadequate, in comparison with others of its size, with only three five inch guns and one twin 40 MM mount to bear on any target. Twenty MM guns are hardly effective, and even their number is small. The 40 MM battery should be doubled, and a fourth gun replaced, sacrificing the magnetic minesweeping equipment, which has not yet been used.[11]

The Destroyer Escorts (DE)

Destroyer escorts such as the *Bowers* were not considered suitable for radar picket duty. As a result, only two served on the radar picket stations and only for a brief period of time. Captain Moosbrugger had considered using more of the destroyer escorts on the picket lines as support ships. However, those available at Okinawa had inadequate anti-aircraft armament. Destroyer escorts with the latest armament, consisting of two 5-inch, ten 40mm and ten 20mm guns were not in the area, otherwise they might have replaced some of the ships assigned to radar picket duty.

Bowers and *Edmonds* were *Buckley*-class destroyer escorts. Armed with one 40mm twin and four 40mm singles, they were no

Bowers DE 637 at NAS Alameda, 5 February 1944.
NARA 80G 216256.

better suited to repel kamikaze attacks than the PGMs that were
sometimes assigned to radar picket duty. They were the only
destroyer escorts so assigned.

Tactics for the Radar Picket Ships

One of the many problems facing the officer in tactical command
(OTC) of the radar picket station was how to determine which of
the possible formations would be most effective in defending
against kamikazes. This might have been less of a problem if the
number of ships on station was consistent and they were all the
same type. However, occupying the RP station might be as few as
one destroyer and one support ship, but at other times there might
be as many as three destroyer types and four support craft
assigned. Frequently the number might even be higher as ships
would report as relief and the ship being relieved might not depart
for several hours. Generally the destroyer types, DD, DM, DMS,
DE, were able to maneuver together. The support gunboats being
of varied types, LCS(L), PGM, LSM(R), found it more challenging
to keep formations intact, particularly when under attack by
enemy aircraft.

How to make use of the support gunboats was another problem that plagued the OTC. It was the practice of the destroyer types to go to high speed and maneuver rapidly, thus hoping to avoid the kamikaze's attack. This required space to move, which frequently placed them at some distance from the gunboats. Most of the support gunboats were LCS(L)s, which were capable of a top speed of about 15 knots, certainly not enough for them to keep up with the destroyers which could easily make twice that speed.

John Rooney, a crewman on the *LCS(L) 82*, interviewed the commanding officer of the *Laffey*, Commander Julian Becton, sometime after the war. The following is an excerpt from that interview:

> I wonder why, when the kamikazes attacked, the destroyers jumped out and went to high speed, leaving the anti-aircraft screen of the LCS's, which couldn't keep up, and it would put the DD's out by themselves taking most of the heat. Why not stay with the AA support?
> "No, the only thing was high speed and maneuvering, and good gunnery. That was the only thing that saved us. You know, when the LAFFEY first got out there . . . the skipper of the CASSIN YOUNG . . . came up on the bridge and called over to me, 'Go as fast as you can, shoot as fast as you can.'"[12]

Speeds of 30 to 35 knots were common when the ships were under attack and it was felt by many destroyer COs that the high speed caused the kamikaze pilots to miss their targets. Some, however, questioned the use of speeds more than 25 knots, claiming that such high speeds were unnecessary. The purpose in using higher speeds was to allow the ship to turn and use its guns to full advantage. Taking an attacking plane on the beam allowed the destroyers to unleash maximum firepower toward the attacker. However, too high a speed might make it difficult for the gunners to follow the targets as the ship might roll excessively. Other destroyer COs saw little relationship between the higher speeds and good defense. *Gregory*, hit on 8 April 1945 at RP Station # 3, was making 25 knots when she was struck by a Sonia. Still another plane missed her when she was at only 20 knots. After she sustained damage from the Sonia, she could only make 10 knots, but two other kamikazes missed her even though she was much slower.

Studies conducted by the Operations Research Group of the U.S. Navy at the end of the war examined the effects of maneuvering as it related to defense against kamikaze attacks. The studies determined that larger ships such as battleships and cruisers could maneuver radically and still remain stable enough so that their gunners could aim effectively. Gunners on the smaller ships, such as the destroyers and LCS(L)s that served on the radar picket stations, would lose the ability to aim and shoot effectively. For the smaller ships it was more effective if they did not maneuver radically. High speed and full rudder were a bad combination for the picket ships.

The same study examined the position of the ship relative to the kamikaze. It was determined that the best method for destroyers was to present their beam to kamikazes attempting a high dive; maximum firepower could be brought to bear and the ship would present a more difficult target. If the kamikaze approached from a low level, presenting the ship's beam would be to the advantage of the plane. In the case of a low level attack it was found that turning the ship to present its bow or stern would minimize the target area. Although the ability to fire on the plane would be diminished, the lesser target area would be more effective. It was recommended that all of the destroyers and smaller ships should turn to present their minimal target to the kamikaze, but not so radically as to throw off the aim of their gunners.[13] The importance of employing these optimum tactics is illustrated by the fact that only 29 percent of attacks on ships using these tactics were successful, and 47 percent of the attacks were successful on ships using other than these tactics.[14]

Every type of ship had an optimum angle for meeting air attacks. LCS(L) ships preferred to head toward the attacking plane. In that position, they presented a smaller target, and if they turned to about 45 degrees to meet the attack, they could fire all of their 40mm guns at the kamikaze. Both 40mms in the bow would face the incoming plane and the aft twin 40mm could swivel around and fire forward as well. The kamikaze pilot would be faced with a narrow target and five or six 40mm barrels firing at him.

Early on, it was determined that ships patrolling in a column would have a difficult time defending themselves from kamikazes attacking from aft, since only the last ship in the column would be able to fire freely. In situations where only two destroyers were on station, they frequently steamed in column and then turned broadside to the target to unleash more firepower. Where three destroyers were present, the preferred formation was triangular or circular in nature.

Tactical Plans for Radar Picket Groups, developed by Commander R.H. Holmes, recommended that the destroyers stay within 1,000-1,500 yards of each other in order to render mutual fire support. Several plans covered various situations. Holmes' plan illustrates some of the considerations necessary to counter different situations.

TACTICAL PLANS FOR RADAR PICKETS
PLAN TWO (Daylight)

1. When the probable direction of attack is uncertain a diamond shaped formation of landing craft support vessels is recommended. The LCS are equally spaced on circle with no ship in the center, but with one designated as guide. This formation would be maneuvered by turn movements to keep attacking aircraft on the beam. At least two and usually three of the LCS should be able to fire without being blocked off.

2. Destroyers steam about 1,000 yards apart in column so that they remain 1,500-3000 yards from the nearest small craft. This spacing is such that the destroyers can take advantage of their speed and have reasonable freedom of movement without too much risk of interference or collision. At the same time they can remain within mutual supporting distance of the support craft. . . .

4. During routine periods this formation can patrol on any convenient courses, small craft at 6 to 10 knots and DDs at 12 to 15 (or faster if desired). A standard patrol plan such as steaming in a square, half an hour on each leg, or on a given course and its reciprocal is generally acceptable. Weather and currents, or conditions for radar navigation will influence the choice of courses to be steered.

5. If only three LCS are present a formation in the shape of an equilateral triangle, each ship 600 yards apart is recommended. The previous paragraphs concerning maneuvers are applicable here also. If only two LCS are on station they should stay in column.[15]

Formations used by the LCS(L) gunboats were determined by the number of ships on patrol. These formations were also used when the support group included PGMs and LSM(R)s. At the beginning of the campaign, when one to two gunboats were available, a column was frequently used with the ships spaced far enough apart to allow turning for maximum firepower. When three or four ships were used, the formations were more definite.

Within a short period of time, the kamikazes determined the angle of attack and direction that seemed most likely to effect a successful crash into an American ship. Planes frequently came in low on the water in order to avoid radar detection. While this made it hard for the destroyers with their air search radar to detect them, the SO2 radar of the LCS(L) could pick them up within twenty miles. It also became apparent that the Japanese liked to attack from astern, thinking that the ships were more vulnerable during that kind of approach.

To counter this type of attack, there were two possible formations utilizing the fire power of four LCS(L)s. One was a diamond formation and the other a box. The diamond formation gave good coverage at all angles, but one ship was always positioned nearer the approaching enemy plane. Spaced at a distance of 500-800 yards, the ships could maneuver radically if needed. Since their primary task was support and defense of the destroyers, this spacing provided maximum coverage for the destroyers when attacked from the bow or stern quarters. The second type of formation used by four LCS(L)s was the box formation. This placed two LCS(L)s at the rear which gave them more fire power to direct against attacks from astern. In this formation, the LCS(L)s were spaced a maximum of 500 yards apart.

It is not clear how the mission of the support gunboats was explained to commanding officers of the destroyers, but many seem to have misunderstood their role. To protect the fighter director ship, other destroyers or destroyer types were assigned for fire support. The gunboats had the same role, i.e., fire support for the fighter director ship. The officer in tactical command (OTC) of the station was free to direct the placement of the ships and the formations, and many did this to their benefit. However, some did not understand how to use the gunboats. Part of the problem lay in the great differences in speed between the destroyer types and the support ships.

Apparently the commanding officers of many destroyers felt that the presence of the smaller, slower ships might hinder their evasive movements when under attack. Not wishing to be in the position of colliding with them, they stationed the gunboats at a distance from the destroyer formation. When the *Luce* was sunk at RP Station # 12 on 4 May 1945, *LCS(L)s 81, 84, 118,* and *LSM(R) 190* were stationed four miles from her and could not lend fire support when she came under attack. The best they could do was to rescue the survivors. The confusion over the role and misuse of the support gunboats was summed up by Lt. P.F. Gilmore, Jr. CO of *LCS(L) 118* in his ship's action report of 8 May 1945:

> It has been the experience of this command having served on Radar Picket duty since 1 April, 1945 to the present and during this period having operated with a minimum of 12 different destroyers that not a single one of them to date has taken advantage of the anti-aircraft fire support which can be rendered by a concentration of fire support craft. On one station we patrolled on a North-South course to a maximum of 19 miles from the destroyer O.T.C. Obviously on such a patrol the whole intent of offering close support to the destroyer is defeated. . . .[16]

Effective Use of the Combat Air Patrol

The picket stations had two important functions. The first was to warn American forces of the approach of enemy aircraft. The second was to direct the combat air patrol to them so that the enemy planes could be shot down. In general two planes, designated as the Radar Picket Patrol (RPP), were kept directly over the ships to provide protection. In the later stages of the Okinawa campaign the number of planes was sometimes increased. Flying near the station at various locations were divisions of CAP fighters ready to intercept the Japanese planes.

Studies by the Operations Research Group suggested that it was far preferable to station the CAP as far as possible from the picket station. This would allow them to intercept the incoming raid at a greater distance. In this manner, the raid could be scattered and the CAP would have more time to shoot them down before they could approach the ships. Scattering the enemy planes would also separate many of them from their leader, making it difficult for them to complete their mission. In the case of kamikaze attacks at Okinawa, this scattering technique was a very important factor. Kamikaze pilots usually had minimal training and were highly dependent on guide planes to get them to their target.

If only one CAP unit were present, it would be best to have it directly over the picket ships. When two CAP units were present, they should patrol on either side of the picket station at a distance of about twenty miles. Greater numbers of CAP units could patrol a radius of twenty-five to thirty-five miles from the ships. This was roughly about half the distance at which incoming aircraft could be detected. The CAP could then be vectored toward the enemy planes and would meet them at the maximum practicable distance of about forty-five miles from the ships, giving them the most time to shoot them down.[17] In practice, the CAP at Okinawa was not always stationed at the best possible location, leading to some disasters on the RP stations.

Friendly Fire

Combat air patrol pilots faced a number of hazards while flying near the radar picket stations, including being fired upon by the ships with which they worked. Part of the problem came from planes that were not a part of the CAP but which passed near the stations without showing proper identification. This became a great problem for many of the weary crews as they were called to battle stations continually, only to find that the reported bogey was an American plane. The destroyer *Caperton* reported:

> It is recommended that additional effort be made to insure that patrol planes do not leave base before a more thorough check of IFF gear is made by having plane orbit base and checked out before being allowed to proceed. This ship was constantly and continually called to battle stations by PBM and TBM patrol planes giving "Bogey indications." In addition to loss of efficiency in fighter direction, the few hours of much needed and essential rest available to the crew were drastically reduced. Peter "Bogey" Mikes [PBM Mariner] and Tare "Bogey" Mikes [TBM Avenger] ranked next after Kamikazes in popularity aboard ship.[18]

Misidentification was not always the fault of the pilots. Many, returning from missions against the enemy, had sustained damage to their aircraft and their IFF equipment and were incapable of identifying themselves to the pickets.

Marine and navy pilots were more familiar with the tactics of the ships, as they had worked with them many times. For army air force pilots, orbiting over navy ships was a new experience. Pilots frequently followed kamikazes as they approached the station and, in some cases, got too close and were hit by friendly fire. Many braved this ordeal, some escaped unscathed but others were shot down by the ships they were trying to protect. Numerous destroyer COs praised the flyers for their courageous attempts to thwart the kamikaze attacks. Unfortunately for the flyers, it was not always possible for the ships to avoid hitting friendly aircraft. Commanding officers had the responsibility of hundreds of crew men and the ship to consider. If they waited too long to identify a plane it might be too late. Far too many ships had been hit by kamikazes with great loss of men and ships to allow this possibility.

Tactics Against Kamikazes

Individual ship's commanding officers all had their own ideas on how best to combat the kamikaze threat. They realized the hazards of firing on the planes at night. Muzzle flashes and tracers could easily be seen by the enemy planes and would give away the location of the ships below. A steady stream of tracers could be followed right into the ship and most COs required that their gunners fire in short bursts. Many felt that it was better not to fire on an enemy plane if it had not spotted them.

It may seem as though the mission of the radar picket ships was to shoot down enemy aircraft, since they did that in great numbers. It was not. The mission was to direct the American aircraft on combat air patrol to intercept enemy aircraft. Therefore, firing at night or otherwise calling attention to the picket ships on station defeated the purpose.

Ships moving at slow speeds reduced their wake and made it more difficult for the enemy planes to spot them. Lieutenant G.W. Mefferd, CO of *LCS(L) 114,* related: "The Marine pilot we picked up said that it was impossible to see our ships from 5000 feet when we were not leaving a wake. He said the camouflage was very effective and it was only by picking up the ship's wake that he knew we were down below."[19]

The angle at which enemy planes tried to crash the ships was also a factor to consider. Planes coming in low on the water were the most difficult to evade. Planes diving on the ships from an angle of 30 to 45 degrees could be evaded by rapid maneuvers. A large volume of fire could also break the concentration of the pilot and, if his plane were equipped with guns, likely make it difficult for him to strafe on the way in.

Commanding officers also agreed on the advantages of mutual fire support. When ships became isolated, they were sitting ducks. Only by staying together in a formation and maneuvering together could the ships hope to shoot down kamikazes by using their combined firepower.

Still another problem faced the commanding officers of the ships. During the kamikaze attacks, many men were topside and could witness the incoming raids. On an LCS(L), for instance, only about fifteen of the seventy-one man crew was below and isolated from the incoming terror.

This led to many problems as men occasionally broke down psychologically as a result of long spells on duty or at battle stations, coupled with the raw nerves caused by knowledge that their ship might be hit. Some, when faced by a kamikaze flying directly toward them, abandoned their guns and went overboard to avoid the crash. This gave the ship little chance to avoid the plane. If men stayed at the guns and continued their fire, the plane might be hit, disintegrate and lessen the impact. In such a manner, many brave men died at their guns.

The terrible toll suffered by the radar picket ships might lead one to believe that their ordeal was in vain. However, it must be realized that while the losses on the picket stations were great, the losses to the invasion fleet and troops ashore would have been far greater had the radar picket stations not been manned. Countless raids, aimed at the American forces on Okinawa, were either stopped cold or diminished in their effectiveness by the radar picket ships and their accompanying combat air patrols. Vice Admiral Richmond K. Turner reported:

The picket system operated efficiently. While eight and nine picket stations were filled, raids were detected at an average distance of 72 miles from the reference point at PT. BOLO, which was a few miles North of the main transport area and close to KADENA and YONTAN airfields. Only seven percent of all raids approached within 50 miles of PT. BOLO undetected; less than one percent approached within thirty miles undetected.[20]

One might expect that the complexity of the campaign and the rigors of radar picket duty would make the task of the radar picket ships insurmountable. This was not the case as courageous and innovative commanding officers rose to the challenge, testing out new tactics and formulating methods of thwarting the kamikaze attacks. LCS(L) skippers, normally assigned to supporting amphibious landings and hunting inter-island barge traffic and suicide boats found themselves as support craft in a huge anti-aircraft campaign. They usually took a day or two to get their bearings. After that, they were able to function effectively.

An overview of the Pacific theater of operation leaves one to conclude that radar picket duty at Okinawa was probably the most dangerous naval assignment of the war. In the short space of four and one half months the Navy losses on the radar picket stations from kamikazes and aerial attacks totaled fifteen ships sunk and forty-five damaged.[21] This figure included ten destroyers, two LCS(L)s and three LSM(R)s sunk and twenty-five destroyers, eleven LCS(L)s, three light minelayers, two LSM(R)s and four high-speed minesweepers damaged. Personnel casualties totaled 1,348 dead and 1,586 wounded. If these figures are compared to the overall naval losses from kamikazes and aerial attacks during the Okinawa campaign it becomes obvious that the radar picket ships faced the most hazardous naval duty of the Okinawa campaign. The overall losses at Okinawa included 28 ships sunk by air attack and 225 damaged. Of the 28 ships sunk at Okinawa by Japanese air attacks, more than half went down on the radar picket stations. Added to this figure must be the losses incurred by the marine, navy and army air force squadrons whose pilots lost their lives while flying combat air patrol missions over the picket ships.

Why the radar picket ships took such losses has been the subject of much discussion over the years. Several factors have emerged that help to explain the situation. First of all, in order to get to the ships and troops at Okinawa, the Japanese had to knock out the eyes and ears of the fleet. This meant destroying the Americans' ability to detect incoming enemy aircraft. It became evident that the radar picket ships were targets. Commander R.M. Pitts, CO of the destroyer *Douglas H. Fox*, noted the following: "From the low direct approach of the enemy planes, it is obvious that they knew the exact location of this station [RP # 5] and were on a mission to wipe it out."[22]   This opinion was echoed later by Capt. A.E. Jarrell when he commented on the sinking of the destroyer *Callaghan* at RP Station # 9A on 29 July 1945: "It was clear that the Japs knew where radar picket station nine able was located [by 29 July]. This location already has been changed. It is recommended that it be changed frequently, and that the night station be in a different position from the day station. . . ."[23]

A second factor contributing to the vulnerability of the radar picket ships was the quality of the Japanese pilots themselves. Many of the kamikazes had minimal flight training and could not hope to avoid the more experienced American pilots who frequently outnumbered them. As a result, they picked the nearest targets of opportunity, the destroyers and support ships operating at some distance from the island. The combat air patrols were so well organized and presented such a great obstacle that the picket ships were the only practical targets. Battleships, cruisers and carriers were preferred, but only by great luck could kamikazes hope to sink them. Destroyers, LCS(L)s and LSM(R)s, on the other hand, might be sunk by a well-placed hit, making them ideal targets for the Japanese planes.

The radar picket ordeal at Okinawa benefitted the American forces overall. The picket ships were able to report Japanese air raids at a good distance from the landing beaches and had successfully vectored the combat air patrol to intercept them. In this manner, many attacks on the ships and men at Okinawa had been thwarted and large numbers of enemy planes shot down. However, the knowledge of these accomplishments did little to assuage the sheer terror of the kamikaze attacks.

CHAPTER 2

The Aerial Combatants

The Combat Air Patrol

From the beginning of the Okinawan campaign, it was obvious that the invasion fleet would need protection against Japanese aircraft attacks. To achieve security for the fleet, combat air patrols (CAP) were organized. In the early stages of the operation, until 8 April 1945, this was primarily the function of carrier-borne aircraft. After that date, the duty was shared with marine fighter squadrons operating from Kadena and Yontan airfields and later from Ie Shima. Army air force P-47s arrived on Ie Shima in mid-May and also participated in the combat air patrols. At any given time, particularly during some of the larger *Kikusui* attacks, the sky over the island and its surrounding waters looked like a hornet's nest of American and Japanese aircraft.

To support land-based operations, the Tenth Army Tactical Air Force (TG-99.2) was created. Placed under the command of Maj. Gen. Frances P. Mulcahy (USMC), the TAF eventually grew in size to include fifteen marine fighter squadrons as well as ten from the army air forces. This was in addition to various other air and support units.

Eventually, sixteen army air force bomber squadrons would be added to the Tactical Air Force. An essential section of the TAF, and the one most directly involved in providing combat air patrol cover for the fleet and its radar pickets, was the Air Defense Command (ADC) under Brig. Gen. William J. Wallace (USMC). The Air Defense Command exercised direct control of four marine air groups and the army air force's 301st Fighter Wing, which gave it control of a total of twenty-five fighter squadrons.

Above Left: Brigadier General William J. Wallace, USMC. *NARA 127PX 121489.*

Above Right: Major General Francis P. Mulcahy, USMC. *NARA 127PX A10563.*

Right: Major General Louis E. Woods, USMC. *NARA 127PX A049726.*

Later in the campaign, on 11 June 1945, Mulcahy was replaced by Maj. Gen. Louis E. Woods.

Headquarters for the TAF were established on Okinawa on 2 April 1945, when General Mulcahy selected a location between the two captured airfields at Yontan and Kadena. By 7 April construction of the camp had developed sufficiently for Mulcahy to leave his temporary headquarters on *Eldorado* and set up his permanent headquarters ashore. The Air Defense Command's Control Center was set up in close proximity to Mulcahy's TAF Headquarters. On 7 April 1945, the ADCCC began operations, exercising control over the fighter groups about to arrive at the Yontan and Kadena airfields. The mission assigned to the Air Defense Command was identified in its *Operation Plan:*

> This command will occupy available airdromes as soon as possible after LOVE Day and will furnish aerial defense of the area occupied by our forces by,
> (a) Commanding all fighter aircraft assigned to TAF in execution of all assigned defensive and offensive missions.
> (b) Establishing Air Defense Command and an Air Defense Control Center as soon as possible.
> (c) Assuming control of air defense including AA artillery and searchlights from Commander Air Support Control Units on order.
> (d) Establishing and operating an early air warning net.
> (e) Furnishing direct defense of the area in conjunction with Fleet aircraft present.
> (f) Being prepared from time of initial establishment for emergency assistance to ship borne Air Support Control Units in handling carrier based aircraft forced to land ashore.[1]

Organization of Fighter Units for the Combat Air Patrol

Prior to the assault on Okinawa, it was expected that the Japanese would attack the Americans at Okinawa from their bases in Kyushu and Taiwan. A ring of radar picket stations had been set up around the island specifically for the purpose of intercepting incoming Japanese aircraft. Partnered with the radar picket ships were the fighter aircraft of the marine, navy and army air force fighter squadrons. Each radar picket station would have a fighter director team on a designated ship and would control the combat air patrol that was flying overhead. When the situation was relatively quiet, forty-eight planes might be deployed over the ships in this manner. During the massed raids of the *Kikusui* attacks, as many as 120 or more planes might be assigned to the duty. In addition to the planes stationed on Okinawa and Ie Shima, the fast carriers of TF 58 and the support carriers of TG 52.1 sent their fighters aloft on CAP missions also. Once the marine air groups and army air force groups became firmly established on Okinawa and Ie Shima, the fast carriers of TF 58 moved north to directly attack the kamikaze bases on Kyushu and other places in the Japanese homeland.

As time wore on, it became obvious that the Japanese were zeroing in on the picket ships, making it necessary to increase the size of the combat air patrol. Original plans had the target combat air patrols assigned to various sectors around Okinawa. Five divisions of fighters would patrol to the north of the island and six divisions would cover the ships off the landing beaches at Hagushi. Another division would operate to the south as protection against air attacks from Taiwan. During the first days of the invasion, it was difficult to coordinate the activities of the combat air patrols. After the initial phase of the operation had been completed, CAP coverage became more consistent and the numbers of planes flying protective coverage in various areas increased.

Originally, the target combat air patrols, assigned to particular sectors, had to be spread out to cover the increased attacks on the picket ships. Regular TCAPs of fifty-six to seventy-six aircraft became the norm, with additional planes scrambling off the fields at Kadena and Yontan when needed. In his original plans, Capt. Frederick Moosbrugger, CTG 51.5, requested a special CAP of four to six planes just to protect the picket ships. These radar picket patrol (RPP) planes were to stay with the picket ships during daylight hours and were not vectored to intercept incoming flights. But this number could not be spared for the duty and, at first, only two were assigned to each of three picket stations. These special radar picket patrols began about 14 April 1945 and always consisted of Corsairs from the marine air groups on Okinawa. In time, all the picket stations had special protective RPPs. They proved their worth time and again by saving many picket ships from kamikaze attacks. Of the 17,595 sorties flown by the CAP between 1 April and 17 May 1945, approximately 1,600 were the two-plane special radar picket patrols.[2] Their effectiveness was greatly appreciated by the picket ships. Commander E.S. Miller, commanding officer of the destroyer *Lowry*, noted:

> The tactics employed by the enemy during the latter part of the period covered [30 April-21 June] were such as to make the

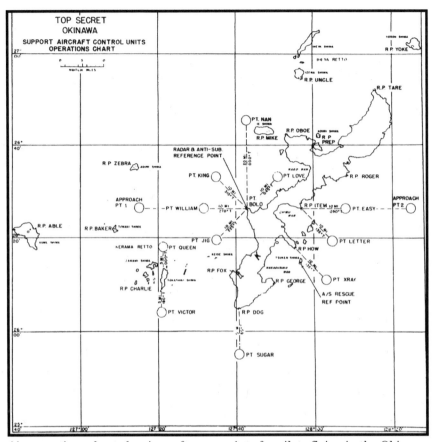

Air operations chart showing reference points for pilots flying in the Okinawa area. *ComPhibsPac Operation Plan No. A1-45* Annex (H), Appendix IV, Enclosure (A).

problem of the intercept officer most difficult. All raids, when intercepted, split. Each unit then pursued its suicidal mission separately by abandoning mutual formation support for the chance of slipping through the combat air patrol at a very low altitude for a final individual suicide run. The low two plane radar picket patrol proved to be a good back stop against this attack and was a splendid morale booster.[3]

Although their performance was exemplary, the two plane RPP was sometimes overwhelmed by the sheer number of kamikaze attacks on some stations.

In addition to regular daytime patrols, a CAP of night fighters was assigned to the picket stations. At the beginning of the campaign, these night fighters flew off the TF 58 carriers and later the carriers of TG 99.2 took over the assignment. Once the island bases were established, the night fighters would come from the marine air groups and army air force squadrons on Okinawa and Ie Shima. Flight times for the regular CAPs and night fighter CAPs would overlap.

The night fighters usually began their patrols about two hours before dark and were up until two hours after daybreak. The regular CAPs took off two hours before sunrise and returned two hours after dark.

Overall, the combat air patrols drew high praise from the picket ships. The destroyer *Ingraham* reported:

> No report on personnel performance would be complete without paying tribute to the magnificent performance of our Combat Air Patrol. Time after time our fighter pilots flew through anti-aircraft fire to make a kill. At times they chased attacking planes almost down to the deck. Their aggressive attacks accounted for many enemy planes that were desperately trying to crash into our ships. The INGRAHAM will never forget the valiant fight by our Corsairs and Hellcats to save the life of the ship.[4]

Many years after the war Don Ball, who served as First Lieutenant on the *LCS(L) 85,* put it succinctly, "I think I'm here because of pilots, they were great."[5]

Perhaps those in the best position to evaluate the performance of the American pilots were the Japanese. According to Comdr. Ryosuke Nomura, "The U.S. Navy pilots were superior in skill and daring to the U.S. Army pilots . . ."[6]

Still another Japanese officer, Capt. Minoru Genda, related that, "In the fighting plane attacks, the American carrier planes were much the best, much bolder and more strongly carried out than other fighters."[7]

Many carriers supplied fighter cover for the picket ships' combat air patrols. The carriers listed below and their squadrons have been mentioned prominently in many ship and aircraft action reports.

Squadron	Plane type	Carrier
VBF-9	F6F-5	*Yorktown CV 10*
VBF-17	F6F-5	*Hornet CV 12*
VC-9	FM-2	*Natoma Bay CVE 62*
VC-13	FM-2	*Anzio CVE 57 (ASW)*
VC-70	FM-2	*Salamaua CVE 96*
VC-71	FM-2	*Manila Bay CVE 61*
VC-83	FM-2	*Sargent Bay CVE 83*
VC-84	FM-2	*Makin Island CVE 93*
VC-85	FM-2	*Lunga Point CVE 94*
VC-87*	FM-2	*Marcus Island CVE 77*
VC-88	FM-2	*Saginaw Bay CVE 82*
VC-90	FM-2	*Steamer Bay CVE 87*
VC-91	FM-2	*Savo Island CVE 78*
VC-92	FM-2	*Tulagi CVE 72 (ASW)*
VC-93	FM-2	*Petroff Bay CVE 80*
VC-94	FM-2	*Shamrock Bay CVE 84*
VC-96	FM-2	*Rudyerd Bay CVE 81*
VC-97	FM-2	*Makassar Strait CVE 91*
VOC-1*	FM-2	*Wake Island CVE 65*
VOC-2	FM-2	*Fanshaw Bay CVE 70*
VF-5	F4U-1D	*Franklin CV 13*
VF-6	F6F-5	*Hancock CV 19*
VF-9	F6F-5	*Yorktown CV 10*
VF-10	F4U-1D	*Intrepid CV 11*
VF-12	F6F-5	*Randolph CV 15*
VF-17	F6F-5	*Hornet CV 12*
VF-23	F6F-5	*Langley CVL 27*
VF-24	F6F-5	*Santee CVE 29*
VF-25	F6F-5	*Chenango CVE 28*
VF-29	F6F-5	*Cabot CVL 28*
VF-30	F6F-5	*Belleau Wood CVL 24*
VF-33	F6F-5E	*Sangamon CVE 26*
VF-40	F6F-5	*Suwannee CVE 27*
VF-45	F6F-5	*San Jacinto CVL 30*
VF-46	F6F-5	*Independence CVL 22*
VF-47	F6F-5	*Bataan CVL 29*
VF-82	F6F-5	*Bennington CV 20*
VF-83	F6F-5	*Essex CV 9*

Squadron	Plane type	Carrier
VF-84	F4U-1D	*Bunker Hill CV 17*
VF-85	F4U-1C	*Shangri-La CVE 38*
VF-86	F6F-5	*Wasp CV 18*
VF-87	F6F-5	*Ticonderoga CV 14*
VF-88	F6F-5	*Yorktown CV 10*
VF(N)-90	F6F-5N	*Enterprise CV 6*
VMF(CV)-112-123	F4U-1D	*Bennington CV 20*
VMF-221	F4U-1D	*Bunker Hill CV 17*
VMF-451	F4U-1D	*Bunker Hill CV 17*

* *Wake Island* was damaged on 3 April 1945 by a kamikaze's near miss. VOC-1 was transferred to *Marcus Island* and VC-87, which had been on *Marcus Island,* was transferred to *Wake Island* which headed for Guam and repairs.

Many of the carrier squadrons listed above flew frequent combat air patrols over and near the picket stations. Some were involved flying CAP nearby and sometimes were engaged over the picket ships although not specifically assigned to them.

The Marine Gun Squadrons Arrive on Okinawa

The assault landings on Okinawa began on 1 April 1945. Situated close inland from the invasion site were two primary objectives, the airfields at Kadena and Yontan. Kadena was only about a mile inland, and Yontan three-quarters of a mile. These were the largest airfields on Okinawa and their capture would deny their use to the enemy, as well as provide a facility for American aircraft to use in the battle for the island. Within the first half of the day, they had been secured. The Japanese strategy of withdrawal from under the guns of American capital ships had made capture of the airfields a relatively easy affair. However, damage to the airfields during the invasion was significant and work had to be done to get them ready for the marine air groups.

Two marine aircraft groups were assigned to the airfields, MAG-31 to Yontan and MAG-33 to Kadena. Immediately following the capture of the two airfields, ground personnel began the task of repairing the airfield's facilities and making them usable for the fighters. Marine Air Group 31 ground crews had arrived on a vari-

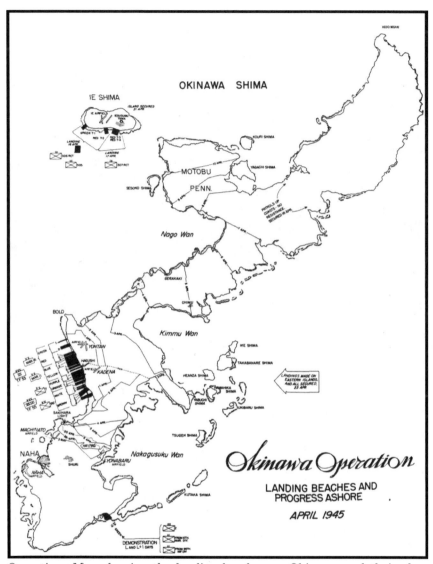

Operations Map showing the landing beaches on Okinawa and their close proximity to the airfields at Kadena and Yontan. *(Opns. In Pacific April, 1945).*

ety of ships, *LSTs 221, 343,* and *781,* along with *Pinckney APH 2, Leo AKA 60, Natrona APA 214* and the merchant ships *SS Whirlwind,* and *SS Afoundria.* After disembarking on 4 April 1945,

This aerial shot of the Hagushi landing area, taken on 3 April 1945, shows the close proximity of Yontan airfield to the water. Smoke from the ships in the anchorage frequently blew inland, making take-offs and landings dangerous. Friendly anti-aircraft fire from the ships sometimes fell on the fields. Kamikazes, attracted by the large number of ships in the harbor, made the area a prime target. *NARA 80G 318530.*

the squadrons' personnel unloaded equipment and supplies from the LSTs and made their way inland to the vicinity of Yontan airfield where they began the work of restoring the airfield. The use of Yontan and Kadena at the earliest possible moment was anticipated by the Japanese who noted that on 4 April 1945 "23 small type enemy planes were seen advancing to the north OKINAWA Airfield [Yontan]."[8]

The task of establishing operating conditions for the airfields was made more difficult by enemy air attacks on 4, 5, and 6 April 1945. Fortunately, the attacks had little effect on the operation as they created no serious damage or loss of personnel. During this period, the aircraft and pilots of the group had embarked on the escort carriers *Breton* and *Sitkoh Bay* at Ulithi. After arriving off the coast of Okinawa the squadrons left the two escort carriers on

7 April 1945, beginning at 1430. Catapulting off *Breton* were thirty-two F4U-4C Corsairs of VMF-224, led by Maj. James W. Poindexter and thirty F4U-4C Corsairs of VMF-311, led by Maj. Samuel Richards, Jr. The thirty-two F4U-1D Corsairs of VMF-441 led by Maj. Robert G. White and the fifteen F6F-5N Hellcats of VMF(N)-542, under Maj. William C. Kellum, were catapulted off *Sitkoh Bay*.

As divisions left the carriers, they flew combat air patrol duty over the ships below. This proved to be a good strategy, as a twin engine Frances bomber attempted a suicide run on *Sitkoh Bay*. Two pilots from VMF-311 spotted the Japanese plane in time and it was shot down within fifty yards of the carrier. The F4U-4C model of the Corsair flown by these pilots had new weapons. Rather than the older armament of six .50 caliber machine guns, these planes were armed with four 20mm cannons, which had more clout. The Frances was one of twelve that had taken off from Miyazaki airfield in Kyushu to attack surface craft in the waters west of Okinawa; only three returned.[9] The Corsairs arrived safely at Yontan late in the afternoon and prepared for their missions. At 0630, the following morning, twelve Corsairs took off on their first combat air patrol.

Marine Corsairs take off from Yontan Airfield, Okinawa at 0630 on 8 April 1945. This was their first combat air patrol at Okinawa. Official USMC Photo by Technical Sergeant Charles V. Corkran. *MAG 31 War Diary 1-30 April 1945.*

April 9, 1945 proved to be a rainy day, but the MAG-31 squadrons were assigned a mission. Adding to the visibility problems caused by the weather was the constant need for patrol ships in the harbor to lay smoke screens in order to protect the anchorage. Since the two airfields were only about a mile from the bay, the smoke blew in and made matters worse. It was the practice of the ships in the anchorage to lay these smoke screens to cover themselves during air attacks. Whenever smoke blanketed the airfields, it was hazardous to take off or land. Colonel J.C. Munn, the commanding officer of Marine Air Group 31, reported that this was the cause of many landing accidents at Yontan. On 9 April while attempting to land under these adverse conditions, three planes crashed on the runway, killing one of the pilots. Still another missed the field completely and landed in the water. Good fortune favored the pilot and he was rescued.

Marine Air Group 33 aircraft, under the command of Col. W.E. Dickey, were delivered to the coastal waters of Okinawa by the escort carriers *Hollandia* and *White Plains* along with their accompanying LSTs and troop transports. Not as fortunate as the MAG-31 squadrons, both VMF(N)-543 and VMF-322 suffered losses before they disembarked. On 2 April 1945 *Achernar AKA 53*, carrying personnel of VMF(N)-543, was struck by a kamikaze. Japanese records indicate that this was the first attack carried out by the Army Special Attack Corps. They had flown from Tokuno Shima with an escort of nine planes from the 66th and 103rd Air Regiments of the Army Third Attack Division.

The special attack planes were piloted by Capt. Minoru Hasegawa and 2nd Lt. Nishi Yamamoto. This group was responsible for the attack on *Achernar* and also attacked other ships at Kerama Retto. On board the *Achernar*, five men were killed and forty-one wounded. Five of the wounded were from VMF(N)-543. A day later *LST 599* was also hit. While anchored off Kerama Retto, she was crashed by a bomb-carrying Tony from the 105th Air Regiment out of Matsuyama Air Base on Taiwan. The 105th had sent out eight Tony special attack planes with five more Tonys as escorts for the kamikazes. On board the LST were the officers and men of VMF-322, seven of whom were wounded by the suicide crash. Damage to the ship was so severe that all the squadron's equipment was lost and the ship put out of action for the duration of the war.

Corsairs from MAG-33 prepare to catapult off *Breton CVE 23* on 7 April 1945. The Corsair on the catapult is from VMF-224, as are the other 200 series planes. The plane on the left, number 327, is from VMF-311. *NARA 80G 265892.*

On 9 April 1945, the F4U-1Ds prepared their departure from the escort carriers. After the Corsairs and Hellcats of VMF-312, VMF-322, VMF-323 and VMF(N)-543 had been catapulted off the ships, they headed for their new home field at Kadena and arrived safely.

Early the next morning twenty-four MAG-33 Corsairs took off to fly combat air patrol over the radar picket ships but soon aborted their mission because of the weather. Rain continued through the day with the aircraft bogged down in mud. Noting the loss of Corsairs and pilots by MAG-31, Marine Air Group 33 made no further attempts to fly that day. The following morning their first missions took off in the midst of heavy rain. First Lt. James Brown, of VMF-323, fell victim to the weather conditions, crashed and died.

Corsairs of VMF-311 Hell's Bells, at Yontan, are outlined by tracers during a
night attack. Photo by Technical Sergeant Chorlest. *NARA 127-GR-118775.*

However, weather did not stop the Japanese and frequent air
attacks on Yontan took place during the period from 4-6 April, with
enemy planes strafing the installations. Enemy air attacks were
not the only hazard for the marine air groups at Kadena and
Yontan. When the anchorage came under attack, every gun on
every ship might let loose at the kamikazes with many of the shells
falling on the fields. A number of men were killed and wounded by
friendly fire in this manner. MAG Corsairs, scrambling to intercept
the enemy aircraft, frequently had to take off right into the guns of
the ships off the beach.

During April 1945, Yontan was strafed and bombed on 4, 5, 6,
15, 17, 20, 21, 22, 26, 27, 28, and 29. Japanese artillery fire hit the
field from the direction of Machinato Airfield during the night and
morning of 11-12 April. In spite of all these attacks, the MAG-31
pilots flew numerous missions during April and shot down sixty-
three enemy planes. A number of these combats took place over the

radar picket stations. Between 8 and 30 April, the pilots of MAG-31 logged 7,253 hours of flight time. However, operational problems and enemy action caused them to lose nineteen of their planes and eight pilots during this period. Construction work was ongoing on the fields, limiting the length of the runway to 2,500 feet. Corsairs, heavily laden with ammo, napalm, rockets and bombs, struggled to lift off in this limited distance.

The bombing at Kadena on 11 April damaged the runway. Other attacks took place on the field throughout April. The Japanese recognized the threat from the planes at Yontan and Kadena and usually sent out bombers to attack the fields just prior to each of their *Kikusui* raids. As early as 4 April, preparations were under way to neutralize the fields. The Japanese reported:

> The enemy, after landing, immediately occupied the airfields in northern and central OKINAWA [Yontan and Kadena]. The Army anticipated that the enemy would rapidly develop these airfields into land bases to take the place of the mobile force, therefore it ordered the heavy bomber units to prepare for airfield attacking. The Navy also thought that its operation would become very difficult if the enemy land air bases are completed . . ..[10]

Attacks on both fields would continue through mid-June and their regularity would not subside until the end of the Okinawa campaign. Still another concern of the MAG pilots was interception by carrier-borne fighters and friendly fire from the ships in the Hagushi anchorage. Since they took off only a mile from the beach, it was impossible not to have jumpy gunners on the ships take them under fire before they could be identified. Hellcats from the carriers frequently intercepted them as well until the "bogeys" were identified as friendly. Carrier-borne fighters were not under the same combat flight controllers, which added to the difficulties in coordinating the fighter squadrons.

Marine fighter pilots chafed at the idea of flying combat air patrols, since they felt their primary mission was ground support of the marines on Okinawa. Major George Axtell, of VMF-323, noted: "A lot of time on CAP and picket ship patrol you just sat and looked at blue ocean. The Navy took the first pick on the patrols. Certain CAP stations were useless, but we grabbed every mission we could in the north because the kamikazes came down from

Kyushu."[11] Pilots never knew what to expect when they returned
to Yontan or Kadena. In their absence the field might have been
shelled, bombed, or might still be under attack. More than one
landing had to be diverted due to these causes, and pilots frequently maneuvered around bomb craters as they touched down.

As the Okinawa campaign progressed, army air force units
began to arrive on the island in preparation for long range attacks
on the mainland of Japan. These units were stationed at the primary airfields on Okinawa and the marine air groups were transferred to smaller fields. Marine Air Groups 14 and 33 moved to
Awase on 31 June and 16 July 1945 respectively. On 1 July, MAG-
31 moved from Yontan to Chimu and fifteen days later MAG-22 left
Ie Shima and joined them.

Thunderbolts to Ie Shima

The first of the army air force fighter groups to arrive on Ie Shima
was the 318th Fighter Group under Col. Lew Sanders. Having
gained combat experience at Saipan, Tinian, Rota, Pagan, Truk
and Iwo Jima, the pilots were ready for their new mission. The
ground echelon left Saipan 6 to 7 April 1945 on board the liberty
ship *S. Hall Young 479* and *Kenmore AK 221* and headed for Ie
Shima. As this excursion was beginning, a skeleton crew remained
behind to prepare the group's new fighters for action. New model
Thunderbolts, the long-range P-47N, had just arrived to replace
the older model P-47Ds that the group had been flying. Pilots tested them out on runs over Truk and Marcus islands for about two
weeks before deeming them ready for the flight to Ie Shima.

Kenmore and *S. Hall Young* arrived in Okinawan waters at
the end of April 1945. The ground echelon of the 318th landed on
Ie Shima on 30 April, and had to stand by as demolition men
cleared mine fields all around them. The next evening, a kamikaze
hit *S. Hall Young*, burrowing into her number 5 hold and setting
off fires. Fortunately the fires were extinguished before the 530
tons of ammunition and rockets were set off. A dozen trucks and
various other supplies and equipment were lost in the attack.

The first of the group's squadrons took off for Ie Shima and
arrived on 13 May. The 333rd Fighter Squadron completed the
1,425 mile flight in seven hours, making it the longest over- water
flight up to that point. A B-29 flew navigation for the Thunderbolts

A P-47N Thunderbolt of the 333rd Fighter Squadron, 318th Fighter Group arrives at Ie Shima after a long flight from Saipan. *NARA A-65021.*

but, three hours into the flight, encountered bad weather and the fighters had to continue on to Ie Shima using their clocks and compasses as a guide. Reports indicate that one plane and pilot were lost.[12] The 73rd Fighter Squadron arrived on the 14th and the 19th Fighter Squadron arrived on the 15th. On 16 May, the 29th Photo Reconnaissance Squadron arrived.

The "Jugs" were quickly put to work at a variety of duties, including bomber escort missions and fighter sweeps from their base up to Kyushu and westward to Korea. On 14 May 1945, only one day after landing, they participated in the combat air patrol. Their primary responsibilities involved flying patrols near Radar Picket Stations # 5, 7, 9, 15, and 16.[13] A few days later, they became the first of the ADC fighter planes to attack the Japanese mainland, hitting targets on Kyushu. From this point on, they would fly regular CAP and attack missions from their base at Ie Shima. Designed for long range missions, the P-47Ns were not seen over the picket ships as frequently as were the marine and navy planes. Army air force pilots found this agreeable, since there were those who felt that radar picket patrol could be unnerving at times. Lieutenant Durwood B. Williams, of the 333rd Fighter Squadron on Ie Shima, had been in the first group of army air force fighters to arrive at Okinawa. He recalled:

> I flew 7 CAP missions during May and 6 CAP missions during June. Several were protecting the pickets. I do not recall how many. I do recall, however, that the duty was hazardous. One could peaceably orbit the pickets as long as no hostile aircraft were reported to be in the area. Once hostiles were reported, you could depend on every Navy gun in the group to fire on you. For Army pilots, undisciplined navy gunners were more feared than were the Japanese. At least, we could shoot back at the Japanese.[14]

Pilots had been given fair warning. In an *Operations Memorandum of 15 May,* Col. Lew Sanders had warned pilots that "Planes must not fly within automatic weapon range of surface craft nor engage in any maneuver near surface craft which might be interpreted as hostile."[15]

Additional fighter groups arrived on Ie Shima in June 1945. Black Widows of the 548th Night Fighter Squadron landed on 8 June. The 34th Fighter Squadron of the 413th Fighter Group flew in on 14 June and three days later was joined by the 1st and 21st Fighter Squadrons. On 27 June the 463rd and 464th Fighter Squadrons of the 507th Fighter Group arrived and the next day the 465th arrived as well.

By this time, the need for their presence over the radar picket ships was minimal, and most of the Thunderbolts were used to the north of Okinawa to escort bombers in attacks on the main islands and to patrol in barrier CAPs near Amami O Shima. The fighter squadrons also headed west and northwest to attack Japanese bases in China and Korea.

From the time of their arrival on 14 May 1945 until 14 July 1945, the army air force units were under the command of the Tenth Army Tactical Air Force. After that date, they were once more back under the commanding general of the Seventh Air Force, a part of the Far Eastern Air Force (FEAF).

Many of the pilots flying CAP near the radar picket stations found themselves in the ocean after bailing out or making water landings. Fortunately the area around Okinawa had numerous ships that could rescue them. Here, Lieutenant D.R. Hagood of VC-13, is picked up by *Ingersoll DD 652* on 20 May 1945. Shortly thereafter, he was returned to his squadron on *Anzio (CVE-57)*. *NARA 80G 344185.*

Rescue Work

Combat air patrol pilots who ran into trouble near the picket stations were more fortunate than were Japanese pilots. While Japan had very limited air-sea rescue capabilities, those of the Americans were much more developed. With over a thousand ships in the Okinawa area, downed airmen had an excellent chance of being rescued. If an airplane went down near any American shipping, the pilot's squadron mates circled his position until help could arrive.

A Martin PBM-5 Mariner shown at Patuxent Naval Air Station on 23 August 1945. Mariners, or "Dumbos" were used as patrol bombers and rescue planes at Okinawa. *NARA 80G 47751.*

In addition to ship rescue, pilots who were not near shipping might be rescued by the "Dumbo" patrol. The patrol was comprised of PBM Mariner aircraft from squadrons VH-1, 2, 3, 4, 5, and 6. Originally based at Kerama Retto, they began to move to a new base at Chimu Wan in July 1945.

Although the first Dumbo flights were conducted by unarmed PBM-3R Mariners, the squadrons began to receive newer, armed PBM-5s in mid-April 1945. The PBM-5s were equipped with eight machine guns and well able to take care of themselves.

The American Aircraft

The American aircraft types designated to protect the invasion forces and ships at Okinawa were several in number and included planes from the marine corps, navy and army air force. During the day, the skies were patrolled by Hellcats, Wildcats, Corsairs and Thunderbolts. At night, the ships were covered by Hellcat and Black Widow night fighters.

The FM-2 Wildcat

By the time of the Okinawa campaign, a new Wildcat had been developed to replace the F4F. Designated the FM-2, it was produced by General Motors in Linden, New Jersey. The newer Wildcat had improved performance over the earlier models and was a capable fighter, although not the best of the American planes. It was able to down most of the aircraft in the Japanese arsenal with the exception of their latest fighters. Faster than most of the dive bomber types such as the Val, the FM-2 sometimes experienced difficulty in turning with them. Vals, flying at a slower speed, were more maneuverable and could out turn the FM-2. Zekes, perhaps the most nimble of the Japanese fighters, could easily turn inside Wildcats. A comparison in *Aircraft Action Report of VC-85* indicates that the "FM-2s had no trouble closing with Vals or Zekes. Jap pilots did not make serious attempts to outrun FM-2s, except in dives. FM-2s turned inside Vals but one Zeke turned inside FM-2s . . . Both types were overtaken in dives, Vals more easily than Zekes."[16]

An FM-2 Wildcat from *Santee CVE-29* on 20 October 1944. *NARA 80G 287594.*

The Sonia also proved to be no match for the Wildcat and many went down under the guns of the American fighter. Zeros were another matter altogether. In general they were faster and had a slightly higher service ceiling. Since the service ceiling of the FM-2 was not as great as some of the planes it encountered this attribute sometimes caused problems. Comdr. Wilbur H. Cheney Jr., commanding officer of the light minelayer *Robert H. Smith*, wrote: "On two occasions during ZEBRA operations FMs controlled by this ship were vectored to within visual range of a high-flying bogie (altitude 29,000 ft.), but were not capable of attaining the altitude necessary for interception. The force was scouted for a half hour on one occasion and 20 minutes on another."[17]

Comparative tests of the FM-2 and the A6M5 Zeke were conducted by the Technical Air Intelligence Center at Anacostia, Maryland in 1944. The test concluded that at most altitudes, the FM-2 could out climb the Zeke, but that the Zeke was faster in level flight. This difference in speed was accelerated above 5,000 feet. At sea level, the Zeke was only six miles per hour faster than the Wildcat. However, as the altitude increased, the speed advantage of the Zeke did as well. The greatest difference in speed was at an altitude of 30,000 feet, with the Zeke Type 52 26 miles per hour faster than the Wildcat. In rolls, turns, dives and zooms, both aircraft were judged roughly equal, with the Zeke having a slight edge in turns and dives and the Wildcat slightly superior in rolls.

The F4U Corsair

Up until a certain point in the war, the Zeke was the supreme fighter. Its speed and acrobatic abilities made it the scourge of the skies and the Americans had to develop fighters to combat it. The first serious challenger to the Japanese in the Pacific skies was the Chance Vought F4U Corsair. Bigger and heavier than the Zeke, it had other characteristics that made it a Zeke killer. The attributes that gave it an advantage over the Zeke's legendary maneuverability were its speed in level flight, climbs and dives. It could easily catch a Zeke, and if the Zeke got on its tail it dove away, leaving the Zeke behind. Since it had less maneuverability, the marine pilots who flew it developed tactics to combat the Zeke's aerobatic qualities. Over Okinawan waters, the Corsair pilots could shoot down anything that they encountered, if they used the correct tactics.

An F4U-1D Corsair at Patuxent River Naval Air Station, 23
June 1945. *NARA 80G 477504.*

VF-10 pilots, flying their Corsairs off the carrier *Intrepid* noted:

> The performance of the F4U-1D has been found highly satis-
> factory against all enemy aircraft encountered, although the
> squadron has had very little experience with GEORGE, JACK,
> or FRANK, the newer enemy fighters. While most Japanese
> planes encountered can outmaneuver the F4U-1D, as long as
> our pilots do not follow the enemy fighters in their maneuvers,
> the enemy can usually be shot down.[18]

The lack of experience with the more advanced of the Japanese
fighters was limited to the area around Okinawa. Japanese planners had kept the better fighters nearer to home to protect the
main islands. VF-84 pilots had encountered the George and felt
that it could not match the Corsair. According to them, the "F4U-
1D has 50 knots superior speed without water injection and without having to jettison belly tank."[19] Pilots from VMF-123 reported
that "they could turn inside a George."[20]

   Corsairs had originally been designed with an armament of
six Colt M2 .50 caliber machine guns. By the time of the Okinawa
campaign, some Corsairs mounted four 20mm cannons, which
sometimes proved to be problematical. At altitudes of 15,000 feet,
the cannons might freeze up, leaving the pilots cursing them.

Troubled by this problem, the pilots checked and found out that the high altitude tests of the cannons had been canceled.[21] This did little to assuage their frustration. Some historians claim that pilots much preferred the machine guns over the cannons because of their higher rate of fire and their dependability.[22] However, many of the aircraft action reports indicate that some pilots favored the 20mm cannon. VMF-314 pilots reported: "All the pilots were very enthusiastic about the performance of the 20 MM guns. They said there is no question about hits, because every hit on any part of a plane appears like a gun flash upon impact."[23]

The most numerous fighter faced by the Corsair was the Zeke, which was a very different airplane. Of much lighter construction, the Zeke could out-maneuver most American aircraft. The Corsair was much heavier, but also faster and capable of absorbing more punishment. Corsair pilots got into trouble if they tried to follow the Zekes in maneuvers as they could easily turn inside the F4U. Pilots who learned to use the attributes of the Corsair were successful against Zekes and other planes that were more maneuverable than they.

Comparative tests conducted in 1944 by the Technical Air Intelligence Center, confirmed that the Corsair was much faster. At sea level it was 48 miles per hour faster and maintained this or greater superiority at higher altitudes. At 25,000 feet it was judged to be 80 miles per hour faster than the Zeke. In rolls, both planes were equal under 200 knots. However, above that speed the Corsair, as with other American planes, had an advantage. The Zeke could also turn much better than the Corsair, gaining "one turn in three and one-half at an altitude of 10,000 feet."[24] In the area of diving, the Corsair was far superior. In the initial stages of the dive both were roughly equal, but in a short while the Corsair easily pulled away. It had marginal superiority in zooms. As with other American fighters, the Corsair pilots were advised not to dogfight with Zekes or to attempt to follow them in loops.

The preferred method of attack was to make an initial high speed dive on the Zeke and then zoom away. If a Zeke was on the tail of a Corsair, Wildcat, Hellcat or Thunderbolt, the recommendation was the same. The pilot should "roll and dive away into a high speed turn."[25]

Japanese pilots recognized the qualities of the Corsair and gained a healthy respect for it. They noted that Corsairs and

Lightnings used the same type of attack, diving on Zekes using hit and run tactics, and then using their speed to escape. By comparison, the Corsair and other American planes were difficult to shoot down when compared to the Zeke and other Japanese aircraft. Self-sealing fuel tanks, armor, and robust construction made them very durable.

Apparently Corsairs were not the easiest of aircraft to fly. The long nose and high landing gear made it difficult to see dead ahead when it was taking off and landing. According to VMF-441 pilot, 2d Lt. Bud Dworzak, "you were wide awake coming in for a landing. You got that thing on the ground, there was a lock on the tail wheel that should have kept it going straight down the runway, but it would take off to the right or to the left, it didn't make any difference to that airplane and you'd be patting yourself on the back, 'you're a hero, you defied gravity again.'"[26] These and other characteristics made the plane particularly difficult to land on carriers. For the early part of the war the navy did not consider them suitable for use on board. Marines usually flew the Corsair from land bases. Changes to the Corsair occurred in 1942 and 1943 that made it more controllable at slow speeds and gave the pilot greater visibility.

The navy began to test its adaptability for carrier use and the first successful landing of a Corsair on the escort carrier *Sangamon* was accomplished in September 1942. By the time of the Okinawa campaign, Corsairs were in use on navy ships, flown by both marine and navy pilots. Of the approximate forty plus navy squadrons flying off the carriers at Okinawa, only four flew the Corsair, the rest flew Hellcats and Wildcats. The four marine squadrons, VMFs-221 and 451, and VMFs (CV)-112 and 123, which were assigned to carriers all flew Corsairs. Toward the end of the war four additional escort carriers, carrying marine Corsair squadrons, were assigned to TF 38. The squadrons on board these carriers were VMFs-351, 511, 512, and 513. In addition to the carrier based squadrons another twelve marine Corsair squadrons flew off the fields at Okinawa and Ie Shima.

The F6F Hellcats

The most successful of the American fighters involved in the battles over the radar picket stations was the Grumman F6F Hellcat.

An F6F-5 Hellcat at Patuxent Naval Air Station, 1 February 1945. *NARA 80G 477448.*

It was faster than the Zeke and, although it could not turn inside one, it was aerobatic enough to seriously challenge the Japanese fighter. Japanese navy ace Saburo Sakai recalled: "The Hellcats were fully as agile as our own planes, much faster, and able to out-climb and out-dive us. Only the inexperience of their pilots saved us. Had they been better, every Zeke would have been shot down in less than a minute."[27] Still another Japanese navy ace, Warrant Officer Takeo Tanimizu added: "I think the F6F was the toughest opponent we had. They could maneuver and roll, whereas planes such as the P-38 and F4U made hit and run passes – they were not very maneuverable."[28]

Comparative tests by the Technical Air Intelligence Center found that the "Zeke 52 climbed about 600 ft/min better than the F6F-5 up to 9,000 feet, after which the advantage fell off gradually until the two aircraft were about equal at 14,000 feet, above which altitude the F6F-5 had the advantage, varying from 500 ft/min better at 22,000 feet to about 250 ft/min better at 30,000 feet."[29] In the speed category, the Hellcat was much faster than the Zeke, clocking 41 miles per hour faster at sea level and 75 miles per hour faster at 25,000 feet. The two aircraft were equal in rolls under 200 knots, but the Hellcat was superior at speeds above that. As with the other aircraft tested, the Zeke was far superior at slow speed turns at low altitudes. As altitude and speed increased, the disparity decreased until they were about equal at 30,000 feet. Hellcat pilots received the same suggestions as the pilots of other American planes. In encounters with the Zeke, dogfights were to be avoided and the plane was to make maximum use of its speed and firepower.[30]

Among the Japanese aircraft were some that caused problems for the Hellcats. Hellcat pilots were impressed with the speed of the Myrt and the difficulty they sometimes had in shooting one down. The Tojo was comparable to the Hellcat, but usually lost in engagements with them. Only the slower planes had a chance to outmaneuver the Hellcat, but with the speed differential, the Hellcat was usually able to make a second pass. Against Vals, Sonias and similar aircraft, the Grumman was a killer. Some of the other Japanese fighters were respected by the Hellcat pilots. "Pilots were impressed with the maneuverability of the Tony and believed that it could out turn the F6F-5 at speeds up to 200kn. below 10,000 feet."[31]

Japanese pilots who faced the Hellcat knew that they had met their match. According to Japanese experts:

> There is no doubt that the new Hellcat was superior in every respect to the Zero [Zeke] except in the factors of maneuverability and range. It carried heavier armament, could out climb and out dive the Zero [Zeke], could fly at higher altitudes, and was well protected with self-sealing fuel tanks and armor plate. . . .
> Of the many American fighter planes we encountered in the Pacific, the Hellcat was the only aircraft which could acquit itself with distinction in a fighter-vs.-fighter dogfight.[32]

The P-47N Thunderbolt

Weighing in at 9,950 lbs. empty, the Republic P47-N Thunderbolts were the heaviest of the fighters over the radar picket stations. Their primary mission involved long-range attacks on the southern islands of Japan; however, on many occasions they flew combat air patrol over the picket ships and barrier CAP north of Okinawa. Eight .50 caliber machine guns and a top speed of 440 miles per hour made the Thunderbolt a deadly adversary. It could catch

The P-47N model differed from the P-47D in that it had squared wing tips, a greater wing span and added ailerons. *NARA 28768 AC.*

whatever the Japanese put in the air with the exception of the *Oka* and, with all eight guns blazing, could demolish anything that flew. With its high speed and heavy weight it was no dog fighter, and so relied on hit and run tactics to make the best use of its attributes.

Technical Air Intelligence Center comparison tests of the Thunderbolt and Zeke 52 had similar findings to other American aircraft such as the Hellcat and Corsair. In turns, the advantage was to the Zeke with one-half to three-fourths of a turn at 10,000 and 25,000 feet respectively.

Thunderbolts were significantly faster than Zekes at all altitudes. For example, the difference in speed at 10,000 feet was 70 miles per hour. In zooms from both level flight and dives, the P-47D was far superior. Aileron roll for the Zeke was a higher rate at lower speeds, but once the aircraft hit a speed of about 250 miles per hour they were equal. At higher speeds Thunderbolts had a significant edge.[33]

An F6F-5N Hellcat from VMF(N)-533 in flight on 27 June 1945. The radar pod is visible beneath the starboard wing. This night fighter belonged to Marine Air Group 22 and was based on Ie Shima. *Official USMC Photo courtesy of the Tailhook Association.*

The Night Belongs to Us

The F6F-5N Hellcat

The night skies over Okinawa belonged to the night fighters. Hellcats from marine squadrons VMF(N)-533, VMF(N)-542, and VMF(N)-543 patrolled in the dark and kept the enemy at bay. At various times, these marine night fighter squadrons operated from Yontan, Kadena, Chimu, and Awase on Okinawa and from Charlie Field on Ie Shima. The first of these to go into operation was VMF(N)-542, under Maj. William Kellum, which began operations from Yontan on 6 April 1945. Numerous shoot downs occurred over the radar picket stations during the early stages of the campaign. Part of the success lay in new tactics developed by the squadrons at Okinawa. Before Okinawa one of the problems facing the fighter director officer was how to get the night fighter to the correct altitude. During the campaign for Okinawa, fighter directors had developed the ability to direct the night fighter to within 500 feet of the enemy plane. At that distance the pilot could usually see the

A P-61 Black Widow shown at Wildwood Naval Air Station, NJ on 8 August 1945. *NARA 80G 383522.*

bogey and was able to shoot it down. From dusk to dawn the F6F-5Ns patrolled the skies in four hour shifts, searching for enemy aircraft. Each patrol included four of the Hellcat night fighters.

The P-61 Black Widow

With the appearance of the 548th Night Fighter Squadron on Ie Shima on 13 June 1945, a new weapon appeared in the night skies, Northrop's P-61 Black Widow. Eighteen of the Black Widows, under the command of Maj. Robert D. Curtis, arrived from Iwo Jima that day and flew their first combat mission on 16 June.

The P-61 was designed as a night fighter from the beginning. It carried a crew of three, a pilot, radar observer and a gunner observer. Armament on the P-61 included four fixed 20mm cannons in the belly and four .50 caliber machine guns in a dorsal turret. They also had the ability to carry 6,400 lbs. of bombs mounted on wing racks. With its special radar gear, the Black Widow was the newest threat to the Japanese intruders. Fortunately for them it entered the Okinawa campaign late, after the major raids had stopped. Between their arrival and the end of the war, the 548ths Black Widows claimed five nighttime kills. Two additional kills were recorded the day after the war ended, when fanatical Japanese pilots disregarded the Emperor's commands and flew final suicide missions.

Comparisons of Japanese and American Aircraft

An overall impression of the characteristics of the planes can be derived from the various aircraft action reports filed by squadron commanders and individual pilots. These action reports include a section entitled "Comparative Performance, Own and Enemy Aircraft." Statistical tables, such as the one on page 80-81, give us an overview of the technical data. However, the pilots themselves give added insights into how it felt to fly in combat against one another. One factor that weighed heavily in these comparisons was the large number of inexperienced pilots sent on suicide missions by the Japanese. At times, this made accurate comparisons of the planes' performances difficult.

In the early years of the war, Japanese aircraft, particularly the Zeke, were the superior fighters. Coupled with the ample number of talented and well-trained pilots, the Japanese had the advantage in the first year or two of the war against Americans. This situation soon was reversed. New American fighters such as the Lightning, Corsair and Hellcat began to turn the tables. As Japan's best pilots were lost and her ability to train new ones and produce new aircraft designs diminished in the latter half of the war, the Americans had the edge in the skies. Planes used in the Special Attack Corps were usually those in need of repair, obsolete types, and trainers. Guide planes for the kamikazes were better aircraft, but even they had difficulty competing with well-trained American pilots flying the latest fighters.

Japanese military leaders, interviewed shortly after the war, made some revealing comments on the relative strengths and weaknesses of the aircraft on both sides. According to Comdr. Ryosuke Nomura IJN, the Japanese regarded the F4F Wildcat, P-40 Warhawk, and Zeke as roughly equal. However, the Corsair and Hellcat were regarded as superior. By the end of 1943, their air losses had convinced the Japanese pilots that they were flying inferior aircraft.[34]

Superior Flight Petty Officer Ichiro Tanaka of the 222 Naval Air Unit, who piloted a Zeke 52 in the Philippines, "considered the

GRUMMAN fighter the most formidable of the ALLIED airplanes, and that the combined two airplane tactics the ALLIES used, were hard to beat."[35] Lieutenant Comdr. Iyozoh Fujita argued that the armament on the Zekes was not equal to that of the Hellcat and that the gun sights in use by the Japanese were technologically inferior to that used by the Americans. The inferiority of the Zeke by the end of the war was apparent to all. In a report dated April 1945, the Technical Air Intelligence Center evaluators reported:

> The Zeke's high rate of turn, general maneuverability, and good flight characteristics are its most desirable combat features. Poor performance, weak armament, high control forces at high speed, and excessive vulnerability make it an undesirable combat airplane The airplane is of very light construction by American standards, and does not have protective armor or self-sealing fuel tanks. These features make it extremely vulnerable as a fighter airplane.[36]

During the battle for Okinawa, the Japanese considered the Frank to be their best fighter with the latest model of the Oscar as second best. Toward the end of the war, the Army K-100 fighter, their last Tony version, held great promise as their best plane. Unfortunately for them the Akashi engine plant was bombed on 19 January 1945, ending production. Only sixty to seventy of the latest Akashi equipped Tony models made it to tactical units.

Japanese aircraft development had made progress throughout the war. However, rather than spending their maximum effort on the production of more advanced fighters, they continued to modify and update the Zeke, a strategy that eventually became costly. The advanced fighters that did get into production were turned out in too few numbers and too late in the war to make a significant impact on its course. In addition, the disruption of supply and production facilities frequently meant that aircraft were subject to many breakdowns due to problems during production.

Although qualitative and quantitative comparisons of the aircraft used by both sides were popular with both the Japanese and the Americans, there were other considerations voiced by the Japanese.

In an article in *Fuji Magazine* in November 1943, Jiro Takeda, the Head of the 2nd Aviation Section of Mitsubishi Heavy Industries wrote

Another question one is often asked is how Japanese aircraft compare with enemy aircraft as regards quality. I think there is very little to choose between them. But the power of an aeroplane is not to be calculated merely by its figures for speed, climbing power, and equipment; it is closely related to the country's method of fighting and to the national character, and depends also on the pilot's spiritual strength and technical ability. The Americans criticized the zero fighter planes we were using at the beginning of the war, and were amazed that we dared to fight with them as we did; and similarly, when we examined the enemy planes we had captured in the south, we were amazed that the Americans should be fighting with such machines. But in each case this betrays a failure to understand the enemy country. It is only when our planes, built by people imbued with patriotic feeling, and themselves filled with the Japanese spirit, are piloted by our heroes burning with loyalty and patriotism that such magnificent results are obtained. . . It is not material things which count most of all in the long run, but the spirit.[37]

The Kamikazes

"Kamikaze," used as a term to identify the Special Attack Corps, is generally thought to be an erroneous pronunciation of the Japanese characters by Japanese-Americans. In the Imperial Japanese Navy, the corps was called the *Shimpu Tokubetsu-Kogekitai*. The characters for *Shimpu* can also be read as "kamikaze," hence the commonly used name in western works. In the Japanese Army Air Forces the units were known as *Shimbu Tokubetsu-Kogekitai*. *Shimbu* translates as a "gathering of courageous forces." Among the pilots and other military men, the shortened name of *To, Tokkotai,* or *Tokubetsu-Kogekitai* was more commonly used. Intercepted Japanese messages usually referred to the units simply as *To*.

The *Ten Go* Campaign

In order to achieve maximum success against the American invasion of Okinawa it was imperative that the Japanese army and navy cooperate. This endeavor resulted in the *Ten Go* Campaign. Although both branches drafted plans for the joint venture, the army plan was adopted. Colonel Ichiji Sugita, former Operations

COMPARISON OF PLANES ACTIVE DURING THE RADAR PICKET ORDEAL

Data	Northrup P-61B Black Widow	Vought F4U-1D Corsair	Grumman F6F-5 Hellcat	Grumman FM-2 Wildcat	Republic P-47N Thunderbolt	Mitsubishi A6M5 Zero Type 52	Kawasaki Ki-61-1 Tony
Wingspan	66'	40' 11"	42' 10"	38'	42' 3"	36' 2"	39' 3"
Length	49' 5"	33' 4"	33' 7"	28' 9"	29' 8"	29' 8"	28' 9"
Empty Weight	23,400 lbs.	8,982 lbs.	9,238 lbs.	5,758 lbs.	9,950 lbs.	4,130 lbs.	5,010 lbs.
Horsepower @ Sea Level	2 x 2,000 h.p.	2,000 h.p.	2,000 h.p.	1,350 h.p.	2,800 h.p.	1,210 h.p.	1,160 h.p.
Speed at Altitude	375 m.p.h. @ 17,000 ft.	425 m.p.h. @ 20,000 ft.	400 m.p.h. @ 20,000 ft.	320 m.p.h. @ 19,400 ft.	440 m.p.h. @ 29,000 ft.	354 m.p.h. @ 21,000 ft.	361 m.p.h. @ 15,800 ft.
Service Ceiling	33,000 ft.	37,000 ft.	37,300 ft.	36,000 ft.	40,000 ft.	39,300 ft.	35,100 ft.
Maximum Range	1,350 miles	1,015 miles	1,040 miles	925 miles	2,350 miles	1,640 miles	2,010 miles
Armament	4 x 20mm cannons, 4 x .50 cal. machine guns	6 x .50 cal. machine guns, 2,000 lbs. bombs	6 x .50 cal. machine guns, 2,000 lbs. bombs	4 x .50 cal. machine guns, 3 rocket rails	8 x .50 cal. machine guns, 2 - 500 lb. bombs, 10 – 5" rockets	2 x 20mm cannons, 2 machine guns, 132 lbs. bombs	4 machine guns or 2 machine guns and 2 x 20 mm cannons 2 x 220 bombs
Crew	3	1	1	1	1	1	1

Data	Nakajima Ki-841a Frank	Nakajima Ki-43-11B Oscar	Mitsubishi Ki-51 Sonia	Nakajima B5N2 Kate	Aichi D3A1 Val	Mitsubishi G4M1 Betty	Mitsubishi F1M1 Pete
Wingspan	37' 1"	35' 6"	39' 8"	50' 9"	47' 5"	82'	37"
Length	32' 3"	29' 2"	27' 8"	34' 2"	35' 4"	64' 5"	32' 3"
Empty Weight	7,940 lbs.	4,170 lbs.	4,125 lbs.	5,439 lbs.	5,760 lbs.	17,400 lbs.	4,490 lbs.
Horsepower @ Sea Level	1,970 hp.	1,105 h.p.	930 h.p.	985 h.p.	1,280 h.p.	2 x 1,825 h.p.	840 h.p.
Speed at Altitude	422 m.p.h. @ 21,000 ft.	347 m.p.h. @ 20,000 ft.	254 m.p.h. @ 9,000 ft.	233 m.p.h. @ 8,500 ft.	281 m.p.h. @ 20,300 ft.	331 m.p.h. @ 16,700 ft.	238 m.p.h. @ 14,000 ft.
Service Ceiling	39,000 ft.	37,100 ft.	27,200 ft.	24,100 ft.	27,200 ft.	30,800 ft.	33,100 ft.
Range	1,795 miles	1,745 miles	1,540 miles	2,240 miles	1,580 miles	3,290 miles	650 miles
Armament	2 x 20mm cannons, 2 machine guns, 2 x 72 lb. bombs	2 machine guns, 2 x 132 lb. bombs	3 machine guns, 4 x 132 lb. bombs	2 machine guns, 1 x 1,760 lb. Torpedo or 1 x 550 lb. bomb	3 machine guns, 1 x 550 lb. bomb	1 x 20mm cannon, 5 machine guns, 2,005 lbs. bombs	3 machine guns, 2 x 200 lb. bombs
Crew	1	1	2	3	2	7	2

Staff Officer at Imperial General Headquarters, would later claim that "the Navy took an extremely negative and indifferent attitude in formulating the *Outline of the Operations Plan of the Imperial Army and Navy* in January 1945. The new operations plan was formulated with the agreement of the Navy only after enthusiastic suggestion by the Army."[38] Captain Toshikazu Omae, who served as Planning Section Chief, Naval General Staff during that period, later reported:

> The actual condition of the Navy's air strength at that time (especially from the viewpoint of training) regrettably would not allow the Navy to participate in the OKINAWA Air Operations which were expected to occur in March or April. The Navy generally desired to avoid the hitherto gradual attrition of semi-trained personnel and did not wish to engage in operations at OKINAWA and other fronts, much less the homeland, until about May, by which time it would have accumulated sufficient fighting strength.[39]

Although both branches of the Japanese military were committed to cooperate against the Americans at Okinawa, coordinating their activities was not easy. Targets to be attacked by the army forces were convoys and troop carriers. These vessels were easier to hit and pilots required less training for the missions. By comparison the navy targets were the carrier task forces, which were more difficult to attack and required greater flying skills. Japanese navy planning called for additional special attack training. According to Comdr. Yoshimori Terai, former officer in charge of Air Operations, Naval General Staff, "From the beginning, air preparations (special attack planes) were not expected to be completed until the end of May. Although we desired to delay the American advance on OKINAWA through the Second TAN Operations (attack on ULITHI Base), but as a result of their failure, we were forced to face the Okinawa Operations unprepared."[40]

The situation was no better for the army. With the failure of the operations against Ulithi and the accelerated advance of the American forces toward Okinawa, the army was caught in the time trap as well. According to Japanese naval officers involved in the planning for *Ten Go,* "the preparations of the 6 Air Army were even more behind schedule than those of the Navy."[41] *Navy Directive No. 5410* of 1 March 1945 detailed the extent of the cooperation.

The Army-Navy Joint Central Agreement on Air Operations

1. Policy

   To destroy the enemy, who is expected to invade the East China Sea and the vicinity, with a display of the combined air strength of the Army and the Navy and at the same time to strengthen the direct Homeland defense. In order to execute the above-mentioned operations, emphasis will be placed on build-up and use of the special attack strength.

2. The principle of air operational guidance in each area:

   a. Air operations in the East China Sea and the vicinity (Formosa, the Nansei Islands, Southeast China, Kyushu and Korea).

      The Army-Navy air forces will immediately deploy in the East China Sea and the vicinity and destroy enemy invading units.

      The chief targets for the Navy air forces will be enemy carrier striking task forces, and for the Army, enemy transport convoys. However, the Army will cooperate as much as possible in the attack against enemy carrier striking task forces.[42]

Navy Directive No. 513, issued by Adm. Koshiro Oikawa on 20 March 1945, spelled out the goals of the *Ten Go* Operation. Its first priority was the destruction of the American carrier task forces that had been attacking Japan. This was to be accomplished by the mass use of conventional and kamikaze aircraft, suicide boats, manned torpedoes and midget submarines. A secondary target was the American invasion fleet operating in and around Okinawa. Of particular importance were the air bases on Okinawa. Should they fall into American hands, the security of the home islands would be further imperiled.[43]

In order to ensure maximum cooperation against the Americans at Okinawa, Gen. Michio Sugawara's 6th Air Army had been placed under the jurisdiction of the Commander in Chief of the Combined Fleet Adm. Soemu Toyoda as of 19 March 1945. *Navy Directive No. 516* of 8 April 1945 outlined an agreement of shared usage of many airbases in Japan and Korea. The army would share their bases at Iwaki, Yabuki, Yokoshiba, Togane,

Oshima, Niijima, and Miyakonojo East with the navy. Navy air bases at Kochi, Oita, Kanoya, Hachijo-Jima, Saishu-To and Tanegashima would be shared with the army. Hamamatasu, Tachiarai and Nittagahara would be used by navy units and the army's 7th and 98th Air Regiments. In addition, Gunzan and Shisen army air bases in Korea could be used by the navy for temporary evacuation of their bases on Kyushu in case of American attack.[44]

During the first few days of Operation Iceberg, American commanders were surprised to find that air opposition to the invasion was relatively light, but this was to change very quickly. With the start of the *Ten Go* campaign a series of ten massed attacks, employing numerous suicide planes and their escorts, would savage the ships at Okinawa. Beginning on the evening of 6 April 1945 and lasting through 7 April, the Japanese launched the first of their ten *Kikusui* (Floating Chrysanthemum) raids. These planes flew from the bases of the Third, Fifth, and Tenth Air Fleets and the Sixth Air Army on Kyushu, the Fifth Air Army at Keijo, Korea, and the First Air Fleet and Eighth Air Division on Taiwan. With so many aircraft attacking at once, it was to be expected that many would break through and that the American ships would suffer great losses. The chart below lists planes of the special attack units or kamikazes as well as planes that flew escort, attack or bombing missions.

Originally conceived as a plan for a decisive battle against the Americans, the *Ten Go* Operation began to run into problems. By the end of May both branches realized that Okinawa would be lost and that the battle would not end the American advance. About that time, the concept of a decisive battle was abandoned and the actions at Okinawa had as their purpose the wearing down of the American forces. Rear Adm. Sadatoshi Tomioka, Chief of the Operations Bureau of the Naval General Staff, termed it a "bleeding operation designed to exhaust the enemy."[45]

Japanese Naval Air Force

Navy kamikaze planes flying against the Americans at Okinawa came from units of the Third, Fifth and Tenth Air Fleets in Japan proper and the First Air Fleet, which was based on Taiwan. They were under the overall direction of the Commander of the

				The Ten-Go Campaign		
Kikusui	Date	Navy	Army	Total Kamikazes	Other Planes	Total Planes
1	6-7 April 1945	230	125	355	344	699
2	12-13 April 1945	125	60	185	195	380
3	15-16 April 1945	120	45	165	*	*
4	27-28 April 1945	65	50	115		
5	3-4 May 1945	75	50	125	225	350
6	10-11 May 1945	70	80	150	*	*
7	24-25 May 1945	65	100	165	*	*
8	27-28 May 1945	60	50	110	*	*
9	3-7 June 1945	20	30	50	*	*
10	21-22 June 1945	30	15	45	*	*
Total		860	605	1,465		

*No data available.

In addition to these *Kikusui* attacks, sporadic small-scale suicide attacks were carried out during this period by 140 navy and 45 army planes. From Formosa 250 suicide attacks were conducted, 50 by navy planes and 200 by army planes. The total suicide sorties against United States surface forces during the Okinawa campaign was 1,900 by navy planes and by army planes 850.

In addition to these suicide sorties, orthodox torpedo and dive bombing attacks were carried out; the total number of sorties is, however, not known except for navy aircraft with a reported 3,700 sorties.[46]

The list above reflects the summary prepared by the United States Strategic Bombing Survey. Figures reported in the *Japanese Monographs* differ, being slightly higher. It should also be noted that this listing ends with the termination of the Okinawa campaign on 22 June. Actual radar picket duty continued on until 13 August, with the Japanese sending small raids to attack Okinawa and the exposed radar picket ships the entire time.

Combined Fleet, Adm. Soemu Toyoda. Toyoda was considered to be one of the most able of the Japanese navy officers. He had graduated first in his class at the Naval Academy in 1905 and gained his Admiral's star in 1931. During the mid-1930s he headed the Naval Affairs Bureau and in that capacity ran afoul of the army high command. From that point on he considered the army to be his enemy. By the end of the Okinawa campaign he became Chief of the Naval General Staff.

The First Air Fleet was commanded by Vice Adm. Takajiro Onishi, and the Third Air Fleet by Vice Adm. Kimpei Teraoka. Vice Adm. Minoru Maeda was the Commander in Chief of the Tenth Air Fleet. Command of the Fifth Air Fleet was under Vice Adm. Matome Ugaki. Headquartered at Kanoya Naval Air Base on Kyushu, Ugaki reported directly to Toyoda. On 1 April, the Tenth Air Fleet was placed under Ugaki's operational control and, on 16 April, the Sixth Air Army came under his direction as well. By the end of the Okinawa campaign, he would also exercise authority over the Third Air Fleet. The tactical designation for his command was the First Mobile Base Air Force.

The Third, Fifth and Tenth Air Fleets operated their aircraft from a number of fields on Kyushu, the southernmost island of Japan. Kanoya was the main base, but others such as Kagoshima, Hakata, Omura, Hitoyoshi, Miyakonojo, Miyazaki, Kokubu, Kushira, Kasanohara, Ibusuki, Iwakawa, Tsuiki, Oita, Izumi, and Usa were regular bases for the kamikazes and other planes flying to attack American targets at Okinawa. In order to confuse American planners pilots flying from Kyushu frequently flew indirect courses to make it seem as though their flights originated on Taiwan.

Kanoya was considered to be an extremely important base. According to reports from the American XXI Bomber Command,

> Kanoya Naval Air Station is by far the most important air headquarters in the Japanese Empire. Damage to installations would cause considerable disruption to Japanese offensive air operations. In addition to being used for staging, the field has served as [an]Army and Navy combat training station. A naval air depot with extensive repair and maintenance facilities services the field, and aircraft assembly has taken place in an integrate [sic] unit. . . .A satellite field, called Kanoya E. adjoins the main field.[47]

Left: Vice Admiral Matome Ugaki, I.J.N., Commander of the Fifth Air Fleet.
Photo courtesy of the U.S. Naval Institute.
Right: Admiral Soemu Toyoda in a photo probably taken in September, 1944.
NARA 80 JO 63365.

South of Kyushu was a string of islands comprising the Amami Archipelago that also held airfields. Among them were Amami O Shima, Tokuno Shima and Kikaiga Shima. Bases for the First Air Fleet on Taiwan included Taichu, Kobi, Matsuyama, Takao, Shinchiku, Tainan, and Giran. Islands of the Sakishima Gunto between Taiwan and Okinawa, such as Ishigaki Shima and Miyako Jima, also held airfields that served as forward staging areas for attacks on American ships at Okinawa.

Japanese Army Air Force

The Japanese army air force units that generated kamikaze attacks during the Okinawa campaign were the Eighth Air Division, which was stationed on Taiwan, the Sixth Air Army based on Kyushu, and a few elements of the Fifth Air Army at Keijo, Korea. The headquarters for the Eighth Air Division on Taiwan was at Matsuyama (Taipei). Its commanding officer was

Airfields used by the Imperial Japanese Navy and the Japanese Army Air
Force during the battle for Okinawa. Adapted from CinCPac-CinCPOA
Bulletin No. 166-45. *Airfields in Kyushu.* 15 August 1945.

Maj. Gen. Kenji Yamamoto. Other army bases on Taiwan included,
Karenko, Toen, Shoka, Heito, Choshu, Giran, Ryutan, Ensui, Mato,
Hachikai, and Kagi. Eighth Air Division planes attacking Okinawa
frequently used the smaller island air bases between Taiwan and

Okinawa. Airfields on islands in the Sakishima Gunto chain, particularly Ishigaki Shima and Miyako Jima, were used as forward staging areas for the attacks.

The Sixth Air Army, under Lt. Gen. Michio Sugawara,[48] established its headquarters at Fukuoka on 18 March 1945 and operated from numerous bases on Kyushu including Nittagahara, Chiran, Kumamoto, Kikuchi, Tachiarai, Miyakanojo, and Kumanosho. Sugawara reported to the commanding general of the Air General Army, Gen. Masakazu Kawabe. The islands to the south of Kyushu, such as Kikaiga Shima, Amami O Shima and Tokuno Shima, were sites of army air bases and were frequently used as forward staging areas for planes flying from Kyushu. During the carrier strikes of 18 March 1945 on the Kyushu airfields, the Sixth Air Army withdrew its planes to Korean bases in an effort to preserve them. From that point on, they began to develop the bases in Korea for use against American forces at Okinawa. Additional units were moved from China and Kyushu to airfields such as Gunzan and Keijo[49] and the Korean fields became rear

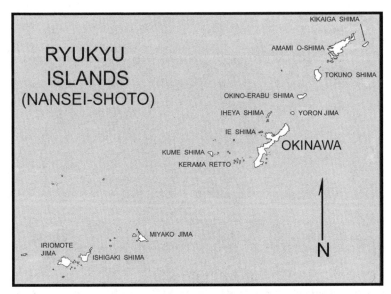

Bases to the north and southwest of Okinawa were forward staging areas for attacks on American forces at Okinawa. Planes flying from bases on Taiwan used Ishigaki Shima and Miyako Jima. Aircraft flying from Kyushu used Kikaiga Shima and Amami O Shima.

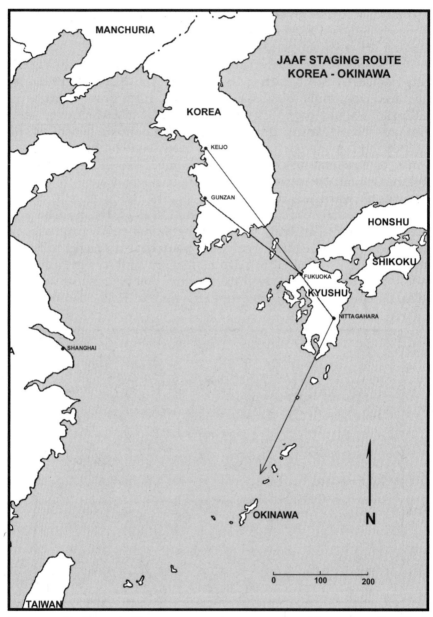

Japanese Air Bases in Korea were used as rear areas. Planes from the Sixth Air Army flew from Gunsan and Keijo, Korea to Fukuoka and then on to Nittagahara. From there they attacked shipping at Okinawa. Adapted from *Magic FES 421,* 15 May 1945.

bases for the attacks on Okinawa. Flying away from attacks allowed the Sixth Air Army to preserve its planes during strikes by American carrier forces and B-29 raids.

Among the Japanese Army Air Force bases, Tachiarai was considered to be the most important. According to the American XXI Bomber Command, the "Tachiarai Army Airfield, which has all-weather runways and complete facilities for the operation of heavy bombers, fighters, and medium bombers, is the most important airport and training station in the Kurume Area. It is one of 8 known Army Air Arsenals in Japan."[50]

Although the overwhelming majority of air units attacking American forces at Okinawa came from the Sixth Air Army and the Eighth Flying Division, one element of the Fifth Air Army also flew a few missions. Lieutenant Gen. Takuma Shimoyama's Fifth Air Army was headquartered at Keijo, Korea. According to his Chief of Staff, Maj. Gen. Ryosuke Nakanishi, the 16th and 90th Fighter Regiments of the 8th Fighter Brigade flew some attack missions against American targets at Okinawa using the light army bomber, code named Lily.[51] The number of sorties flown by these planes was relatively small and was estimated at between thirty and forty.

A standard procedure for the Special Attack Units was to advance to the island bases from Kyushu in order to give them greater range. This was the practice at the beginning of April, but increasing American attacks on the islands made it difficult to advance the planes, particularly to Tokuno Shima, without significant losses. To counter these attacks, the Japanese fitted their aircraft with extra tanks to fly directly from their bases on Kyushu whenever possible.

Unlike the navy, which included special attack planes in each unit, the army set up separate units comprised solely of kamikazes. Patriotic pilots "volunteered" for these units. Toward the end of the Okinawa campaign, army volunteers for the special attack units began to fall off, and men from training and tactical units were involuntarily transferred into them. In the beginning each unit had twelve airplanes assigned to it but, as attrition set in, the number declined.

By June of 1945, units with as few as six planes were being formed. Plans for the formation of up to two hundred units were on the books and were completed by the end of the battle for Okinawa.

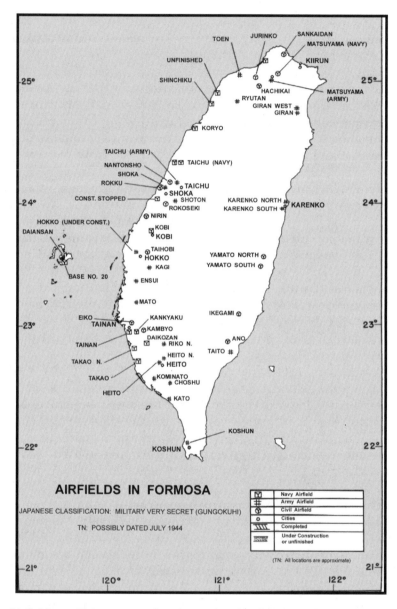

AIRFIELDS IN FORMOSA

JAPANESE CLASSIFICATION: MILITARY VERY SECRET (GUNGOKUHI)

TN: POSSIBLY DATED JULY 1944

⊠	Navy Airfield
⊞	Army Airfield
⊕	Civil Airfield
○	Cities
⅏	Completed
▨	Under Construction or unfinished

(TN: All locations are approximate)

Airfields on Taiwan served as bases for the Japanese Army Air Force 8th Air Division and the Imperial Japanese Navy First Air Fleet. Adapted from CinCPac-CinCPOA Bulletin No. 102-45. *Translations Interrogations Number 26 Airfields in Formosa and Hainan.* 25 April 1945, p. 6.

Less than one-third of these actually flew missions at Okinawa. The rest were kept in reserve for the anticipated invasion of the homeland.

By March of 1945, the Sixth Air Army had a total of fifteen special attack units. Nine of the units were ordered to Kyushu to counter the American invasion of Okinawa and six remained in eastern Japan. This placed a total of sixty Army suicide planes on Kyushu's bases; however, of the units only three, the 20th, 21st and 23rd Shimbu Units, were considered combat ready. With the expectation that additional units would be used in the *Ten Go* operation, their number was increased, and the Sixth Air Army added another ten for a total of twenty-five.

Such a rapid increase meant that the units were comprised of insufficiently trained pilots destined to fly obsolete planes in poor condition. American pilots encountering these planes would report back that the pilots seemed to lack experience and skill.

In order to coordinate their attacks on the American forces set to land on Okinawa, the Commander of the Mainland Defense Army issued an order on 19 March 1945, placing the Sixth Air Army under the command of the Combined Fleet Commander, Admiral Toyoda. This would insure maximum effectiveness for the two branches in their battle against the invasion forces.

In practice, Admiral Toyoda's Navy staff planned the attacks and informed General Sugawara and Admiral Ugaki. Sugawara and Ugaki then worked out the details of the operation between them. It was up to Sugawara to determine the specifics of army participation, such as the number of planes, attack routes, and tactics.

One of the most important aspects of the joint venture was fighter support between the bases on Kyushu and the targets at Okinawa. Since the navy had more planes available, this cooperation was vital. At first this proved problematic, as communications between the army and navy on Kyushu were not in place. In addition, up to this point, there had been little cooperation between the two branches, illustrated by competition for resources and frequent disagreements over strategy. This competition made it difficult to produce a unified military effort.

Air Brigade Commanders met in Fukuoka on 25 March 1945 to determine their strategy for the anticipated campaign. The army recommended that:

(1). As soon as the strength has been concentrated and preparations advanced, the 1st Attacking Group (59th Air Regiment, 5 suicide plane units) will secretly move to the Southwestern Islands (KIKAI-GA-SHIMA will also be used) and make preparations to be the 1st wave of the attack.

(2). The 2nd Attacking Group (101st Air Brigade, 102nd Air Brigade and 2 suicide units) will be concentrated at MIYAKONOJO, while the 3rd Attacking Group (103rd Air Regiment, 65th Air Regiment, 66th Air Regiment, and 2 suicide units) will be at CHIRAN and BANSEI. Both groups will prepare for the future attacks.

(3). Two heavy bomber regiments will make preparations at KUMAMOTO and TACHIARAI for future attacks against enemy fleets. According to these instructions all matters were to be promoted rapidly.[52]

In general, the army was to attack transports and the navy would attack warships. This was considered the most practical division of responsibilities. Army pilots were used to attacking stationary ground targets, not ships moving at high speed. Naval aviators had more training in hitting moving targets such as ships. Furthermore, the slower transports were a better target for the less experienced army pilots.

The suggested plan proved to be unworkable; the army was not yet ready to begin the *Ten Go* Operation. Losses and delays in plane movements caused the plan to change. The initial attack would be executed by the Third Attacking Group which consisted of two regiments of the Sixth Air Brigade. On 28 March, some of the brigade units advanced planes to Tokuno Shima. Eight planes from the 103rd Air Regiment and ten from the 66th Air Regiment were ready for the beginnings of the *Ten Go* Operation. On 29 March the missions began. Three companies of planes from the 65th, 66th and 103rd Air Regiments attacked American shipping early in the morning, at about 0600. Although Japanese reports claim that three warships and one transport were hit, American sources indicate that no ships were damaged that day.[53] Over the next several days, additional planes would be advanced to the islands south of Kyushu and be prepared to attack when ordered to do so.

By the morning of 1 April, as the American invasion of Okinawa began, the Japanese Army Air Force had placed a total of

The Aichi D3A, Navy Type 99 bomber was frequently used as a kamikaze plane during the battle for Okinawa. This plane carried the Allied code designation "Val." Many of the radar picket ships were attacked by them. *NARA 4292 AC.*

twenty-five planes on Tokuno Shima from the 65th, 66th and 103rd Air Regiments and eight suicide planes from the 20th *Shinbu Unit.* As dawn broke over the islands of Kerama Retto, they launched their attack. Over the following weeks and months numerous other planes would follow.

Planes used by the Japanese Army Air Force included the fighters Tojo, Oscar, Nate, Frank, Tony, Nick, reconnaissance planes Dinah and Sonia, and the bombers Lily, Helen, Sally, Peggy, and Mary. Some Japanese naval officers considered these planes to be superior to those used by the navy. The planes most frequently used for kamikaze missions were the Sally, Oscar and Sonia. American analysis of the special attacks by army aircraft differed from Japanese sources and indicated that Oscars and Tonys were the main types used for suicide missions.[54] Older planes such as Nates created a number of maintenance problems, as parts were difficult to obtain and the engines were generally worn out. Japanese maintenance and repair personnel were in short supply. Many had been stranded on by-passed islands and were unable to rejoin air units. Additionally, a large percentage of aircraft mechanics had been lost in the Philippines and their replacements were poorly trained. At home, the labor pool was in equally bad shape and the quality of aircraft production dropped.

Army units flying from bases on Kyushu had additional problems. They were continually under attack by American aircraft flying from Okinawa, the Marianas, Iwo Jima and off the carriers. These attacks had knocked out rail service and aviation gas had to be trucked in, thereby limiting missions. Some of the gas was of poor quality which shortened the flying range of the aircraft.

CHAPTER 3

The Ordeal Begins

Radar picket duty at Okinawa began eight days before the actual invasion of the island. On 24 March 1945, *Pritchett,* with Task Unit 54.1.1 under Rear Adm. P.K. Fischler, arrived in Okinawan waters and was assigned to Radar Picket Station # 5, which lay forty-three miles east of Point Bolo (Zampa Misaki). *Pritchett* arrived on the station at 0610 and four Hellcats from *San Jacinto* were assigned to fly CAP over her. A few hours later, at about 0910, *Pritchett's* radar picked up an incoming bogey to the northwest and sent the CAP to intercept it. The bogey escaped and *Pritchett* remained on station until dusk and then returned to her task unit. Just after dawn, two Myrt 11 reconnaissance planes of the 102nd Hikotai, 752nd Air Group had flown from Kanoya on a scouting mission. They reported the location of the American ships.

One of the first ships assigned to radar picket duty and the first casualty of the radar picket ordeal was the destroyer *Kimberly* under Comdr. J.D. Whitfield. She had been patrolling station King 7, about forty miles southeast of Okinawa. At 0535 on 26 March 1945, she received orders to report to RP Station # 9 which was nearby. Approaching the location for RP Station # 9, she picked up a bogey on her radar screen and went to general quarters. At 0617, two Vals from the First Air Fleet on Taiwan zoomed in for the attack. *Kimberly* went to flank speed and opened fire. The two enemy planes banked and flew out of range. One of them turned back and began a run on the destroyer. For several minutes both ship and plane maneuvered radically, the Val attempting to get into a position for a stern run and the destroyer attempting to keep her guns bearing on the target. Apparently the pilot was experienced, as the ship's report indicated that he performed a number of

Kimberly DD 521 was one of the first ships to serve on a radar picket station at Okinawa. Almost as soon as she arrived at Radar Picket Station # 9 on 26 March 1945 she was hit by a kamikaze and damaged. *NARA 80G 68240.*

maneuvers in order to avoid the anti-aircraft fire. The pilot finally managed to get on the destroyer's tail and, in spite of its radical turns, the ship could not avoid the kamikaze. The plane was hit a number of times and apparently headed for a crash on the destroyer's bridge. As it passed over the stern, it went out of control and crashed into the aft 40mm gun mount, killing four men and wounding thirty-three. Another seventeen were listed as missing.

Fires started by the plane and its 200 pound bomb were quickly extinguished. Although she was not completely disabled, the destroyer had two of her 5" guns put out of action, along with a 40mm mount. Commander Whitfield requested permission to transfer the casualties and the ship left the station about 0951. Her damage was significant but she was able to stay at Okinawa for a few days and engaged in screening activities. On 1 April, she departed Okinawa for repairs at Mare Island. She was out of the war, but repairs were finished in time for her to make it to Tokyo

Bay for the surrender in September. Sent in to replace her at RP Station # 9 was another destroyer, *Sproston*, which reported to the station at 0940 on 26 March and soon encountered enemy action. At about 2250 that evening, she picked up bogeys on her radar and increased speed to twenty-five knots. Five minutes later she sighted a twin engine plane 2,000 feet overhead and took it under fire with her 40mm and then her 5" guns. At 2300, hits on the plane were observed and it began to burn. The crew was sure the plane was shot down but did not observe the crash. Within a few hours, at 0320 on the 27th, they took another plane under fire and drove it off. *Wickes* relieved *Sproston* at 0812 on 28 March.

The beginning of action at Kerama Retto set Japan's plans for defense of Okinawa into motion. American intelligence had already intercepted Japanese messages relating to the invasion. On the afternoon of 31 March the Commander of the Okinawa Area Special Base Force (Navy) issued the following "redraft of a Naval Secretariat message" of the 30th:

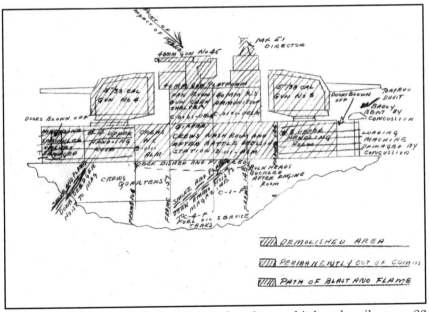

Sketch of damage to *Kimberly DD 521* after she was hit by a kamikaze on 26 March 1945 at Radar Picket Station # 9. *USS Kimberly DD 521 Serial 014 Action Report 12 April 1945*. Enclosure A.

The Combined Fleet ordered TEN #1 Operation [defense of
the Ryukyus] into effect on 26 Mar., and that operation is now
in progress. Since the success or failure of that operation will
form the basis for the operations immediately following, its success or failure will determine the fate of the nation.

All officers will impress upon their subordinates the great
importance of the operation and that, whether one is at the
front or in the rear, there is no better time than today for giving one's life for one's country. Raise your spirits higher and
higher and make your performance of duty leave nothing to be
desired.[1]

Throughout the campaign for Okinawa the Americans would
be aware of Japan's plans. In April of 1942, MacArthur had acti-
vated a comprehensive intelligence operation known as the Central
Bureau. Headquartered in Melbourne, Australia, the Central
Bureau consisted of a number of signal intelligence units from the
American and Australian armies as well as from the Royal
Australian Air Force. Intelligence developed from intercepted
Japanese communications came to be known as ULTRA.
Intercepted messages were translated, analyzed and forwarded to
the War Department's Military Intelligence Service which sent it to
the appropriate military commands.

This information frequently prevented the Japanese from
catching the Americans by surprise and, on many occasions,
allowed the American forces to launch preemptive strikes on
Japanese airfields. Because of this, Japan's ability to mount aerial
attacks was slowed and the number of aircraft in the raids less
than they had planned.

Just prior to the invasion, the XXI Bomber Command sent B-
29s from the 73nd and 314rd Bombardment Wings in the Marianas
to attack the airfields on Kyushu. According to *Headquarters XXI
Bomber Command Tactical Mission Report, Missions No. 46 and
50*, these planes had three primary goals: "(1) to destroy airfield
installations; (2) to draw enemy fighters from the Okinawa Area;
and (3) to keep enemy fighters at their home bases on and near
Kyushu."[2]

The Japanese had developed a new code book for their JN-25
code and placed it into effect on 1 February 1945. However, the
Central Bureau's ULTRA program had continually deciphered
their coded messages with increasing rapidity. By the time of the

Okinawa campaign, translation of intercepted messages was virtually contemporaneous.

Wickes had replaced *Sproston* on the morning of 28 March at
RP Station # 9, which was located seventy-three and one-half miles
to the southeast of Point Bolo. With the attack on *Kimberly* in
mind, the crew was particularly watchful for aircraft coming from
Japanese bases on Taiwan or the mainland. On 31 March, a night
raid at 0125 caused the ship to fire, but with negative results.
American intelligence noted that naval aircraft attacking from
Kyushu were using Kikaiga Shima as a staging base and those
from Taiwan were using Ishigaki Shima.[3] In order to keep the
Japanese at bay, British carriers designated as TF 57, under Rear
Admiral Sir Philip Vian, and American escort carriers of TG 51.2,
under Rear Admiral Calvin T. Durgin, hit the fields in the
Sakishima Gunto continually between 26 March and 1 April.
Attacks by the British and American carriers would continue into
April.

Sunday, 1 April 1945

Dawn broke at about 0640 on Love Day (1 April). Gentle breezes
blew across the water onto the beaches at Hagushi as marines and
soldiers loaded onto landing craft. The temperature was seventy-
five degrees. The big guns of the capital ships fired salvo after salvo
inshore with a deafening roar. Near the shoreline, the gunboats
lined up for their initial rocket runs on the landing sites. At 0800,
the LCI(G)s, LCI(R)s, LCI(M)s, and LCS(L)s began their assault,
firing at the beaches and inshore targets with rockets, mortars,
40mm and 20mm gunfire. The invasion of Okinawa was underway.

As soon as the troops were safely ashore, the ships turned to
other diverse duties. For many of the destroyers, LCS(L)s and
LSM(R)s, the new assignments would prove to be their greatest
challenge. Until 13 August, the U.S. Navy would use them as isolated sentinels in the face of the kamikaze onslaught.

Radar picket duty was assumed by eleven destroyers as soon
as the initial landings at Okinawa were completed. Stations to be
patrolled were RP Stations #s 1, 2, 3, 4, 7, 10, 12, 14, and 15. At
about 1000, *Bush* received orders to report to RP Station # 1, which
was located fifty-one miles north of Point Bolo. Radar Picket
Station # 1 was considered to be a critical area since it was in a

direct path between Japan and the invasion site. *Bush* arrived on station at 1330 and began her patrol. It would be one of the few uneventful days she would experience on radar picket duty. A number of Japanese planes were spotted visually and on radar, but none came within range of her guns. *Luce*, patrolling nearby on RP Station # 2, also spotted enemy planes. The following morning, *Bush* was ordered back to Kerama Retto for fuel. She was relieved by *Pritchett.*

Wickes was on patrol at RP Station # 9. At about 0549 a Japanese torpedo bomber attacked the ship with a torpedo. Smoke from the ship's gunfire was so thick that no one on board saw the torpedo drop, but its screws were picked up by the ship's sonar. *Wickes* maneuvered sharply and the torpedo missed. As the plane came around for a second run and tried to crash into the ship, *Wickes* turned to bring its guns to bear. Fortunately, the kamikaze crashed into the sea close off the starboard quarter. A second plane approached but was driven off by the ship's guns. Later that day, *Wickes* was reassigned to RP Station # 7.

Bennett was assigned to RP Station # 10, which lay seventy-three and one-half miles west-southwest of Point Bolo. Arriving at the station at about 1000, the ship soon had bogeys under fire. Between 2130 and 2359, Japanese aircraft were observed flying on an easterly course toward their targets. The Japanese planes flew low over the water at an approximate altitude of 500 feet, and all were driven away by the destroyer's guns. It is likely that the planes were from the 17th Air Regiment at Karenko South airfield on Taiwan and the 24th Air Regiment on Miyako Jima. The 17th had sent out eight kamikazes and six fighter escorts. The 24th had added two planes to the group. Eight of the planes from the 17th did not make it back to base.[4]

Earlier that day, the 22nd and 43rd Bombardment Groups of the 5th Air Force had flown missions against both Giran and Karenko airfields. A total of thirty B-24s and eighteen B-25s, flying from the Philippines, had hit the two bases but some of the enemy planes were still able to begin their missions.

Relatively little action had been seen by the ships on their first day of radar picket duty, with most of the attacking aircraft driven away and no damage or loss of life incurred by the American navy. The Japanese had lost one torpedo bomber to the radar picket ships. Their Sixth Air Army's Third Attack Division was hindered in its plans, having sent out only two planes from Tokuno Shima and thirteen from Chiran. On the evening of 1 April, the Japanese had tried to move the Third Attack Division into position in the southern offshore islands, but most of the planes were blocked by the American carrier fighters and only a part of the division had made it to Tokuno Shima. The First Attack Division had moved its kamikaze units to Chiran, but they were unable to take off on their mission.

Monday, 2 April 1945

Pritchett had been reassigned to RP Station # 15. At 0543, the ship was attacked by a single engine plane which was painted black. The low flying plane had not been picked up by radar and was able to come in on the ship's port quarter. It dropped a 500 pound bomb from masthead height which landed twenty to thirty yards off *Pritchett's* port beam, causing a temporary loss of the ship's SG-1 and Mark 4 radars. As the plane passed over *Pritchett*, the ship's gunners opened up and hit it with a 40mm round. The damaged plane escaped to the east. At that point, *Pritchett* was ordered to report to RP Station # 1 to relieve *Bush*, which she did at 0755. Within an hour, *LCS(L)s 62* and *64* joined her.

The destroyer *Bennion* was patrolling at RP Station # 2 early on 2 April when her radar picked up an approaching Japanese Betty at 0155. The radar controlled guns took it under fire and drove the Betty off. At 0334, another Betty approached from the east only fifty feet off the water. This attack was no surprise as the ship's radar had picked up the plane when it was nine miles out. A single shot from one of *Bennion's* 5"/38 guns exploded the plane and it went down 4,200 yards from the destroyer.

LCS(L)s 84 and *87* joined the *Bennion* at about 0650. The ships came under attack again at 1828 that evening when two planes, thought to be Vals, approached them from the northeast. One came within range and was hit by a five inch shell from the destroyer; it went down in flames. The second plane lost altitude and headed to the east where it crashed a few minutes later. Since the LCS(L)s had not opened fire, it was not clear why the second plane went down.

Although the ships on the other stations had escaped harm and had not seen a great deal of action, the Japanese had managed to cause some damage. Japanese army planes from Tokuno Shima had taken off in the early morning hours and slipped through the net, attacking ships in Kadena Bay. The Army's Third Attack Division had sent in seven planes to accompany two special attack planes from the 66th Air Regiment. The 103rd Air Regiment had supplied two other special attack planes. Transport ships *Dickerson, Goodhue, Telfair,* and *Henrico* were hit. *Dickerson* was severely damaged and subsequently scuttled. *Henrico* was out of service for the remainder of the war. These incidents marked the first successful suicide attacks by Japanese forces in the Okinawa campaign. Captain Minoru Hasegawa and Sub-Lt. Nishi Yamamoto of the 66th Air Regiment were credited with leading the flights.[5]

Tuesday, 3 April 1945

Pritchett, having suffered minor damage in the previous day's attack, continued her patrol at RP Station # 1 with *LCS(L)s 62* and *64*. Hardly had the day begun when the station came under attack. *Pritchett's* radar picked up several raids coming in from the north at a high rate of speed. At 0121 she opened fire on the first of the attackers and it turned away. Eight minutes later, four enemy planes approached the ship. As two circled overhead, the others came in for the attack. Gunners on *Pritchett* found the range and one of the planes went down in flames 2,300 yards to starboard. For the next twenty minutes, the remaining three planes made continual attacks on the destroyer, approaching from opposite sides to confuse the gunners. At 0142 one came in from the starboard bow and dropped a 500 pound bomb as it passed over. It struck the fantail and exploded under the ship's stern, causing a great deal of damage. About the same time, *LCS(L) 64* spotted a plane coming into her port side at 0145. The plane, believed to be a Zeke, dropped a small bomb off the port side which exploded and rocked the ship but caused little damage. It was driven off by the ship's guns.

From that point on, continued attacks occurred. For the next fifteen minutes another group of four planes took turns attacking the picket ships. Most were driven off by their gunfire but, at 0156, *Pritchett's* gunners picked up another incoming raid and splashed a twin-engine Frances 7,000 yards from the ship. The Frances was one of eight from Air Group 762 that had taken off from Miyazaki

Airfield. Many Japanese planes remained in the area for the next few hours. *LCS(L) 64* spotted another plane about to attack her at 0405 from her port side; she fired her port twin 40mm and 20mm guns. As the plane passed over her bow, her starboard guns opened up and the plane went down in flames one hundred yards from the ship.

The destroyer *Bush* had spent the first day of April on RP Station # 1 and had been relieved by *Pritchett* the next day. Since *Pritchett* had sustained damage during the attack on the station, *Bush* was ordered back to RP Station # 1 on 3 April. She relieved *Pritchett* at 1330 and began her patrol supported by *LCS(L)s 62* and *64*. *Pritchett* headed back to the anchorage for repairs and supplies. About that time, twenty Judys and twenty-four suicide planes scrambled from Kanoya and Kokubu # 1 airfields in Southern Kyushu. Thirty-two Zeke and eight George fighters were flying cover for them.[6] At 1700, the station came under attack. Heading for *Bush* were four Judys, which were taken under fire. As *LCS(L) 62* attempted to close the distance and lend fire support, one was shot down by *Bush* and the remaining three fell victim to the six VF-84 Corsairs from *Bunker Hill* that were on combat air patrol.

Bennion, LCS(L) 84 and *87* continued their patrol on RP Station # 2. It was to be a dangerous day and night for the picket ships, with a number of attacks on the station. At 0143 *Bennion's* radar picked up a plane coming in from the west at about 600 feet. It was taken under fire but escaped destruction and disappeared into the night. Twenty-two minutes later another plane approached from the east at about 300 feet but it was also driven away by the ship's guns.

About the same time the *LCS(L) 84* came under attack by a single plane. The Japanese plane turned off after coming under fire by the gunboat's twin 40mms. At 0305 still another plane was picked up on the destroyer's radar, closing at about 160 knots at an altitude of 900 feet. This plane was driven off, as well as another at 0424. The next two attackers were not so fortunate and *Bennion* added two Zekes to her score.

Cassin Young relieved *Colhoun* on RP # 3 on 3 April. Late in the afternoon, at 1709, she observed the CAP shoot down two Japanese planes over the station. Shortly thereafter, *Cassin Young* opened fire on several planes that approached her position, driving them away with her gunfire. *LCS(L)s 109* and *110* patrolled the station also but did not get in on the action.

 Radar Picket Station # 4 was under patrol by *Mannert L. Abele* and *LCS(L)s 111* and *114*. The destroyer had a close call late in the afternoon. About 1600, several Judys approached the station; two were taken under fire and driven away. Three more enemy aircraft commenced their attack at 1630. While one of the Judys circled high overhead drawing fire, a Zeke came in on a suicide run. It was taken under fire and shot down within 200 yards of the ship. *LCS(L) 111* spotted a Judy closing on the destroyer and took it under fire. Both the gunboat and the destroyer scored numerous hits, deflecting the plane in its attempt to crash into the destroyer. Just prior to reaching the *Abele*, the plane dropped a bomb. Both the plane and its bomb passed closely over ship, with the bomb landing about one hundred feet to port. The Judy continued on for a short distance and crashed into the sea. A fourth plane came in from the starboard bow on another bomb run. Again *Abele* narrowly escaped as the bomb passed over her and exploded in the water. The plane also passed over the destroyer while under fire and disappeared. By 1750 the attack was over and the Japanese planes had retreated.

 Wickes continued her patrol at RP Station # 7. Japanese planes were numerous during the nighttime hours but none approached within firing range of the ship. At 1715, the four Corsairs flying CAP over the station were vectored to the west to intercept Japanese planes that had been picked up by *Wickes'* radar. The Corsairs shot down one Zeke and one Judy, with a probable on a second Judy. The remainder of the night was uneventful for *Wickes*.

Wednesday, 4 April 1945

Staff Officers of the Combined Fleet and the Imperial Headquarters Naval Staff had been preparing for the invasion of Okinawa for some time. They had determined that support of the 32nd Army there was of paramount importance. It would be necessary to mount a large scale air attack on the American fleet in order to disrupt the landings of additional men and supplies, as well as to diminish the fleet's capabilities to conduct naval bombardment of the Japanese positions. All the operational units of the

Sixth Air Army, Tenth Air Fleet, Eighth Air Division and the First Mobile Base Air Force would be committed to the attack. This would include aircraft from southern Japan as well as from Taiwan. The attack was originally scheduled to begin on the evening of 5 April but the date was changed to 6 April because of inclement weather.[7] This gave the radar picket ships a brief rest before the main attack began.

The flurry of messages surrounding the planning for the special attacks was intercepted by Task Force 58 monitors. After identifying the procedures that the Japanese used in planning special attack operations, the Americans were able to intercept many of their raids. As a result the first attack, *Kikusui* # 1, was met with a large number of American aircraft thereby lessening its effect.

The main target of the kamikazes and conventional aircraft would be the ships carrying troops and supplies and their support ships. A secondary target would be the carrier task forces that were engaged in striking the Japanese air bases. Rather than sit and wait, the carriers of TF 58 sent their planes to attack Kikaiga Shima and Tokuno Shima in a preemptive strike.

Wickes patrolled RP Station # 7. At 0725 her radar picked up bogeys about fifty miles out, and she vectored her CAP of four VF-84 Corsairs from *Bunker Hill* to intercept them. The Corsairs encountered four Zekes at 11,000 feet and shot two down, with a third listed as a probable. At 1700, *Wickes* once again sent the CAP planes westward to intercept incoming planes, but they could not make contact.

Thursday, 5 April 1945

Ships patrolling on RP Stations # 7, 12, and 14 had a quiet day, but this was not to be the case on other stations. *Bush*, patrolling on RP Station # 1 with *LCS(L) 64*, reported a number of planes headed southward, but none came within range of her guns. Japanese records indicate that these planes were six special attack aircraft from the 6th Air Army at Chiran and their escorts.[8]

Colhoun, along with *LCS(L)s 84* and *87*, patrolled RP Station # 2. During the night hours no enemy planes were detected. Later in the day, at 1430, *Colhoun* received word that a Corsair pilot from *Bennington* had gone down in the area and she was requested to make the rescue.

Sixteen Corsairs from VMF(CV)-112-123 had taken off from *Bennington* to attack the Japanese airfield at Tokuno Shima. After three runs on the airfield the plane, piloted by 1st Lt. Junie B. Lohan of VMF-112, was hit by anti-aircraft fire. Lohan managed to get within thirty miles of Okinawa before his plane went in. His squadron mates circled the downed flyer and dropped lifeboats. One pilot, 2d Lt. R.B. Hamilton, headed out in search of a destroyer. He found *Colhoun* and requested her assistance. The destroyer turned her CAP over to *Cassin Young*, steaming nearby on RP Station # 3, and headed for the downed flyer. Within the hour, the pilot had been snatched from the cold Pacific waters. Lohan spent the next couple of hours with a hot shower and a meal. Little did he know that this would be only the first of his rescues. By 1729, *Colhoun* was back on RP patrol. The next day *Colhoun* would be sunk and Lohan was picked up by *LCS(L) 84*. Eventually he was returned to Yontan Airfield and finally made it back to the *Bennington* on 14 April.

A division of F6F-5E Hellcats from VF-33 on the escort carrier *Sangamon* were patrolling the area. Led by Lt. Comdr. Paul C. Rooney, the planes were about to return to their base when incoming bogeys were picked up on *Colhoun's* radar. Since they were at the end of their patrol they were given the option of returning to their ship or engaging the enemy. The Hellcat pilots immediately decided to intercept the bogeys and were turned over to the fighter director officer on *Colhoun*.

Colhoun's radar had picked up the raid coming in from the southwest at 1807. About the same time, *LCS(L) 84* reported a seaplane diving on her, but the gunboat drove it off. *Colhoun* directed the VF-33 Hellcats toward the bogey which located the enemy plane below them at 3,000 feet. It was a Paul, a twin float, single engine monoplane that the Japanese navy used for reconnaissance. This one was on a suicide run and unaware of the Hellcats coming up behind it.

The Paul went into a shallow dive, heading for the picket destroyers. Rooney opened fire at 1,000 yards and scored some hits but the plane kept going. As the Paul turned slightly to port, Rooney fired again, hitting the cockpit and the wing root. The plane caught fire, turned to starboard and went down. Rooney took his division back to *Sangamon* arriving in the dark at 1925 and landing under hazardous conditions.[9]

Not all the danger came from above. On RP Station # 10, *LCS(L) 115* spotted a submarine about thirteen miles to the north of *Hudson*. She proceeded to the area and attempted to ram the sub which quickly dove. At 0214 the ships closed on the sub which had disappeared below the surface. An antisubmarine patrol plane was called in for assistance and the ships investigated the area. *Hudson* picked up the sub on her sonar and began her attack at 0428 and continued until 0836 when no further contact was made. The DD was credited with a probable sinking of the sub. At 0916 the ships returned to accompany *LCS(L) 116* which had remained on radar picket duty.

Friday, 6 April 1945

April 6 would prove to be a hazardous day for the picket ships. American intelligence was aware of the planned air attacks. On the 5th, CINCPAC had sent the following message to all units:

X Day for KIKUSUI # 1 Operations now established as 6th April. Beginning around 0400(I), April 6th, large scale air attacks expected against Blue surface and land forces in Okinawa general area by planes from Kyushu and Formosa. It appears that practically all operational air strength of Jap Army and Naval Air Forces including that of 1st, 3rd, 5th, 10th and 13th AIR FLEETS, plus 3rd and 8th AIR ARMIES will be involved in these attacks, many of which will be suicide attacks. Air Bases at Miyako, Ishigaki, Amami Oshima and Kikai Island will probably be used for staging. All types of air attacks will be made and mining will be attempted throughout the 6th and probably subsequent thereto. Evidence 32nd ARMY on Okinawa will commence an all out land attack 7th April in order to annihilate Blue land forces.[10]

The warning was based on messages intercepted from the Japanese Combined Fleet Headquarters. On 4 April the command had sent out messages directing the various air units to specific targets. Convoys would be the main targets but the Japanese would also search for and attack the American carrier strike force if possible.

On RP Station # 1, *Bush* and *LCS(L) 64* continued on their patrol. *LCS(L) 62* had been ordered back to the transport area and reassigned to patrol there until 9 April, leaving the station with only two ships. Unfortunately, this was to be a bad move, as the Japanese were launching their first *Kikusui* attack against Okinawa. Coming in from Japanese airfields would be 355 kamikaze aircraft bent on destroying the American fleet. Accompanying them would be another 344 aircraft engaged in regular attack, escort and bombing missions. The majority of these would be naval aircraft coming from airfields in southern Kyushu such as Kanoya, Kokubu #1 and # 2, Kushira, and Miyazaki. Sixth Air Army planes would fly from Bansei, Chiran, Tokuno Shima, and Miyakonojo West. Standing in their way were the picket ships at RP Stations # 1, 2, and 3 and the Corsairs, Hellcats, and Wildcats of the combat air patrol. This confrontation would be one of the great air battles of the war with so many enemy aircraft shot down that VF-82's aircraft action reports would refer to it as a "Turkey Shoot."[11]

Enemy air activity at RP Station # 1 began about 0245 and continued for nearly an hour. *Bush* had four aircraft in her vicinity. All were taken under fire at various times during the next hour and one dove on the ship. The plane passed closely over her and a few minutes later a light was seen on the water about ten miles away, leaving the destroyer to conclude that she had splashed the plane.

Colhoun, patrolling on nearby RP Station # 2, had been menaced as well. Between 0247 and 0600, she experienced a total of eleven attacks, all of which involved bombs dropped by enemy planes. Fortunately none hit her. Another close call occurred at 0600 when a Betty approached the ship and dropped a torpedo, which missed its mark. First Lt. Junie B. Lohan, the rescued marine pilot, now began to appreciate how perilous the situation on the ship was. He had been accustomed to fighting kamikazes in the air and now had to stand by as sailors manned their guns in a desperate effort to drive them off.

Combat air patrol coverage of the ships began at 0700, as two divisions of fighters reported to the station. At 0830, an Irving was intercepted by the CAP and shot down near the destroyer. At 1030, the *Colhoun* turned over control of the CAP to *Cassin Young*, which was patrolling on RP Station # 3. As the day progressed, the CAP was kept busy. Around noon, a division of four Corsairs from VMF(CV)-112 off *Bennington* was on patrol. Led by Maj. Herman

Hansen Jr., the marine flyers soon had their hands full. Accompanying Hansen were 2d Lts. George J. Murray, James M. Hamilton and R.W. Koons.

Hamilton and Koons sighted the first Jap. They swept down through the clouds after the enemy. Hamilton climbed on his tail. Moving better than 350 knots in a screaming dive he chased the Zeke right into the water. Hamilton pulled out just in time. The Jap plane hit and exploded. Almost the same instant the Jap jumped. The chute blossomed, but there was no trace of the Nip.

A while later Hansen and Murray spotted a Jap plane darting in and out of the clouds. When the Jap pilot tried to split S away Hansen climbed on his tail, opened fire. However, in putting negative Gs on his plane he jammed the machine gun link ammunition and put five guns temporarily out of commission.

Suddenly Hansen realized he was going to fly directly into the Jap. "It looked like a certain collision," he recalled. "I pulled back on the stick. I barely cleared the tail and fuselage with my prop. I figure I wasn't more than 12 inches above him. I could see the rivets in the plane. There were two yellow stripes on the wings, where patches had evidently been placed. I saw the pilot clearly. Lashed beneath the plane was a big bomb. It was suspended by a makeshift arrangement of wires or ropes. The wires or ropes flapped in the wind."

When Hansen overshot, Murray closed. Opening fire 2500 feet away he sailed into the Nip with guns blazing. When Murray was about 25 feet away, the Nip flamed, rolled over and crashed into the sea.[12]

San Jacinto had launched sixteen F6F-5 Hellcats of VF-45 at 0925 that morning. After an uneventful patrol the planes prepared to return to base. At 1200, one of the divisions, led by Lt. (jg) D.E. Paul, was ordered north to assist the ships at RP Stations # 1, 2, and 3. The Hellcats were vectored to intercept an incoming raid after arriving over the picket ships about 1240. Two minutes later they spotted three Myrts to the southeast of the station. Paul went after the closest Myrt, but the other two had already started their dive on the destroyers. The ships shot down the first Myrt as Paul changed his aim and got on the tail of the second. Paul's guns found the range. He hit the engine area and set it aflame. The Myrt kept on course and Paul had to break off from the chase because of the intense AA fire from below. He watched as the plane headed in toward the destroyer and splashed short of its target.

The situation calmed down until later in the afternoon. About 1430, *Bush's* radar picked up an incoming flight of planes thirty-five miles to the north. *Colhoun* picked up the raids a few minutes later. Within the next quarter hour three more groups had been detected and the ships prepared for action. Nearby picket destroyers had turned over a four plane CAP to *Bush* and she put it to work. *Colhoun* reported that the attacking planes seemed to concentrate on RP Stations #1 and #3. She observed that "From forty to fifty planes appeared to be orbiting and attacking the *Bush* in station one and from ten to twelve the [*Cassin*]Young in station three."[13] *Bush* shot down two of the planes in the first group and the CAP finished off the other two.

At 1500, the destroyer drove off the second group of attacking planes. The third group of enemy planes approached from the port side and was taken under fire. At 1513, lookouts on *Bush* spotted a Jill coming in dead ahead. These Jills were from a group of fifteen that had taken off from Kushira Naval Air Base on Kyushu earlier that morning. Maneuvering to bring her guns to bear, *Bush* was unsuccessful and, at 1515, the plane crashed amidships on the starboard side. Its bomb exploded in the forward engine room causing a great deal of damage. Flooding began, and within a few minutes, the destroyer was listing ten degrees to port. A call was sent out to other ships in the vicinity informing them of the attack and requesting assistance. Flooding caused *Bush's* emergency power generators to fail and some of the ship's five-inch and 40mm guns were rendered inoperable. The men worked to save their ship and hoped that they would not be attacked again. To this point, *LCS(L) 64* had not received word that *Bush* had been hit.

Colhoun picked up the radio transmission from *Bush* and realized that she was in trouble. She could see that at least twenty to thirty planes were still over *Bush* and headed to her assistance at thirty-five knots. The CAP, running low on fuel, had shot down six planes but had to return to base. Another CAP division was vectored to the scene, shot down several planes and then ran low on fuel as well. At about 1545, contact was made with two other CAP groups, placing a total of twenty planes over the ships. The melee overhead did not lessen the predicament of *Bush*, *Colhoun*, and *LCS(L) 64* below.

Belleau Wood had launched fourteen Hellcats from VF-30 about 1455. They arrived in the vicinity of RP Stations # 1, 2, and 3 about 1530 and over the next hour and one-half encountered an estimated sixty to seventy enemy aircraft in small groups. Squadron reports indicated that these were definitely kamikazes as their pilots seemed to have little ability. One group of about twenty Vals, each carrying two 500 pound bombs, took no evasive action when attacked by the Hellcats. None of the planes had tail gunners and, when under attack, continued to fly directly toward the radar picket station.

Of the twenty Vals, only one escaped the VF-30 pilots and made a run on the radar picket ships. By the end of their patrol, VF-30 had shot down forty-six Japanese planes. Ensign C.C. Foster shot down two Tojos, one Zeke, and four Vals to become the high scorer for the squadron. Ensign K.J. Dahms shot down five and one-half enemy planes and Ensign J.G. Miller got five. Several other pilots each shot down multiple Japanese planes and the mission was described as "Turkey Shoot Number Two."[14]

Once again, *San Jacinto* sent her planes aloft. At 1500, sixteen VF-45 Hellcats took off to conduct a CAP over the area. Two divisions, led by Lts. C.B. Knekey and James B. Cain arrived over the *Cassin Young* at about 1550. Cain's division was then sent on to cover *Colhoun* and the action began. In a running gun battle over the picket ships, which at various times had the planes over *Cassin Young, Bush, Colhoun,* or *Bennett*, VF-45 Hellcats shot down a total of twenty-four Japanese aircraft. Most of the Japanese planes were either Vals or Zeros, along with a Jill, Hamp and Oscar. High scorers for the flight were Lt. James B. Cain who was credited with three and one-half planes. Ensigns Henry Nida and N. Bishop and Lt. (jg) Wolverton had three each, and Lts. (jg) D.R. Paul, D. Thompson, E.F. Swinburne and Ens. D.L. Krier each had two. The Hellcats returned to *San Jacinto* at 1815. As with so many of the gun battles that took place during the campaign, a number of the pilots reported that they had run out of ammunition or had burned out their guns. There was no shortage of enemy aircraft at which to shoot.[15]

Bennington launched eleven of her VF-82 Hellcats at 1513. This flight, led by Lt. R.E. Britson, headed north for RP Stations # 1 and 2, upon receiving word of the large air battle. One Corsair from *Bennington* joined them as they arrived in the area over *Bush* and *Colhoun* at about 1630 and quickly jumped into the fray. The squadron later reported:

> Primary danger to our pilots was collision or getting in the path of a friendly planes' fire. 3 Japs were seen to blow up when hit; 14 burned and crashed in the water, and 8 dove in the water before breaking into flame. A sample of the action was told by Lieut. GREGORY who kept a tally of planes he observed crashing on his plotting board - there were 28 marks on it when he returned to base. Of these 28, GREGORY estimates he had 20 in his sights during the action and actually fired on 12 or 15 but found it necessary to break off to avoid hitting our planes which were near.[16]

One of the VF-82 pilots, Lt. R.H. Jennings, Jr., spotted a Val heading for one of the destroyers. Jennings chased the Val toward the ship and was relieved when the DD ceased firing as he closed in and shot it down. During the pursuit, Jennings was so low that he believed that one of his wing tips hit a wave. He finished the day with three Vals to his credit, as did his squadron mate Lt. H.A. Gregory. Lieutenant (jg) S.P. Ward shot down two Vals and a Frank. The squadron's top gun for that day was Lt. (jg) C.E. Davies who was credited with one Oscar and two and one-half Vals.[17] Every other pilot in the group of eleven was credited with one or two kills as well. By around 1830, the planes had begun to run out of ammunition and the flight headed back to base, arriving on *Bennington* at 1900. They had accounted for twenty-six enemy aircraft destroyed; most were Vals, but several Franks, Oscars, Jills and Zekes were also shot down. These planes were obviously on a suicide mission. VF-82 reported, "Of all the enemy planes encountered, not one returned fire; all remained on course, boring in toward the surface vessels."[18]

Hornet had launched seven Hellcats from VF-17 and another nine from VBF-17 at 1219. One of the planes ditched soon after take-off and one other developed hydraulic problems and had to return to the carrier. One of the Hellcats orbited the ditched plane until its pilot was picked up and returned to the carrier. This left thirteen planes heading for the RP stations. At about 1500 one of the divisions, led by Lt. G.W. McFedries, was vectored toward an incoming bogey and spotted a Val at 3,000 feet. Ensign C. Dikoff dove on it and shot the plane down. The division reformed and headed back to their orbit point. They spotted *Bush* under attack. However, before they could intercede, the destroyer took her first kamikaze hit. Pursuing a Kate which had just dropped a bomb near the destroyer, Ens. F.R. Chapman shot it down after two of his division mates overran the plane. As Chapman pulled up, he saw another Kate diving for the *Bush*. He fired into the plane's side and then got behind it. After hitting the enemy plane with a number of rounds the Kate smoked, burst into flame and went down.

At about the same time another *Hornet* division, led by Lt. (jg) C.E. Watts, arrived in the vicinity and was vectored to meet a new group of bogeys heading for the station. They found two Vals at 1,500 feet. The two enemy planes split apart, one heading for the deck and the other remaining at altitude. Lieutenant (jg) G.M. Covelly and Ens. C.L. Toburen dove after the lower Val, and Toburen came up behind the Val. His gunfire hit the starboard wing root and the plane caught fire and went down. Above them, the second Val had been shot down by the combined fire from Watts and Lt. (jg) W.H. Gaerisch.[19]

Later in the day, at 1528, *Hornet* launched sixteen more F6F-5 Hellcats. This flight, led by Lt. (jg) R.D. Cowger, was comprised of seven planes from VF-17 and eight from VBF-17. Another VBF-17 plane soon joined them, making a total of four divisions. The additional Hellcat came from a division led by Lt. (jg) B.A. Eberts which had taken off a few minutes earlier. The planes comprising this division headed for Point Nan which was located ten miles northwest of Ie Shima and about twenty-five miles south of RP Station # 1. No sooner had they arrived at their orbiting point than *Bush* vectored them north to intercept incoming Japanese planes. Within minutes numerous Zekes and Vals appeared, flying in scattered formations toward RP Station # 1 and Okinawa. Cowger and his wingman, Lt. (jg) Pace, arrived on the scene just as the first kamikaze hit *Colhoun*.

> Before they [Cowger and Pace] got into effective range, the section, at 4000' altitude, saw the DD take a suicide bomber on her fantail. A few minutes later, a second DD, which was operating close by, was taken under bombing attack by a group of Vals. Lt.(jg) PACE, sighted one Val pulling out of his run, low on the water. He had just dropped a bomb on the DD. PACE nosed down, made a tight 180° turn to get on the Val's tail and opened fire at 8 o'clock from above. PACE was closing fast, fir-

ing long bursts into the forward cockpit and engine, when an
unidentified plane from the U.S.S. BENNINGTON [VF-82]
opened fire on the Val from directly astern. Under this two
plane attack, the Val flamed and hit the water.[20]

Cowger and Pace went after a Val and Cowger splashed it. He then
reformed his division and sent the other divisions to orbit at different altitudes. With so many enemy planes inbound toward the station, Cowger ordered the pilots to operate independently.

The three other divisions of VF-17 planes were led by Lt. (jg)
S.O. Bach, Lieutenant R.L. Junghans, and Ens. B.A. Smith.
Throughout the battle they had cruised from Point Nan to areas
around RP Stations # 1 and 2, battling Zekes, Vals, Judys and
Myrts. When they finally ran out of time and ammo, the sixteen
planes headed back to *Hornet*. Their score for the day was thirty-
two and one-half enemy aircraft destroyed and six damaged.[21] The
division led by Eberts, which was minus one plane, accounted for
two Kates.

At about 1635, *Colhoun* arrived on the scene, just as the CAP
was retiring from the area. Without the assistance of the CAP, the
ships were in great peril. *Bush* was smoking and down by the stern.
Five Zekes and seven Vals circled her waiting for a chance to
attack. The Zekes were probably from Kanoya and Kokubu # 1 and
the Vals flew from Kokubu # 2. *LCS(L) 64* was ordered to close
Bush and evacuate personnel. At 1650 the gunboat tied up to the
destroyer, which was now dead in the water. Two Vals circled the
ships in preparation for an attack. *Bush* cast off the lines and told
the gunboat to maneuver and protect herself. Both ships fired on
the Vals driving them off. The gunboat then stationed herself a few
thousand yards from *Bush* so as to provide more effective anti-aircraft fire.

At about the same time, four FM-2 Wildcats from VC-13
joined the melee. Lieutenant (jg) Douglas R. Hagood went after a
Val that was making a suicide run on *Colhoun* and shot it down.
Still another Val attacked *Colhoun* and was splashed by Lt. (jg)
Thomas N. Blanks while Lt. (jg) William E. Davis scored on a Zeke.
Davis then went after a Val but flew too close to the AA from the
destroyer and had to pull out. He found another Val to take under
fire and the plane went down. Within the next few minutes, Blanks
got another Val and Hagood splashed a Zeke. Ensign Eugene D.

Pargh shot down a Zeke and two Vals. Calls for help from the destroyers put more CAP planes over the station and the battle expanded. The VC-13 planes finally ran low on fuel and returned to the *Anzio*. At 1720, the first of two suicide planes crashed into *Colhoun*. Marine 1st Lt. Junie Lohan, now a spectator to the battle, described the scene:

> Out of the clouds came . . .a Zeke, diving straight at our port side. Everyone started running, but I was too fascinated to move. I stood by the rail on the main deck forward of amidships watching him come in. It was a horrible sound. The Zeke hit near me, wrecking the forward fire room. Many men were wounded and hurt. . . . I looked for Doc Casey and began to help him with the wounded. We carried the worst cases into the wardroom. . . . We were moving the wounded to a safer place when the Jap came in from the starboard side. The bomb burst hit the fire room - killed all but two men. The scenes were horrible. Burns were terrible. . . .
>
> The last Jap came in from the starboard - aimed right for the bridge. He got through the AA fire and hit the port side of the bridge. It was hell again - even worse. The Jap pilot was blown overboard by the blast. I could see him floating by, face upward. He looked not a day older than 14 years of age.[22]

At about the same time another kamikaze crashed into *Bush*. Still another Zeke made a run on *Colhoun* and passed over, crashing into the water between the two destroyers. A Val, attacking from the starboard bow, was shot down fifty yards from the ship. Two more Zekes attacked, one from the port bow and another from the starboard quarter. The Zeke on the port bow was hit but kept coming and, although damaged, it hit *Colhoun* on the main deck near the number forty-four 40mm mount.

A Zeke and two Vals attacked *Colhoun*. Both Vals were shot down close aboard, but the Zeke, coming in from the starboard bow, crashed the destroyer's starboard side and went into the forward fireroom. Its bomb exploded, breaking the ship's keel and causing extensive damage. The crew fought valiantly but a third attack at 1725 spelled doom for the destroyer. Three more planes commenced their attack, a Zeke from the port bow, a Val on the starboard bow and another Val on the port quarter. Damage to *Colhoun* had been significant and all her guns were under manual

Colhoun DD 801 zig-zags after being hit by a kamikaze on 6 April 1945. She sustained another strike and was sunk later that day. *NARA 80G 317257.*

control at that point. The Zeke was hit and went into the water 150 yards off the port beam. The Val came in from the starboard bow, hit the after stack and bounced off the # 3 gun, spreading gasoline over the decks. Its bomb exploded in the water near the aft end of the ship, holing it. The third Val missed *Colhoun* and proceeded to *Bush,* crashing into her. Two more Vals attacked the ships and dropped bombs that missed *Colhoun. Bush* took two more kamikaze hits from Zekes at 1730 and 1745.

Believing that the ship might break into two salvageable halves, the commanding officer continued his efforts to keep the ship afloat. Heavy swells began to take their toll and, at 1830, the sounds of the ship breaking up became apparent. The order was given to abandon ship and men went into the heavy seas. Within a short time, *Bush* went to the bottom. Many men clung to float nets and balsa rafts until they were picked up later by *LCS(L)s 24, 36, 37, 40, 64, PCE(R) 855,* and *Pakana ATF 108.* Fourteen officers and men on *Bush* were killed in action, seventy-three were missing, and 246 survivors were rescued. She was the first ship sunk on radar picket duty. *Pakana* reported that many of the survivors were in very poor condition, having suffered from shock and exposure after nearly ten hours in the water. A number had to be given artificial respiration. Many were too weak to assist in their own rescue, and three men from the tug went over the side to secure lines to them to assist in their rescue. The tug launched a whaleboat and rescued additional survivors. By the end of the ordeal, *Pakana* had rescued four officers and thirty enlisted men.

The LCS(L) gunboats arrived on the scene to render assistance to the stricken ship where they could. Bob Wisner, communications officer on *LCS(L) 37*, later recalled:

> We went over to where the *Bush* had been sunk and the *Colhoun* was being sunk and some of us tied ropes around our waists and went out in the water to get the men who were dead and wounded. We got aboard quite a few people, we picked up more dead than alive . . . We piled all the dead people on the fantail. That next morning, when the sun came up, I looked out over the horizon and it was just filled with people in their jackets, sagging in their jackets, terrible sight to see all those dead people out there, it was a terrible sight.[23]

Colhoun DD 801 (right) is obscured by smoke as another kamikaze closes in on *Bush DD 529* at Radar Picket Station # 1 on 6 April 1945. The kamikaze can be seen aft of the *Bush* just above the smoke trail. *NARA 80G 317258.*

Stationed about 6,000 yards from the two destroyers, *LCS(L) 64* found herself the next target. At about 1725 two planes approached from her port bow. All guns turned in their direction and, as they passed over the bow, they were met with a fusillade of fire. A Zeke turned in towards *64* and made a head-on run. The gunboat made a hard left turn to bring all of its guns to bear and splashed it twenty feet off the starboard quarter. It exploded upon impact but the ship was not damaged. It was a close call for the gunboat. Crewman Gordon H. Wiram would later write:

> I could see the plane kept trying to swerve so as to crash down on us. I looked as long as possible until the last moment when I knew that the aircraft would collide with our ship. I curled up into the tightest ball possible and flat on the deck with as much steel between me and the plane. Every muscle in my body was rigid and my eyes were clenched . . . thinking that the worst was about to happen. There was a strong thud. The ship shook like a strong earthquake! . . . thank God it missed me."[24]

On board *Colhoun*, the crew took all necessary measures to insure her survival, jettisoning extra topside gear and attempting to plug the holes in her hull. At about 1800, a damaged Hamp made a run on the ship and crashed her on the port beam, in spite of being hit by guns # 1, 2, and 41. Little damage to the hull was sustained from this crash and the ship's company continued with their work.

By 1900 the decision was made to abandon ship. At 2015, the *LCS(L) 84* came alongside the starboard side of *Colhoun* and evacuated 217 enlisted men and eleven officers. Among those rescued was marine 1st Lt. Junie B. Lohan, the pilot who had been picked up by the destroyer. The seas were heavy and, as the gunboat came alongside *Cassin Young* to transfer survivors, she was pounded against the destroyer before she could complete her task. She took the survivors back to the transport area the next day.

Lohan described the experience:

> . . . an LCS came alongside and we piled over the side, stretcher cases first. The Captain, gunnery officer, first lieutenant and some volunteers stayed behind to try to keep the ship afloat.
>
> Worst of all was the tiring ride in the LCS. We knew if we were hit again the LCS would take us all. Luckily we got

through the night and next morning we were aboard another ship.

I don't think I'll ever forget the sight of the other ship as we came upon them. It was wonderful. A lot cried, too.[25]

LCS(L) 87 rescued another fifty-six men from the ship.

At 2355 *Cassin Young* was ordered to sink *Colhoun* and commenced firing on her. The destroyer went down within the hour in 200 fathoms. Radar picket duty had claimed its second destroyer.

LCS(L)s 109 and *110,* patrolling RP Station # 3 with *Cassin Young,* also saw some action that day. At 0515 *LCS(L) 109* was attacked by a twin-engine Sally. Several of the gunboat's 40mm shells were seen to hit the belly of the plane when it was 800 yards off the ship. The plane turned away. Shortly thereafter, at 0547, *110* took a Judy under fire as it passed over the ship. The gunners were on target and the plane was splashed by the twin 40mms. At 0900 the two gunboats were ordered back to Nago Wan anchorage.

Bennett began her day patrolling RP Station # 4 with *LCS(L)s 111* and *114.* By the end of the day, she would be at RP Station # 1, assisting *Bush* and *Colhoun.* At 1536 the fighter director officer on *Bennett* contacted *Cassin Young* and four Hellcats were put on station over the destroyer to intercept enemy planes. Shortly thereafter, the ship was attacked by two Vals. *Bennett's* gunners accounted for one and the CAP for the second. At 1635 another plane was spotted coming in and was taken under fire. It missed and crashed to port of the ship. Five more planes came in at 1740 and the ship vectored the CAP to intercept them. One made a run on *Bennett* but missed and splashed in the ocean. In all, five were shot down by the American fighters. *Bennett* shot down another kamikaze at 1803. *LCS(L) 39* also got some gunnery practice; she took a Zeke under fire at 1813 and drove it off. About that time, word was received that *Colhoun* had left RP Station # 2 to aid *Bush,* and *Bennett* moved over to RP Station # 2 where she was attacked by two Judys. The CAP shot both down. At 1830 when she received word that *Colhoun* was hit, *Bennett* and the gunboats set out for RP Station # 1 to assist the damaged destroyer. Arriving on station about 1940, they spent the remainder of the night there assisting the stricken ships and searching for survivors.

Hudson continued her patrol at RP Station # 10 along with *LCS(L)s 115* and *116.* The station was approached by bogeys at

1215 and 1702 but both turned away. At 1829 a Betty came in from the west and was fired upon by both *Hudson* and *LCS(L) 115*; it splashed at 1835. The gunboat received credit for the kill.

Saturday, 7 April 1945

Kikusui 1 continued into 7 April. Nineteen ships had begun patrols the previous day, but by 0900 on the 6th, four of the LCS(L)s had been sent back to the anchorage, leaving only fifteen ships on station to face the beginning of the largest kamikaze raid the campaign would see. The seventh of April found a total of twenty-two ships assigned to the duty, including three LSM(R)s. Commander Task Force Fifty-One asserted: "The gunboat types proved valuable additions by their AA armament, and by the fact that they are a difficult target to hit."[26] While this would prove to be true for the LCS(L)s, it would not be so for the LSM(R)s.

    Luce was assigned to RP Station # 1 along with *LSM(R) 189, 192,* and *LCS(L) 33*. The ships arrived on station to find the water covered with oil slicks and a lot of floating debris from the previous day's disaster. *LCS(L) 33* sighted the body of a dead Japanese flyer. *Bennett* had been assisting the ships at the station since the preceding evening. During the early morning hours she had come under attack, driving off one plane at 0323 and shooting down another about 0400. Other enemy planes approached *Bennett*. A night fighter shot one enemy plane down at 0600 and drove off a Val at 0637. Shortly thereafter, *Bennett* vectored the CAP to intercept other planes; the CAP reported splashing one at 0810. *Bennett* picked up three other Vals at twenty-five miles and vectored the CAP in their direction. The CAP shot down two and damaged the third. The enemy plane escaped from the CAP and crashed in flames into *Bennett's* starboard side amidships; three men were killed and eighteen wounded. *Bennett* was escorted back to the anchorage by *LCS(L) 39* and *Sterrett*.

    Radar Picket Station # 2 was patrolled by the high speed minesweeper *Macomb* and *LCS(L)s 32* and *51*. Two divisions of VF-23 Hellcats were patrolling near RP Station # 2. They had taken off from *Langley* at 0503. One of the pilots, Ens. R.C. Leverence, caught a Val northeast of Iheya Shima and shot it down with a burst to the wing root area. Later, about 1900, *Macomb* heard a report that *Gregory*, on nearby RP Station # 3, had been attacked and hit by a kamikaze. She headed for the station and stood by to assist the destroyer until 0700 the next morning. *LCS(L)s 32* and *51* arrived there at 1454 and began their patrol. The ships went to general quarters many times that day but the enemy did not come within firing range. Lieutenant H.D. Chickering, commanding officer of *LCS(L) 51*, later wrote:

> The raids seemed ceaseless, our guns were always manned and the gunners literally slept at them. As Captain I seldom left the bridge. For a week, we fired on, or reported, dozens of raids, and lost count very quickly. The radio reported continuous fighting, hits and sinking on all stations.[27]

LCS(L) 32 went to general quarters at 1850 and ten minutes later opened fire on an incoming plane. No hits were reported and the plane disappeared.

Cassin Young began her day at RP Station # 3 and was relieved by *Gregory* at 0630. At about 1045, she vectored four Hellcats from her CAP to intercept three enemy planes coming in from the north. The F6F-5s, from VF-82 on *Bennington*, spotted two Franks and a George headed toward the picket ships at an altitude of about 200-300 feet. Lieutenant A.G. Manson shot down the George and flight leader Lt. R.B. Dalton and Ens. C.C. Robbins shot down the two Franks. The navy pilots then saw two more Franks; they were attacked and shot down by Lt. Manson and Lt. (jg) L.B. Murray. None of the navy flyers sustained any damage to their planes.[28]

At 1150 the *Gregory* again vectored CAP aircraft to intercept incoming Japanese planes. This CAP consisted of two VF-29 divisions from *Cabot*. The eight Hellcats, led by Lt. Comdr. Willard E. Eder, were first sent after the VF-82's planes, but arrived just in time to see the two Franks splashed by Manson and Murray. They were then vectored north where Lt. Malcolm V.D. Martin and Lt. Comdr. Eder spotted two Judys 1,000 feet above them at 4,000 feet. Eder shot one of the Judys down with only forty rounds of ammunition. Martin shot the wing off the other and it went down in flames.

Another VF-29 division, under Lt. Van Vranken, was vectored northwest to intercept a single Judy. Lt. (jg) Joseph L. Chandler closed to within 800 feet and opened fire. At 300 feet, he had to swerve to avoid pieces of the plane which was on fire and coming apart. It went into a spin and exploded before it hit the water.[29]

Twelve Frances bombers had taken off from Miyazaki in the early afternoon. At 1436 *Gregory* vectored eight F4U-1D Corsairs from VF-84 off *Bunker Hill* to intercept them. Lieutenant Comdr. R.E. Hill spotted a Frances bomber and came up from underneath. He hit the plane's port engine, causing it to go down in flames. Another Frances was attacked by Lt. J. Littlejohn who quickly splashed it. Lieutenant C. Kendall caught a Judy, one of twelve that had left Kokubu # 1 earlier that afternoon. It had been chased by Lieutenant Schaeffer but escaped. However, as it exited some cloud cover, Kendall shot it down. With the excitement over for the day and their ammunition running low, the planes returned to their carrier.[30]

The destroyer *Gregory* headed out for Radar Picket Station # 3 to relieve *Cassin Young*. At 1234 she observed four Corsairs from the VF-10 Grim Reapers Squadron on their way back to *Intrepid*. As they watched, the plane flown by Lt. Comdr. Walter E. Clarke, the commanding officer of the squadron, collided with another of the Corsairs flown by Ensign Croy. Croy's plane spun in and no trace of him was found. Clarke put his plane down 4,000 yards astern of the *Gregory* and was picked up. He was transferred to *Cassin Young* later that day and returned to his ship.

Gregory arrived on station and relieved *Cassin Young* at 1454. At 1737 a Val was observed about eighteen miles away. It seemed to be closing on the ship and, at 1739, was only nine miles away. Since the CAP directed by *Luce* at RP Station # 1 was reported to be after it, the ship held fire. By 1743 the Val was too close for comfort and *Gregory* opened fire, hitting it several times and driving it off course. The plane passed over the ship and crashed in the water fifteen feet to port. At 1845 *LCS(L) 38* arrived to supplement the patrol and within an hour went to general quarters but saw no action.

Early in the morning of 7 April, *Wickes* refueled and headed out to RP Station # 12 where she arrived at 0630. At 0716 a Japanese fighter came in from the northeast and made a suicide run on the ship. It was hit by a number of rounds and crashed in the water close aboard the port quarter. Debris showered the aft end of the ship but no injuries or damage resulted. *LCS(L)s 11* and *13* joined *Wickes* at 1245 to supplement the destroyer's efforts. All three ships were ordered back to the transport area to replenish supplies and returned back to RP Station # 12 at 0108 the next morning.

On this day and the following, Domei News Agency announced a reorganization of the Japanese Army Air Forces. Previously they had been under the command of local ground forces, but from this point on they would be under the overall command of the Air General Army, headquartered in Tokyo. General Shozo Kawabe was appointed as Commander in Chief.[31]

Sunday, 8 April 1945

Luce patrolled RP Station #1 with *LSM(R)s 189* and *192* on 8 April until she was relieved by *Cassin Young* at 1300. At 1715 she was joined by *Lang* and *LCS(L)s 33* and *57*. Two Oscars attacked *LCS(L) 33* at about 1809. The first Oscar came at the ship from the port beam and was taken under fire. According to the ship's action report, the pilot was killed while his plane was about 200 yards from the ship, enabling the gunboat to maneuver out of its way. It passed over the *33* and crashed close to the starboard bow, about twenty feet away. The second Oscar was driven off by the ship's gunfire.[32] To the south of the station, six Corsairs from VMF-224 spotted three more Oscars heading for the picket ships. The enemy planes were flying at 2,500 feet and the American planes climbed to intercept them. First Lt. A.C. Satterwhite and his wingman, Second Lt. R.M. Tousley, followed one through a series of dives, turns, and loops and finally shot it down. Second Lts. R.E. Torgerson and J.B. Bender shot down a second and Captain F. Mick and his wingman, 2d Lt. R.C. Bray, shot down the third. "The VMF-224 pilots expressed the opinion that all three enemy pilots were very inexperienced and did not attempt any aggressive action."[33]

Radar Picket Station # 3 was also hazardous. *Gregory* and *LCS(L)s 37, 38,* and *40* were patrolling there. Eight combat air patrol planes covered the station during the day but saw no action. At about 1830, after the CAP had retired from the scene, enemy aircraft made their appearance. *Gregory* reported three Sonias approaching her position, with a fourth plane in the area. It soon became obvious that *LCS(L) 38* was the target, and the destroyer steamed toward her at twenty-five knots in order to join their firepower against the enemy planes. Two planes attacked the ships and were turned away.

Shortly thereafter, the third plane made several attempts to approach the destroyer but was driven off. On its third run, at 1813, the enemy plane came directly into the destroyer, striking her amidships on the port side, near the waterline. Fortunately, it hit the ship's gig, which took the brunt of the impact. The destroyer temporarily lost power and headway and began to flood in the forward fireroom and engine room.

The damage was quickly brought under control and the ship was again fully operative. Another of the Sonias came in from the port side but was turned away by the ship's gunfire. The remaining plane made a steep dive toward *Gregory* and was taken under fire by *LCS(L) 38* and the destroyer. It strafed the ship and dropped a bomb which did not explode. Two of the ship's crew were wounded. After being hit by fire from both ships, the plane passed over the *Gregory* and splashed to port at 1827. The only damage to the destroyer from this plane was a lost radio antenna. The LCS(L) and the destroyer proceeded to RP Station # 2 to inspect the damage. *Gregory*, accompanied by *Macomb*, made it back to Kerama Retto the next day under her own power and was repaired.

Monday, 9 April 1945

Ships on the radar picket stations to the north of Okinawa, (# 1, 2, 3, and 4), would do some shifting around during this day. The attacks on *Sterrett* at RP Station # 4 would make this tactical arrangement necessary.

Sterrett had been patrolling RP Station # 4 with her support gunboats, *LCS(L)s 24* and *36*. Four Hellcats from VF(N)-90 on *Enterprise* had taken off on a CAP mission at 1715. They headed for RP Station # 4 and arrived at 1815. *Sterrett* picked up incoming bogeys and vectored Lt. D.E. Runion and his wingman Lt. (jg) W. "J" Squires to intercept them.

After some difficulty, they spotted the ships firing on them and came in for the kill. A Val was circling the station at 1,500 feet and made a dive on *Sterrett*. Squires got on its tail and followed it through a hail of anti-aircraft fire until his bursts hit the starboard wing root. The Val turned off to starboard, pointed down and hit the water close to the bow of the destroyer.

Shortly thereafter, at 1849, as the ships were steaming in a column, a combination of five Vals and Nates attacked them. Four headed for the destroyer and one for *LCS(L) 36*. A Nate came in aft of the formation chased by two Hellcats from the CAP which shot it down. Still another came in behind the *36* and was taken under fire. The plane was hit numerous times and crashed directly in front of the gunboat. It passed over so closely that it took off a good portion of the ship's mast, damaging her radio and radar antennas. *Sterrett*, assisted by the gunboats, shot down two of her attackers but the third hit her in the starboard side at the water line. *LCS(L) 36* had taken the planes under fire as well and scored direct hits on the first plane, which crashed off the starboard side of *Sterrett*. Fortunately the damage to *Sterrett* was not great and the flooding was localized. The hit caused some of her fuel tanks to rupture, spilling diesel fuel into two compartments. None of her crew were injured. Since the ship was maneuvering at high speed, sea water entered the compartment and put out the fires. The ships were ordered back to the anchorage for repairs and damage assessment. They were escorted by other destroyers and *LCS(L) 24*. Although the damage was not great, *Sterrett* was out of the war. She had to return to Pearl Harbor for repairs.

Tuesday, 10 April 1945

At a planning session of the Japanese Combined Fleet, held on 8 April, the start of *Kikusui # 2* was set for the 10th. The Japanese army air force ordered its special attack units to prepare for the assault. This attack would involve a total of 185 planes flying as kamikazes, as well as 195 others flying cover and conventional missions.

The tenth of April was rainy and cloudy with low visibility. Squalls from the north increased along with the wind and sea. As a result, many CAPs were grounded and the Japanese kept most of their patrols and attack aircraft on the ground as well. The poor weather provided the picket ships with a breather from the constant calls to general quarters.

The inclement weather was acceptable to the Japanese. April 10 was one of the *To Shi Bi* or ten death days according to the Japanese calendar. For the superstitious, no good could come from launching an attack on this day.[34]

Wednesday, 11 April 1945

Radar Picket Station # 1 was patrolled by *Cassin Young, Purdy, LSM(R) 192, LCS(L)s 33, 57, 114,* and *115* on 11 April. At 1459 an incoming plane was picked up on radar and *Cassin Young* vectored the combat air patrol to intercept it. The aviators were on target and one Tojo went down. *LSM(R) 192* departed at 1345.

Hudson patrolled on RP Station # 3 with *LCS(L)s 37, 38, 111, 118,* and *LSM(R) 199.* At 2100 two Japanese planes approached the station. A night fighter was vectored to intercept them and shot one down. The second turned away from the ships.

Radar Picket Station # 7 was patrolled by *Brown* and *LCS(L)s 15, 16,* and *24.* Throughout the day the station was covered by planes from *Shamrock Bay, Manila Bay, Makassar Strait,* and *Rudyerd Bay.* As the day ended, the four plane CAP of VC-96 Wildcats from *Rudyerd Bay* was sent home at 1745. At 1837 observers on *Brown* spotted two Zekes trying to escape from a CAP not under their control. In desperation, one made a run on the station with one of the CAP planes on his tail. The Zeke was taken under fire by the ships and splashed about fifty yards off the starboard beam of *Brown* after being hit by fire from the destroyer and the gunboats. Two other Zekes were shot down by the CAP aft of the formation. These planes were a part of the flight of fifty that had taken off from Kanoya and Kokubu # 1 airfields on Southern Kyushu. Thirty of the planes had to turn back for various reasons and only twenty made it through to attack the American forces.

To the south, the airfields at Tainan, Takao, Kagi, and Taichu were hit by B-24s from the 5th Air Force. The Philippine-based bombers would hit the fields again on 12 and 14 April.

Thursday, 12 April 1945

Kikusui # 2 was originally scheduled to begin on 10 April, but bad weather had postponed it until 12 April. Vice Adm. Matome Ugaki, Commander in Chief of the Fifth Air Fleet, was anxiously awaiting its launch. The first attack in the *Ten Go* campaign had been deceptive. Ugaki was misled by many exaggerated reports of losses inflicted on the American fleet. According to those reports sixty-nine ships had been sunk or seriously damaged between 7 and 8 April. Among those allegedly sunk were two battleships, three

cruisers and three destroyers. Still another battleship was reported as damaged.[35] In actuality, twenty-eight ships had been hit,
with only eight of them sunk. One battleship, *Maryland*, had taken
a hit. A single bomb put her number 3 turret out of commission.

The largest among the seriously damaged were destroyers,
with *Bush* and *Colhoun* sunk and *Leutze, Morris, Mullany,
Newcomb*, and *Bennett* damaged so severely that they were out of
action for the duration of the war. This was hardly a death blow to
the American navy, but Ugaki's intelligence reports led him to
believe that several more such attacks might force the Americans
to abandon their campaign at Okinawa. They rated their chances
as even.[36] One of the greater concerns were the marine fighter
squadrons at Yontan and Kadena.

Although Japanese estimates of 130 aircraft were low (MAG-
31 and MAG-33 had about 220), the Japanese still felt that the
presence of these planes placed their special attack forces in jeop-
ardy. Ugaki's diary indicated this total on 12 April, and it is likely
that his figures reflected only the aircraft of MAG-31 which had
arrived on 7 April.[37] MAG- 33's fighters did not land at Kadena
until two days later. Ugaki's intelligence reports probably reflected
sightings between the 7th and 9th. Had he been aware of the latest figures, it is possible that he might have placed Yontan and
Kadena even higher on his list of priorities.

The marine flyers had more serious problems than the
Japanese. According to Air Defense Command reports for 12 April:

> Biggest hazard of all was our own anti-aircraft batteries which
> continually fired on our own planes when taking off and until
> they were out of range. All batteries that could be communi-
> cated with by Lieutenant Colonel Mallory and Major Kirk were
> notified that our planes were taking off, yet they continued to
> fire.[38]

The Americans, however, had been forewarned of the impend-
ing attack. An enlisted Japanese naval aviator, Flight Petty Officer
Sata Omaichi, flying his Jack out of Kikaiga Shima, had been shot
down on 6 April by the CAP from TG 58.1. The destroyer *Taussig*
picked him up. He boasted of the coming attack and how it would
wipe out the American fleet. The Military Intelligence Service had
also been picking up messages from Ugaki's command giving

details of the attack.[39] As a result, Rear Adm. J.J. Clark CTG 58.1, sent the following message to all units on 11 April:

> BE PREPARED FOR VERY HEAVY AIR ATTACKS TOMOR-
> ROW COMMENCING BEFORE DAWN X INDICATIONS
> ARE THAT THE JAPS WILL MAKE ANOTHER MAJOR
> EFFORT TOMORROW USING ALL TYPES OF PLANES
> INCLUDING OBSOLESCENT TYPES AND TRAINERS X
> SUCH TYPES OF PLANES AS NAVY CLAUDE, ZEKE
> MODEL 21, VAL, SUZY, KATE, NELL, DAVE AND ALF AND
> ARMY TYPES NATE, IDA AND SONIA ARE PROBABLE AS
> WELL AS CURRENT OPERATIONAL TYPES X UNFAMIL-
> IAR TRAINER TYPE BOTH TWIN AND SINGLE ENGINE
> AND BOTH MONOPLANE AND BIPLANE CAN BE
> EXPECTED IN SUICIDE ATTACKS X SOME OF THESE
> LOOK LIKE OUR SUGAR NAN JIGS [SNJ].[40]

Participating in *Kikusui # 2* would be a total of 185 Special Attack aircraft, including 125 from the navy and sixty from the army. Another 195 planes would fly regular escort and attack missions. Most of the planes came from the combined Third, Fifth and Tenth Air Fleets and the Sixth Air Army based on Kyushu and the islands just to the south of Japan such as Tokuno Shima and Amami O Shima. Additional aircraft of the Eighth Air Division would attack from Taiwan.

Among the messages intercepted by American intelligence was one that referred to Betty bombers "equipped for Cherry Blossom attacks."[41] An *Oka*, captured at Yontan and shipped to Anacostia for study, had a cherry blossom symbol on the nose. It was deduced that the allusion to cherry blossoms must indicate an attack using *Okas*. This was the first reference to the piloted bomb that Military Intelligence Service reported and from this point on, the Americans would know what it meant.

Patrolling RP Station # 1 on 12 April were *Cassin Young*, *Purdy*, and *LCS(L)s 33, 57, 114*, and *115*. It was a bright, clear day with calm seas but it was to be a disastrous day for the ships at RP Station # 1. By the end of the day five of the six ships would be hit by kamikazes, with one of them, *LCS(L) 33*, going to the bottom. Only *LCS(L) 114* would escape damage. In the melee, twenty to twenty-five Japanese planes would be shot down by the ships and the CAP.

Marines inspect an *Oka Type 11* at Yontan Airfield, Okinawa, 11 June 1945. *NARA 80G 323641.*

Langley provided a morning CAP of VF-23 Hellcats which returned to base around noon. Beginning at 1112, a series of raids were detected coming in from the north. By 1243 *Cassin Young* had three divisions of VF-10 Corsairs from *Intrepid* under her direction. The Grim Reaper divisions were vectored out to intercept the Japanese planes. Lieutenant W.J. Schub's division spotted fifteen Vals and Nates heading for one of the destroyers and went after them. Moments after Schub's division went on the attack, they were also spotted by 1st Lt. William Nickerson who was leading another division. The Vals and Nates scattered as the eight Corsairs cut through their formation, knocking down most of them. When the action was over, twelve of the enemy had been splashed.

Wildcats from *Petroff Bay* joined the battle. One division, led by Lt. L.V. Lieb, was at 15,000 feet when they spotted a Zeke being chased by some Corsairs. With their superior diving speed, the F4Us continually overran their opponent, giving Lieb his opening.

In a 12 o'clock run, Lieb hit the Zeke's engine with a burst before he also overran it. His wingman, Lt. (jg) Reid, hit the plane in the cockpit, killing the pilot. The Zeke spun in from 17,000 feet.

Two more Zekes were under pursuit by Corsairs. Ensigns C.J. Janson and P.R. Baumgartner, comprising the second section of Wildcats, got into the fray. One of the Zekes made a pass at Janson and this gave Baumgartner his opening. He hit the Zeke's engine from the side and it broke off the fight; it was followed down and finished off by a Corsair. Baumgartner was surprised to see bullets hitting his engine and instrument panel. As he had been engrossed in watching his section mate, a Zeke had managed to sneak in on his tail. The navy pilot did a controlled half spin and came in from in front of his attacker. A quick burst missed but the Zeke broke off the engagement. Baumgartner's Wildcat was in trouble and he prepared to ditch near two of the destroyers. Adding insult to injury, the destroyers promptly opened fire, not recognizing him as friendly. With no choice in the matter, he continued down, ditched and was picked up unharmed by *Purdy*.[42]

A third VF-10 division, led by Lt. Frank M. Jackson, was vectored to intercept another group at 20,000 feet. It was a large raid consisting of thirty to forty Zekes and Oscars.

> The division attacked the Jap formation from the rear and were joined shortly afterwards by some FM-2's. Lieut. JACKSON was immediately jumped by 3 Zekes, but his wingman, Ensign TUCKER, shot one of them down and got enough hits on the other two to chase them away. JACKSON got on the tail of another ZEKE, when the Jap did a tight wingover and ended up in a head-on pass at JACKSON. JACKSON's guns were truer and the Jap went down in flames. Sighting another Zeke, JACKSON made a diving turn onto its tail. An FM-2 pilot, apparently not seeing JACKSON and chasing the same ZEKE, slid under JACKSON's plane and a midair collision resulted. JACKSON was eventually able to get out of his plane and parachuted to comparative safety near a Jap held island.[43]

Jackson had collided with the Wildcat flown by Ens. C.J. Janson of VC-93. The collision broke one wing off each plane. Jackson was picked up uninjured by *Hudson* at 1515, but Janson's body was not recovered.

An F4U-1D Corsair from VF-10 flies over Okinawa on 10 April 1945. The squadron, known as the "Grim Reapers," was based on the *Intrepid CV-11*. *NARA 80G 316035*.

At 1337 *Purdy* opened fire on an attacking Val. This plane came in high, dive bombing *Cassin Young* which also took it under fire. The bomb exploded close aboard the starboard side of *Cassin Young* without causing damage. With both ships firing on the plane, it pulled out, circled and crashed into the starboard quarter of *Cassin Young*. The great number of planes attacking the station that afternoon made casualties unavoidable. Arrayed against the six picket ships were a combination of approximately forty Vals, Kates, Zekes, Oscars, and Bettys. The Zekes were all carrying bombs and they, along with the Bettys, had taken off from Kanoya. The Kates had scrambled from Kushira about the same time. Overhead, the VF-10 division led by Lt. W.A. Nickerson, was on its way back to *Intrepid* when they spotted a combination of ten Jills, Vals and Judys heading for *Purdy* and her support ships. Nickerson, with Ens. Brauer, got on the tail of a Jill which was diving on *Purdy* and they shot it down. The two subsequently went after a Judy but the plane's rear gunner shot Nickerson down. He was picked up at 1614 by *LCS(L) 114*.

Lookouts on *Purdy* spotted a Val making a run on her from the starboard quarter. She and *LCS(L) 114* took it under fire and splashed it 2,500 yards out. *Cassin Young* headed back to port for repairs and *Purdy* began to accompany her but was directed back to the station. At 1442 another Val being pursued by the CAP, came in from the starboard side and went down in flames as it was caught between *Purdy* and the CAP. In the next ten minutes two more Vals went down under the destroyer's guns. Still another Val attacked at 1500. The plane was being chased by three fighters from the CAP but managed to get through the hail of antiaircraft fire from *Purdy* and *LCS(L) 114*. It splashed only twenty feet from the side of the destroyer and ricocheted off the water, striking the side of *Purdy*. The plane's bomb pierced the destroyer and exploded inside the ship causing *Purdy* to lose steering and communications. Ten of her men were blown overboard. The ship regained control and headed back to the anchorage carrying thirteen dead and fifty-eight wounded men. She had shot down four kamikazes, had assisted with three others and been hit by the eighth.[44] Her CO, Comdr. Frank L. Johnson, would later observe: "The prospects of a long and illustrious career for a destroyer assigned to Radar Picket Station duty is below average expectancy. That duty is extremely hazardous, very tiring, and entirely unenjoyable."[45]

In the midst of the melee, *LCS(L)57* spotted a group of eight planes to her starboard at 1347, one of which made a bombing run on the ship. The plane dropped its bomb 200 yards off the starboard side but it did not explode. The ship's gunners had been firing on the plane from the time it was 4,000 yards out. Repeated hits on the plane were observed and, after dropping its bomb, the plane went down fifty yards from the gunboat. Eight more planes attacked the ship from the starboard side in two waves of four planes each. One peeled off and commenced a wave-top strafing run from dead ahead. Taken under fire by the forward twin 40mm gun, the plane was hit repeatedly and the pilot was killed. At the last moment it pulled up and struck the forward 40mm gun tub, careening off to crash in the water twenty-five yards to port. The gun was knocked out by the attack. At 1352 the ship's gunners accounted for two Nates but a third came in at wave top height on the port quarter. Although it was hit, the Nate exploded about ten feet from the ship and blew an eight foot hole in her side. Four men were blown overboard. With both of her twin 40mm guns out of action, the ship was in dire straits. Areas below the decks began to flood and, within a short time, the *57* was listing ten degrees to starboard.

The last kamikaze crash had knocked out the *57's* steering and Lt. Harry L. Smith, the ship's commanding officer, sent two men aft to the emergency steering compartment. *LCS(L) 33* came to her assistance, picking up men from *LCS(L) 57* who had been blown overboard. At 1420 a Nate made a run on the *57* from the starboard bow.

In hot pursuit was one of the CAP fighters. Both the gunboat and the American plane hit the Nate with their fire and it splashed 300 yards off the starboard bow of the *57*. Ten minutes later another Nate, also under pursuit by the CAP, circled the ship and crashed into the forward single 40mm mount killing two men. This left the gunboat with only a couple of 20mm and .50 caliber guns in operation. *LCS(L) 57* began to list heavily to starboard and requested permission to leave the station in an attempt to make it back to port for repairs before the ship sank. The *57*, fighting for her life, did not realize that the *LCS(L) 33* nearby was also under attack.

> After proceeding five miles noticed that LCS(L) 33, which had been ordered to standby, was not following, and being unable to contact her by radio, returned to battle area. Received message from LCS(L) 115 indicating that she was picking up survivors of LCS(L) 33 . . . which had been hit and was burning...DD 734 passed close aboard heading south; advised this ship by semaphore to follow her to port. This was attempted but could not keep up. . . . Since DD 734 was apparently unable to help, turned northward again, returning to battle area. Since both destroyers had left, friendly aircraft which had covered them during large part of the attack, covered the four LCS(L)'s now grouped together.[46]

LCS(L) 57 arrived at the anchorage at 0020 the next morning. Her dead and wounded were transferred off the ship. The gunboat was sent to Kerama Retto the next day and later to the Philippines for repairs. She was out of the war. *LCS(L) 57* had shot down four Nates and had been hit by three others. Her valiant effort did not

LCS(L) 57 at Kerama Retto after sustaining damage in a kamikaze attack while on radar picket duty. *NARA 80G 330114.*

go unnoticed and the ship was later awarded the Presidential Unit Citation.

At 1500 *LCS(L) 33* had been attacked by two Vals, one of which came in from the port side and the other from starboard. The Val coming in from the port side made a strafing run on the ship and was shot down 5,000 yards off the port beam. The second Val hit the gunboat amidships and exploded, breaking the fire main and making it impossible to fight the many fires which were started. The ship's power was also knocked out and even her Johnson pumps were on fire. Within a few minutes, *LCS(L) 33* was a ball of fire and listing thirty-five degrees to port. Lt. (jg) Frank C. Osterland would later write:

> A third plane dove down along the ship's starboard side and leveled off just above the wave tops. It struck Dolly Three [LCS(L) 33] full force, forward of amidships. There was a terrific crash and gasoline was sprayed over the ship. Fires immediately engulfed much of the superstructure.

Many of the crew topside were temporarily rendered unconscious by the concussion. The Captain was thrown violently
against the conning tower and suffered a broken vertebra. The
mortally wounded ship began to list in the water and go out of
control. All engines were shut down. Below decks in what
would very quickly become a steel coffin, we were deafened by
gunfire and tossed about by the wildly maneuvering ship. Then
came a terrific crash when the plane struck and suddenly, for
me, there was only darkness, stillness and emptiness. I was
lying on the deck of the radio/radar room which was my Dolly
Three battle station. I had apparently been thrown off my feet,
unconscious, under the radar console and against the bulkhead. There was a deep dent in my helmet that hadn't been
there before, and I knew that I'd received a hard blow to my
head and that my nose was bleeding.[47]

Osterland could hear the order to abandon ship being given. In a
dazed condition he crawled out of the radio room and made it to the
deck. There he saw the terrible condition of the ship and its crew.
Many were already in the water and in need of help. Osterland
dove in and assisted in getting the men together to make it easier
for them to be rescued. After an hour *LCS(L) 115* picked them up.
Along with the survivors from *LCS(L) 33, 115* also rescued a
Japanese pilot who had managed to survive the battle over the
picket station. The order to abandon ship had been given at 1505
as the ship's magazines began to explode. *LCS(L) 115* picked up
seventy survivors. Only three men were listed as missing. At 1648
Purdy sank the ship with two rounds from her five inch gun.
LCS(L) 33 became the third ship and the first gunboat sunk on RP
duty.

Compared to the other ships, *LCS(L) 115* escaped with minor
damage. With her companion gunboats under attack, she headed
toward *57* to render aid. At 1427 a Val attacked her, strafing the
ship as it came in for a suicide run. The gunboat zig-zagged as the
crew took the plane under fire. It narrowly missed the ship, going
into the water twenty-five feet off the port side. The only damage
to the ship came from the strafing which wounded two men. A half
hour later, at 1455, another Val dove on the gunboat from the starboard side. The enemy plane was taken under fire and maneuvered
radically in an attempt to crash the gunboat, narrowly missing the
ship's forward twin 40mm mount. It crashed into the water one

hundred feet off the port beam; the gunboat continued toward *LCS(L) 57*.

LCS(L) 114 was the only ship to escape damage that day. At 1337 she fired on the bogey closing on *Cassin Young* but the destroyer splashed it. A few minutes later four Zekes came within range. She fired on them but they were too high. When *57* and *Cassin Young* were hit by suicide planes, she headed to their aid. At 1425 an Oscar approached from the north and *Cassin Young* took it under fire. The enemy plane was splashed 1,000 yards off the port quarter. Within seven minutes another Zeke headed towards *Purdy*. *LCS(L) 114* fired upon the enemy plane and the destroyer finished it off. Simultaneously, another plane approached from behind the ship. *LCS(L) 114* took it under fire and drove the Japanese plane into the guns of *Purdy* which shot it down. At 1500 the gunboat observed the devastating hit on *LCS(L) 33* which led to her sinking. The gunboat continued on patrol picking up men from *Purdy*. At 1640 *114* was ordered to take the wounded survivors back to the transport area.

The gunboats and the destroyers took their toll on the enemy planes. According to the action report of *Purdy* for that day:

> One shipboard enlisted observer who kept a tally of the "splashes" made by friendly fighters, surface ships including LCS type, and by suicide hits, stated that he counted a total of 22 splashes during the 86 minute air action. It is believed that at least 20 and probably about 25-30 Japanese planes were destroyed in the above action.[48]

The commanding officer of *LCS(L) 114*, Lt. G.W. Mefferd, concurred, adding that five were shot down by the CAP and seventeen by the combined fire of the six ships.[49]

Although night was approaching the attacks did not stop. Three divisions of VMF-221 Corsairs had taken off from *Bunker Hill* about 1418 to fly CAP in the area near RP Stations # 1 and 2. At 1620 one division, led by Capt. F.B. Baldwin, was vectored north to intercept an incoming raid. First Lt. J.E. Jorgensen was first to spot three Vals headed straight for RP Station # 1. The Corsairs had to climb to catch them as they were flying at 9,000 feet. Jorgensen hit one of the Vals in the wing roots and it caught fire and went down in flames. First Lt. A.B. Imel got behind another of the Vals and his fire hit its gas tanks; it burst into flame and went down. He then went after the third Val but found he was out of ammunition. Baldwin took up the pursuit. As the enemy plane's rear gunner fired on him, Baldwin hit the Val in the left wing root and it was engulfed in flames. He turned off as Capt. D.L. Balch from the other VMF-221 division shot at the plane. It spiraled downward in flames and crashed into the ocean. Baldwin was given credit for the kill.

Balch's division had been flying cover over *Purdy*, which radioed to the planes "keep the Japs away as we cannot fire."[50] Second Lt. E.K. Nicolaides went after two Zekes which were only about a quarter mile away. He overran one Zeke but turned back in on its tail. Meanwhile, Balch hit the plane with two bursts before he also overran it. Nicolaides finished off the Zeke with shots to the cockpit, tail and wings. The Zeke dove into the ocean from 9,000 feet. Balch climbed to engage another Zeke and hit it in the engine, cockpit and tail. It caught fire and headed for the destroyers, splashing so close to one that flames momentarily engulfed the ship's deck.

At 2044, *PCE(R) 852* arrived at the radar picket station to offer assistance. She took eight casualties from the LCS(L)s and transported them back to Hagushi.

Patrolling on RP Station # 2 were *Stanly, Lang, LCS(L)s 32, 51, 116, and LSM(R)s 197* and *198*. With many enemy planes in the area, the ships were constantly at general quarters. Because of the activity at RP Station # 1, *Stanly* was ordered to proceed to that station at 1351 to assist *Cassin Young*. As the ship proceeded to her new assignment she fired on five Vals that passed overhead on course to Okinawa. Although the formation was broken up, none of the planes was shot down.

At 1200 two divisions of FM-2 Wildcats from VC-93 were launched from *Petroff Bay*. One division was sent to fly CAP over RP Station # 2, while the other orbited west of the station at 15,000 feet. The first division led by Lt. R.E. Friedrich, was at 5,000 feet over RP Station # 2 and under the control of *Stanly's* fighter director officer, when the pilots spotted a column of four Vals cruising towards the station. They maneuvered their Wildcats so that they would be in position for a side run on the planes. Friedrich had the first crack at the enemy and came in on the third Val, hitting it from forty-five degrees and then swinging in to get on its tail. The

Val increased speed and began to dive and Friedrich fired again, hitting it in the wing root and cockpit. It went into a tight spin and hit the water. Meanwhile, Friedrich's wingman, Lt. (jg) R.C. Sullivan, came up on the tail of the second Val. At a range of only fifty feet he let loose with four two-second bursts, hitting the Val in the engine and wing roots. Sullivan's Wildcat had superior speed and he overran the Val, peeling off to the right. As he looked back he saw the Val hit the water. The second division, led by Ens. R.R. Parsons, went after the fourth Val which was heading north at 200 knots. He fired at 1,200 feet but was out of range. Parsons closed the distance and fired a couple of short bursts which hit the Val's internal service tank and the plane went down. Shortly thereafter, Sullivan made a run on the first Val. The Japanese pilot was more skillful than his companions and made a number of evasive moves. Sullivan caught the Val as it climbed, fired into its cockpit and it went down.

After forming up, the Wildcat division went back to patrol at 3,000 feet and soon spotted two more planes, a Val and an Oscar. Friedrich made a side run on the Val and scored some hits. The Val turned and he fired again, hitting the wing roots on both sides; the Japanese plane exploded and went into the water. Parsons came in from behind the Oscar and found that it had too much speed. He pushed the Wildcat to full power and closed the gap. The Oscar maneuvered wildly in an attempt to escape the Wildcat's guns. Several bursts hit the engine and it flamed and spun out of control, hitting the water.

The division reformed at 4,000 feet and saw anti-aircraft fire to port. Upon investigating, Friedrich spotted a Zeke about to make a bombing run on *LCS(L) 32*. He got in a burst from the side then turned on its tail. Friedrich hit the Zeke's engine with another burst and it flamed, pulled up, and splashed astern of the LCS(L). The Wildcat division spotted another Val at 3,000 feet and the four made a flat side run scoring many hits. Lieutenant (jg) H. Foster III circled behind the Val and finished it off with a quick burst; it broke into flames and went in. Below them, another Val headed for *Stanley*. However, *LCS 51*, following behind the destroyer, took the Val under fire and drove it off. A few minutes later, Parsons and Foster spotted an Oscar at 9 o'clock making a run on one of the destroyers. Braving the hail of AA fire from the destroyer, Foster got on the Oscar's tail and followed it toward the ship. He closed to

An FM-2 Wildcat from VC-93 landing on *Petrof Bay CVE 80* on 19 May 1945. *NARA 80G 378860.*

200 feet and fired, hitting the Oscar's wing root and cockpit. Foster turned off as the Oscar, now in flames, headed toward the deck and splashed a couple of hundred feet from one of the DDs.

A Corsair was hot on the tail of a Zeke heading for the ships. It overran the enemy plane and turned off, giving Foster his chance to attack. Gunning his engine to full power, he got behind the Zeke, hit it in the engine and wing root, and it went down.

By the end of the melee, the division led by Friedrich had shot down a total of ten planes, with Friedrich and Foster splashing three and Parsons and Sullivan two each.

At 1426 another Val made a suicide run on *Stanly* from the port quarter. Taken under fire by the 5-inch and other guns of *Stanly*, as well as those of *Lang,* the Val was knocked off course, passed over the ship and crashed in the water off the starboard quarter.

A Betty, piloted by Flight Petty Officer 1st Class Shosun Ito, approached RP Station # 2. Ito had taken off from Kanoya with eight other *Oka* carrying bombers earlier that day. As he approached the picket ships the *Oka* pilot, Flight Petty Officer 2nd

Class Kosai, readied himself for his final mission. Ito spotted the *Stanly* below him to port and Kosai climbed into the *Oka*. Kosai's *Oka* glided down, ignited its rocket engine and crashed into *Stanly* on the starboard bow, passed completely through and exploded in the water to port.

Men on the destroyer were not sure what they had encountered but they knew it was something different. They had been one of the few ships to be hit by a Japanese *Oka* piloted bomb. The craft had been designed to attack much larger ships with heavier construction and its high rate of speed caused it to pass right through the destroyer's relatively thin sides before exploding.

In a later assessment of the *Oka*, the commanding officer of *Stanly,* Comdr. R.S. Harlan, described the problems encountered in combating the new weapon:

> From the scraps of the jet-propelled plane that were left on board, we observed that they are constructed largely of plywood and balsa, with a very small amount of metal, most of that being extremely light aluminum. Because of this construction there is a great doubt in my mind as to whether Mk. 32 or Mk. 40 projectiles work against this type of plane.[51]

Overhead the CAP downed two Japanese planes, but another *Oka* came in on *Stanly's* starboard beam. The ship's gunners managed to hit the attacker which was too high to make a successful crash.

Passing over the ship, it attempted to bank and make a second run on the ship but was shot down 2,000 to 3,000 yards to port. The only damage from this attack was a ripped ensign. A Tony made a suicide run on the destroyer at 1515 and was shot down by the guns of *LCS(L) 32*, crashing astern of the destroyer.

At 1530 *Stanly* was ordered back to the transport area to assess damage.

As she was about to leave, her CAP and four additional Corsairs engaged five Zekes overhead. One of the Zekes left the dogfight and made a bombing run on the destroyer. Both the bomb and the plane missed, crashing alternately on the port and starboard bows and not causing any damage. *Stanly* would spend five days at Kerama Rhetto getting repaired before she was ready to fight again.

On this day, *Lang* would fare better than many of the ships in the area. At 1313 her radar picked up incoming raids and she closed with *Stanly* for mutual support. For the next hour she fired on numerous enemy planes but none came within range of her guns. A Val made a run on her at 1430 and dropped a bomb off the starboard quarter. It did not explode and the Val was shot down as it tried to depart the area. *Lang's* men were surprised to see an *Oka* hit the water 500 yards to port; no one had seen it attack the ship. At 1504 they observed a second *Oka* crash off their port bow; they had not seen or fired on the rocket plane until the last moment. With *Stanly* departing the area, control of the CAP passed to *Lang*. At 1622 *Lang* vectored a division of Corsairs to intercept three Vals closing on the station; the CAP shot the Vals down. *Bryant* reported on station at 2305 to replace *Stanly*.

Over at RP Station # 3, *Hudson, LCS(L)s 37, 38, 111, 118,* and *LSM(R) 199* continued their patrol. During the first six hours of the day the destroyer spotted nine separate raids heading south toward the anchorage. At 0118 *Hudson* was attacked by two planes, one from the port beam and one from starboard. However, the enemy planes were taken under fire and driven away. At about the same time, another plane dropped eight bombs that bracketed *LCS(L) 38*. The closest was 1,000 yards off her starboard quarter and she suffered no damage.

Enterprise had launched one of her VF(N)-90 Hellcat night fighters around midnight. Normally under control of the fighter director officer on *Eldorado*, this plane was turned over to the control of *Hudson*. At 0215 *Hudson* vectored the plane south where it caught and shot down a Peggy. Still another plane made a run on *Hudson* at 0558 and was driven off by gunfire from the destroyer and *LCS(L) 111*. *LCS(L) 38* was a target again, but her attacker's single bomb fell 250 yards to starboard and she escaped damage. Later in the day, between 1315 and 1500, continual raids appeared over the northern radar picket stations. A division of VF-84 Corsairs spotted two Zekes heading for the picket ships. They came in from behind and shot both planes down. Lieutenants (jg) J.A. Pini and A.L. Brooks were credited with the kills. By now the CAP was continually overhead and estimates are that they shot down at least eleven planes, consisting of three Kates, five Vals, two Zekes and a Betty. The close proximity to the ship and the sharp-shooting of the CAP planes made it unnecessary for *Hudson* to fire.

Other Japanese planes passed through the area for the next few hours and, at 2128, a Betty attacked *Hudson* and was shot down. At 2250 one of *Bennington's* VF-82 night fighters shot down another Betty fifteen miles northeast of the station.

Wickes arrived at RP Station # 4 about 1145, joining the high speed minesweeper *Ellyson* and *LCS(L)s 12, 39, 40,* and *119.* Three divisions of the CAP were overhead and the destroyer took control of them. At about 1400 one of the divisions began to run low on fuel and went back to its base. The other two were vectored to the west to intercept an incoming raid. It was fairly even, two of the CAP planes were shot down, as well as two or three of the Japanese. At 2231 *Ellyson* fired on an approaching bogey with uncertain results. Compared to the action at RP Station # 1, the ships at RP Station #4 had a relatively easy day.

Brown, along with *LCS(L)s 15, 16,* and *24,* patrolled RP Station # 7 on 12 April. Overhead the CAP was furnished by fighters from the escort carriers *Shamrock Bay, Makassar Strait,* and *Rudyerd Bay.* This revolving assignment saw from two to four planes on station from 0950 until 1745. A dogfight began over a nearby radar picket station between CAP fighters and two Zekes. One Zeke escaped the battle and made a suicide run on *Brown.* Taken under fire by the destroyer and the gunboats, the plane went down off the destroyer's starboard beam. *LCS(L) 24* observed the CAP shoot down a Zeke off her stern at 1420. Between 2004 and 2111 several bogeys appeared in the area and CAP planes, not under the direction of *Brown*, took up the chase.

The weather at RP Station # 12 was clear and the sea calm. Patrolling there were *Jeffers* and *LCS(L)s 11* and *13.* An incoming raid was spotted at 1345 and eight minutes later the three ships fired on ten Vals flying 12,000 yards to starboard. The planes quickly shifted course and prepared to attack the ships. *Jeffers* was attacked by one enemy plane that came in on the port beam for a suicide run. Although the plane was shot down one hundred yards away, parts of it continued on and holed the ship three feet above the water line. A gash two feet by seven in the hull was not enough to slow the ship down, however, the force of the explosion knocked two men overboard. Both men were picked up by *LCS(L) 13.* A second Val came in on the port beam and was shot down by the combined fire of *Jeffers* and the LCS(L)s. *LCS(L) 11* spotted another Val closing on her and splashed it only 300 yards from the ship.

At about 1202 *Belleau Wood* launched twelve VF-30 Hellcats for a CAP over RP Station # 12 and over its task group. One division of Hellcats was assigned to *Jeffers*. They soon spotted eight bandits at 7,500 feet and went in for the kill. Lieutenant (jg) R.B. Carlson was the high scorer for the day, shooting down a Tony and two Zekes. The squadron's action report details his exploits:

> He [Carlson] first jumped a TONY . . . scoring hits in the right wing root and severing the wing from the plane which crashed out of control. His second victim was a ZEKE. . . . he went into a tail run, scored hits in the fuselage and wing roots which fired the gas tank, and the enemy plane crashed into the sea. Nearing the Task Group screen he engaged in a long tail chase with another ZEKE, firing bursts whenever possible. . . . By this time the chase had entered the gunfire radius of the Task Group, then under attack, and the planes were taken under fire by battleship and anti-aircraft weapons. At this point the ZEKE went into a steep dive and crashed into the sea.[52]

At 1352 *Belleau Wood* launched twelve more VF-30 Hellcats for a CAP about twenty-five miles southeast of RP Station # 12. After the enemy planes had passed by RP Station # 12 they intercepted them and shot down four Vals and one Oscar.

Mannert L. Abele had been hit at nearby RP Station # 14 and the ships from RP Station # 12 were ordered to her assistance at 1450. A few minutes later *Jeffers* observed a Betty drop an *Oka* piloted bomb which zeroed in on her. *Jeffers* let loose with all of her guns, hitting the *Oka* several times. At the last moment she gave the ship hard left rudder and the rocket plane undershot the ship, crashing into the water fifty yards to port. It disintegrated and the fuselage bounced off the water and landed on the starboard quarter. Fortunately it did not explode and *Jeffers* escaped without serious damage.

Four Corsairs reported for CAP duty at 1555. *Jeffers* and the LCS(L)s arrived at RP Station # 14 at 1646, but *Mannert L. Abele* had already gone down. Still on station were *LSM(R)s 189* and *190*. The ships cruised the area looking for survivors. By 1705 the men had been rescued and the LSM(R)s transferred them to *Jeffers*. *LCS(L)s 11* and *13* went back to RP Station # 12 and *Jeffers* and the LSM(R)s headed back to Kerama Retto. Aboard were twenty-

two officers and 230 men from *Mannert L. Abele* who had been rescued. Four had died and were buried at sea.

Mannert L. Abele had been patrolling on RP Station # 14 since
8 April. During that period she had seen little action. On station
with her were *LSM(R)s 189* and *190*, one patrolling on either side
of her at a distance of about 2,000 yards. At 1320 the destroyer was
advised by the CIC that enemy planes were closing on her position
from sixty miles away. She went to general quarters and sighted
three Vals approaching her. The group split, with two coming in
from one side as a decoy. They were fired upon and turned away.
The third Val made a run on the starboard side of the ship and was
hit by its fire. It then attempted to crash *LSM(R) 189* but failed as
the ship took it under fire and splashed it. About the same time
LSM(R) 190 shot down a Val which crashed close aboard.

Two Kates made a run on *189* and both were shot down; *190*
accounted for a second Val. It was a close call for *189*. The Kate had
clipped the conning tower, knocked two men overboard and caused
minor injuries for two more. By 1400 the ships had numerous
enemy planes overhead and requested CAP support. Four Lilys
approached the destroyer at 1415 and one began a run on the ship.
It was turned away at 9,000 yards after being hit by fire from the
destroyer's guns. A few minutes later, three Zekes approached from
the northeast. Two made a run on the ship and one was shot down.
The second crashed the destroyer at the after fireroom on the starboard side. Its bomb exploded in the engine room causing the ship
to lose headway.

High overhead, a Betty bomber, piloted by Sub-Lt. Kitataro
Miura, approached the radar picket station. Miura's plane was one
of the nine Bettys that had taken off from Kanoya Air Base in
Southern Kyushu about noon. Slung beneath each of the bombers
was an *Oka* piloted bomb. As they approached the ships ringing
Okinawa, American fighters were vectored toward them and shot
some of them down. At 1445 the crew of the plane began their
preparations. They awakened *Oka* pilot Sub-Lt. Saburo Doi and
informed him that his date with destiny was at hand. Doi climbed
into the *Oka* and, at an altitude of about 19,000 feet, the craft
dropped from the mother ship and sped towards its target.
Jubilation overcame the crew of the Betty as they realized that Doi
had hit his target. Too distant to determine the type of ship they
had hit and under fire from the ships below, they turned and head-

ed back to Kanoya, radioing ahead that they had sunk a battleship. *Mannert L. Abele* was no battleship but it was still a significant victory for the crew. The Betty landed at Kanoya to a hero's reception.[53] Of the nine Bettys with *Okas* that set out for the American fleet, only four made it back to base.

Mannert L. Abele had been hit amidships by the *Oka* and her keel was broken by the explosion. She went to the bottom within three minutes. Other Japanese planes strafed the survivors in the water and dropped a bomb on them. The CAP had not yet arrived and the enemy planes were free to attack. If a CAP had been overhead, the sinking might have been averted, but with so many Japanese planes in the area that was still questionable. As the number of incoming raids began to grow, the *Mannert L. Abele* had requested a CAP which was sent to them from *Petrof Bay*. Unfortunately, the planes had their hands full, shooting down nine enemy planes. In the confusion of the air battle, the CAP wound up over another destroyer five miles away and was not able to protect *Abele*. The destroyer again requested a CAP and it was promised, but it came too late.

Lieutenant J.J. Hoblitzell III, *Abele's* engineering officer, was at his station behind the throttle board in the engine room when the first plane hit. Men were thrown about by the blast which broke one of the propellor shafts. As Hoblitzell and his engineering gang began to shift some of the engine functions, the ship was hit by the *Oka*, knocking men off their feet once more. Water began to flood the compartment and the men headed for the nearest ladder, only to find the door at the top jammed. Above on the deck the ship's damage control officer, Lt. G.L. Way, had been blown overboard by the second blast but had managed to grab a line and clamber back on board. He noticed a jammed dog on the door and its wheel was turning as the men tried to open it. With the aid of a crewman, he broke off the dog and the hatch opened, allowing the men to scramble to safety.

On deck Hoblitzell found WT1/c Kirsch sitting in the amidships passageway. The blasts had burned him badly and he was blinded. Crewmen came to the rescue and led Kirsch to safety and Hoblitzell turned to close the fuel oil valves to the # 3 and # 4 boilers. Looking aft, he saw the ship buckle amidships and the stern rise. The call came to abandon ship and he went over the side. A talker's flared helmet gave him added buoyancy and he joined F1/c

Mannert L. Abele DD 733 underway on 1 August 1944. *NARA 80G 382764.*

Ellenburg who was clinging to an air accumulator tank. The two made their way to a nearby raft with other crewmen and were picked up a half hour later.

Lieutenant Walter S. Snowdon, *Abele's* communications officer, was serving at his battle station as officer of the deck during the attacks. After the *Oka's* explosion had thrown him to the deck in the pilot house, an eerie calm overtook the ship. All Snowdon could hear was a hissing sound as steam escaped from the engineering spaces. Communications throughout the ship were out and he went to the starboard wing of the bridge just in time to see the ship break in two, the stern rising high in the air. The order to abandon ship had been given and, as Snowdon clambered towards a nearby 40mm gun platform, he was washed overboard. He swam to a nearby floating raft and joined several of the crew. As they watched, a Zeke few over and dropped a bomb 500 yards away, shocking but not seriously injuring them. One of the LSM(R)s shot down a Japanese plane which crashed nearby and exploded, blowing the pilot and his open parachute 200 feet in the air. The lifeless pilot and his parachute slowly settled back into the ocean and disappeared. As other action occurred overhead, the men were startled to see the fins of two sharks cruising only twenty-five yards away. When they splashed their feet in the water, the disturbance seemed to chase the sharks away.[54] Most of *Abele's* crew were rescued, but seventy-nine had been killed and another thirty-five wounded.

Nearby, lookouts on *LSM(R) 189* spotted a Kate coming in from her port beam. Although the ship's guns hit her a number of times, she still crashed into the ship, damaging her conn and rocket launchers and wounding a number of men. After clearing the damage she continued on patrol, picking up 108 survivors from the *Abele* by 1650.

Gallantry was in evidence that day. Lieutenant James M. Stewart, commanding officer of *LSM(R) 189*, wrote:

Retracing its steps, the *189* searched the ocean surface for the survivors from the *Abele*. We located grim men. Many of them had banded together and watched the *189* and *190* fight off the

Damage to rocket launchers on *LSM(R) 189* after kamikaze attack. *NARA 80G 316002.*

planes. Captain Parker, Skipper of the *Abele*, from one group sent us to pick up another group first - it included their ship's doctor. He knew we "small boys" had no doctor and that one was urgently needed for his injured crew.[55]

Friday, 13 April 1945

News of the death of President Franklin D. Roosevelt spread throughout the fleet this day, casting a pall on an already difficult situation. At Kanoya, Vice Admiral Ugaki took notice of Roosevelt's death. He believed it to be a result of the first *Kikusui* raid and felt that the Japanese should send a letter of condolence.[56] The propaganda branches of the Japanese military agreed and sent the following message aimed at the American forces:

American Officers and Men

We must express our deep regret over the death of President Roosevelt. The "American Tragedy" is now raised here at Okinawa with his death. You must have seen 70% of your CV's

An F6F-5 Hellcat from VF-40 on *Suwannee CVE 27* on combat air patrol off Okinawa on 27 April 1945. *NARA 80G 394414.*

and 735 of your B's sink or be damaged causing 150,000 casualties. Not only the late President but anyone else would die in the excess of worry to hear such an annihilative damage. The dreadful loss that led your late leader to death will make you orphans on this island. The Japanese special attack corps will sink your vessels to the last destroyer. You will witness it realized in the near future.[57]

The high speed minesweeper *Hobson*, along with the destroyer escort *Bowers* and *LSM(R)s 189*, *190*, and *191* patrolled RP Station # 14. *LSM(R)s 189* and *190* were ordered back to base at 0549 and 0644 respectively. *Bowers* was sent to investigate a possible submarine sighting at 1420 but it proved negative.

A division of Hellcats from VF-40, led by Lt. Comdr. J.C. Longino, had taken off from the escort carrier *Suwannee* at 1530 and arrived at RP Station # 14 at 1640. At 1715 *Hudson* reported bogeys in the area and vectored the CAP to the enemy planes. To cover their bases, Longino sent one section with Lts. (jg) Hartman and Clement to 1,000 feet while he and his wingman, Lt. (jg) Monteau stayed at 3,000 feet. Hartman spotted a Sonia cruising above Longino and Monteau at 5,000 feet and notified his leader. Longino and Monteau quickly turned and climbed to altitude, getting on the Sonia's tail. Longino took it under fire and the Sonia maneuvered in an attempt to avoid destruction. By this time, Hartman and Clement had climbed to get in on the action. With four Hellcats on its tail, the Sonia had no chance as Longino, Clement, and Hartman scored hits. Hartman came around again and made the final kill.

The division of VF-40 Hellcats reformed and within minutes found four more Sonias. They climbed to meet them and Longino made the first kill. Clement and Hartman both were on the tail of another, scoring hits as Longino came in from 6 o'clock and finished it off. Monteau was on the tail of another Sonia, hitting it from behind in the left wing tank. The plane exploded and went in. The last Sonia fell under his guns as well as he made another 6 o'clock run and flamed its left wing tank. Monteau and Longino finished the day with two kills each and Hartman was credited with one. The division remained on CAP over the ships until 1830 but did not have enough fuel to make it back to their carrier. They landed safely at Yontan and returned to *Suwannee* the next day.[58]

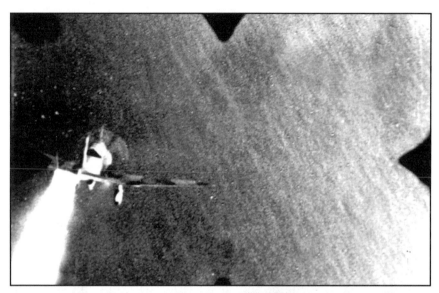

Photos taken by the gun camera on Lieutenant Commander J.C. Longino's Hellcat. This was Longino's second kill for the day. A Sonia is shown going down in flames after being hit by gunfire from the VF-40 Hellcat. The division of Hellcats from *Suwannee CVE 27* shot down a total of five Sonias that day while flying CAP over the ships at Radar Picket Station # 14. *Aircraft Action Report VF-40 13 April 1945.*

Carrier Air Group-40 pilots and officers discuss the mission of 13 April on board the *Suwannee CVE 27*. From left to right are Lieutenant Earl E. Hartman, Captain Delbert S. Cornwell, Commander Schermerhorn Van Mater and Lieutenant Commander James C. Longino, Jr., the Commanding Officer of CAG-40. *NARA 80G 344400.*

The losses during the first two weeks of radar picket duty had been terrible. On the radar picket stations three destroyers and one LCS(L) had been sunk. In addition, eight other destroyers, one high-speed mine sweeper, one LSM(R) and two LCS(L) were damaged in the air onslaught. On board the ships 235 men died and another 304 had been wounded.

Although the radar pickets had given their all, the magnitude of the attacks was overwhelming. Many kamikazes had slipped through to wreak havoc at the Hagushi and Kerama Retto anchorages, as well as the adjacent waters. Five ships had been sunk and thirty-nine damaged. Particularly hard hit were the destroyer types, with twelve destroyers, six destroyer escorts, one high-speed mine sweeper, and three light mine layers suffering in the air attacks. The battleships *Maryland* and *Tennessee* and the cruiser *Indianapolis* were also hit. Japanese flyers especially prized carriers. The carrier *Hancock* and the escort carrier *Wake Island* were damaged as well. Added to the personnel losses suffered by the radar picket ships were an additional 946 killed and 1,496 wounded.[59]

CHAPTER 4

"They came in droves. . ."

It is not clear at which point in time the Japanese became cognizant of the activities of the radar picket ships. Perhaps they were too preoccupied with the overall campaign to stop the American landing on Okinawa in the early days of April, or perhaps because of their failure to stop the invasion despite the magnitude of their first massed raid, the Japanese air forces had neglected to identify the specific locations of the radar picket ships. By the end of *Kikusui # 2*, however, the radar picket ships had not escaped their attention. They noted that at "the same time [*Kikusui # 2*], measures were adopted by the enemy to counterattack our attack units by employing radar patrol ships."[1] This led to the decision to utilize kamikazes during the evening hours when they would have fewer CAP planes with which to contend. Additional attacks on the bases at Yontan and Kadena would ensure air supremacy over the area.[2]

To combat the night-time attacks, the TAF began to utilize the marine night fighter squadrons based on Okinawa. Beginning in the evening of 14 April F6F-5N Hellcat night-fighters from VMF(N) 543 began operating in the night skies around Okinawa. The first flights that evening began at 2045 and lasted until 0550 the next day. During the daylight hours, a new two plane radar picket patrol would begin flying continuous cover over three of the radar picket stations. A few days later, on 16 April, the coverage was increased to five radar picket stations.

Saturday, 14 April 1945

On RP Station # 1, the light minelayer *J. W. Ditter*, *LCS(L)s 51*, and *116* patrolled without incident. At 1612 the destroyer *Laffey* relieved *J. W. Ditter* and within twenty minutes picked up eight planes approaching from the north. She notified *Bryant* on RP Station # 2 which controlled the CAP and the fighters were vectored to intercept the Japanese planes. The CAP splashed all eight. At 1650 *Laffey* picked up three or four more bogeys. *Bryant* turned over control of the CAP to *Laffey* which vectored them toward the planes. They shot down three Zekes.

Patrolling RP Station # 3 were *Hudson* and *LCS(L)s 38, 111,* and *118.* Overhead a division of F6F-5 Hellcats from VC-30, based on *Belleau Wood,* was on patrol. The Hellcats were led by Ens. J.J. Noel. At 1410 the *Hudson* picked up incoming bogeys and vectored them twenty miles to the northwest for interception. There the Hellcat pilots found two Bettys at 8,000 feet and another at 4,000 feet. The Bettys were part of a flight of seven that had taken off from Kanoya.

Flying cover for the twin engine bombers was a Zeke at 19,000 feet. Ensign H.A. Lee took off after the Zeke. He made a high side run on the enemy plane, fired a burst into the engine and it began to smoke. The pilot soon bailed out and the Zeke went down. Noel caught one of the Bettys from the side and got several bursts into the starboard wing and engine. It soon exploded, breaking the wing off and sending it spiraling toward the ocean. The other Betty tried to avoid destruction by diving from 8,000 feet. It was unsuccessful as Ens. K.W. Curry caught up with it, hitting its wing root and fuselage. The Betty went down. The third Betty, under attack by Ens. R.L. Rhodes and flying at 4,000 feet, plummeted into the sea after being hit in both engines. One of the Bettys had been carrying an *Oka* which it jettisoned in order to escape. The *Oka* was seen to hit the water without making any attempt to fly. The VF-30 Hellcats returned to *Belleau Wood* at 1443. Later in the day, at 1854, two enemy planes approached the station. *Hudson* vectored the CAP to intercept them; one was shot down and one escaped to the south.

Radar Picket Station # 4 was patrolled by the high speed minesweeper *Ellyson,* the destroyer *Wickes,* and *LCS(L)s 12, 39, 40,* and *119.* In the early morning hours, between 0310 and 0417, enemy planes were in the area but none attacked the ships; one fell victim to a night fighter at 0310.

Randolph launched two divisions of VF-12 Hellcats at 1330. As they arrived in the vicinity of the station one division, led by Lt.

H.E. Vita, spotted a Zeke below them which had just evaded some other Hellcats. Vita dove toward the Zeke and fired on it from an 11 o'clock position, hitting the Japanese plane with several bursts. The Zeke continued on its course, attempting to escape from the Hellcats, and Vita was able to get behind him and fire again. The cockpit area of the plane burst into flames and it crashed into the sea.

Sunday, 15 April 1945

Kikusui # 3 was scheduled for 15 to 16 April and would include a total of 165 kamikaze aircraft. Of these, 120 would be navy and 45 army. They were from the First, Third, Fifth, and Tenth Air Fleets, and the Sixth Air Army and would fly from the fields north of Okinawa on Kyushu and Tokuno Shima, as well as from Taiwan to the south. At least three hundred other aircraft would fly regular attack and escort missions as well.

Ugaki issued the following order for the attack:

"TEN Operation Order 145." dated 16 April

X Day for Kikusui # 3 Operation is the 16th. All units will operate as follows:

(1) At dawn the forward fighter unit and the Army fighter unit will carry out strafing attacks on the Yontan and Katena airfields.

(2) [Word missing] medium bomber unit will attack Naha and [word missing] around Okinawa.

(3) Medium bombers and flying boats will carry out night patrols in accordance with previous orders. When they have located the enemy carrier group, medium bombers will carry out night attacks.

(4) [Word missing], medium bombers and torpedo bombers will cooperate with Army [medium bombers] in bombing the Yontan and Katena airfields.

(5) [Word missing] will also carry out strafing attacks on the Yontan and Katena airfields.

(6) The reconnaissance unit will take off and find the enemy striking force and thereafter will endeavor to maintain contact and to cooperate with the units scheduled to attack during the day.

(7) The fighter unit which is to cooperate with the Anchorage Attack Unit will operate as follows:

(a) The [word missing] unit will take off at [time missing] and provide cover along the route to be taken by the attack unit.

(b) The [word missing] unit will take off at [time uncertain] and provide cover over [place names missing].

(8) The Anchorage Attack Unit (including ten torpedo bombers) will take off from its bases so as to complete its attacks between 0930 and 1000; the objective of the attacks will be Katena roadstead.

(9) The attack unit which is to attack the enemy striking force and its covering fighter unit will take off [word missing] and carry out daytime attacks on the striking force.

(10) #11 Force fighters will carry out [word missing] against the striking force.

(11) Army forces which are to assist in this operation are as follows:

Forward fighter unit — 12 planes
Covering fighter unit — 30 planes
Airfield bombing unit — 8 planes
Suicide attack unit — about 30 planes[3]

Poor weather and American carrier planes delayed the start of the main attack until about 1630 on 15 April. At 1400 on the 15th, eighty American planes from Task Force 58 pulled a surprise raid on the southern Kyushu airfields, delaying the *Kikusui* raiders. Destroyed in the attack were fifty-one aircraft on the ground, with another twenty-nine shot down.[4] The Japanese were not sure if the American planes had come from the carriers or from Kadena and Yontan, since they carried auxiliary gas tanks. In actuality, the first long range marine raids from the Okinawa fields did not occur until 10 June.[5] Although the assumption by the Japanese about the origins of these raids was incorrect, they made sure that Yontan and Kadena were on their hit list. In a message sent to all units under his command on 15 April, Admiral Ugaki claimed that suppression of the American planes at Yontan and Kadena would be the deciding factor in the success of *Kikusui # 3*.

The army's 100th Air Brigade sent eleven fighters to raid the marine airfields. At 1840 they strafed the fields, damaging planes and equipment at both Yontan and Kadena. Eight of the Japanese planes did not make it back and one made an emergency landing at Kikaiga Shima. A few minutes after that attack, ten Zekes roared in from the Kyushu airfields and continued the bombing and strafing. At 2100 the 60th Air Brigade followed up the earlier attack by sending four heavy bombers to attack Yontan. All four of the Japanese bombers made it back to their base but they had been badly shot up. An hour later eight Betty bombers made still another attack. MAG-31 reported ten planes damaged. In a final attack, four Zekes and twelve Judys bombed and strafed the marine airfields the next morning at 0300. They dropped 500 pound bombs on the runways and started several fires

Bryant and LCS(L)s 32 and 35 patrolled on RP Station # 2 on 15 April. Overhead the CAP, vectored by Bryant, splashed seven Zekes in the afternoon. Bryant's radar was giving her problems and she started repairs, turning over control of the CAP to Laffey on nearby RP Station # 1. Laffey vectored the CAP to intercept some incoming bogeys and three more Zekes went down. Two enemy aircraft closed on Bryant at 2100 and were driven off by gunfire.

Wickes patrolled Radar Picket Station # 4 with LCS(L)s 12, 39, 40, and 119. Flying CAP near the station was a division of VMF-323 Corsairs which had taken off from Kadena at 1705. At about 1830, they were vectored to pick up an incoming bogey and spotted it at 6,500 feet. Lieutenants Joe Dillard, Harold Tonnessen and Francis Terrill all dove to the attack and soon splashed a Val. At 1845 a PBM with engine trouble appeared on the ship's radar. After being identified the PBM landed in the water six miles north of the station and taxied toward Wickes; the problem was reported to its base. At about the same time two bogeys were spotted coming in from the north. At first the ships held fire since the planes were being chased by American fighters. The CAP got one and then the gunboats shot down another. The Val that attacked Wickes had strafed it, wounding three men slightly. With the immediate danger over, LCS(L) 39 was assigned to stand by the PBM until it was repaired.

Radar Picket Station # 7 was patrolled by Brown and LCS(L)s 114 and 115. Two Hellcat night fighters, from VF-84 on Bunker Hill, saw the only action that day. They were vectored to a bogey at 0200 by Brown. The two night fighters located the plane, a Zeke, and shot it down.

The ships at RP Stations # 10, 12, and 14 had a quiet evening. One of the reasons for limited Japanese sorties from the Taiwan airfields may have been bomber attacks by units of the 5th Air Force in the Philippines. On 15 April, B-24s hit Taichu, Shinchiku, and Nantonsho airfields. Later that day and into 16 April, the 345th and 38th Bombardment Groups sent thirty-six B-25s to hit the fields at Jurinko and Toen. On the 16th, the 380th Bombardment group hit Giran airfield with their B-24s.

Monday, 16 April 1945

Radar Picket Station # 1 was to be the scene of one of the most spectacular ship versus kamikaze battles of the war. Patrolling on RP Station # 1 was *Laffey*, along with *LCS(L)s 51* and *116*. A two plane RPP had been assigned to the station, and by 0600 two divisions arrived, bringing a total of ten Corsairs over the ships.

Three divisions of VF-10 Corsairs from *Intrepid* had taken off earlier that morning and headed for RP Station # 1. The Grim Reapers squadron had already distinguished itself during the campaign for Okinawa in previous air battles. The three divisions, led by 1st Lt. George Krumm, Lt. (jg) Phil Kirkwood and Lt. Comdr. Walter E. Clarke, arrived in the vicinity of RP Station # 1 at about 0600. Krumm's division was directed to orbit the station at a high altitude, keeping them out of the action. Kirkwood's division was vectored north, where they encountered a number of Vals and Nates. They shot down four planes before they became separated. Returning to the vicinity of the picket ships, they got into a dogfight with a number of Vals and Nates. Ensign Albert Lerch shot down four planes and Ensign Heath one. Heading south, they encountered other planes and Lerch added three to his total and Heath two more. Between the two pilots they had shot down ten planes.

Lerch's appearance at that battle was a strange twist of fate. He had originally been flying with VF-87 on *Ticonderoga*. A broken leg hospitalized him for a while, and by the time he recovered, his ship and squadron had departed. He was then reassigned to VF-10 on *Intrepid* and preceded his former squadron mates into combat at Okinawa.

Meanwhile, Lt.(jg) Kirkwood and Ensign Quiel accounted for ten more, with Kirkwood splashing six and Quiel four. The division led by Lt. Comdr. Clarke headed northwest from the station and encountered a large number of Tonys and Zekes. Clarke shot down three and Lt. (jg) Farmer four. Ensigns James and Eberhard each shot down one.

Ensign Albert Lerch poses with his Corsair on board the *Intrepid CV 11* on 5 June 1945. A member of the VF-10 Grim Reapers squadron, Lerch was credited with shooting down seven enemy planes. *NARA 80G 49349.*

Another division of Grim Reapers, under Lt. George Weems, was vectored to the north to cover the area around Kikaiga Shima. They splashed four Zekes. The Grim Reapers returned to *Intrepid* having shot down thirty-three enemy aircraft, with one more listed as a probable. It would be their last mission. Later that day, *Intrepid* was put out of action by a kamikaze attack.

In spite of the successes of the CAP planes overhead, problems arose for *Laffey*. She lost communications with her two plane CAP at 0730 and could not reestablish them. A Val that closed on the ship at 0744 would have been easy pickings for the two plane CAP, but instead it was driven off by the destroyer's guns. Reports indicate it was splashed by the CAP after turning away from the ship. Four more bogeys were spotted at a distance of twenty miles and the CAP was vectored to intercept them. At about 0818, three Vals were shot down by the CAP forty miles from the ship after a wild dogfight. Shortly thereafter, at about 0827, *Laffey's* ordeal began. Her action report for the day gives the summary:

> During this time [0827-0947] the ship was under incessant and concentrated attack, with enemy planes so numerous and so well dispersed that organized interception by CAP became impossible after a few attempts. Radar operator reported seeing up to 50 bogies on scope, converging from north, northeast, and northwest. CAP was apprized of situation by our fighter director officers and told to watch out for our AA fire. To complicate matters, CAP was in process of being relieved when bogies were closing fast. The CAP undoubtedly intercepted and splashed a large number of planes outside of our gun range, and in several instances the fighter pilots waded right into our own AA fire to splash their victims.[6]

The first attack on the ship began at 0830 as a formation of four Vals split in two and approached the ship from both sides. Two of the Vals came in on the starboard bow and were splashed, one at 9,000 and the other at 3,000 yards. On the port side, the first Val was shot down by the destroyer at a range of 3,000 yards and the second came under the combined gunfire of the destroyer and *LCS(L) 51*; it went down near the gunboat. Two Judys attacked *Laffey*, one from port and one from starboard and both were shot down. The plane coming in from port strafed the ship, wounding several crewmen before it exploded close aboard. Some minor damage was incurred from the blast. At 0839 another Val came in off the port bow and was taken under fire. It struck a glancing blow on top of gun mount three and crashed in the water aft of the ship, exploding on impact. At 0845 a Judy made a run on the ship from the starboard beam and was shot down. A second Judy came in from the port bow and crashed into the area near gun mounts # 43 and 44. The ensuing fires put the guns out of commission. A minute or two later, a Val crashed into gun mount # 3 (a five inch gun) and put it out of commission as well. The following entry was made in *Laffey's* action report on 29 April 1945:

> This plane was followed by another on the starboard quarter which dropped [a] bomb two feet inboard of deck edge to starboard aft of mount three and then crashed into the side of mount three. Shortly thereafter an unidentified Jap plane came out of the sun in a steep glide, then leveled off when just above [the] water and dropped a bomb which landed on the port quarter above the propellor guard.[7]

The bomb exploded and jammed the rudder, causing the ship to circle. *Laffey* could only evade her attackers by adjusting engine speed. Two more enemy planes crashed into the ship, striking the after deckhouse. A Corsair chased an Oscar almost into the ship and both of the aircraft hit the destroyer's mast. The Oscar splashed close to starboard and the Corsair's pilot made altitude and bailed out. Still another CAP plane chased a Judy almost to *Laffey*. It splashed very close to the ship and the explosion from its bomb knocked out power to the number 2 gun mount (5-inch gun). Within the next few minutes, the remaining guns on *Laffey* had accounted for bringing down another Judy, an Oscar, and a Val.

Lieutenant L.E. Forkner was leading three divisions of F6F-5 Hellcats. The VF-45 planes had taken off from *San Jacinto* at 0755 with instructions to head for RP Station # 1 where *Laffey* was already under attack. Heavy radio traffic prevented communications with the force fighter director so the planes proceeded toward *Laffey's* position, knowing that the destroyer was in need of help. As they passed over Izena Shima, approximately eight miles from *Laffey's* position, Lt. (jg) C.F. Bywater sighted three Zekes 1,000 feet above and headed for them. Forkner, with Lts. (jg) H.N. Swinburne, L. Grossman, N.W. Mollard, Willis, and Bywater engaged the enemy planes. Forkner and Willis shot down a Zeke and it crashed near *Laffey*.

As Forkner and Willis were engaging their Zeke, Swinburne and Grossman firewalled their Hellcats and caught up with anoth-

er Zeke that was in a dive. Using the superior diving speed of the
Hellcat, they soon caught up with the enemy plane and flamed it.
As the two pulled out from the engagement with the Zeke, they
spotted a Kate heading across their position from starboard to port,
some three miles distant. Obviously intent on making a bombing
run on the ships at RP Station # 1, the Kate was on course, but its
pilot was unaware of the two Hellcats closing behind him.
Swinburne hit the plane in the engine and cockpit setting it afire.
It splashed short of the destroyers. As Swinburne was finishing off
the Kate, Grossman went after a Tony. Aware of his pursuer the
pilot of the Tony increased speed, only to find the Hellcat closing.
The Tony began a turn to starboard just as Grossman's bursts
raked the fuselage and flamed the engine; the plane headed for the
sea from 3,000 feet and hit the water.

Meanwhile Bywater, following Forkner, spotted another Zeke
and got on its tail. The enemy plane maneuvered in an attempt to
escape the Hellcat's guns. After being hit by a burst, the plane
began to flame and picked a target of opportunity. An LSM was
cruising below and the Zeke made a wing over in an apparent crash
dive, but putting itself in perfect position for another shot; Bywater
hit the plane and it exploded, sparing the LSM. This dogfight put
Bywater almost at sea level and he pointed his Hellcat skyward to
join his comrades. He regrouped with three Hellcats above, then
realized that they were not his division. They spotted another Zeke
below them and headed down to intercept it. The enemy plane
maneuvered violently and the three Hellcats overshot it giving
Bywater his opening. Bywater cut his speed, got on the Zeke's tail
and soon flamed it with bursts to the engine. The Zeke rolled over
and plummeted to the water from 5,000 feet. Bywater rejoined his
division. His adventures for the day were over.

Although Bywater's flight was filled with action, other pilots
were put to the test as well. Lt. (jg) Mollard shot down two Zekes
and a Val after teaming up with a Corsair from another squadron.
The Corsair ran out of ammo and Mollard escorted him back to
Yontan and headed back. However, his adventures were not over.
On the way back to RP Station # 1, he spotted action over some
minesweepers and DDs near the northern tip of Okinawa and went
to investigate. There he observed five Vals in the vicinity of the
ships and, with his one remaining gun, splashed one. He then
headed north and rejoined his division, which had been busy as

well. At 0920, the second division, led by Lt. (jg) Mosley, was sent to investigate a parachute and spotted a Zeke cruising overhead. He climbed, got on its tail and hit it with a single burst. The Zeke flamed and splashed from 3,000 feet. Mosely reformed his division which spotted *Bryant* on fire below. The DD had been hit by a kamikaze while en route from RP Station # 2 to aid *Laffey* and the division orbited the ship to provide protection.

Swinburne and Grossman were orbiting *Laffey* and spotted a Betty with an *Oka* heading toward the destroyer. The squadron's action report indicates that twenty Corsairs were on its tail, but most broke off and went after the *Oka* once it was dropped. For whatever reason, the *Oka* could not fire its engines and spiraled aimlessly into the water. This left the Betty with the two VF-45 Hellcats and two Corsairs on its tail. Although the Betty had been hit several times by various planes, Grossman was the one who delivered the *coup de grace*. He managed to maneuver to the port quarter of the bomber and hit its port engine and wing with several bursts. The engine flamed and the Betty went into a shallow glide, first ricocheting off the water and then regaining some altitude. Grossman let loose again and this time the wing tore off the Betty and it splashed in. The crew survived the crash and emerged from the fuselage where three sat on the wing. Still another Japanese flyer was in the water. As Grossman flew over, the man in the water shook his fist at him. Minutes later, the Betty sank.

Laffey was still not out of danger, but she was well covered by the combat air patrol. At 0930, Major Wiffen and Lieutenant Carl of VMF-312 shot down a pair of Vals near the station. Three divisions of Corsairs from VMF-441 arrived overhead as additional support. Throwing themselves into the battle, the twelve marine pilots shot down sixteen and one-half planes during the action. Beginning at 0946, a Val dropped a bomb to port and passed over the destroyer. Closely trailed by 2d Lt. Marion I. Ryan and 1st Lt. Charles H. Coppedge, it was splashed in front of the *Laffey*. Another Val dropped a bomb which destroyed a 20mm gun group. It went down under the guns of Ryan's Corsair. Still another VMF-441 Corsair trailed a Judy which came in from the port bow. Between the Corsair and the ship's guns, the enemy plane didn't stand a chance. The Judy splashed close to the ship. VMF-441 distinguished itself this day. Lieutenant William W. Eldridge was the high scorer, splashing four enemy planes, while Capt. Floyd C.

Marine pilots from VMF-441 celebrate after shooting down fifteen and one-half Japanese planes over the radar picket ships. Kneeling from left to right are Captain Floyd C. Kirkpatrick, and Second Lieutenants Clay H. Whitaker and Charles H. Coppedge. Standing left to right are Second Lieutenants Will H. Dysart, William W. Eldridge and Selva E. McGinty. The plane behind them is Corsair # 422, "Palpitatin' Paulie," which was flown by Kirkpatrick. *NARA 208-AA-PAC-10046.*

Kirkpatrick and 2d Lt. Selva E. McGinty each got three.[8] Second Lt. Charles E. Coppedge shot down two planes and 2d Lts. Will H. Dysart and Clay H. Whitaker both got one and one-half. Second Lt. Larry Friess was killed in action and 2d Lt. Marion I. Ryan's plane was shot down. He was picked up by a patrol boat. Ryan was credited with one and one-half planes.

A summation of *Laffey's* ordeal was provided by her action report.

> During the eighty minute action the ship was attacked by a total of twenty-two planes, being struck by eight enemy planes, seven of which were with suicidal intent, the eighth being the

Val who dropped a bomb on the fantail and then knocked off the starboard yardarm as he passed over the ship.

Five of the seven planes which struck the ship inflicted heavy personnel and material damage. Besides the planes which crashed into the ship with their bombs still aboard, four bombs were dropped on the ship, three of which struck the fantail. The ships gunnery personnel shot down nine of these twenty-two attacking planes.[9]

Laffey set about tending to her dead and wounded and making whatever repairs she could. She had suffered thirty-two dead and seventy-one wounded. By this time, two dozen navy Hellcats and marine Corsairs covered the station and the ships were not subject to further attacks.[10] *Barber, Wilson, Snyder, Ringness,* and *Wadsworth* were ordered to RP Station # 1 to assist *Laffey. Barber* picked up fifty wounded. *PCE(R) 851* arrived and rescued thirty-six from *Laffey* and one from *Macomb.*

The high speed minesweeper *Macomb* had been cruising nearby looking for a downed flier when *Laffey* requested her help. After an hour of difficult towing, *Macomb* was relieved when the fleet tugs *Pakana* and *Tawakoni* arrived on the scene and took *Laffey* back to safety at Kerama Retto.

During the attack on the radar picket station, *LCS(L) 51* also saw her share of action. Under the command of Lt. H.D. Chickering, *LCS(L) 51* had been blooded at the invasion of Iwo Jima and her crew was battle hardened. Although the early part of the attack concentrated on the destroyers, the gunboats soon became targets. At 0815 a Val made a suicide run on *LCS(L) 51,* coming in on the starboard beam. The gunboat shot it down by a combination of fire from its 40mm, 20mm and .50 caliber guns when it was only 300 yards off. Thirty-five minutes later the gunboat caught another Val lining up for a crash dive on *Laffey* and splashed it. Still another Val attacked the gunboat from the port bow but was shot down. At 1010 a fifth Val made a suicide run on the ship from the port side. On board *51,* Gunners Mate 3/c Frances F. Ryers stood at his 20mm cannon station even though he had run out of ammunition. With little else to do, Ryers watched as the kamikaze came directly at him. "You could really get a good look at the pilot . . . . he was sitting straight up in there, holding on to his joy stick, and he looked like he was just staring at me." Ryers "just stared back."[11]

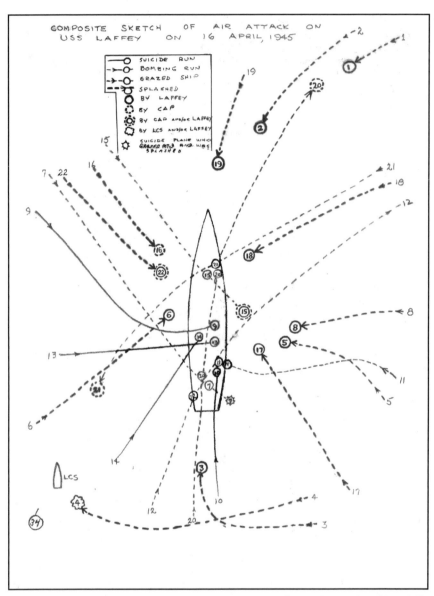

Sketch from *Laffey's* action report showing series of attacks on the ship while it was on Radar Picket Station # 1 on 16 April 1945. *USS Laffey Report of Operations in Support of Landings by U.S. Troops in Kerama Retto–Okinawa Area March 25 to April 22, 1945, Including Action Against Enemy Aircraft on April 16, 1945,* p. 26B.

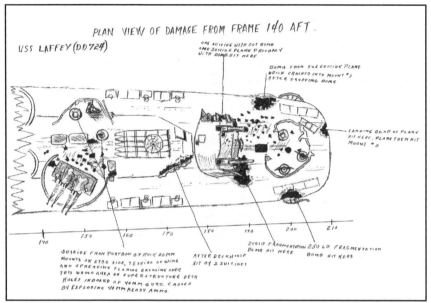

Sketch from *Laffey's Action Report* showing damage to her aft end sustained by kamikaze attack at Radar Picket Station # 1 on 16 April 1945. *USS Laffey DD 724 Report of Operations in Support of Landings by U.S. troops in Kerama Retto–Okinawa Area March 25 to April 22, 1945, Including Action against Enemy Aircraft on April 16, 1945*, p. 26B.

Other gunners did have ammunition, and the plane was shot down close aboard. When it exploded, the plane's engine was propelled forward and smashed into the side of the gunboat, embedding itself in the hull. Fortunately, the impact occurred above the waterline and the deck bead absorbed most of the force.

The LCS(L) continued in its support role, firing on planes that were attacking *Laffey* and scoring hits on many. It caught a Zeke heading across its bow toward *Laffey* and splashed it, making six planes shot down by the gunboat that day. As soon as the action ended, the *51* went alongside *Laffey* to help in fire fighting and rescuing survivors. At 1150 the gunboat received permission from *Laffey* to head back to the anchorage to drop off wounded men. For her actions that day, *LCS(L) 51* was awarded the Presidential Unit Citation.

LCS(L) 116 was also in peril that day. She fired on an approaching Val about 0755; but it was out of range. At 0905 a for-

The engine from a Japanese Zeke kamikaze plane was imbedded in the side of *LCS(L) 51* after it was shot down by the ship at Radar Picket Station # 1 on 16 April 1945. *NARA 80G 359030.*

mation of Vals approached the ship. Three made a run on the gunboat. The *116* took them under fire driving off two, but the third crashed into the stern of the gunboat and exploded. The aft twin 40mm was put out of action and the ship suffered eleven dead and nine wounded. As they tended to their casualties, two more Vals attempted to crash into the ship. One had been damaged by a Hellcat, and the ship's forward 40mm gun finished it off. It splashed 200 yards to port. The second Val was hit by the ship's gunfire and overshot it, taking off her antenna and going into the water one hundred yards off the starboard beam. Two of her men were transferred to *Preston* but died shortly thereafter. Other dead and wounded were transferred to *LCS(L) 32* and *Macomb. LCS(L) 32* began to tow *116* back to the anchorage and at 1830 the task was taken over by the rescue tug *ATR 51*. Overhead the three VF-45 divisions reformed and headed back to base. Along the way, at about 1030, Forkner spotted a Val over a destroyer and made a run on it. He had to turn off in the face of gunfire from the ships. They landed at 1145. The tally for the two VF-45 divisions was fourteen Japanese planes, with Mollard the high scorer having downed two Vals and two Zekes.

Radar Picket Station # 2 was patrolled by *Bryant* and *LCS(L)s 32* and *35*. At 0900 they received word that the ships at RP Station # 1 were in need of assistance. Overhead, CAP coverage was effective and the ships suffered no early attacks at RP Station # 2. The three set out for RP Station # 1 and were soon targets themselves. Initial attacks were driven off by the ships' gunfire; however, at 0934, six enemy planes attacked the destroyer. The first two, a Betty and a Zeke, were splashed by the ship's guns. At 0915 another Betty was shot down by Lieutenants Sharp and O'Neal of VMF-312. A column of three Zekes then lined up and made a run on the ship. The first went down under fire from the ship's main battery,

The damage to the aft 40mm gun tub on *LCS(L) 116* is evident. She was hit by a kamikaze at Radar Picket Station # 1 on 16 April 1945. *NARA 80G 342580.*

but the second, although hit by the destroyer and *LCS(L)s*, crashed into the port side of *Bryant* near the radio room. Its bomb exploded causing damage and starting fires.

Bryant managed to get the fires out and regained her steering but she was out of the fight. Twenty-six of her men were dead, eight unaccounted for and thirty-three wounded. At 1145 she headed back to Hagushi and *LCS(L)s 32* and *35* continued on toward RP Station # 1. *PCE(R) 853* arrived at 1623 and evacuated *Bryant's* casualties.

Bunker Hill launched eleven VMF-451 Corsairs at 1357. A division led by Maj. H.H. Long engaged two Vals heading in the direction of the picket ships. As they went into action against the enemy planes, the destroyers below opened fire. First Lt. R.H. Swalley shot down the first of the Vals. Long followed the second one through the anti-aircraft fire as it headed toward a destroyer. Long's fire was accurate and the Val burst into flame, but a 5" shell from the destroyer hit his Corsair. It went into a spin and Long bailed out but was picked up safely a half hour later by *LCS(L) 111*, which had been patrolling nearby on RP Station # 3. He suffered some bruises but was back on his ship within a few days.[12]

Radar Picket Station # 14 was patrolled by the destroyer *Pringle*, the high speed minesweeper *Hobson*, *LSM(R) 191*, and *LCS(L) 34*. Numerous raids appeared on the radar screens at dawn and, about that time, two Corsairs arrived on the station to fly radar picket patrol. At 0730 a division of VMF-323 Death Rattler Corsairs led by Major Axtell took off from Kadena and headed for RP Station # 14. First Lt. Jim Feliton and his wingman, 2d Lt. Dewey Durnford, arrived on station within a half hour and were soon vectored toward an incoming bogey. Thirty miles north of Ie Shima they found a Lily heading for *Pringle*. Feliton's wingman, Durnford, dove toward the water and followed the plane as it headed toward the destroyer. By this time, *Pringle* had taken the Lily under fire and Durnford finished the job, hitting the fuselage of the plane. It nosed over and splashed. The other two planes, flown by Maj. Axtell and his wingman 1st Lt. E.L. Abner were jumped by two Jacks and two Zekes about the same time. Axtell's engine, flaps and main tank were hit and he went briefly out of control before recovering. Durnford and Feliton were then vectored toward another bogey thirty miles west of Yontan. In the squadron's action report it was recorded that:

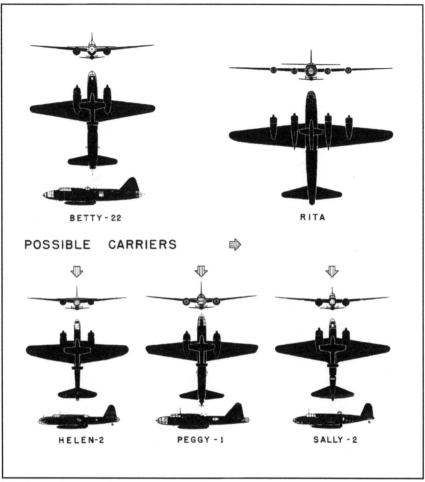

BETTY-22

RITA

POSSIBLE   CARRIERS

HELEN-2   PEGGY-1   SALLY-2

Not long after the *Oka* made its appearance, American intelligence identified the types of medium and heavy bombers that might possibly serve as the mother plane. Technical Air Intelligence Center. *Summary # 31 Baka.* June 1945, p. 4.

. . . Lieutenant Durnford sighted a Helen at 8000 feet. Climbing with full power, Durnford initiated a stern attack. The Helen took violent evasive action and jettisoned his bomb, which Lieutenant Durnford noticed to be unusual, in that it was equipped with fins, small clipped wings, stabilizers, and rudders. This miniature glider bomb was carried under the belly.[13]

Feliton's guns had jammed and Durnford made the kill, hitting the Helen's left engine on the first run and shooting off the left wing on the second run. It was Durnford's first experience with the *Oka*, and he reported back to base that the bomber had dropped a "papoose." Durnford did not realize the uniqueness of his situation. He had encountered an *Oka* carried by a Helen rather than by the usual Betty mother ship.

At around 0830 a division of VMF-224 Corsairs from Yontan, led by 1st Lt. M.J. Crawford, were patrolling near the station. Two of the pilots, 2d Lts. W.H. Donovan, Jr. and H.S. Kovsky, were vectored to the north to intercept three unidentified planes. Donovan shot down a Val and then Kovsky got a second. When turning to go after a third they observed a Hellcat shooting it down. The absence of a gunner in the rear seat confirmed that the planes were kamikazes. A few minutes later, Crawford and his wingman, 2d Lt. G.M. Washburn, got behind a Val and their gunfire set it ablaze. They watched as its pilot bailed out without a parachute.

A single Zeke was spotted on radar closing the formation at about 0900 and was taken under fire. *Pringle* and *Hobson* shot it down about 2,000 yards off the destroyer. Shortly thereafter, at 0910, three Vals attacked the station. At a range of 10,000 yards the three planes began to weave and maneuver to throw the gunners off target. Both *Hobson* and *Pringle* fired on the planes and one of the Vals went down. Sonarman 1/c Jack Gebhardt was at his battle station in the chart house on board *Pringle* when the Val passed over his head by about ten - fifteen feet and crashed into the base of the number 1 Stack. Its 1,000 pound bomb penetrated the hull and exploded, breaking the keel of the destroyer. The ship erupted in a huge ball of fire. According to Gebhardt,

> . . .it seemed like the world ended as the Chart House rumbled and years of dust crashed down from the overheads. I sensed the Pringle was severely damaged and tried to get off the Bridge through the starboard door, but the door was jammed and the access ladder was blown away. I managed to bend the door from the top and slide out onto the open bridge area. I looked toward the stem and the ship was a burning hulk with men stumbling dazed and bleeding from the flying debris, smoke and flames. I looked forward and saw men going over the side. Just then someone yelled "ABANDON SHIP" and I saw a 40-mm ammo magazine under the bridge on fire so I

went to the Starboard side of the bridge and worked my way
down to the main deck. The Bridge splash shield was blown
away so I climbed down to the gun deck where I took off my
shoes and hat and laid them neatly against the bulkhead as if
I was coming back! People can do strange things when in a
stressful circumstance. I put on my life jacket, the type that
inflates with a rubber tube and prepared to go over the side.
But when crawling off the bridge I forgot my tin helmet so went
back to the Chart House to get it. While searching for my helmet I saw more men going overboard, and without thinking
dove into the water and swam away from the ship as fast as I
could. I don't know how far I swam, but it seemed like several
hundred yards before stopping to look back and see the *Pringle*
engulfed in flames, broken in half sinking amidships. The bow
and stern were pointed sharply upward and I heard screams as
she slipped under the water and disappeared. It all happened
in less than 5 minutes after the Japanese plane hit *Pringle* and
disappeared.[14]

As Gebhardt watched, Japanese planes came in and tried to strafe
the men in the water, but they were driven away by gunfire from
the other ships. Sharks were in the vicinity and the ships fired
20mm cannons into the water to scare them off. It would be nearly
eight hours before Gebhardt would be picked up by *LCS(L) 34*.
Pringle suffered sixty-five killed and 110 wounded.

Moments later a Val attempted a crash into the *Hobson* but
was shot down close aboard. Its wing went flying over the ship's
bridge. Its bomb, estimated to be a 250 lb. device, penetrated the
minesweeper's starboard bulkhead amidships and exploded, causing internal fires and damaging much equipment. During this
time, repeated requests for CAP coverage had been made but no
planes were assigned to the station. In all likelihood the giant air
battle, some fifty miles to the east over RP Station # 1, had all
available aircraft engaged in action. Other marine aircraft were in
the vicinity and shot down some of the enemy planes in the area.
At 0900 Captain Rolfus and Lieutenants Seaman and Allen, of
VMF-322, shot down two of the three Vals that they encountered.
The fourth pilot in the division, Lieutenant Peterson, was shot
down by one of the Vals. He parachuted safely and was picked up
shortly.

As *LCS(L) 34* and *LSM(R) 191* headed toward the damaged
ships to assist them, they came under attack themselves. At 0945

LCS(L) 34 and *Hobson* picking up survivors of the *Pringle* after she was sunk by a kamikaze at Radar Picket Station # 14 on 16 April 1945. The photo was taken from *LSM(R) 191* by Lieutenant (jg) L.R. Russell. *Courtesy of L.R. Russell.*

LCS(L) 34 was attacked by three Vals. The first, making a run on the gunboat from the bow, was splashed after being fired upon by the forward 40mm and 20mm guns. A second Val came in from aft and was also hit. The attacking plane turned away, and when last seen it was smoking, leading observers to believe that it was shot down as well. The third Val was driven off.

More Japanese planes came in over the station. At 0946 a Betty and six Vals were spotted to port. The *LSM(R) 191* came under attack first. Gunnery officer Lt. (jg) L.R. Russell watched as one of the enemy planes made a run on the landing ship. His men shot it down. A second plane was turned away by the ship's gunfire. Another attacked the *Hobson* at 1002 and was driven away. Three minutes later a Val made a run on her from the port side and was shot down.

After the action was over, *Hobson, LSM(R) 191,* and *LCS(L) 34* cruised the area looking for survivors. *Hobson* picked up 136 survivors, while *LCS(L) 34* got thirty-one and *LSM(R) 191* picked up eighty-four. *PCE(R) 852* arrived on the scene and transferred her medical officer and corpsmen to *Hobson* to assist in caring for the wounded.

Back at Kanoya, Vice Admiral Ugaki once again received exaggerated reports of Japanese successes. According to these reports the Japanese had sunk two large ships, either battleships or cruisers, damaged several carriers and sunk four transports.[15] *Intrepid* was the only carrier hit during this period and the only other warships suffering damage were the destroyers and gunboats on the radar picket stations. Ugaki was surprised when Kanoya was attacked by P-51s for the first time that day. He correctly deduced that they were flying from Iwo Jima. This was the first long range P-51 attack on Kyushu undertaken by the VII Fighter Command.

On 16 April, Vice Admiral Turner sent the following dispatch to the radar picket ships:

THIS DISPATCH IS FOR THE PURPOSE OF GIVING
SPECIAL HONOR TO THE SHIPS WHO ARE AND HAVE

Five survivors from *Pringle* swim toward *LSM(R) 191* for rescue after their ship was sunk at Radar Picket Station # 14 on 16 April 1945. The photo was taken from *LSM(R) 191* by Lieutenant (jg) L.R. Russell. *Courtesy of L.R. Russell.*

BEEN ON RADAR PICKET DUTY X DD'S, DE'S , LSM'S AND
LCS'S REPEAT LCS'S ARE ALL ON THIS DISTANT GUARD
WHOSE WORK IS DOING SO MUCH TO HELP OUR
TROOPS MAKE THIS OPERATION A SUCCESS X WE ARE
PROUD OF THE MAGNIFICENT COURAGE AND EFFEC-
TIVENESS WITH WHICH THESE VESSELS HAVE DIS-
CHARGED THEIR DIFFICULT AND HAZARDOUS DUTY. [16]

Tuesday, 17 April 1945

Kikusui # 3 had taken its toll on the picket ships, but the Japanese
had suffered great losses as well. According to *Japanese
Monograph # 51*, "Immediately after the 3rd General Attack and
opening the new TEN operation, the Army lost almost all of its
Special Attack Units and only a few planes were left."[17] Additional
special attack planes would have to be brought down to Kyushu
from the northern air bases. To the south of Okinawa, the British
carriers launched strikes on the fields at Ishigaki Shima and
Miyako Jima on 16 and 17 April. No sooner had the British carriers departed than American escort carriers followed up with two
more days of attacks.

Alarmed over the increasing kamikaze attacks from Kyushu,
Admiral Nimitz directed the XXI Bomber Command in the
Marianas to temporarily change its mission. Major Gen. Curtis
LeMay had been sending his B-29s to attack Tokyo and other
Japanese cities. From 17 April through 11 May, LeMay would con-
centrate 75 percent of his air power on the Kyushu and Shikoku
airfields. The main field at Kanoya alone would be hit fifteen times
and its eastern field seven times. Kokubu and Oita were hit nine
times during the period and Miyazaki and Miyakonojo eight. Izumi
and Kushira were hit six times and Usa, Saeki, Matsuyama and
Nittagahara suffered four air strikes. Also hit were the bases at
Tomitaka, Omura, Ibusuki and Chiran.

In all, a total of 2,104 sorties would be flown against the fields
on Kyushu and Shikoku.[18] The first strikes were aimed at
Tachiarai, Kokubu, Izumi, Nittagahara and the two fields at
Kanoya. They were hit by 134 B-29s on 17 April. Many of these
strikes would miss the fields and hit nearby villages, and the effort
was not completely successful in keeping the kamikazes at bay,
although the Japanese did sustain a great deal of damage to their

aircraft and facilities during the period. Some of the ships would experience a brief respite from the deadly attacks. Those patrolling at Radar Picket Stations # 1, 10, and 12 went to general quarters a few times during the day but saw no action.

Radar Picket Station # 2 was patrolled by *Twiggs* and three LCS(L)s. Six F4U-1D Corsairs from VF-84 had taken off from *Bunker Hill* at 0834. They arrived at RP Station # 2 at 0930 and came under the control of the fighter director officer on *Twiggs*. Soon after arriving on station, they spotted a George heading into the station and Lieutenants Freeman and Horner commenced the attack. As they closed in on the plane it dropped a bomb and, shortly thereafter, Freeman scored hits on it. The George peeled off to port and splashed.

Twiggs vectored the planes to intercept a Betty at 0950. Lieutenant Wallet got on its tail and succeeded in setting fire to its port engine. Following the Betty to the deck at a range of only fifty yards, his Corsair was caught in the explosion when it hit the water. The force of the blast blew the tail off Wallet's plane and it flipped over. His body was not recovered. [19]

The magnitude of the explosion would indicate that the Betty was probably carrying a full bomb load, but there was no indication that it had been carrying an *Oka*. At 1220 the planes landed back on *Bunker Hill*.

Radar Picket Station # 4 was patrolled by *Wickes* and *LCS(L)s 12, 16, 39, 40,* and *119.* A CAP of eight F6F-5 Hellcats from VF-47 had taken off from *Bataan* at 0530.

At about 0815 one of the divisions, led by Lt. John W. Wright, was vectored fifty miles northwest of the station by *Wickes*. They got into a dogfight at 10,000 feet after arriving at an area just south of Tokuno Shima. The division spotted a Zeke and went after it. It cut across them and dove for the deck. Lieutenant (jg) Walter C. Clapp, closely followed by his wingman, Ens. Rudolph Sykora, trailed it down to 5,000 feet. As the Zeke pulled up, Clapp hit it with a burst and the plane exploded. Now it was Wright's turn. He headed off after another Zeke and it turned to avoid his fire, pulling up in a half loop as Wright's bullets found their mark. Continuing on upward, the Zeke was hit again at the top of the loop and flamed. Its pilot escaped death by parachuting into the sea as his plane went down.[20]

Wednesday, 18 April 1945

The experiences of the first two and one-half weeks of April had given Capt. Frederick Moosbrugger great concern. With many ships damaged by kamikazes, it was uncertain if the schedules of radar picket assignments could be kept. From 1 through 17 April, Japanese air raids had damaged or sunk fourteen destroyers, four high speed mine sweepers, five LCS(L)s and one LSM(R). On 18 April, he sent a communique advising ships assigned to picket duty that "IN CASE DESTROYERS MENTIONED ABOVE ARE NOT ON DESIGNATED STATIONS REPORT TO DESTROYER ON THAT STATION."[21]

Radar Picket Station # 2 was patrolled by *Luce*, *Twiggs*, and *LCS(L)s 12*, *25*, and *61*. Overhead at any given time were from one to three divisions of CAP. This was the first night of radar picket duty for *LCS(L) 61* and her crew approached the assignment with nervous anticipation. Having recently arrived from the states, the ship had first anchored in Kerama Retto where its crew had seen the hulks of destroyers and LCS(L)s that had been damaged by suicide attacks. Reality set in, however, and as *LCS(L) 61* additional officer Lt. (jg) Powell Pierpoint recalled: "The sea stories were strange and wonderful to the ear. Suicide planes, suicide boats, suicide swimmers, more suicide planes – salvage and survivors. For a fact the laughs were over."[22]

Hudson relieved *Cowell* at RP Station # 12 at 1115. *LCS(L) 11* and *LCS(L) 13* continued patrolling the station. At about 1835, the station was approached by three Bettys. The four plane CAP was vectored to the west to intercept them. Two of the three were shot down at 1845 and 1910, but the third escaped over Kume Shima. At 1945 the marine Corsairs, which had been flying CAP, headed back to their base at Yontan. Another enemy plane approached the ships at 2015 but was out of range and escaped toward Taiwan.

American intelligence reported:

> (1) On 18 April the 1st Mobile Base Air Force reported that 2,086 sorties were flown against Allied forces in the Ryukyus from 16 Mar through 17 Apr. That figure probably includes roughly two-thirds of Japanese offensive and reconnaissance sorties in the Ryukyus during the period. It apparently does not include (i) sorties flown by the Sixth Air Army from

Kyushu, or (ii) sorties flown from Formosa by either Army or Navy Units.

(2) The report states that from 16 Mar through 5 Apr, the 1st Mobile Base Air Force made 152 suicide attacks and 291 other attacks. Beginning on 6 Apr, when the Force undertook the first of the three "Kikusui" operations so far carried out (6, 12 and 16 Apr), suicide attacks predominated. The report is not complete but it appears that during the period 6-17 Apr the Force made more than 425 suicide attacks and only 168 other attacks. During the same period it apparently flew at least 600 sorties for fighter cover, a substantial number of reconnaissance sorties and 13 mining sorties.[23]

Friday, 20 April 1945

From 20 April through 1 May, a new arrangement of picket patrols was tried. On most of these days one of the patrol gunboats, usually an LSM(R), was stationed two-thirds the distance from Point Bolo to RP Stations # 1, 2, 3, and 4. This would keep the gunboats out of the immediate action but would also give them a chance to pick up strays that had slipped past the picket ships and the CAP. They would also be close enough to aid any ships damaged on the station.

On RP Station # 2 were the destroyers *Luce* and *Ammen*, and *LCS(L)s 12, 25, 61,* and *118.* Two thirds of the way to the station, *LSM(R) 196* kept her lonely vigil. *LSM(R) 189* joined the station later in the day. A few minutes after midnight a bogey was reported coming in from the north, but the position of *Luce* nearby made it impossible to fire on it. The enemy plane disappeared from the radar screen as it approached Izena Shima. At about 0012, the plane suddenly reappeared on the starboard quarter of *Ammen* and dropped a one hundred pound bomb which exploded in the water near the starboard quarter, wounding eight crewmen. The attack had been so sudden that gunners were unable to target the plane and it escaped.

Saturday, 21 April 1945

Luce, Ammen, LCS(L)s 12, 25, 61, and *LSM(R) 189* patrolled on RP Station # 2. *LSM(R) 196* patrolled two-thirds of the way from Point Bolo to the station. At about 1644, a large number of bogeys were detected to the north at a distance of fifty miles, and *Luce* directed the CAP to intercept them but the enemy aircraft evaded the CAP. *Russell* relieved *Ammen* at 1735 and, within a few minutes, planes were spotted coming in from her port side. At 1748 she directed the two plane radar picket patrol to intercept them. One Val was splashed by her CAP at 1750 and the *Luce's* CAP shot down two more at about 1800. *Bennion* relieved *Luce* at 1819. At 2025 she fired on a plane with undetermined results.

Brown, Putnam, LCS(L)s 16, 38, 82, and *PGM 20* were patrolling on RP Station # 4 with *LSM(R) 198* two-thirds of the way from Point Bolo to the station. At 2058 the destroyers picked up four enemy planes heading for the station. They were taken under fire and *Putnam* was credited with splashing one plane and shared another kill with *Brown*. Other bogeys approached the ships between 2122 and 2142 but were too distant to take under fire.

At Kanoya, Admiral Ugaki spent a good portion of the morning in his bunker, protected from the B-29 raids. LeMay's XXI Bomber Command sent 217 B-29s to raid both of the Kanoya fields as well as those at Oita, Usa, Kokubu, Kushira, Tachiarai, Izumi, and Nittagahara.

Sunday, 22 April 1945

Radar Picket Station # 1 was patrolled by *Cowell, Little, LCS(L)s 24* and *35, PGM 9,* and *LSM(R) 191* on 22 April. *LSM(R) 192* patrolled two-thirds of the way from Point Bolo to the station. At 0117 the ships went to general quarters as an enemy plane was picked up coming in at a distance of eighteen miles. It turned away at ten miles and the situation subsided.

As daylight arrived, the CAP began its patrols over the ships. Most of the day was uneventful but things changed late in the afternoon. Enemy planes began to appear about 1711. A Val approached the station from the north and *Little* and *Cowell* took it under fire. *Cowell* vectored the CAP to intercept the Val and it was splashed. A few minutes later, at 1756, several bogeys approached from the west and northwest and the CAP was vectored to meet them; they splashed one enemy plane.

Radar Picket Station # 3 was patrolled by *Daly, Henry A. Wiley, LCS(L)s 81, 111, PGMs 10* and *17* with *LSM(R) 197* two-thirds of the way to the station. Flying CAP over the picket ships were six VMF-224 Corsairs from Yontan. Late in the afternoon, at about 1730, raids were picked up coming in from the north. The marine pilots headed toward the enemy planes and splashed five Vals within the next half hour.

First Lts. H.R. Mabey, D.A. McMillan, E.E. Luther and 2d Lts. J.B. Bender and H.E. Winner were each credited with one kill. Only one of the planes had a rear seat gunner and the marines reported that the enemy pilots were poor flyers. Later in the evening, at 2005 and 2108, other enemy planes passed near the ships but at a range of ten to twenty miles, they were too distant to engage.

Radar Picket Station # 14 was patrolled by *Wickes, Van Valkenburgh, LCS(L)s 15, 37, 83,* and *LSM(R) 195* with *LSM(R) 199* two-thirds of the way to the station. A ten plane CAP of MAG-31 Corsairs circled nearby.

Late in the afternoon, at about 1700, enemy aircraft began to approach the station. Ten came in from the north and the CAP was sent to intercept them. At around 1745 one of the planes slipped past the CAP and made a run on *Wickes.* It was shot down and splashed some distance from the ship. Within another half-hour, at 1816, a large raid was detected approaching from the north. Estimated at from ten to twenty planes in groups of two or three, it spelled trouble for the picket ships. Two more CAP fighters joined the station and the Corsairs were vectored to intercept the attack.

Fourteen miles northwest of the ships they found some incoming Vals. VMF-441 pilot, 2d Lt. Frederick Kolb Jr., shot down two Vals with a third Val listed as a probable and 2d Lt. Elliot F. Brown got another Val.[24] Kolb's F4U-1D Corsair developed problems and he had to ditch. Later *Cowell,* on RP Station # 1, sighted Kolb bouncing on the waves in his life raft and picked him up at 1913.

Four more American planes joined the fray. At 1828 a Val eluded the CAP and made a run on *Wickes* which took it under fire. When the plane was 1,500 yards off the ship it changed course and headed for *LCS(L) 15,* which was cruising astern of the destroyer. At 1831 the Val struck the port side of the gunboat aft of the superstructure. Its bombs blew holes in both sides of the ship and within three minutes the gunboat went to the bottom. Crewman Harold J. Kaup RM 3/c was on his station in the radio room.

He recalls the action:

. . .I realized the "bogie" must be very close, for this reason I put my helmet on. At that moment we were hit somewhere aft, there was an explosion. We lost all power in the radio room and it began filling with smoke. In the darkness I fumbled for the dog wrench for the porthole. Meanwhile someone had opened the hatch into the passageway outside the radio room. There were flames out there.

I finally succeeded in opening the porthole to get some fresh air and light inside. Looking out I saw people in the water and the deck on the starboard side directly below the porthole was already covered with water. . . . When I stepped down on the deck the water was about crotch deep and my life jacket was nowhere to be found. By this time the ship was listing badly to the starboard and the fantail was under water. The bow was clear of the water. I went over the side without a life preserver of any kind. Initially I clung to a 40mm ammunition can. . . .Finally someone . . . helped me get to the wooden potato locker that was floating in the area. There were several of the wounded laying on the locker and a number of others clinging to its sides.

The ship in the meantime with its bow in the air turned 180 degrees pivoting on its fantail and went down stern first.[25]

Kaup was rescued by *Van Valkenburgh*. He was fortunate since fifteen of his shipmates had been killed and eleven were wounded. The gunboats circled the area picking up survivors while *Wickes* maneuvered to protect them. They were later transferred to *Van Valkenburgh*.

As word of the attack was radioed back, additional planes were sent to intercept the Japanese aircraft. The original CAP had consisted of Corsairs from VMFs-224 and 441 flying out of Yontan. They were subsequently joined by VMF-323 Corsairs from Kadena and Hellcats of VF-12 and VBF-12 flying off *Randolph*.

Two divisions of Hellcats had taken off from *Randolph* at 1427. One division, led by Lt. (jg) J.M. Franks, was orbiting about ten miles northeast of the northern tip of Okinawa. The other division, led by Lt. (jg) R.D. Gatlin, was orbiting about ten miles west northwest when they were vectored to intercept incoming bogeys. They encountered a total of seven Nates and the battle was on. One of the major problems for the Hellcat pilots was the relatively slow speed of the Nate. They had to avoid overshooting their target and this allowed one of the Nates to come up behind Ens. W.L. Smart.

Smart used full throttle combined with water injection and easily pulled away from his adversary. By the end of the battle, all seven Nates had been shot down. Franks got one and Gatlin shot down two. Smart was credited with two kills and Ball and Northcutt each got one.[26]

Three divisions of Death Rattler Corsairs of VMF-323 had taken off from Kadena in mid-afternoon. The first two divisions were led by Maj. George Axtell and the third by Maj. Jefferson Dorroh. When *Wickes* picked up the large raid coming into the station, she vectored the three VMF-323 divisions to intercept them. Axtell's division was first on the scene and found a large flight of Vals. Within minutes the Corsairs dove on them. Axtell managed to splash five Vals and damage another three. His wingman, 1st Lt. Ed Abner, shot down two and damaged two more. Another member of the division, 1st Lt. Charles Allen, was credited with one kill and one probable. Leading Axtell's second division was 1st Lt. Jerry O'Keefe. O'Keefe and his wingman, 1st Lt. Bill Hood, went after the Vals with spectacular results. O'Keefe shot down five Vals and Hood got two Nates and one Val. Hood was credited with damaging or sharing the kill on four more Vals. Next, Dorroh led his three plane section into the Vals. By the end of the day, Dorroh had shot down six Vals and was credited with a probable on the seventh. The two other pilots in Dorroh's division, 1st Lts. Normand Theriault and Charles Allen also took their toll. Allen had one kill and one probable and Theriault shot down three Vals and shared another Val with three other Corsairs.[27]

Between 1900 and 1920 the CAP Corsairs returned to their base at Yontan. The pilots from VMF-224 had accounted for five enemy aircraft, and those from VMF-441 another three. The marine squadrons had taken a heavy toll of the enemy, shooting down thirty-three and three-quarters Japanese planes with two probables and four damaged.

Thus ended 22 April in the battle for Okinawa. It had been a bloody day for the Japanese and reinforced their superstitions. April 22 was one of the *To Shi Bi* or ten death days and it lived up to its name.[28] Over the radar picket stations forty-one of their planes were shot down with another three listed as probables. Still other planes had been damaged.

The following day, Major Gen. Francis P. Mulcahy USMC, commanding general of the Tenth Army Tactical Air Force,

Majors George Axtel and Jefferson Dorroh of VMF-323, MAG-33 at Kadena, Okinawa in May of 1945. *NARA 80G 373360.*

received the following communique from Lt. Gen. Simon B. Buckner, Commanding General of the Tenth Army:

> HEARTIEST CONGRATULATIONS TO YOU AND YOUR FIGHTER COMMAND FOR HAVING SHOT DOWN YESTERDAY EVENING A FORCE OF 32 ENEMY PLANES THAT WOULD OTHERWISE HAVE BEEN IN A POSITION TO INFLICT SERIOUS DAMAGE TO OUR SHIPPING AND GROUND FORCES HERE X MORE POWER TO ALL XX BUCKNER.[29]

Monday, 23 April 1945

Raids by B-29s the previous day had disrupted activities at a number of the Kyushu bases. The XXI Bomber Command had sent out over eighty B-29s to hit the fields. The runways at Kanoya were damaged and the field was out of service for a few days. Air Group 762, an important carrier medium bomber squadron, was sent to

Miho and Miyazaki in order to avoid damage from the attacks. Miyazaki also came under attack, as well as Izumi, Kushira, and Tomitaka.[30]

Patrolling on RP Station # 3 were *Daly*, *Henry A. Wiley*, *LCS(L) 81*, *111*, *PGM 10*, and *PGM 17*. *LSM(R) 197* patrolled two-thirds of the way from Point Bolo to the station. *LCS(L) 111* left the station at 0505. A RPP of two VMF-224 Corsairs flown by Maj. R.C. Hammond, Jr. and First Lieutenant Van Salter flew over the station. At 0625 a bogey was spotted on the *Daly's* radar screen. She vectored the two Corsairs out to intercept it and at 0630 they splashed the Val five miles astern of the destroyer. Major Hammond was credited with the kill.

At 1620 VMF-224 scrambled four Corsairs from the field at Yontan. 1st Lts. H.R. Mabey, and D.A. McMillan and 2d Lts. E.L. Rafferty and C.V. Troland, found seven Vals headed toward the picket ships from the northeast. Troland and Rafferty had been flying at 7,000 feet and dove to 2,000 to shoot down the first two.

Major General Francis P. Mulcahy USMC congratulates members of the VMF-323 Death Rattlers after their aerial victory. *NARA 127PX 119257.*

Mabey and McMillan dove to attack two others and watched another pair of Corsairs overshoot them. Mabey caught one of the Vals as it attempted a wingover. They continued on toward the picket ships and observed another Val avoid the fire from two Corsairs. Mabey got behind the enemy plane and shot down his second Val of the day.

Tuesday, 24 April 1945

Allied intelligence reported the relocation of units of the Sixth Air Army. Intercepted communications between the Sixth Air Army in Kyushu and some of their bases in Korea indicated that a few of their units were using Korean bases as rear staging areas. According to the National Security Agency reports:

> (1) The 22nd Flying Regiment (Frank single-engine fighters), a Sixth Air Army unit, addressed at Keijo, W. Korea, on 27 and 30 Mar.
> (2) The 90th Flying Regt (Lily twin-engine bombers), under the 8th Flying Brig and previously located in China, addressed at Gunzan, SW Korea, on 19 and 20 Apr.
> (3) The 8th Flying Brig, also previously in China, addressed at Gunzan on 19 April.[31]

Wednesday, 25 April 1945

Mindful of the importance of the airfields on Okinawa to the defense of the American fleet, the Japanese identified their role:

> At the same time, the enemy air bases in OKINAWA began their full operation. The success of our TEN operation depended upon their control and our Central Authorities paid considerable attention toward this matter. Accordingly, the Army planned continuous night attacks against the enemy air bases with 2 heavy bomber units. On the night of the 25th, 4 planes from the 110th F [110th Air Regiment] carried out an attack.[32]

Thursday, 26 April 1945

The National Security Agency reported:

Early this month the operational bombers of the Thirteenth Air Fleet (HQ Singapore) were transferred to Formosa to participate in the Ryukyus operation. Orders of 25 and 26 Apr now direct that all operational fighter strength of the Thirteenth Air Fleet (including available pilots and ground crews) be returned to the command of the Combined Fleet (HQ probably Kanoya, S Kyushu). The fighter units "will be transferred at once to such Kyushu bases as the commander of the 1st Mobile Base Air Force may direct, and will come under the tactical command of that Force." On 27 Apr the 1st Mobile Base Air Force assigned the units to bases at Kasanohara, Kagoshima and Izumi.[33]

In order to slow the attacks on the ships at Okinawa, the XXI Bomber Command unleashed its B-29s from the Marianas. From 26 through 29 April, the 73rd, 313th and 314th Bombardment Wings would send a total of 537 B-29s to bomb the fields at Chiran, Izumi, Kanoya, Kanoya East, Kokubu, Kushira, Miyazaki, Miyakanojo, Nittagahara, Oita, Saeki, Tomitaka and Usa. Many of the bombs would target the runways and make it difficult for the Japanese to get their aircraft airborne. Delayed action fuses would add to the problems of the Japanese, with bombs fused to delay detonation at one, two, six, twelve, and twenty-four to thirty-six hours.[34]

Friday, 27 April and Saturday, 28 April 1945

The fourth *Kikusui* attack had been scheduled for 25 to 29 April but inclement weather postponed the start until the 27th. By this time, the supply of potential suicide planes was beginning to dwindle. A total of 115 Japanese planes, sixty-five from the navy and fifty from the army, made up the number of special attack planes flying against the Americans. Other Japanese planes would accompany them as escorts and some would fly regular missions.

Kikusui # 4 would have a different emphasis than the first three *Kikusui* raids. They had been primarily aimed at the convoys and the airfields on Okinawa with the American carrier task force as a secondary objective. *Kikusui # 4* would have the American carrier task force as its primary target. When they failed to locate the Task Force 58 carriers on 21 April they postponed the start of the operation. Inclement weather put off the attack for several more days. In addition, B-29 raids against Usa, Oita, Saeki, Tomitaka, Imabara, Nittagahara, Miyazaki, Kokubu, Kanoya and Miyakanojo on the 26th had disrupted plans for the attack and destroyed some of the Japanese planes. One hundred ninety-five of the heavy bombers had been sent out by the XXI Bomber Command against the fields. They had been accompanied by P-51s, which finished their day by strafing the field at Kokubu.

On 28 April, the Japanese fighter force at Kokubu was sent to Kasanohara to avoid these attacks. Kokubu, bombed by the Americans on 26, 27, and 28 April, was badly in need of repair and would not be usable until 1 May. Other units would send their aircraft to the rear as well. They would advance to the more forward bases at the beginning of the next attack.[35]

The National Security Agency reported intercepting Japanese navy messages on the 27th and 28th of April indicating that "airfields of Kokubu, Miyazaki and Kushira, and possibly Kasanohara, had been rendered unserviceable, apparently by B-29 attacks."[36] In order to lessen the effects of these heavy bomber raids, the Japanese began to hold back some of their fighter strength to protect the fields. In addition the Jacks from Air Groups 302, 332, and 352, which had been operating against the B-29s in the Tokyo area, were transferred south to Kanoya to fight off the American bombers.[37]

The ongoing operations at Okinawa, including the previous *Kikusui* operations had taken their toll on the Japanese. American intelligence reported that the number of planes available to the First Mobile Base Air Force at the beginning of the Okinawa campaign had diminished.

The following rates of serviceability are derived from available April status reports on units of the 1st Mobile Base Air Force, which at the beginning of the Ryukyus operations had a strength of more than 500 planes:

Fighters	45%
Dive bombers	46%
Torpedo bombers	49%
Medium bombers	45%

The same status reports indicate that only a small percentage of the pilots of the units reported were fully trained:

Class A	6% (pilots suited for any operation)
Class B	10% (pilots suited for daytime operations)
Class C	19% (beginners)
Class D	65% (classification recently added to status reports; may include pilots who have not completed normal training)[38]

The number of planes available for suicide missions was in serious decline. To make the remaining Zekes more effective, the Japanese began to equip them with 1,100-pound bombs and radar.

On 27 April, Radar Picket Station # 1 was patrolled by *Aaron Ward*, *Mustin*, *LCS(L) 11*, and *LSM(R) 191*. The first raid began at 2128 when *Aaron Ward's* radar picked up four incoming planes at a distance of fifteen miles. When they were within 8,700 yards, the ship opened fire and hit one of them, causing it to go down in flames. Since it was at a great distance and in the dark, the plane was listed as a probable. The other three aircraft turned away. A second raid occurred at 2145 when a plane was taken under fire and driven away, as was the third raid at 2207. Between 2215 and 2243, three other planes closed on the formation. At 2243 *Mustin* took one of the planes under fire and all three turned away. *Aaron Ward* spotted two planes coming in at 2243. When they reached a range of 6,600 yards, she fired, splashing one. The other escaped.

Early the next morning, 28 April at 0023 and 0030, three or four more planes passed by the station heading south but were too distant for the destroyers to engage. One of them made a run on *LCS(L) 61* from dead ahead, passing over the ship before its crew had time to react. The plane did not return after it was taken under fire by the aft twin 40mm gun. By this time, night fighters were overhead and, at 0033, were vectored to meet an incoming flight of three Japanese planes. Another bogey at 0046 was also intercepted by night fighters. At 0049 two to four more planes approached the formation and were driven away by fire from *Mustin*. Additional planes came into the area at 0204 and 0215 and were also driven off. *Aaron Ward* picked up two incoming planes at 0240. Two Bettys flying from Kanoya dropped their bombs on the formation. They missed all the ships and then tried a suicide run on *Aaron Ward*. Both were splashed about 2,500 yards off the starboard beam by the ship's 40mm and five inch guns. *Ward* finished the night with one probable and three planes shot down. At 1100 on the 28th, the *Aaron Ward* was relieved by *Bennion* and *Mustin* was relieved by *Ammen*. *LCS(L) 61*, which had been cruising two-thirds of the way to the station, closed with the other ships on RP Station # 1 and they continued on patrol. *LCS(L) 11* was relieved by *LCS(L) 23* during the day and left the station. Late in the afternoon, at about 1830, the ships came under attack.

First Lt. Joe Dillard from VMF-323 was flying south of the station with his wingman, 2d Lt. James Bierbower. After three and one-half hours of routine patrolling, *Bennion* vectored them toward an incoming Kate armed with a torpedo. The Kate was one of ten that had flown from Kushira earlier in the day. With two Corsairs on its tail, the Kate did its best to escape but it was futile. Dillard finished it off with a burst to the wing root and, at 1845, the enemy plane hit the water.

Also covering the ships were three divisions of Corsairs from VMF-311 at Yontan. Three more divisions of FM-2 Wildcats from VC-83 cruised the area to the south near Ie Shima. *Bennion's* radar picked up several large raids coming in from the north and vectored the Corsairs to intercept them. The aerial sharpshooters were on target as usual and a combination of twelve Vals and Zekes went down to a watery grave. Two Vals each were splashed by 2d Lts. Donald H. Clark and William P. Brown and Capts. John V. Blakeney and Ralph G. McCormick each got one Val. Other members of the division, 2d Lts. Roland T. Hammer, Robert K. Sherrill, Lawrence K. Whiteside, Thomas M. Kirby and Theodore A. Brown each splashed one enemy plane. Eight more of the enemy went down under the guns of other CAP planes in the area.

Captain Floyd C. Kirkpatrick and 2d Lt. George E. Lantz of VMF-441 at Yontan, had been flying radar picket patrol over the station. They caught a Zeke making a run on the ships and shot it down. Another Japanese plane, an Oscar, circled directly overhead, making tracking and firing on it difficult. The plane made a dive on *Bennion*, coming in from astern at a steep angle. Continued hits from 20mm and 40mm guns did not stop the plane and, as it crossed over the fantail of the destroyer, debris was scattered over the deck. Its wing hit the number 2 stack and the plane continued on, crashing into the water off the starboard side; it was a close call for *Bennion*.

One division of Death Rattler Corsairs from VMF-323 had taken off from Kadena at 1615 and headed for RP Station # 1.

Bennion directed the Corsairs to orbit to the south of the station over Izena Shima. There, 1st Lts. Vernon Ball, Francis Terrill, Bill Hood and Ed Murray spotted four Vals from Kokubu # 2 cruising south at 15,000 feet and went after them. With no rear gunners to protect them, the Vals were splashed in short order, with each of the pilots getting one kill. The absence of a rear gunner usually indicated that the planes were on a suicide run. Their immediate task completed, the division was then vectored to the west, where they ran into four more Vals and an Ida. These too, went down under the guns of the Death Rattlers. The division returned to base, with nine and one-half planes to its credit. Credit for one of the Vals was shared with a Corsair from Yontan.[39]

Two divisions of VC-83 Wildcats had been launched from the escort carrier *Sargent Bay* at 1515. They were due to return to base about 1815 but were alerted by *Bennion* that there was a bogey in their area. The divisions, led by Lts. D.O. McNinch and H.C. Cook, became involved in the action. They found a Val, which Cook eventually shot down after it took a series of evasive maneuvers.

At about 2200, a Kate made a run on the support gunboats. They were cruising in a line three miles to starboard of the destroyers with about 800 yards between them. First in line was *LCS(L) 31*, followed by *LCS(L)s 61* and *23*. Powell Pierpoint, XO of *LCS(L) 61* described the action:

Roger Peter One had been alerted for a good part of the night and the DD's had taken bogies under fire several times. It was an active night all over the Picket Line and we had been at Red & Green for a long period. Our private bogie had not been reported to us by any source until our own Radarman, A.H. Bleiler, RdM2/c, picked him up and tracked him in. LCS 61 was second ship in a column of three and the bogie was closing from ahead, from right to left and an angle of about 201 to the axis. The lookouts and fire control man sighted him visually while he was still on the starboard side of the column and started tracking. Fire was not opened until he cleared the ship ahead. The number 2 40MM gun with Larry Fabroni, FC 2/c, at the director was right on from the first shot. As soon as he realized he was being fired on the Jap turned in toward the 61 but he was much, much too late. We had him on fire before and he fell within 100 yds. on our port beam. 18 rounds of 40MM ammunition were expended. And that was that. The OTC investigated the wreckage, discovering two bodies. Just as easy as falling

off a log. We had visions of our take running into the dozens.
We were soon to be disillusioned, but our first conquest gave us
a world of confidence. Bring on the bogies. We were ready and
waiting for them.[40]

LCS(L) 23, steaming third in the column, had also fired on the
plane and was give credit for an assist. At 2320 a bogey made a
flyby of the station. *Bennion* described the plane as a reconnaissance aircraft that was obviously assessing the results of the day's
raids.[41]

April 28 was a clear day with excellent weather. In the morning hours, as the ships patrolled at RP Station # 2, they were covered by a radar picket patrol of two Corsairs directly over them and
another twelve in the area patrolling from 10,000 to 30,000 feet.
The afternoon CAP had two Corsairs near the ships and six more
nearby to intercept raids. At 1539 *Daly* vectored the six Corsairs to
intercept incoming bogeys.

From the beginning they knew that this was a large raid, but
the Corsairs radioed back that they were attacking a flight of
between thirty-five and fifty Japanese aircraft, mostly Zekes. Vice
Admiral Ugaki wrote: "The entire fighter strength was sent over
Okinawa, and they fought Sikorski fighters [Corsairs] in the air
over Ie Shima and surely shot down three of them." [42] Between
1555 and 1612, the first two sections of the CAP splashed twelve of
the enemy planes with another four to six listed as probables. The
third section reported in at 1628 that they had splashed seven,
with four to five probables. Low on fuel and ammunition, the
planes returned to their base, having routed a vastly superior
enemy force.

Unfortunately for the ships at RP Station # 2, the day was not
over. At 1700 another raid, estimated at between eight and ten aircraft, was reported to be one hundred miles away and closing on
the station. At 1719 the ships went to general quarters and began
to organize for the anticipated attack. *Daly* stationed herself
behind *Twiggs* with the support ships nearby. At 1730 the two
destroyers maneuvered to take a small flight of Vals to starboard
under fire. As they did this, another larger flight of Vals from
Kokubu # 2 came in on suicide runs from the port side. *Daly*
splashed three at ranges from 200 to 1,000 yards. A fourth Val followed. It made a run directly at *Daly's* bridge, was taken under fire

and hit repeatedly.

As the plane passed over the destroyer's Number 2 torpedo tube it lost a wing and crashed into the sea twenty-five yards off the port side of the ship. The explosion knocked out the ship's radar and damaged the engineering plant. Two men had been killed and fifteen seriously wounded. Among the dead was the ship's medical officer. A fifth plane, following right behind the fourth, was shot down 700 yards astern. About the same time, *Twiggs* was attacked by two planes, one of which she shot down. Both crashed into the water very near to the destroyer, causing a great deal of damage. *Twiggs* hull plating was blown in and her hull opened from frames 46 to 60. She was fortunate in that only two men were wounded. By 1739 the attack was over.

Overhead, the station's RPP, assisted by planes from the CAP at RP Station # 3 reported splashing six planes. Lieutenants Kenneth Royson and Victor Armstrong of VMF-312, were flying CAP over the station when they spotted eight Nates heading for the ships. Armstrong got two and Royson was credited with one.

At 1910, *Van Valkenburgh*, cruising on RP Station # 1, came to the aid of *Daly*, transferring her medical officer and a Pharmacist's Mate to assist the wounded. At 2003 *Gainard* relieved the ships at RP Station # 2. *Twiggs* and *Daly* headed back to the transport area.

Patrolling RP Station # 10 on 27 April were *Macomb*, *J. William Ditter*, LSM(R)s *193*, and *195*. At 0502 *Ditter* picked up four bogeys on her radar and tracked them as they approached the station. The first plane made an attempt to crash *Macomb* and was shot down 50 yards astern of the ship. *Macomb* and *Ditter* took two other planes under fire and splashed them both. The fourth plane turned away and fell victim to the CAP.

At 0929 *Brown* relieved *Macomb* and took charge of the four plane CAP that was on patrol near the station. LSM(R) *193* was relieved by LCS(L) *53* which reported at 1200. During the daylight hours, a series of four-plane CAPs orbited the station, flying out of the marine fields on Okinawa. Bogeys were reported splashed by planes from other stations and the CAP over RP Station # 10 was on alert, but had no enemy aircraft to intercept. At 1805, an hour after the CAP had returned to base, three Vals were reported closing on the station at a distance of fifty-four miles. Within the hour they were in orbit ten miles off the station and other enemy planes were on the way. *Brown* and *J. William Ditter* began to fire on the incoming raid at 1936 and one plane went down in flames; the others flew off.

At 2055 the ships again opened fire on six enemy planes, one of which made a suicide run on *Ditter*. As it passed down the starboard side of the ship the plane was hit by 20mm and 40mm shells but continued on course. Passing aft of the ship, it turned and attempted to crash, but it went down thirty feet off the port side of the minelayer. A short while later, at 2105, a plane dropped a torpedo aimed at *Brown* which passed astern of the ship. Two other torpedo bombers closed the station and were taken under fire by *Brown* and *Ditter*. A fourth plane in the raid was caught between *Ditter* and *LCS(L) 53*. It was shot down and splashed thirty feet to starboard of the gunboat without causing damage. The last plane in the group fell victim to the combined gunfire of the ships. By 2153 the radar screens were clear and the ships continued on patrol.

Patrolling Radar Picket Station # 12 were *Wadsworth* and *LSM(R)s 190* and *192*. The ships were attacked at 2007 on the 28th. *LSM(R) 190* shot down one plane. A Kate then made a run on *Wadsworth* from astern, strafing the ship as it passed over. It banked to the left and attacked again on the port beam, dropping a torpedo which missed the ship. Its wing snagged the ship's gig and a life float as it passed over, crashing into the water only ten feet from the side of the destroyer. No damage to the ship occurred but it had been a close call. Another Kate followed the first and was shot down only thirty feet off the port bow. At 2130 two more planes approached the station and the destroyer knocked down one and drove off the other.

Radar Picket Station # 14 was patrolled by *Robert H. Smith*, *Bache*, *LCS(L)s 62, 64, 83*, and *LSM(R) 196*. At 1730 on the 28th VMF-323 launched two divisions from Kadena. Major George Axtel led one division and Capt. Joe McPhail the other. The Death Rattlers' divisions orbited the area near RP Station # 14 and soon found their prey. First Lt. Jerry O'Keefe, leading a section in Axtel's division, was the first to spot the enemy. With his wingman, 2d Lt. Dewey Durnford, O'Keefe headed for some bogeys and soon reported back to Axtell that they were Japanese. The division turned and dropped down, coming at the five Nates from behind.

Within a few minutes, all five of the Japanese planes had been splashed, with Durnford and O'Keefe getting two and Axtell one.[43] A Nick fighter, caught between the guns of a CAP plane and *Bache*, went down at 1836 after it had been hit by both. It had approached within 6,000 yards of the ship. The station's CAP had accounted for ten of the enemy aircraft, with several others listed as probables. At 2150 two bogeys were reported headed for the station and *Bache* took them under fire. One disappeared from radar, leaving the observers to assume she was splashed. The second plane escaped to the south. It had been a busy day for the ships at RP Station # 14, *Robert H. Smith* reported that "the raid designations went as high as Raid 42."[44]

General Buckner sent a message of praise for the marine flyers to General Mulcahy. It stated:

> AGAIN I DESIRE TO COMMEND YOU AND YOUR COMMAND AND AIR CREWS FOR DECONTAMINATING THE OKINAWA ATMOSPHERE AND TURNING THIRTY FIVE MORE JAP AVIATORS OVER TO THE TENDER MERCIES OF THE ATTRACTION OF GRAVITY.[45]

Sunday, 29 April and Monday, 30 April 1945

In an effort to render more aid to the ships and hopefully cut the death rate, a new plan was adopted for the radar picket stations. As of 30 April, *LSMs 14, 82, 167, 222, 228,* and *279* were reassigned to LSM Flotilla Nine. Their assignment would be as towing and medical ships specifically for the radar picket stations. As such, they would be stationed about one-third of the way from Point Bolo to RP Stations # 3, 7, 9, 10, and 12. Each ship would carry a medical officer and supplies. Positioned two-thirds of the way to RP Stations # 3, 7, 9, 10, and 12 would be LSM(R)s which would have a similar assignment, including the presence of a medical officer. The LSM(R)s were designated as survivor and medical ships. Both the LSMs and LSM(R)s were required to report in to the senior destroyer on the radar picket station and make their availability known. In addition, other LSM(R)s would continue to act as close support ships for the destroyers on RP Stations # 2, 3, 4, 9, and 14. These ships, with the exception of *LSM(R) 190*, would not carry medical officers.

Radar Picket Station # 1 was patrolled by *Bennion, Ammen,*
LCS(L)s 23, and *31* on 29 April. *LSM(R) 189* would patrol two-
thirds of the way from Point Bolo on both days. In short order, it
became obvious that the picket ships were now considered a target.
According to *Ammen's* action report:

> On the night of 29-30 April 1945 an attack obviously was
> launched from Japan with the sole intention of hitting this par-
> ticular picket station. From time of first contact it came
> straight on in. Another raid to the east headed for the adjacent
> easterly station (No. 2) and a third raid to the west went to the
> adjacent station (No. 14) to the west. All planes in each raid
> attacked their respective pickets and none went farther south
> toward Okinawa.[46]

The first raid consisted of seven planes and was first spotted at
0155 on the 30th. At 0200 *Ammen* was targeted by two planes
which came in from the starboard side and tried to crash her. The
destroyer maneuvered violently at flank speed, executing a hard
right rudder at the last moment. Both planes overshot her. They
crashed into the water about 200 feet to port of the ship. *Ammen*
and *Bennion* continued to fire on incoming planes, either turning
them away or shooting them down. Another plane attempted to
crash *Bennion* but was shot down just off the fantail, showering the
aft end of the ship with pieces of airplane and tearing off the lifelines on the port side. Two more Japanese planes were shot down
by the combined fire of the destroyers. Of the total number of
planes in the raid, only one was left. As the enemy plane tried to
leave the area of the station *Bennion* vectored a night fighter to
intercept it. It shot down a Zeke twenty-five miles southwest of the
station at 0315.

Radar Picket Station # 2 was patrolled by *Morrison, Gainard,*
LCS(L)s 11, 19, 81, 87, 88, and *111. LSM(R) 194* patrolled two-
thirds of the way from Point Bolo on both days. She was joined by
LSM(R) 191 at 2200 on the 30th. At 0549 *LCS(L) 87,* patrolling
near Iheya Shima, spotted a Val making a run on it from a low altitude. The gunboat turned broadside to the plane and took it under
fire. Her 40mm guns found the range and the plane went down
2,000 yards to port. Other raids were reported in the vicinity during the day, but none closed the station.

During the night of the 29th to the 30th, a number of new raids came in from the north. At 0220 *Gainard* took an enemy plane under fire with her 40mm guns and it turned off and crashed in the water several miles from the ship. At 1051 *Ingraham* relieved *Morrison* which shifted over to RP # 1 to relieve *Bennion*. The only event for the day was a tragic one, with *Gainard* shooting down a marine Corsair from VMF-311 that had been flying CAP over the station. The disaster took place about 1510. The two CAP Corsairs which had been flying cover over the station were relieved by another pair and ordered back to their base at Yontan. For some reason, they unexpectedly made a low level run twenty-five feet off the water that took them near *Gainard's* starboard quarter. One of the destroyer's quad 40mm batteries opened fire on the Corsairs, mistaking them for Japanese Graces and shot one down. The second escaped and made it back to base full of holes. *Ingraham* recovered the body of 1st Lt. William K. Ouellette of VMF-311 and was given permission to bury him at sea.

Patrolling on RP Station # 3 were *Hudson*, *Van Valkenburgh*, *LCS(L)s 18*, *52*, *110*, and *LSM(R) 198*. *LCS(L) 86* was positioned two-thirds of the way to the station. April 29 was uneventful. Early the next morning, *LSM(R) 198*, *LCS(L)s 18*, *52*, and *110* steamed in a column as directed by *Hudson*. Surface radar on *LCS(L) 110* picked up an incoming bogey at five miles distance. At about 0300, a Frances light bomber came in from the port quarter and the three gunboats opened fire, all scoring hits. As the plane splashed close to the formation, loud explosions were heard and the plane continued burning for twenty minutes.

The Frances was one of a flight of eight that had left its base in southern Japan late in the evening of the 29th. Each of these planes carried a crew of three and their mission was to attack shipping around Okinawa.[47] Later in the morning, at about 0800, lookouts on *LCS(L) 110* spotted a Japanese survivor in the water and fished him out. Aviation Radioman 3/c Yokire Kato was the only one of his crew to survive. He was in good condition and was turned over to *Van Valkenburgh* for custody and transport back to the anchorage.[48]

Patrolling RP Station # 4 were *Cowell*, *Harry F. Bauer*, and *LCS(L)s 54*, *82*, and *109*. *LSM(R) 199* patrolled independently two-thirds of the way to the station. In the afternoon, about 1635, incoming raids were detected. The Japanese had sent out thirty-three fighters from the Fifth Showa Special Attack Unit at Kanoya. They were equipped with bombs and their target was the American task force east or southeast of Okinawa. One of the planes was piloted by navy Lt. Yasuo Ichishima. The previous week, on 23 April, he had written:

> My life of twenty-five . . . years is approaching its end, but I do not feel like a person who is going to die tomorrow. I have already come to the southern end of Japan; tomorrow I shall dare fierce anti-aircraft fire and dive through enemy fighters into an enemy ship – but somehow I cannot feel that any of this is real.[49]

Ichishima's unit was not successful and he died on the mission. Of the thirty-three fighters that left Kanoya that day, only five made it back.[50]

At 1650 *Bauer* spotted four Zekes and a Lilly medium bomber. The planes ducked into the clouds and were hidden from sight until the Lily emerged at 1705 and made a run on the *Bauer*. The plane was hit repeatedly and its bombs exploded. It crashed into the sea 5,000 yards from the ship and the pilot was blown out of the plane. His parachute was later found, but not his body. Within a few minutes one of the Zekes came in from the starboard beam. The plane took a number of hits to the fuselage and engine cowling. With its engine knocked out and the pilot probably killed, the plane rolled over and crashed into the water twenty-five yards off *Bauer's* starboard beam. Almost immediately a second Zeke made a run on the ship. *Bauer's* two 40mm quad guns took it under fire and scored, turning it away. The Zeke flew to the west in flames and probably crashed out of sight. The third Zeke to attack the ship made its run about the same time. All guns unloaded on the plane and it was seen to catch fire at a range of 2,000 yards. Observers on the ship believe that the pilot was dead as the plane passed over the after stack and crashed seventy-five yards to port. These attacks were considered to be suicide runs as none of the planes seemed to be equipped with machine guns.

Cowell was also under attack at the same time. At 1703 a Zeke tried to crash her on the port bow. *Cowell's* gunners were on target and the Zeke crashed into the water 1,000 yards off the ship. Overhead, the CAP accounted for two more Zekes. The gunboats

LCS(L) 33, shown here in early 1945, was sunk at Radar Picket Station # 1 on 12 April 1945 by a kamikaze. *NARA 80 GK 2681.*

cruised nearby but all of the planes were too distant for them to engage. By 1817 the area was clear.

April had been a disastrous month for the radar picket ships. The Japanese raids had taken their toll. On the radar picket stations, four destroyers had been sunk and sixteen others damaged by kamikaze attacks. Two LCS(L)s had been sunk and four hit. In addition, four high-speed minesweepers and one LSM(R) had also sustained damage in the attacks. Casualties on these ships were high, with a total of 416 men killed and 529 wounded.

In spite of their vigilance, the picket ships and their CAP cound not stop all of the Japanese planes. During the last two weeks of April, in addition to the radar picket ships, thirteen other ships were hit. Among them was the carrier *Intrepid*, which suffered ten killed and eighty-seven wounded.[51]

On 29 April, a Japanese army Lily from the 90th Flying Regiment crashed on Okinawa. Among the items taken from the plane's wreckage were three sets of orders indicating that the plane was using the field at Gunzan, Korea as a rear base. Earlier orders had designated areas at Gunzan for use by the 16th and 90th Flying Regiments. Planes were to fly from Gunzan to Fukuoka on

Kyushu. From there they would stage forward to Nittagahara and then on to Okinawa. On the return trip they would land at Nittagahara and then proceed back to their base in Korea.[52]

War weary men went through their daily assignments in spite of their exhausted condition. Called to general quarters continually, they began to feel the intense strain of being at death's edge twenty-four hours a day. Gunners Mate 3/c Earl Blanton of *LCS(L) 118* recalled:

> I did not remove my clothes for twenty-one days . . .We'd get so doggone sleepy we could hardly stand it. We'd actually stand up and our knees would buckle and you'd catch yourself so you wouldn't fall down. You'd do what you could to keep awake. It was just terrible. . . Time didn't mean a whole lot when you're on four on and four off. . . There just wasn't time to worry about changing clothes. . . .There was always a raid, always GQ....Back on the aft gun, the port and starboard engine exhaust and smoke from the diesel generators and engines all that diesel smoke was blowing across that aft area all the time.[53]

CHAPTER 5

"The dead were the luckiest of us all...."

Foul weather would make May a difficult month for the planes flying on combat air patrol and radar picket patrol. Major P.L. Shuman, the commanding officer of VMF-311, reported:

> Weather conditions, throughout the month, were the most hazardous ever encountered even by the most experienced pilots. Winds up to 30 knots on the ground and 80 knots aloft, blew from every octant except 3151 to 3601. For almost a quarter of the time ceilings were below 1000' and many landings were made in driving rains with negligible visibility and ceilings of less than 100'. Precipitation, recorded by aerology was just under 14 inches, of which 7 1/2 inches fell during a period of five days at the end of the month. The difficulty of maintaining aircraft operational under these conditions can easily be imagined.[1]

The poor weather was welcomed by the ships on the radar picket stations. They received a break from the constant calls to general quarters and the hazards of Japanese aerial attacks. No enemy planes threatened the picket ships for the first two days of May. This would be but a brief respite, as the launch of *Kikusui #5* was imminent.

Thursday, 3 May and Friday, 4 May 1945

Kikusui # 5 began on 3 May and lasted into 4 May. Flying against the American ships were a total of 125 special attack planes, including seventy-five from the navy and fifty from the army. Still others would fly regular missions of escort and attack. This massed raid was planned to coincide with a counter attack by the Japanese 32nd Army which "expressed its gratitude for the air cooperation received here to fore. At the same time, [it] asked for further air cooperation by attacking the enemy Naval bombardment group and also the supply dumps along the coast."[2]

The Japanese army and navy recognized the futility of sending its fighter and light bomber aircraft into suicide crashes on the American battleships but were determined to do it anyway in order to show support for the army. Attacks on the supply dumps were considered an impossibility during the day due to the presence of the marine air groups at Yontan and Kadena. It was decided to execute night attacks against these targets using the heavy bomber units of the Japanese army.[3]

The ships and men at Okinawa were fortunate. American military intelligence had intercepted enough radio transmissions to identify 4 May as the beginning date for *Kikusui # 5*. This information had been reinforced by the appearance of enemy search planes the evening of 3 May, indicating that the Japanese were attempting to pinpoint the locations of ships for the next day's attack. To hinder the Japanese air units, the XXI Bomber Command conducted B-29 strikes on the airfields at Chiran, Ibusuki, Kanoya, Kanoya East, Kokubu, Matsuyama West, Miyazaki, Oita, Omura, Saeki, Tachiarai, Tanega Shima, and Tomitaka. A total of 225 bombers hit the fields on 30 April and from 3 to 5 May.[4] Records of the Naval Security Group note:

> The Blue air strike during the morning apparently caught a considerable number of planes at Kyushu bases awaiting the start of KIKUSUI # 5 operations. The strike precipitated a mass movement of aircraft from Kyushu to Miho, Hiroshima and other more secure bases on western Honshu; these planes began returning to their original bases during the afternoon, just in time to encounter the afternoon B-29 strike.[5]

Radar Picket Station # 1 was patrolled by *Morrison*, *Ingraham*, *LCS(L)s 21, 23, 31*, and *LSM(R) 194*. The morning of the 3rd was still a bit cloudy but the weather cleared by mid-day. Bogeys began to appear near the station late in the afternoon. At 1600 *Morrison* vectored the CAP to intercept two Dinahs which were closing the formation at a high altitude; both were shot down.

Occasional bogeys were in the area for the remainder of the evening but none came within range of the ships' guns.

Early on 4 May, at 0150, an enemy plane made a bomb run on *Ingraham* at a low altitude. Its bomb missed and the plane flew off unscathed. From then until daybreak, a number of enemy aircraft were reported in the area, but none came close enough to engage. A twelve plane CAP reported on station at 0540. At 0715 *Morrison* picked up a bogey at forty-five miles and sent a division of Corsairs to intercept it. One Oscar was splashed. Within minutes a Val was picked up on radar and another CAP division sent in its direction. The Val initially evaded the CAP and appeared off the port beam of *Morrison* where it made a suicide run with four Corsairs on its tail. It was hit by the destroyer and the American planes as it passed over the DD, grazing the number two five-inch gun and splashing twenty feet astern of the ship. At about the same time, a PBM Mariner landed nearby, having run out of fuel. Two other Mariners circled overhead covering the downed plane.

More bogeys appeared in the area about 0732 and the CAP was vectored to intercept them. Within a few minutes the melee was on. Nicks, Nans, and Vals could be seen falling out of the sky in the distance as the CAP planes found their victims. The circling Mariners were attacked by a fighter and they shot it down. CAP fighters chased another enemy plane into the guns of *Ingraham* and it was splashed to starboard of the destroyer. At 0742 *Ingraham* headed for the Mariner to rescue its crew. Meanwhile, the CAP splashed several more of the enemy planes. As *Ingraham* approached the floating Mariner another Zeke attacked it. The plane was shot down after being caught between the fire of the destroyer and the circling Mariners.

Taking place in the sky above was one of the great air battles of the Okinawa campaign. Among the CAP fighters flying overhead were six divisions of VF-9 Hellcats off *Yorktown*. The first flight of three divisions was launched at 0510 and was under the leadership of Lt. Eugene A. Valencia. Valencia was already an ace, having shot down seven enemy aircraft at Rabaul, Tarawa and Truk. His division mates, Lts. (jg) Harris E. Mitchell, James B. French, and Clinton L. Smith were veteran combat pilots as well. Only a few weeks before, Valencia's division, known as the "Flying Circus," had splashed fourteen enemy planes, with another three listed as probable kills. Their assignment was to cover RP Station # 1, which

Lieutenant Eugene Valencia at Guam on 19 May 1945. *Photo by J.G. Mull PhoM3/c. NARA 80G 329441.*

was directly in the path of incoming enemy aircraft from southern Japan. As the three divisions arrived on station, the fighter director officer on *Morrison* set them to orbit at different altitudes. Valencia's division was at 20,000 feet, with Lt. (jg) Caldwell's at

12,000 and Lt. Bert Eckard's at 8,000. At 0715 Valencia's division was ordered down to 8,000 feet and Eckard's up to 20,000. Within minutes the two divisions under Caldwell and Eckard were vectored north in search of incoming bogeys, but they made no contact and returned to orbit the ships. At about 0800, as Valencia's division dropped down in altitude, they spotted a Frank and a Dinah making a run on the ships. Valencia came in behind the Frank and hit it with two bursts in the cockpit. It caught fire and crashed into the sea. At the same time, Mitchell made a stern run on a Dinah which he hit in the starboard wing. The Dinah began to roll to port and Mitchell hit it again in both wings causing it to flame and crash. Minutes later a large formation of enemy planes was sighted to the north at altitudes from 3,000 feet down to fifty feet and the battle was on. Valencia and Mitchell spotted five Vals heading for the ships and engaged them. Valencia raked the fuselage of the first from one end to the other and it turned into a ball of flame as it exploded.

Mitchell went after a Frank at 1,200 feet and caught it from behind. A burst from the Hellcat's guns flamed both wings, sending the Frank into the water. A second Frank appeared below Mitchell heading toward the destroyers and he fired two bursts, hitting the enemy plane's engine and fuselage. Undaunted by the damage to his plane, the Japanese pilot kept on course, narrowly missing a destroyer as his plane passed over and exploded in the water. Valencia spotted more Franks going after the ships and he followed them in as one dropped a bomb and then strafed one of the destroyers. After dropping its bomb, the Frank made a wing over and headed for one of the gunboats. Valencia followed and caught the enemy plane as it turned and came toward him. Hitting it in the engine and fuselage, he set the Frank afire and it rolled over and hit the water. Valencia then spotted a Nate and closed in, only to find that he had run out of ammunition. Fortunately Corsairs from another squadron were in a good position and he guided them toward the Nate which they promptly shot down.

Other VF-9 pilots had their hands full as well. Lieutenant (jg) James B. French caught up with an Oscar heading for a destroyer and got on its tail. It lowered its wheels in an effort to make the Hellcat overshoot it but French did the same, firing a burst into the plane's fuselage. He turned off as the Oscar pulled up and then crashed past the destroyer in a large ball of fire. French soon splashed a Frank and then teamed up with some other planes to shoot down a Zeke. After joining Smith and Valencia overhead, they found a Nate ten miles from the station and French shot it down after his two companions overran the plane. Soon after, he assisted in another shoot down.

Lieutenant (jg) Clinton L. Smith, the last of the four members of the division, spotted a Frank making a bomb run on the destroyers and followed it in, hitting it in the engine and fuselage and flaming it. Ten minutes elapsed and Smith found another target. This time it was a Judy making a run on a destroyer. Smith caught up with the Judy just as the DDs found the range. Caught between the ships' fire and the Hellcat, the Judy flamed and went into the sea. Smith narrowly escaped being hit by friendly fire as he pulled up sharply and sped away. Valencia's division formed up to head back to *Yorktown,* but were so low on fuel that they could not make it. They had to land at Yontan instead. Smith's Hellcat had only ten gallons of gas left. After refueling, they returned to their ship.

Valencia's division was not the only one in action over RP Station # 1. Another VF-9 division, led by Lt. Bert Eckard, had been held back by the fighter director until the appropriate moment. They were vectored down to 700 feet to intercept a Val and Eckard splashed it. His wingman, Lt. (jg) Emmett B. Lawrence, got on the tail of another Val and hit its starboard wing with two short bursts, setting it on fire and causing the plane to crash into the ocean.

The division led by Lt. (jg) Caldwell had been orbiting at 20,000 feet and, toward the end of the sky battle, headed down to 10,000. There, Ens. Paul A. Anderson pulled up behind a Zeke that was headed for *Ingraham* and fired bursts into its engine and wing. Fuel in the wing tanks ignited and the plane splashed near *LCS(L) 31* at 0833. Ensign Theodore M. Smyer, another member of Caldwell's division, doggedly pursued a Zeke, making two runs on it before hitting its engine with three bursts and sending it down to the water. As his first Zeke went down Smyer spotted another passing him and got in a few hits before it escaped. The last member of the division, Ens. Martin Lally, caught a Frank broadside at the same time other American planes fired on it. Lally got credit for a quarter kill.

Yorktown had launched a second flight of VF-9 Hellcats at 0630 to provide CAP for RP Station # 1. The flight was led by Lt.

Franger with two other divisions led by Lt. Edward C. McGowan and Lieutenant Kussman. They arrived over RP Station # 1 at about 0730 and orbited the battle scene until Kussman's and Franger's divisions were vectored to the north at about 0750 to cover the ships at RP Station # 14.

McGowan's division joined with Valencia's in the fight at RP Station # 1. At 0845 McGowan was flying at 4,000 feet when he noticed a Tojo 1,000 feet below him heading toward *Ingraham*. He dove and turned on the Tojo's tail, hitting its fuselage and cockpit with a couple of bursts. The Tojo flamed and went into the sea. A few minutes later, McGowan caught up with an Oscar headed into the picket ships at an altitude of 300 feet. The Oscar turned sharply to the right with McGowan on his tail, firing furiously. Within minutes the Oscar had splashed. Still another Oscar passed within his sights and McGowan scored some hits but the plane escaped, only to be shot down by another American fighter.

The VF-9 divisions over RP Station # 1 had shot down twenty-six planes, including seven Franks, six Vals, five Oscars and three Zekes. Single kills included a Dinah, Nate, Judy, Peggy and Tojo. Valencia was credited with three and one half, Mitchell and French with three and Smith and McGowan with two kills. Young, Eckard, Lawrence, Anderson, Smeehuyzen, Sledge, Isaacson, Smyer, Darrow, and Reiner each got one.[6]

Morrison sent out word about the size of the raid and within the next hour nine more divisions were on the scene, placing at least forty-eight Corsairs and Hellcats over the ships. As each division reported, they were vectored out to meet the enemy. Within a short time, so many enemy planes had arrived at the station and the action overhead was so confused that the destroyers stopped trying to get through to the planes. Pilot to pilot talk jammed the airways as the battle raged. An incomplete count by *Morrison* indicated that at least thirteen planes had been shot down.

The downed Mariner that had landed near *Morrison* was still not out of danger. Another Val selected it as a target. Chased by four Corsairs, the Val changed course, first attacking one of the Mariners circling above and then turning toward *Morrison*. It went down at 0745, 2,500 yards off the destroyer after being hit by fire from the CAP and the ship. Still another Val made a run on *Morrison* at 0810. Chased by a division of Corsairs, the enemy plane strafed the destroyer on the way in, passing from port to starboard and crashing twenty-five yards off the ship. The Val grazed the bridge on its way across, causing minor damage. The ships on station had to use great discretion in firing on the enemy planes. Most of the Japanese planes were involved in dog fights or being chased by the CAP and the ships did not want to hit American planes.

After taking off from Kadena at 0730, two divisions of VMF-323 Corsairs had been directed to orbit the skies over Ie Shima. One division was soon vectored toward RP Station # 12 to assist the ships there, leaving one division behind. The division remaining over Ie Shima was led by Capt. Joe McPhail with wingman, 2d Lt. Warren Bestwick; the division also included 1st Lt. John W. Rusham and his wingman, 1st Lt. Bob Wade. Over Ie Shima the four spotted a Nate and pursued it. Rusham came in too fast and overshot his mark, but McPhail had the right angle and hit the Nate with a burst. It rolled over, caught fire and hit the water. Bestwick developed engine trouble and McPhail covered him as he returned to the field at Kadena, promising to return as soon as he was safely down.

About the same time, Rusham and Wade took notice of the battle at RP Station # 1, since *Morrison* had been hit and was on fire. Approaching RP Station # 1, they spotted a number of Vals menacing the picket ships and took them on. Rusham's first bursts tore part of the starboard wing off the first Val. He came around for another pass and this time flamed the plane, sending it into the water. As he broke off from the first Val, a second appeared in his sights and was promptly shot down.

Meanwhile, Wade had splashed a Val and headed up to join Rusham. The pair then double-teamed a Nate which escaped Rusham's guns only to fly into those of Wade. Wade's burst was aimed at the cockpit and apparently killed the pilot; the plane headed for the water and splashed. Rusham, on the tail of another Val, fired a burst and flamed it. Wade came in for the kill only to see the plane explode in his face. Rusham chased another Val down to the deck, scored some hits and then ran out of ammunition. Wade zoomed by firing his guns but also ran out of ammunition. In an attempt to avoid the two Corsairs, the Val made a tight turn. He was too close to the water and his wingtip caught a wave and he crashed into the sea. With their guns empty, Rusham and Wade returned to Kadena, after chalking up many Japanese planes between them. Rusham finished the day as the Death Rattlers high scorer, having shot down four Vals and damaging three others.[7]

Marines from Yontan also got in on the action. Vectored north at 0810, nine Corsairs from VMF-224 went into action. By the end of the day they would shoot down ten of the enemy planes. At 0815 Lt. C.H. Rushfeldt was the first to score, shooting down a Val which was approaching the station at an altitude of fifty feet.

At about 0825 *Morrison* was again a target. A Zeke, chased by a division of Corsairs, strafed the ship on the way in. Gunfire from the Corsairs and the ship caused it to splash fifty yards to starboard. Two more Zekes had been orbiting overhead at about 6,000 feet. Suddenly they made wing overs, coming at the destroyer from out of the sun. The enemy planes leveled off at about fifty feet and made their final run on the ship. Although they were chased by the CAP and also hit by the destroyer's guns, both crashed into *Morrison*. The first hit the base of the forward stack and its bomb went off. The second hit the deck near the number three 5-inch gun. *Morrison* was gravely injured from these two kamikaze hits. Her number one boiler exploded, sections of the bridge were heavily damaged, power and light to the forward part of the ship was knocked out and the starboard shell plating near the aft engine room was ruptured as was the forward engine room. Serious fires began in several locations.

Other enemy planes came in for the kill. 1st Lt. F.P. Weldy and his wingman, 2d Lt. C.K. Jackson of VHF-224, spotted six Daves approaching the ship from starboard. The twin float biplanes were from a group of twenty-eight that had taken off from Ibusuki earlier that day. Their slow speed and low altitude made it difficult for the speedy CAP fighters to intercept them. Only eight would return to their base. Jackson shot down one of them and then turned into another and shot it down also. Weldy then fired into a Dave but it continued on toward the *Morrison*. Explosive shells from the ship failed to detonate since the planes were constructed of wood with fabric coverings. At 0834 the Dave crashed into *Morrison's* number three 5-inch gun igniting the powder in the upper handling room and causing a massive explosion. A second Dave landed in the wake of the destroyer in order to evade the Corsairs that were on its tail. It made a touch-and-go landing 500 yards astern *Morrison* and then took off. Coming in low over the fantail, the Dave crashed into the number four 5-inch gun and ignited its powder. This proved to be the death blow for the ship. Water rushed into a number of compartments and *Morrison* rolled over to starboard and sank stern first in 325 fathoms. One hundred and fifty-two men went down with the ship.

At about the same time that *Morrison* was under attack, other divisions of VMF-224 engaged a combination of eight Vals, Nates and Zekes to the south of the station. Major Hammond shot down two Vals and his wingman, 2d Lt. M.M. VanSalter, shot down a Nate. About fifteen minutes later, at 0830, Capt. J.H. Carroll and 2d Lts. Franklin, M.S. Bristow and T.A. Gribbin attacked five Zekes that were headed for the picket ships. Carroll shot down the first Zeke and Bristow fired into the cockpit of another and it burst into flame. Gribben followed another Zeke through anti-aircraft fire from *Ingraham* and splashed it 200 feet from the destroyer. For his actions Gribben received the Navy Cross.

LSM(R) 194 was cruising along in a column with the three LCS(L)s when the support group came under attack at 0832. *LCS(L) 21* was attacked by three planes, all of which were shot down, but had managed to strike the ship. None of the hits were solid. The planes only skimmed the gunboat which suffered minor damage. A small fire was quickly extinguished.

At 0833 Lieutenant (jg) Reiner and Lieutenant McGowan of VF-9, got on the tail of a Val with a bomb which was making a suicide run on *LCS(L) 21*. McGowan got a few shots off before a Corsair mistakenly took him for the enemy. It fired on the Hellcats, forcing them to break off the chase. Hit repeatedly by *21* and *194* and on fire, the Val swerved at the last moment and crashed into the stern of *LSM(R) 194* at 0838. With the aft steering and engine rooms on fire, the boiler blew up. The bomb ruptured water lines and knocked out the fire and sprinkler systems; this spelled the end for the rocket ship. Within minutes she began to settle by the stern and the order to abandon ship was given to all but the 40mm gun crews. As soon as the crew was off, the gunners and commanding officer left the ship. She went to the bottom stern first. Overhead, Reiner and McGowan went after an Oscar, and Lt.(jg)Young and Ens. Darrow chased two others which they shot down. At about the same time, at 0840, *LCS(L) 21* took a Pete under fire and splashed it close to the ship. She then headed toward the site of the LSM(R)'s sinking to pick up survivors. As she cruised the area, the *194's* magazine exploded underwater. *LCS(L)*

21 was only a few hundred yards from where the ship had sunk and sustained some minor damage from the explosion. The *21* picked up forty-nine survivors and *LCS(L) 23* picked up twenty. *PCE(R) 851* arrived and took the casualties off *LCS(L) 23* and brought them back to the anchorage.

LCS(L) 21 spotted another formation of enemy float planes on the horizon. To alert the CAP they fired their 40mm guns in the direction of the planes. The CAP spotted the float planes and all were splashed. At 0940 *LCS(L) 21* proceeded to pick up survivors of *Morrison*. After the war W. H. Stanley, a gunners mate on board *21,* described the rescue:

> I was surprised there was anyone alive. They had every kind of wound and burn. I helped pull one aboard whose feet were blown off and when we laid him on the deck, I pushed his legs together because his guts were coming out. We tried to pull one aboard that we knew was dead because he was floating face down. When we lifted him up by his life jacket, we saw that his whole face was blown away.[8]

The total number of *Morrison* survivors on board the gunboat numbered 187, of which 108 were injured. Also on board were the survivors from *LSM(R) 194*. With her decks and below deck areas crowded with the injured and wounded, she headed to port.

Ingraham came under attack at 0822 when a Val was sighted off the starboard bow. Her 5-inch battery made short work of the plane. At 0823 a Hellcat chased a Betty toward the ship and the ship's gunners splashed it fifty yards astern. Debris from the splash hit the ship and one of the plane's propellers put a hole in the deck. *Ingraham* took another plane under fire and it veered away and crashed near *LCS(L) 31*. The CAP fighters and *Ingraham's* gunners made short work of another enemy plane at 0833. Shortly thereafter, float biplanes appeared near the formation and one landed in the water near the destroyer; Hellcats finished it off. From 0838 to 0840, the action accelerated. With *Morrison* and *LSM(R) 194* sunk, the Japanese turned their attention to *Ingraham*. In the space of a few minutes the destroyer shot down four more planes, but the fifth crashed into her. The Zeke that hit her had taken off from Miyakonojo Airfield in Southern Kyushu that morning. Piloted by Kanichi Horimoto, it crashed into the port side of *Ingraham* at the waterline. Its bomb went off in the forward diesel room and heavily damaged the number one boiler. Power to the forward 5-inch mounts was knocked out, as well as their fire directors.[9]

LCS(L) 31 had her share of the action as well. A Zeke made a suicide run on her port beam at 0822. As it approached the *31,* it was hit repeatedly by fire from the ship's 40mm and 20mm guns. Its port wing was shot off and it passed over the ship's conning tower. The Zeke's wing clipped off the halyard for the ship's ensign and it crashed into the water ten feet to starboard. A second Zeke came in from the port side. This one was also hit repeatedly, and its port wing hit between the conning tower and the forward twin 40mm mount, killing two men and injuring another. The starboard wing slashed a two by six foot hole in the pilot house and destroyed the starboard 20mm gun. After passing the ship it exploded in the water, killing three more men and wounding another.

Another Zeke made a run on the *31* and was shot down at 0832 and, shortly thereafter, a Val made a successful attack on the ship. It crashed across the main deck aft of the conning tower. Gasoline splashed over the deck causing a number of small fires. The impact from the crash knocked out the fire director tub for the aft twin 40mm gun and destroyed the port 20mm gun. With most of its guns damaged or out of commission, the ship still managed to shoot down another Zeke that was headed for *Ingraham*. The plane was hit by the gunboat's aft starboard 20mm gun and splashed twenty-five yards off the ship. A sixth plane was hit by the *31's* 40mm gun and went down 1,500 yards astern of the ship.

During the time of the action, the *31* observed the CAP shoot down fourteen float-type biplanes, later identified as Petes. *Ingraham* estimated that forty to fifty enemy planes had attacked the station. Anti-aircraft fire from the ships probably accounted for about 19 planes with the CAP accounting for another 25.

Ingraham had been badly damaged. When the fleet tug *Pakana* arrived on the scene at 1230 the bow of the DD was nearly underwater. The tug took *Ingraham* in tow and had her at Kerama Retto by 1900. The high speed transport *Clemson* was ordered to the station to assist in searching for survivors. She took seven dead and seven wounded from *LCS(L) 31* and then continued to search the area, picking up three bodies from *Morrison* and a dead Japanese pilot. The wounded from *LCS(L) 31* were in serious condition and the *Clemson* headed back to Hagushi, where she transferred them to the hospital ships *Mercy* and *Solace*. *PCE(R) 851* arrived on the scene and received thirty-six casualties from *Ingraham*.

At 1318 *Sproston* closed on the station and took over control of RP Station # 1. *LCS(L) 23* and *Nicholson* reported for duty soon after. *LCS(L) 31*, loaded with survivors, was ordered to transport them back to the anchorage. Sharp-shooting gun crews on *LCS(L) 31* had shot down six planes. The ship received a Presidential Unit Citation and her CO, Lt. (jg) Kenneth F. Machacek was awarded the Silver Star.

There were few benefits to being damaged in a kamikaze attack, but *LCS(L) 31* managed to get one. Her single 40mm bow gun had been knocked out in the attacks. At Kerama Retto she was told to replace it and was given permission to cannibalize another LCS(L) that had been damaged too badly to be repaired. Its stern-mounted twin 40mm became her new bow gun, giving her the most advantageous firepower for radar picket duty. Since the single 40mm guns were a temporary fit and the forward mount was already wired for the director and twin 40mm, it was an easy switch.

Lowry, Massey, LCS(L)s 11, 19, 87, and *LSM(R) 191* patrolled RP Station # 2 on 3 May. Lieutenant Leslie H. Kerr Jr. of VF-23 off *Langley*, spotted a twin-engine Dinah making a reconnaissance flight over the ships at 27,000 feet. Pulling his F6F-5 Hellcat up from below, Kerr got on the Dinah's tail and hit it with a single burst of 250 rounds, sending the plane down in flames;[10] the time was 1618.

Early the next morning, at 0224, *Massey* took an enemy plane under fire and turned it away. On 4 May *Lowry* picked up incoming raids at 0736. She fired on one enemy plane at 0833 and it crashed into the sea near *Massey*. A second plane made a run on *Lowry*. It headed directly for her stern and then made a wing over in an attempt to crash the bridge area of the ship. However, the pilot's aim was off. His right wing caught the number three 5-inch gun mount and the plane was thrown over the ship's superstructure and crashed into the water amidships on the port side. The plane and its bomb exploded, killing two men and injuring twenty-three, and the ship suffered some minor damage. The remainder of the day was uneventful. At 0224 the next morning, *PCE(R) 852* took *Lowry's* casualties aboard and transported them back to Hagushi.

The escort carrier *Shangri-La* had launched twelve VF-85 Corsairs at 0630 that morning. Assigned to cover RP Station # 2, they arrived there at about 0830. At 0842 *Lowry* picked up another incoming raid and vectored the three VF-85 divisions to the north to intercept them. They found the enemy planes seven miles north of Iheya Shima. Upon making contact with the bandits, the F4U-1C pilots found two types of aircraft, biplanes and Zekes.

One division, led by Lt. J.S. Jacobs, went after eight biplanes consisting of Pete float biplanes and Willow intermediate trainers. Lashed under each of the Willows was a bomb. Jacobs and his wingman, Ens.W.R. Green, closed on them and Jacobs shot down the first and went after a second. He scored hits on the biplane but it continued on, crashing near a destroyer. At about the same time, Green hit another Willow with a full deflection shot and it landed on the water in flames. Green and Lieutenant Lawrence Sovanski strafed it and it exploded. Green turned and came up behind a Pete, hit it with a quick burst, and it splashed. Immediately he maneuvered his plane behind another Pete and it too went down. Sovanski and his wingman, Ens. M.M. Fogarty, increased the toll of biplanes. After hitting one Willow, Sovanski assisted in destroying the one previously hit by Green. At that time he spotted another eight biplanes above him and got behind one, hitting it and causing it to explode. On the tail of still another, Sovanski had to hold his fire as a Corsair passed in front of his guns. Once the F4U had cleared, he hit the trainer with several bursts and it exploded. Meanwhile his wingman, Fogarty, had taken out a Pete. In the midst of the melee, Hellcats from *Yorktown* zoomed through the mass of planes and added to the kills.

Fifteen miles to the north, the other two divisions of VF-85 Corsairs tallyhoed two groups of twelve to sixteen Zeke-52s at 17,000 feet. The division led by Lt. (jg) J.D. Robbins ran into trouble. They had cruised in the direction of the bogeys at 22,000 feet and their cannons had frozen, forcing them to break off the fight. The only plane with operating guns was that of Lt. (jg) Saul Chernoff. His wingman, Ensign E.L. Myers went after a group of Zekes but failed to notice a second group. Chernoff came in under the second group and shot down three before noticing that three more were after him. He did a split S maneuver but one of the enemy planes hit him and damaged his engine. With his plane smoking, the Zeke apparently thought he was done and at 1,000 feet gave up the chase. Chernoff was able to escape and headed back toward Okinawa where he made a water landing. He survived the water landing and was picked up two and a half hours later by *LCS(L) 11*. Lieutenant F.S. Siddall, from the same division, was also shot down and rescued uninjured.

The other Corsair division that had been vectored to meet these Zekes was led by Lt.(jg) R.A. Bloomfield. They also had gun problems, but Lt. (jg) D.W. Lawhon's cannons worked and he shot down a Zeke. Heading for lower altitudes, Lt. (jg) L.W. Moffitt managed to unfreeze his guns and put some rounds into another Zeke. Lawhon finished it off.

Overall, the VF-85 pilots had splashed thirteen planes, including five Zeke-52s, five Willows and three Petes. Two of their F4U-1C Corsairs had been destroyed, but both pilots were rescued. Chernoff had three kills, Sovanski, Jacobs, Lawhon and Green two each and Fogarty one. Sovanski and Jacobs shared another.

Many planes had been shot down by the CAP but several managed to get through the net of fighters and approach the ships. Reports of heavy enemy air activity at RP Station # 1 reached RP Station # 2 about 0800. At 0831 two Zekes were spotted heading for destroyers; one crashed near *Massey*, and the other splashed off the port beam of *Lowry*. The main parts of the plane bounced off and landed in the water fifteen feet off the side of the ship. The explosion of the plane's bomb killed two men and wounded twenty-three, causing some minor damage to the destroyer, but she was not mortally wounded. Overhead, the CAP could be seen engaging the enemy in the massive air battle spanning the radar picket stations. A Val broke free from the Corsairs trying to down it and made a run on *Massey* from astern. Hit repeatedly, it lost a wing but kept coming, passing over the ship's forecastle and crashing seventy-five feet off the port bow. Observers on the ship could not see the pilot's head, leaving them to believe that he had been killed on the approach.

LCS(L)s 11 and *19* also had their share of the action. Two Nates were sighted at 0840 closing on the ships. The first came under heavy fire and pulled up short, having been discouraged by the ordinance aimed in his direction. This was his mistake as he was then picked off by one of the CAP Corsairs. The second continued his run and was hit by fire from both gunboats, splashing about midway between them. By 0955 the enemy had departed the immediate area and the ships secured from general quarters.

On 3 May, RP Station # 3 was patrolled by *Sproston*, *Wadsworth*, *LCS(L)s 18, 52, 86*, and *LSM(R) 197*. *Drexler* relieved the *Sproston* at 1502. May 3 was relatively calm, but on the morning of 4 May things changed. At 0831 *Drexler's* radar picked up incoming bogeys. *Wadsworth* vectored two divisions of the CAP north to intercept them and they reported splashing eighteen. The ships lost contact briefly when the planes were hidden by cloud cover. Suddenly a Zeke was spotted a few miles off beginning a run on *Wadsworth*. Both destroyers took it under fire and it crashed close aboard *Wadsworth's* port beam. A second Zeke began its approach from the opposite side of the destroyers but turned away at five miles. An analysis by the CO of the *Drexler* indicated that this was "a coordinated attack with one diving out of the clouds on the port side and the other making a low approach on the starboard side. Apparently they were not timed together and the second Zeke, for some unknown reason did not press home it's attack, but fled."[11]

Radar Picket Station # 7 was patrolled by *Wickes*, *LCS(L) 13, 16*, and *61*. *Hudson* relieved *Wickes* at 1117 on the 3rd. While 3 May was uneventful, 4 May would prove to be the opposite. One bogey approached the station at 0330 but did not come within range. Reports of the raids on the other stations began to come in and several raids passed the station at a distance during the morning. In the early evening, at 1854, twelve bogeys headed toward the station from the southwest. *Hudson* vectored the CAP to meet them and they splashed three Dinahs and eight Judys.

The jeep carrier *Sangamon* was cruising near the station and the one remaining intruder, a Tony from the 105th Air Regiment at Giran South airfield, Taiwan, made a run on her. *Sangamon's* gunners shot it down. At 1920 three more enemy planes came in from the southwest and headed for the carrier. *Fullam*, screening carriers in the area, splashed the first. The second crashed near the carrier and the third, a Nick carrying a bomb, crashed in the center of *Sangamon's* flight deck, causing a large explosion and raging fires.

The picket ships headed to the aid of the stricken carrier. The carrier requested water and, at 2010, *Hudson* maneuvered next to the ship and played her hoses on the hanger deck. The close proximity of the ships caused damage to the destroyer from *Sangamon's* bridge superstructure and gun sponsons. Crewmen on the carrier began to jettison extra gear and damaged aircraft. A Hellcat was pushed over the side of the carrier and landed on the fantail of *Hudson*. At 2025 the destroyer stood clear of the carrier and the three LCS(L)s maneuvered alongside. LCS(L)s, equipped with extra fire fighting equipment, were well suited for the task. They too were battered by the carrier's hull. *LCS(L) 13* broke her mast as ammo on the carrier began to go off. Lines were run from some of the planes on deck and *13* helped pull several of them over the side. Ammunition and star shells exploded across the bow of *61* and another jettisoned Hellcat nearly landed on her. The ships of RP Station # 7, having helped to save the carrier, resumed their patrol at 2345. The next day they received the following congratulatory message:

THE SUPPORT SHIPS OF ROGER PETER SEVEN ARE TO BE CONGRATULATED FOR A SUPERB JOB LAST NIGHT X YOU WERE CERTAINLY RESPONSIBLE TO A LARGE DEGREE IN SAVING THE CARRIER X REQUEST DUN-GEON SIX SUBMIT NAMES OF ALL COMMANDING OFFI-CERS INCLUDING DUNGEON THREE AND ALBERT FOURTEEN.[12]

Lieutenant (jg) Billy R. Hart, and Lts. Homer O. White, Jr. and James W. Kelley, commanding officers of *LCS(L)s 13*, *16*, and *61*, all received the Silver Star for their work that night.

Macomb, *Bache*, LCS(L)s *89*, *111*, and *117* patrolled RP Station # 9. The daylight hours of 3 May were peaceful, but in the early evening the station came under attack. *Bache* picked up a large number of incoming planes at seventy miles and the ships went to general quarters. Communications difficulties with the CAP slowed down the interception of the planes until they were only nine miles from the ships. The CAP consisted of a division of Corsairs from VMF-323 at Kadena. It was led by 1st Lt. C.S. Allen and included 1st Lts. J. Strickland and J.A. Feliton and 2d Lt. T.G. Blackwell. They located a single Judy carrying a torpedo about ten miles from the station. After some maneuvering by the division, Blackwell found that he was in firing position and hit the Judy in the wing roots, cockpit and fuselage; it exploded and crashed in the ocean. The other enemy planes managed to slip by the CAP and split into two groups to attack. Three Judys made a run on the formation.

Bache shot down the first at 1829 and it crashed off her port quarter. The second headed for *Macomb* and hit the minesweeper in the number 3 gun turret. Gas from the plane ignited and set off a cartridge in the number three gun. Its 500 pound bomb passed through the ship and exploded in the water on the port side. Joe Bazzell, Chief Pipe Fitter on *Macomb,* was near the after deckhouse when the plane struck. His clothes caught fire and he quickly put them out. Bazzell then headed aft where he and eight other men were trapped on the fantail until fire control parties were able to reach them. Many of the crew had been killed or wounded, but it could have been much worse had the bomb exploded inside the ship. As it stood, the toll was four killed, three missing and fourteen wounded. *LCS(L) 89* picked up four of the *Macomb's* crew who had been blown off the ship and *117* recovered one body. The gunboats had been unable to fire on the attacking planes since *Macomb* and *Bache* were in their line of fire.

At about 1836 *LCS(L) 111* picked up a Wildcat pilot, Lt. (jg) C.H. Harper of VC-96. Harper had taken off from the *Rudyerd Bay* with his division and arrived at the station at about 1600. After about one hour and forty-five minutes of inaction, the planes received permission to strafe the enemy airfield at Kume Shima and return to their carrier. As they were preparing to leave the area, they were called back to the station to intercept the incoming raid. They shot down four Judys but Harper's plane was hit by anti-aircraft fire from one of the destroyers. The damage to his plane made his wheels come down and his engine quit. Coming in off the stern of *LCS(L) 111* with his wheels down, the Wildcat looked like a Val and was taken under fire by the gunboat also. His plane landed in the water and he was quickly picked up.

The ships patrolling RP Station # 10 on 3 May were *Aaron Ward, Little, LCS(L)s 14, 25, 83,* and *LSM(R) 195.* Poor weather saved them from attack until late in the afternoon on 3 May. The gunboat formation steamed about five miles south of *Aaron Ward* and *Little.* At 1833 two bogeys were picked up at twenty-seven miles and the four Hellcats on CAP were vectored to meet them, but they slipped by. Realizing this, the Hellcats turned and gave pursuit as the two Vals closed on the ships. Warned by *Aaron Ward* to turn away so the enemy planes could be taken under fire, the

Hellcats banked left. The two Vals did likewise, preventing the ships from firing on them for fear of hitting the friendly aircraft. Suddenly the two Vals broke away from their pursuers and one began a run on *Aaron Ward*. It was taken under fire and *Ward* splashed it one hundred yards to starboard.

The impact with the water caused the plane to disintegrate, and its momentum caused the engine, propeller and part of the wing to ricochet off and land on the ship's deck. The second Val began his run and was gunned down 1,200 yards to port. About the same time a Zeke carrying a bomb came in on the port side. In spite of being hit by fire from the *Aaron Ward*, it released its bomb and then crashed into the ship. Fires and explosions killed and wounded many crewmen and the ship began to slow down as the after engine room and fire rooms flooded. Her rudder was jammed and she circled tightly to port. Other enemy aircraft approached the stricken vessel and were turned away by its guns.

Shannon was sent to aid *Aaron Ward* and the other ships on station closed to protect her. At 1859 another raid came in on the station. *Aaron Ward* shot down another Val at 2,000 yards. At 1904 a Betty tried to line up for a run on the minelayer but found it difficult due to the circling of the ship. *Ward's* gunners splashed the Betty at 5,000 yards. Immediately thereafter, two Vals chased by the CAP, made their attack on the minelayer. One was shot down by CAP and the second was damaged by fire from *Aaron Ward*. It passed over the ship, clipping the top of the number one stack and tearing off the radio antenna. It crashed in the water on the starboard side of the ship. Another Val came in on the port beam at 1913. Although hit repeatedly, it succeeded in crashing the ship on the main deck. It released a bomb as it neared the ship which exploded a few feet to port, holing the hull near the forward fire room. Her engines were knocked out and *Aaron Ward* was dead in the water. A second Val hit the ship a few seconds later, followed by a Zeke at 1916.

Within a few minutes *Aaron Ward* had taken three more kamikaze strikes. Smoke and fire obscured vision and through the haze came another plane which crashed into the ship at the base of the number two stack. A bomb carried by this plane did even more damage. Within a short period of time *Aaron Ward* had been hit by five kamikazes and shot down four more. Her chances of survival were

Aaron Ward DM 34 off Kerama Retto after being damaged
by kamikazes at Radar Picket Station # 10 on 3 May 1945.
NARA 80G 330112.

slim, but heroic efforts on the part of her crew and supporting vessels saved her. *LCS(L) 14* took another kamikaze under fire as it
made a run on *Ward* and splashed it close to the minelayer. The
LCS(L)s came alongside her, taking off the wounded and assisting
with the fires. By 2024 the fires were under control and within
forty minutes *Aaron Ward* was being towed back to Kerama Retto
by *Shannon.*

   Little had even worse luck. By the end of her ordeal she would
be at the bottom of the ocean. The destroyer estimated the number
of planes in her area to number between eighteen and twenty-four.
She suffered her first kamikaze hit at 1843 when one crashed her

port side. A few seconds later, her gunners knocked down a second plane close aboard, but a third plane got through the hail of gunfire and hit her on the port side near where the first plane had crashed. At 1845 a Zeke crashed her starboard side at almost the same time another Zeke crashed her in a vertical dive. Their timing was perfect and *Little* was mortally wounded. Fires and explosions overtook the ship and she began to flood. Her keel had been broken by the attacks and she listed heavily to starboard. At 1851 the CO of *Little*, Comdr. Madison Hall, Jr., gave the order to abandon ship. Sometime after the war, crewman Melvin Fenoglio, Y3/c, would write:

> It took less than a minute for us to scramble to the main deck. There our eyes met a weird site. Fragments of steel lay about the deck Gaping holes in the sides of our proud ship met our eyes. One side of our own gun mount had disappeared and it took little imagination to understand what had happened to the men inside. What brought a lump to our throat was the sight of the corpsmen administering first aid and pitifully inadequate bandages to the injured. Officers walked briskly about

Aaron Ward DM 34 at Kerama Retto on 5 May 1945 after being hit by a kamikaze on radar picket duty. *NARA 80G 330113.*

the decks silently drawing gray blankets over still warm and bleeding bodies . . . In many respects the dead were the luckiest of us all. They neither had to abandon nor to remember.[13]

Four minutes later *Little* went to the bottom in 850 fathoms. Crewman Doyle Kennedy had been at his battle station on the aft 20mm gun. When the twin engine plane hit *Little* one of its engines was blown back into his gun tub, pinning his legs and causing burns. Freed by a shipmate, he eventually went into the water when the call to abandon ship was given. One of his shipmates was burned severely and Kennedy held him up until he died.[14] The support gunboats began the task of rescuing the survivors.

LSM(R) 195, following the LCS(L)s toward the stricken ships, lost her starboard engine and fell behind the formation. Within a few minutes two planes made a run on her. A Nick came in from starboard and was taken under fire by her 5"/38 gun and 40mm guns. Simultaneously a second plane, identified as either a Nick or a Dinah, closed the ship from port. Although it was taken under fire by the 20mm guns, they were not powerful enough to stop its run and the enemy plane crashed into the port side of the *195*. The midship and forward rocket magazines were damaged in the crash, as well as the forward crew's quarters. Rockets went off, scattering shrapnel all over the deck and causing additional fires and explosions. Unfortunately, the impact had knocked out the fire main and auxiliary pumps on the LSM(R), and the fire spread unabated, setting off more rockets. At 1920 the order was given to abandon the furiously burning ship. Fifteen minutes later she went to the bottom. The destroyer *Bache* appeared on the scene and began picking up survivors.

One of the problems for the LSM(R) was the unsuitability of her armament. On board *LCS(L) 14*, Ray Baumler watched from his battle station as the rocket ship was hit. He later recalled:

> Having that single 5"/38 gun on the stern brought the ships nothing but trouble. I feel sure they did not have an issue of Radio Proximity fused ammunition and without them they were large sitting ducks. Regardless of the lack of radio proximity fuses, the rate of fire from that single gun was painfully slow. I saw an LSM(R) attacked from the stern that did not get off more than 2 or 3 rounds before it was crashed. You could almost go out and have a cigarette between firings.[15]

The LCS(L)s also had their hands full. At 1909, after *LCS(L) 14* observed the crashes into *Aaron Ward, Little,* and *LSM(R) 195,* she spotted a plane making a run on *LCS(L) 25.* It splashed forty yards astern *25* after coming under fire from both *25* and *14.* The impact caused the plane's engine to break loose and it ricocheted off the water and broke the mast off the gunboat. Part of the plane's wing and other debris showered the ship, causing additional damage. One man was killed, eight wounded and two blown over the side. At 1916 *LCS(L) 14* saw two planes making a run on *LCS(L) 83,* both of which missed and crashed into the water close aboard. *LCS(L) 83* headed for the sinking ships and was attacked by a plane from astern. Tracer bullets from the plane went over the conn, but the ship's gunners were on target and it splashed behind the gunboat. As *83* attempted to pick up survivors from *Little,* an Oscar came from port and tried to crash her. Under fire by almost every gun on the ship, the plane swerved at the last minute, crashing into the water near the bow. *LCS(L) 83* maneuvered among the sinking ships, saving many from *Little* and taking on board others from *Aaron Ward.* The commanding officer of *LCS(L) 83,* Lt. James M. Faddis, described the courage of his crew in his ship's action report:

> They had previous to that day seen the LCS 15 sunk by a suicide plane. They had seen several suicide dives on Destroyers. They had seen the LSM 195 hit and burning. They had seen the DD and DM hit repeatedly. The chances of stopping the suicide attacks seemed remote yet while picking up survivors they were calm, stood to their guns and poured out a murderous fire. The men on number one 40, with the plane barely 50 feet away, were loading and firing unceasingly. Neither noise nor smoke nor confusion bothered the men. They stuck to their guns and fired like demons.[16]

This series of enemy attacks described above seem to have taken the ships by surprise. Although raids were spotted at a distance, many apparently slipped through the CAP and got to the ships before they were able to react. They had almost no warning of the attack. By 4 May the greatest danger to the ships at RP Station # 9 had passed. *Bache,* carrying survivors from *LSM(R) 195,* headed back to Hagushi to transfer them. Continuing on patrol at RP Station # 9 were *LCS(L)s 117* and *111.*

By the following day a new group of ships had been assigned to RP Station # 10. *Cowell*, *Gwin*, *LSM(R) 192*, and *LCS(L)s 54*, *55*, and *110* patrolled there. Theirs would not be a peaceful mission either. Early in the morning, at 0944, *Cowell* picked up a bogey at a distance of twenty-six miles and vectored the CAP to intercept it. They reported shooting down a Dinah a minute later. Late in the day, four special attack planes of the 19th Air Regiment and the 105th Air Regiment took off from Giran South field on Taiwan. Joining them as a guide was one plane from the 47th Independent Air Company at Taito and a sixth plane from the 43rd Independent Air Company at Giran South. An additional eleven special attack planes and nine land based army bombers would join them that day from the Eighth Air Division's fields on Taiwan.

At 1910 *Cowell* picked up a group of six to eight bogeys headed for the station. The CAP, operating at dusk and with short warning, was unable to cover them; the ships were on their own. When the bogeys closed to four miles, *Gwin* and *Cowell* took them under fire and went to twenty-five knots. Two planes peeled off from the group and attacked the support ships. Gunners on *LCS(L) 110* caught a Judy coming in from the starboard beam and knocked it out of the sky. The second, described by *LSM(R) 192*'s crew as an Oscar, attacked from dead ahead. With short notice, the LSM(R) barely had time to get to general quarters.

Bob Landis, SK 1/c, was below decks working on his books when the GQ horn went off. Landis dropped everything and headed for his battle station as loader on the number three 20mm gun which was located on the stern. He arrived on deck just in time to see the plane as it went over the area near his station. Landis recalled "I saw this plane back on the stern and it just sort of slid off the stern and I remember one fellow was hit on the hand, I think he was hit by one of the lines."[17] The plane, hit by 40mm and 20mm fire, banked in an apparent attempt to crash the aft 5"/38 gun mount. Its wing struck the port rocket launchers and it was knocked off course and hit the water astern of the ship. It was a close call for the LSM(R) which sustained minor damage and escaped with a minor injury to one crewman.

At about the same time, *Cowell* took under fire and splashed a single engine fighter off her port quarter. Still another plane made a run on *Gwin* from astern. Under fire by *Cowell* and *Gwin*, the plane managed to hit *Gwin* amidships on the deck, starting fires. *Cowell* soon shot down another plane and *LCS(L) 55* reported bagging one as well. *LCS(L) 54* reported splashing an Oscar that made a run on her from forward. By 1930 the action was over. In the short space of twenty minutes, the ships had downed many of the Japanese army air force planes from Taiwan.

At 0145 on 4 May, large raids were reported closing on RP # 12 from the west and northwest. It was estimated that the enemy aircraft were headed for the Hagushi area since they did not make attacks on the ships at RP Station # 12. Two that did approach were driven off by the destroyer's gunfire.

Four divisions of VMF-323 Corsairs had taken off from Kadena at 0730. Two of the divisions, led by Capt. Bill Van Buskirk and 1st Lt. Joe Dillard, headed for RP Station # 12. The others, led by Capt. Joe McPhail and 1st Lt. V.E. Ball, headed north to cover the skies over Ie Shima and the nearby RP Stations # 1 and 2. Meanwhile, the division led by Dillard did its part. Dillard splashed two Dinahs and a Val and then teamed up with his wingman, 1st Lt. Aquilla Blaydes, to take out another Dinah and Val. First Lt. Francis Terrill, leader of the second section, shot down a Val and two Dinahs in the area. His wingman, 1st Lt. Glen Thacker, splashed a Betty. Terrill and Dillard formed up and headed back to Kadena while Thacker and Blaydes made one more sweep. Thacker spotted a Helen above him and splashed it before heading back.

At RP Station # 12, *Luce* picked up an incoming raid of from four to six planes at a distance of thirty-nine miles and vectored the two divisions to intercept them. Communications were difficult, with the radio channels in constant use. The CAP reports indicated that they had eliminated a number of enemy planes, but not all. Lookouts on *Luce* spotted two Vals making a run on her from her port side at 0805. Taken under fire at a range of 8,000 yards, the two planes split apart and approached the *Luce* from opposite sides. One of the Vals took evasive action, crossed the bow of the destroyer and banked sharply, crashing into the water close aboard the starboard side amidships. Its bomb exploded, temporarily knocking out power in the ship and making it difficult to fire on the second plane which was approaching from the port side. The enemy plane was taken under fire by *LCS(L) 118* which succeeded in knocking off a wing, but this did not stop it. At 0811 it crashed into the ship near the number three 5-inch gun. The ship's port engine was knocked out and the hull holed. Crewmen on board the destroyer reported that other planes hit the ship as well. Lieutenant John Welsh and Omer Edmond S 1/c reported a float biplane aiming for the port side near the number three 5-inch gun mount and Freeman Phillips and Richard LeBrun, both SM 3/c, saw two more Japanese planes headed for the port side in the vicinity of the number five 5-inch gun.[18]

In the confusion it was uncertain how many kamikazes had hit *Luce*. All that was certain was that she had been mortally wounded. Within minutes the ship began to list to starboard and at 1814 her CO, Comdr. J.W. Waterhouse, gave the order to abandon ship. Communications on the ship had been destroyed and men below decks did not get the word. This probably added to the heavy casualty list for the ship.

Aboard *Luce* pandemonium reigned. Numerous men had been killed in the initial explosions and many were seriously wounded by the crash of the kamikazes. On the fantail, at the number 3 20mm gun, was James C. Phillips, SC 1/c. He fired on an incoming Zeke until his gun jammed and then watched as it hit the ship. His friend Virgil G. Degner BKR 2/c, who was serving as loader on the gun, was decapitated in the explosion, as was Dale McKay S 1/c who manned the nearby number four 5" gun.

The wounded, along with the uninjured, abandoned the ship. Many acts of heroism accompanied the disaster, with Lt. Derry O. Moll receiving the Bronze Star for his work in aiding wounded men. Oil covered the water and many men clung to floating ammo cans and other debris in order to survive. As they watched, *Luce* pointed her bow skyward and slid beneath the surface, sucking down a number of men who had held on to her or had not managed to swim clear.

For the survivors the ordeal was not over. Japanese planes began to strafe the men in the water until marine Corsairs drove them off. Sharks began to move in on the groups and many were killed by them. Lieutenant Cliff Jones watched as two sharks killed the ship's barber just as he was about to be pulled from the water.[19] It was a terrible ordeal for the crewmen of *Luce* who had been on radar picket duty almost continuously from 1 April to 4 May.

Flying CAP just to the south of the station was a division of Corsairs from VMF-311. At 0805 they spotted a combination of eleven Vals and Oscars. First Lt. Norman Turley shot down a Val and an Oscar. First Lt. Billy Cooney shot down two Vals and 1st Lt. Jack M. Rothweiler shot down another Val.

LSM(R) 190 was steaming nearby and observed the attack on *Luce*. Shortly after the destroyer was hit, a Dinah flew over the rocket ship and dropped a bomb which missed it. By 0750, the two VMF-323 divisions at RP Station # 12 were vectored to intercept incoming bogeys. Captain Van Buskirk's division saw the first action. Van Buskirk and 1st Lt. Cy Dolezel spotted a Dinah heading for *Luce* and got on its tail. They splashed the twin engine fighter and then observed a Val heading for *LSM(R) 190*. Van Buskirk flamed it but it still hit the LSM(R), crashing into the 5"/38 gun mount. Shrapnel killed the ship's gunnery officer and severely wounded the commanding officer, Lt. Richard H. Saunders. With the CO out of action, the communications officer, Ensign Tennis, took command in the conn.

The blast had damaged the ship's fire mains and fire-fighting was difficult. As the flames spread to the powder and handling rooms, a Val crashed the ship from port, setting the engine room on fire. An auxiliary fire pump which had been the ship's main avenue of defense against the raging fires, was disabled by this crash. Under attack by a third plane, the ship continued to maneuver. This plane, a Dinah, dropped a bomb which missed the ship, but a fourth plane was on target. Its bomb hit the ship near the Mk. 51 Director tub. Still another plane made a run on the ship, but the Corsairs drove it off. With no possibility of stopping the fires and with the ship beginning to list, the ship's XO, Lt. (jg) Harmon, consulted with the wounded CO and the order was given to abandon ship. At 0840 *LSM(R) 190* slid beneath the waves and *LCS(L) 84* began the task of rescuing the survivors. *PCE(R) 852* arrived at the station and took on board 118 casualties from the two ships. A Japanese flying officer who had survived the crash of his Betty was also picked up. The VMF-323 division continued its flight overhead and 2d Lieutenants Harold Hohl and Bill Drake each shot down a Val. The Death Rattlers finished the day with a total of twenty-four and three-quarters planes destroyed and eleven more damaged.

Another division of Corsairs from VMF-312 at Kadena had been orbiting over Point King, which lay about thirty miles east of the action. The fighter director on *Panamint* vectored them westward to assist the ships. They arrived in the area just in time to see the *190* get hit by the Val. The division, led by Capt. William K.

Perdue, requested permission to attack. They spotted enemy aircraft above them engaged by Corsairs.

A Nate broke free from the melee and turned in Purdue's direction. After slowing his airspeed, he got on the tail of the Nate and quickly hit it with a single burst; the Nate flamed and went down. A second Nate was chased into his guns by other Corsairs and Purdue shot it down also. His wingman, 1st Lt. Billy Anderson, spotted another Nate at 200 feet heading for a destroyer. He dove on the Nate and shot it down close to the water. Anderson saw another Nate preparing for a bombing run on a destroyer about twenty miles in the distance. With the Corsair's superior speed, he was able to intercept it and his fire hit the plane, causing its bomb to miss the destroyer. Looking above him, he noticed a Corsair chasing another Nate which turned toward him. It was a critical mistake for the Japanese pilot as 650 rounds from Anderson's guns hit the Nate and sent it flaming into the sea.

Another pilot from the division, First Lieutenant Ernest A. Silvain, spotted a Val making a run on a nearby LST and went after it. He fired on it at 650 yards and it burst into flames. The Val peeled over on one wing and went into the water. At about the same time, Corsairs from VMF-224 at Yontan were patrolling near RP Station # 12. First Lt. C.H. Rushfeldt encountered the first enemy plane about 0815; it was a Val coming in from the west. He turned behind the plane and shot it down.

At 0822, *Henry A. Wiley* was ordered to RP Station # 12, to assist *Luce.* She headed for the station at twenty-five knots and was soon under attack. Between 0852 and 0858, she turned away a pair of Jills with her gunfire and a few minutes later, at 0859, splashed a Betty at 3,000 yards. Just prior to being taken under fire, the Betty launched an *Oka* which was fired upon by the ship's 20mm guns. It hit the water seventy-five yards astern of the minelayer. A second *Oka* headed for *Wiley* and was taken under fire at two miles. Although it was not hit, near misses drove the piloted bomb off course and it crashed into the water 1,200 yards from *Wiley.* The impact caused the warhead to separate from the body of the *Oka* and continue on course to the ship. It passed over *Wiley's* fantail before finally exploding without causing any damage. At 0910 a Jill made a torpedo run on *Wiley.* What followed was a daring, but not unusual, act on the part of a marine pilot. According *Wiley's* action report:

. . . a Marine Corsair flew directly over this ship (and was not fired on) from starboard, and dove through this vessel's intense AA fire to machine gun the JILL – the JILL splashed at 1500 yards, and although this vessel's AA fire would probably have destroyed him, the heroic act of this Marine Corsair made doubly sure that the JILL failed his mission. This was a very heroic act on the part of this Marine pilot and this ship wishes to acknowledge a job very well done.[20]

The Corsair pilot was 1st Lt. Melvin L. Jarvis of VMF-322 stationed at Kadena. His Corsair did not escape unscathed. When he landed his Corsair looked like a Swiss cheese, with a number of holes in the cowling, port wing, empennage and tail wheel. Based on the recommendation of the commanding officer of *Henry A. Wiley*, Comdr. P.H. Bjarnason, Jarvis received the Navy Cross for his actions.

Normally the gunboats would be considered valuable support for the destroyers at the picket stations. This was not to be the case on RP Station # 12 that day. In his *Action Report of 1 August 1945*, the commanding officer of *LCS(L) 81*, Lt. C.C. Lockwood, indicated that the support vessels had been assigned a position four miles away from the destroyer and were thus unable to lend their firepower.[21] The best they could do was to pick up the survivors from the *Luce*. Only one of the gunboats, *LCS(L) 118*, was attacked. At 0819 a Betty made a run on her from dead ahead and was shot down when it was only 1,000 yards off. The "small boys" had been spared, the Japanese had bigger targets on which to focus their efforts. At day's end the support craft headed back to the anchorage to transfer the survivors.

After the war Earl Blanton, GM 3/c on board *LCS(L) 118*, wrote:

. . .we were picking up the men from the Can (*Luce*). There was a lot of heavy black oil around and they were covered with it. The water was dotted with their heads. Some were waving their arms but none were crying out. Everyone but just enough men to man the guns were helping to get them aboard. There were a lot of wounded around. One fellow's whole face was gone and he was swelled up from broken bones and burns and was floating among the survivors. Another man had his arm gone but was still conscious. They were cut and torn and burned and broken and they were naked or their clothes hung on them in rags and they were all covered with black heavy oil except where the blood was running from their cuts and wounds. The ones who were not wounded helped their shipmates aboard. Most of them just sat down shaking like a leaf. They would look at you and their eyes seemed to say "Thanks buddy."[22]

Shea, Hugh W. Hadley, LCS(L)s 20, 22, 64, and *LSM(R) 189* patrolled RP Station # 14 from 3 to 4 May. Early on the morning of the 4th, about 0200 and again at 0425, *Shea* took intruders under fire and drove them off. Smoke screens generated at the Hagushi anchorage during the night of 3-4 May began to drift in the vicinity of RP Station # 14. *Shea* reported that by about 0900 visibility in the area was limited to around three miles, in spite of the clear weather. Reports of enemy aircraft approaching the station began to come in around 0749 and the ships went to general quarters.

The two divisions of VF-9 Hellcats that originally had been sent to cover RP Station # 1 appeared over RP Station # 14 about 0830. Within ten minutes Lt. (jg) Albert S. Smeehuyzen spotted an Oscar north of the station at 4,000 feet. The Oscar headed right for his division and Smeehuyzen dove to meet it. As the planes approached each other head on, he fired, hitting the pilot and sending the enemy plane spinning out of control.

At about the same time, Ens. Leroy O. Sledge and Lt. Franger made a run on a Val which split S'd away from them. Sledge then came in from the starboard side of the Val, which split S'd again in an attempt to avoid him, but it dove too close to the water and crashed in. About the same time Ensign Jerrold A. Isaacson shot down a Peggy bomber. The VF-9 Hellcats had splashed seven planes and damaged one.

Earlier in the day, at 0730, the escort carrier *Steamer Bay* had launched a division of VC-90 FM-2 Wildcats as part of the area's combat air patrol. They orbited over RP Station # 12 some sixty miles to the south. Soon they were sent north to cover RP Station # 14 which had reported many incoming raids. Over RP Station # 14, they orbited at 10,000 feet and at 0830, were vectored toward some incoming bogeys that were about ten miles out. One of the VC-90 pilots, Lt. F.J. Gibson, spotted a twin engine plane about five to ten miles to port and the division set out to engage it. Fire from the picket ships below made them turn off and they circled to make another run on the plane. As they closed on it, they identified

it as a Dinah. What surprised them more was that it dropped an
Oka.[23] CompRon Ninety's action report indicated:

> On closing in enough to see the plane all pilots positively iden-
> tified it as a Dinah. (Knowing that all reports of Baka bombs
> thus far have been connected with Betties, a careful interroga-
> tion has been made of all pilots and this plane was positively
> identified as a Dinah). . . . The attacks were begun at 8 to 9000
> feet and the kill made at 6000 feet.
> Lt (jg) E.E. McKeever, leader of the second section, was
> slightly below the other planes when the Dinah dropped the
> Baka Bomb. . . .The Dinah did not appear to have the custom-
> ary smooth green house aft but instead had a ball turret in the
> rear of the cockpit very similar to that appearing on the Sally.[24]

Gibson and his wingman, Lieutenant (jg) D.S. Paulsen, got on the
tail of the plane. Paulsen's burst killed the rear gunner and Gibson
fired into the plane's starboard wing root; it began to burn. Paulsen
hit it again in the right engine and the plane plummeted to the sea.
Meanwhile, the other section, led by Lt. (jg) E.E. McKeever, saw
the *Oka* drop. At first he thought it was a bomb, but as the *Oka* fell
its rocket engines ignited and it took off. McKeever gave chase but
the *Oka* easily pulled away from him and headed for *Shea*. At 0859,
as the pilots watched, the *Oka* flew through the destroyer and the
warhead exploded on the other side.

Earlier that morning a flight of seven bombers carrying *Okas*
of the 7th Cherry Blossom Unit had taken off from Kanoya. Along
with them were twenty bomb-laden fighters. Ten Type 97 carrier
borne attack planes (Kates) and twenty-eight reconnaissance seaplanes from the field at Kushira and the seaplane base at Ibusuki
had joined the attack.[25] High over RP Station # 14, Sub-Lt.
Susumu Ohashi, acting on directions from his bomber's pilot,
climbed into his *Oka*. At 0856 Ohashi's rocket plane dropped from
the mother ship and headed for *Shea*. The minelayer had no
advance warning, and the first she knew she was under attack was
when the *Oka* was sighted closing on her from starboard. Less than
five seconds later, the *Oka* struck *Shea* on the starboard side of the
bridge superstructure. Its body spiraled down through the ship and
out the opposite side of the hull, exploding ten to fifteen feet from
the ship. The minelayer's relatively light construction had saved
her since *Okas* were designed to punch through the heavier armor

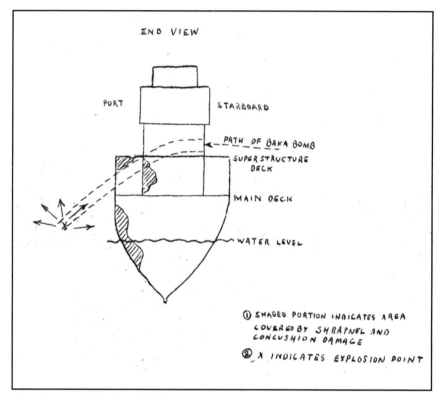

Sketch from *USS Shea DM-30 Action Report of 15 May 1945* showing damage from an *Oka* piloted bomb that hit her while she was on Radar Picket Station # 14 on 4 May 1945.

plate of larger ships. Although the ship had two holes from the entrance and exit, the major damage came from the explosion which buckled and ruptured a number of frames and plating. For *Shea* it was a close call, but she was still in action.

Kikusui # 5 was over, but it had taken a heavy toll on the radar picket ships. *Morrison, Little, Luce, LSM(R)s 190, 194*, and *195* had been sunk and *Ingraham, Lowry, Macomb, Aaron Ward, Gwin, Shea, LSM(R) 192, LCS(L)s 25* and *31* had all been hit with varying amounts of damage. *LCS(L) 21* had been damaged by the underwater explosion of the magazine from *LSM(R) 194*. On the radar picket stations, 475 men had lost their lives and 484 had been wounded.

Military Intelligence Service reported:

Kikusui # 5 Operation, on 3-4 May, was slightly larger than the effort on 27-29 Apr. Japanese sorties are estimated at 350, and 249 Japanese planes were claimed destroyed. Damage to Allied ships, resulting almost entirely from suicide attacks, was heavy. The principal victims were destroyers in the radar picket and small ships near shore, despite the fact that Japanese operational orders had called for efforts against carriers and transports. It thus appears that Japanese suicide pilots either (i) were mistaking destroyers for larger units or (ii) decided that they had a better chance of success if they attacked before encountering the heavier fighter cover over major Allied vessels.[26]

Saturday, 5 May and Sunday, 6 May 1945

By this time the reality of the situation had set in. No longer optimistic about their chances of achieving victory on Okinawa, the Japanese assessed the situation:

> The 32nd Army reported that since almost all of their strength had been exhausted in the drive which had progressed as far as Northern YAHARA, they had ceased all offensive operations at 1800 on 5 May and retreated to their former position. The situation on OKINAWA is believed to be hopeless.[27]

Nevertheless, *Kikusui # 6* was in the final stages of preparation.

In an attempt to slow down the new attack, the XXI Bomber Command sent forty-five B-29s to hit Oita, Tachiarai, Chiran and Kanoya. On 6 May the 5th Air Force hit Matsuyama air field on Taiwan with their B-24s.

On 6 May, the radar picket assignments changed. The old series of stations was no longer to be operative and RP Stations # 5, 7, 9, 15, and 16 would cover the invasion force at Hagushi. Installations at Hedo Misaki and other locations had come into operation. With the capture of Tori Shima and other islands, more land based radar would eliminate the need for some of the radar picket stations.

On the 6th, between 0154 and 0405, several bogeys plagued the ships at RP station # 12. A night fighter chased one toward *Brown* which took it under fire at 0350. Results were inconclusive. Two VMF-224 Corsairs from Yontan came on duty at 0722 and were kept at a low altitude over the ships. They were vectored toward two incoming planes and encountered a Tojo and a Tony ten miles from the station. The Tojo made a strafing run on *LCS(L) 81*, then veered off and headed for the *Brown*. First Lt. A.C. Satterwhite shot the tail off the Tojo and it was last seen on fire and losing altitude. Chased by another Corsair, flown by 1st Lt. R.O. Hansen, the Tony attacked *Brown*. It was shot down by combined fire from the destroyer and the Corsair. It was a narrow miss for the destroyer. Hansen was credited with a probable and *Brown* with an assist. At 0915 the CAP was sent back to base and the ships were directed to the anchorage. RP Station # 12 was to be inoperative.

Monday, 7 May through Wednesday, 9 May 1945

To help keep the Japanese preoccupied, the XXI Bomber Command sent forty-one B-29s to hit Usa, Oita, Ibusuki, and Kanoya; they claimed thirty-four aircraft destroyed at Usa and Oita.

Radar Picket Station # 9 was patrolled by *Ammen*, *Putnam*, *LCS(L)s 56*, *87*, *89*, and *LSM(R) 198*. The two days passed without incident. *William D. Porter* relieved *Ammen* at 0830 on the 9th. *LCS(L) 117* relieved the *87* at 1530. At 1820 enemy aircraft were detected in the area, but the four-plane CAP sent in their direction missed them. The two-plane CAP from Yontan's VMF-224 was then vectored toward them. They caught three green-colored Willow biplanes heading for the picket ships. Second Lts. J.B. Bender and M. Waldman attacked them. Bender shot down two and Waldman got the third. When the action was over, Bender looked in vain for Waldman's Corsair but it was nowhere to be seen. *Putnam* reported that it had observed the Corsair crash eleven miles from her. Two of the LCS(L)s were sent to search for the pilot but found only an oil slick. Later in the day, at 2030, the ships again went to general quarters. *Porter* and *Putnam* took a plane under fire at 2048 and *Putnam* reported splashing it 7,000 yards away. A second plane turned and left the area.

Thursday, 10 May and Friday, 11 May 1945

From 10 to 11 May the Japanese launched their next attack, *Kikusui # 6*. Participating in this attack were a total of 150 Special

Attack planes, seventy from the navy and eighty from the army. Joining them were other aircraft from the Imperial Japanese Army Air Force and the Imperial Japanese Naval Air Force which flew regular missions.

The strategy for this attack was outlined in the Operational Instructions which was later detailed in *Japanese Monograph # 86*:

Operational Instructions for Operation KIKUSUI No. 6.

  a. Reinforcement of the Fighter Units.

     The strength of our fighter unit had decreased considerably since only a few ZERO fighters are in flying condition and a large number of GEORGE 11's (Navy SHIDEN fighter) have crashed immediately after the take off because of faulty mechanism and flimsy construction.

     Since we cannot expect immediate assistance from the Army fighter unit, a part of the heavy fighters will be transferred to the above mentioned fighter unit to newly organize the 13th Fighter Unit.

  b. Attacks Against Small Enemy Ships.

     The attacks against enemy ships in the vicinity of OKINAWA will be made more frequently in order to facilitate our landing on OKINAWA.

     Since a large number of the planes of the 10th Air Fleet assigned to the fighter unit . . . were destroyed, we are assuming that in the coming operations, the main body of this fighter units will be composed of Army fighters.

     Hereafter, the SHIRAGIKU trainers and recon. seaplanes will be withheld so that they will be available for the operations to be conducted during the moonlit nights next month.

  c. Since it is believed that if the above mentioned ships are attacked an enemy task force will advance north to give assistance, 60 special light attack planes will be readied to attack the task force.

  d.The attacks against small enemy ships will be carried out in force during May to facilitate the landing operation of our force.

Two divisions will land after the airborne unit alights on the enemy's northern [Yontan] and central [Kadena] airfields.[28]

Japanese assessments of their own air power seemed to be realistic. Continued American bombing of the Japanese factories had made it difficult to maintain production schedules. On 10 May, LeMay sent forty-two B-29s to hit Matsuyama West, Usa, Miyazaki, and Kanoya. He followed up the next day with a fifty plane strike by B-29s which hit Oita, Saeki, Nittagahara, Miyazaki, and Miyakanojo. The purpose of the missions was to destroy enemy aircraft on the ground and crater the runways to keep the planes from taking off.

To the south, the 5th Air Force sent their B-24s to hit Daikozan airfield on Taiwan. In order to prevent the bombing of single facilities that would put a company out of business, Japanese production units were dispersed, leading to further delays in completing much needed aircraft.

> The air-raid damage and the frantic reshuffling of supplies available directly within Japan threw our internal transportation facilities into chaos. The hindrance of transportation and the loss of raw materials reduced aircraft-factory assembly lines to a meaningless crawl. Further, those aircraft which we did manage to produce under these difficulties were less effective than usual, for the inferior materials employed in their manufacture reduced flight performance and increased the time spent in maintenance and overhaul. Vital equipment failed all too often, and our pilots cursed the planes which consistently failed them just as they attacked the great enemy air fleets.[29]

Estimates of the number of planes rejected during the closing phase of the war ran from thirty to fifty percent.

Admiral Toyoda recognized the need to make a decisive move if the situation at Okinawa were to be improved. Returning to Kanoya on 8 May, he surveyed his forces to determine the next course of action. The 8th Cherry Blossom Unit was best prepared to carry out the attacks. Recognizing that the marine squadrons at Kadena and Yontan were a major obstacle to the success of *Kikusui # 6*, he decided to attack them again. Mitsuo Yamazaki and Koji Katsumura, *Oka* pilots of the Thunder Gods Corps (Air Group 721), were assigned the initial assault on the bases. Both were to crash their piloted bombs onto the runways in order to prevent the Corsairs from taking off. They were scheduled to attack at 0500 on the 11th. Fortunately for the marines, one mother plane developed engine trouble and the other encountered cloud cover which prevented the attack from being carried out. Other planes from the Sixth Air Army, including "four medium bombers, six fighters and 20 suicide planes"[30] were scheduled to attack the airfields as well. Another fifty army planes would participate in other attacks.

In order to more effectively coordinate the attacks on Okinawa, the Combined Naval Force reorganized the air fleets. The National Security Agency reported: "At 1841I on the 10th, the Combined Naval Force announced that effective at 2400I on the 11th there was to be established a Combined Base Air Force, to be called the "TEN Air Force." The new Force is to comprise the 1st Mobile Base Air Force and the Third Air Fleet and is to be commanded by the commander of the 1st Mobile Base Air Force [Vice Admiral Matome Ugaki]."[31] Ugaki noted "how much we can increase our fighting strength and how far we can take advantage of this new setup has to be seen."[32]

Patrolling RP Station # 5 on 11 May were *Douglas H. Fox*, *Harry F. Bauer*, *LCS(L)s 52, 88, 109, 114,* and *PGM 20.* Early in the morning of the 10th, the ships went to general quarters twice, but no planes closed on the station. At 0740 on the 11th numerous raids were reported coming in from the north. A CAP of four Corsairs from VMF-441 at Yontan circled overhead, awaiting their chance at the intruders. Four more Corsairs from VMF-323 at Kadena flew CAP nearby. At 0801 *Bauer* opened fire on a Dinah coming in from the northwest and it turned away. *Bauer* called to the CAP from VMF-441 and vectored them to the north. The division, led by Capt. Addison R. Raber, included 2d Lts. Willis A. Dworzak, Charles C. Whipple and 1st Lt. Robert J. Kane. *Bauer* indicated that the enemy plane was still miles ahead of them but the ship's radar was off. As they scanned the skies, they spotted a Dinah flying southward at 9 o'clock. Whipple spotted the enemy plane first and the division turned to meet it. As they flew toward the Dinah, it abruptly made a 90 degree turn, placing it in the path of Dworzak. He checked with his section leader, Whipple, and was given permission to attack. Dworzak later recalled:

> I dropped my belly tank and I had that throttle right up there . . . and I'm chasing that sonofagun and I'm getting close enough where I can get a gun sight on him . . . it was a twin

engine, I didn't know if that sonofabitch had a tail gunner or
not. I didn't want him shooting at me. . .so I squeezed the trigger and to my horror I can see the tracers are going out [to the
left] they should have been boresighted at 300 yards . . . You
could see some of the high explosive incendiary . . . you could
see them flash when they hit . . . so I moved the cross hairs, the
pipper, over to the starboard engine and just held down the
trigger and everything happened at the same time, the guns
started shooting, his left wing flew off and he entered the
clouds just as I overtook him, damn near hit him . . . they don't
fly so good with only one wing, he was spiraling down and when
he hit he exploded and went up in flames.[33]

The gunboats, which were cruising in a wide V formation,
spotted a Betty overhead and opened fire. At 0803 *Bauer* spotted
two more planes closing on the formation at a low altitude. Two
Oscars were taken under fire and the first of the pair was splashed
1,200 yards to starboard of *Bauer*. All the ships fired on the second
and scored numerous hits. It headed for the conn of *LCS(L) 88* in a
bombing run. Hit by gunfire from *PGM 20*, the plane peeled off and
went down in flames close to the starboard side of *LCS(L) 88*. It
released a 200 pound bomb just before crashing. The bomb struck
the aft 40mm gun mount of *88*, starting some fires and blasted the
mount clear of the ship. A bomb fragment shot toward the conning
tower, striking the commanding officer Lt. Casimir L. Bigos in the
head and killing him instantly. Just as the plane was closing the
ship, the order for left rudder had been given and the blast jammed
the ship's rudder in that position. Without rudder control, the ship
cut its engines. Seven men and the CO had been killed and nine
wounded, two of whom would later die of their injuries. Most of the
casualties were among the aft 40mm gun crew. *PGM 20* closed on
the stricken ship and her doctor ministered to the wounded who
were subsequently transferred to her.

At 0821 four more enemy planes were spotted orbiting to starboard of *Bauer* and were taken under fire. After one Tojo went
down in flames, a Zeke made its run. *Bauer* maneuvered violently
to bring all guns to bear and thwart the attack. The Zeke, hit
numerous times by the ship's guns, climbed and turned into the
ship, strafing it as it approached. It passed over *Bauer* and hit the
water thirty yards off the starboard quarter. Its bomb exploded but
had no effect on the minelayer. Still another Zeke closed on *Bauer*

Damage to *LCS(L) 88* after kamikaze attack of 11 May 1945 at Radar Picket Station # 5. *Photo courtesy of Art Martin.*

at 0833 and almost crashed her. *LCS(L) 52* took the Zeke under fire and scored some hits. Gunners on *Bauer* managed to knock its tail off when it was near the ship, and the Zeke passed close over taking off some lifelines and clipping the deck. It crashed in the water close aboard the port side. *Bauer* reported: "During the last three runs, the CAP reported splashing the fourth fighter type plane (a ZEKE). Thus of the seven attacking planes in the area, none got away. Neither FOX nor support craft fired on latter attacks, shooting at planes overhead which were believed part of CAP. None were splashed."[34]

Captain Thomas J. Cushman Jr. of VMF-312 was credited with shooting down the Zeke. He and his wingman,1st Lt. C.W. Baldwin, had been flying radar picket patrol and saved the ships from this attack. This was a fortunate kill for the ships as the fighter was carrying a 500 pound bomb which it jettisoned in trying to escape from the Corsairs. The Zeke was one of thirty-seven that had flown off the field at Kanoya earlier that day. Only ten made it back to their base.

First Lt. C.W. Martin Jr. and his wingman, 2d Lt. E.L.Yager, were flying near the station when they were vectored to incoming bogeys near Izena Shima. The VMF-323 pilots cruised through a hazy sky and eventually heard aircraft below them. They dove, broke through the haze and spotted a Tojo lining up for a bombing run on the picket ships. Martin came in from above, fired into the Tojo's cockpit, and it went down

Patrolling RP Station # 9 were *William D. Porter, Bache,* and *LCS(L)s 23, 56, 87,* and *LSM(R) 198. Bache* relieved *Putnam* at 0830. Late in the day, at 2025, a bogey was picked up at twenty-two miles from the station. As it approached the ships, *Porter* and then *Bache* took it under fire. The twin engine plane passed down the port side of *Bache* about 3,000 yards from the ship and crashed in flames.

Radar Picket Station # 15 was patrolled by *Evans, Hugh W. Hadley,* and *LCS(L)s 82, 83, 84,* and *LSM(R) 193.* On the 10th the ships were attacked by a single plane at 1935 and both destroyers fired on it. *Evans* reported that it had been splashed. Enemy aircraft were in the area throughout the night of the 10th to 11th, and the ships were constantly at general quarters.

Morning came on the 11th and with it came a supporting CAP of twelve planes. Bogeys were reported approaching from the northeast about 0740. A few minutes later a Jake twin float plane, one of two flying from the base at Ibusuki, appeared out of the haze and both destroyers took it under fire.

The plane went down 1,200 yards from the ship and *Hadley* was credited with the kill. When the Jake hit there was a huge explosion, indicating that it was probably carrying a large bomb. At 0755 bogeys were detected at fifty-five miles, heading straight for the station. *Hadley* vectored a division of Corsairs to intercept them. Within minutes other incoming raids were spotted, and the remaining two CAP divisions were vectored in their direction as well.

The statistics were lopsided. *Hadley* reported "Our Fighter Director Officer in CIC has estimated that the total number of enemy planes was 156 coming in at different heights in groups as follows: Raid ONE 36, Raid TWO 50, Raid THREE 20, Raid FOUR 20 to 30, Raid FIVE 20; Total 156 planes."[35] Since subsequent reports on the *Kikusui* attacks indicate that 150 special attack planes took part, it would seem that most of the *Kikusui* attacking force was headed directly for RP Station # 15. This would prove to be the largest radar picket station battle of the Okinawa campaign.

Sixteen F4U-1C Corsairs from VF-85 had taken off the escort carrier *Shangri-La* in the early morning. The four divisions, led by Lt. Comdr. Ted Hubert, arrived on station and within an hour were vectored to the north to meet the enemy. Lieutenant Joe Robbins and his wingman, Ens. Frank Siddall, were flying at about 5,000 feet when they spotted sixteen Zekes about 1,000 feet below them. The division of Corsairs dove on the Japanese planes, scattering them on their first pass. Robbins hit a Zeke and it splashed. As he pulled up, another Zeke came into his sights and he fired. The enemy plane flamed and its pilot bailed out. Robbins and Siddall pursued a third Zeke for ten miles until it turned and came at them head on. Robbins burst hit the Zeke and it exploded. Within minutes the two chased another Zeke but had trouble closing. Robbins finally managed to get enough rounds into the plane and it went down, bouncing once off the water before finally splashing.[36]

By 0755 the CAP had engaged the incoming planes, and estimates based on their communications indicate that they probably shot down forty to fifty planes. The CAP aircraft were so tied up with the large numbers of planes that there was no protection for the ships. Estimates claimed that the nearest friendly aircraft were at least ten miles from the station.[37]

Many aircraft began to fly past the station headed south. *Hadley* splashed four before the others turned their attention to the ships on the radar picket station. Planes in groups of from four to six began to attack each of the ships. *Hadley* was able to close on the support ships several times during the attack, but the maneuvering left the two destroyers miles apart at times. Between 0830 and 0900, gunners on *Hadley* splashed twelve more enemy planes.

Two VMF-323 Corsairs, flown by 1st Lt. Ed Keeley and 2d Lt. Larry Crawley, had been in the midst of engaging eleven incoming bandits when they spotted one making a run on *Hadley*. Both fliers had already seen action that day and between them had shot down seven planes. They got on the tail of the kamikaze and fired off a few bursts before running out of ammunition. In an attempt to keep the plane from hitting *Hadley,* they flew so close that they forced the enemy plane off course and it splashed on the other side of the destroyer.

The commanding officer of *Hugh W. Hadley*, Comdr. Baron J. Mullaney, praised their skill in *Hadley's* action report for the day. He wrote:

It can be recorded that the aviators who comprised the Combat Air Patrol assigned to the Hadley gave battle to the enemy that ranks with the highest traditions of our Navy's history. When the leader was asked to close and assist us, he replied, "I am out of ammunition but I am sticking with you." He then proceeded to fly his plane at enemy planes attacking in attempts to head them off. Toward the end of the battle, I witnessed one Marine pilot attempting to ride off a suicide diving plane. This plane hit us but not vitally. I am willing to take my ship to the shores of Japan if I could have these Marines with me.[38]

By the end of the battle, Keeley had shot down a Tojo and three Nates and Crawley a Dinah and three Nates.

Evans began tracking and firing on incoming planes about 0830. Three Kates made a run on the ship and all were splashed within three minutes, the first at 6,000 yards, the second at 4,000 yards and the third at 500 yards. *Evans* and *Hadley* closed to 3,500 yards for mutual support. At 0835 both destroyers fired on an incoming plane and shot it down. Two Zekes came in on *Evans* starboard side and both were splashed. A Tony aimed for *Hadley* but ran in front of *Evan's* guns and went down in flames close aboard *Hadley*. Both ships had scored hits on this plane. A few minutes, later another Tony dove on *Evans,* dropping a bomb which landed close aboard the starboard bow. This plane was hit by *Evan's* 5-inch guns and went down as well. At 0849 *Evans* shot down an Oscar, then a Jill. A Kate made a run on the destroyer a few minutes later and dropped a torpedo which passed twenty-five yards ahead of the ship. Taken under fire by *Evans* and *LCS(L) 82*, it too went down in flames.

Another Tony dove on the *Evans* from port at 0845 and both destroyers and *LCS(L) 82* scored hits on it. It splashed between the two destroyers. At about the same time, *LCS(L) 83* took a plane under fire and splashed it astern of *Evans*; at 0846, she shot down a Val 6,000 yards to port. *LSM(R) 193* spotted a Kate trying to gain altitude to make a dive on her. At 0859 she opened fire with her 5" and 40mm guns and shot it down near *LCS(L) 84*. An Oscar dove on the *Evans'* port quarter at 0901 and was hit when it was still 4,000 yards out. It dropped a bomb, which missed the ship, and then attempted a suicide crash and missed as well, hitting the water 1,500 yards to port of the *Evans*. At about the same time,

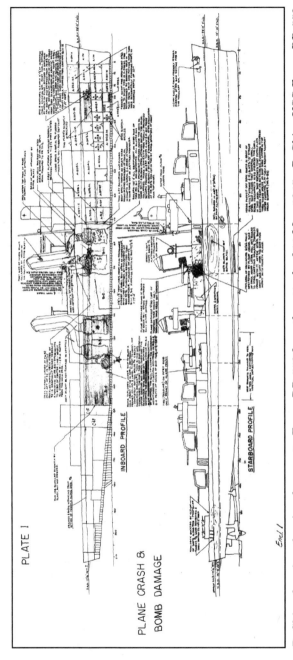

BuShips drawing showing damage to *Evans DD 552* from the attack of 11 May 1945. *BuShips USS Evans DD 552 Report of War Damage Okinawa Gunto 11 May 1945.*

gunners on the other side of the ship shot the wing off a Jill and it went into the sea. *Evans* splashed another Tony at 0904, but a few minutes later a Judy found its mark. It hit the destroyer on the water line on the port side, holing it and flooding part of the ship.

Minutes later, *LCS(L) 83* caught a Hamp making a run on her bow and shot it down. Another Tony went down in flames to port after being hit by the *Evans'* 5-inch battery. Two minutes later the ship was crashed again by a plane that dove on it from port. Although the plane was hit by gunfire, it managed to impact at the *Evans'* waterline. Its bomb exploded inside the ship causing more damage. Immediately after, an Oscar dove on the destroyer and dropped a bomb just before it crashed into it. The bomb penetrated the deck and exploded in the forward fireroom; both boilers blew up. Another Oscar crashed into the main deck, starting fires. The bodies of two Japanese pilots were later found in the galley and on deck.

With her boilers blown up, the *Evans* was dead in the water but still afloat. Two planes made a run on *LCS(L) 83* and were driven off by the ship's gunners. *LSM(R) 193* drove off two planes and then caught another Hamp making a run on her which she splashed at 0912. Three more planes came in toward the support craft at 0914. *LSM(R) 193* shot down one and the two others went down under the guns of the LCS(L)s. A final attacker came at *Evans* at 0925. Two Corsairs chased it down to the ship. Caught between the guns of the ship and the CAP, the enemy plane went off course and crashed close aboard the destroyer without causing further damage.

With her fire mains damaged, *Evans'* crew fought the fires with buckets and extinguishers. *LCS(L) 84* came to her aid, although she too was under attack. She had taken her first plane under fire at 0835 when it came in from the port side. Her first splash of the day came at 0900 when she shot down a Zeke. Manning the aft twin 40mm gun was Fred W. Waters who later recalled: "He splashed 10 feet off our starboard bow covering the ship with water and flaming gasoline. The complete starboard bow and gunnels were afire, one man had been blown overboard and one man received lacerations and was set afire. . ."[39] Nine minutes later the *84* shot down her second Zeke and a few minutes later she downed a Tojo. *LCS(L) 82* had her hands full as well. An Oscar dove on her starboard bow at 0910. Fire from the gunboat disinte-

Casualties from *Evans* being brought aboard *PCE(R) 855* from *Ringness APD 100* on 11 May 1945. *Photo by A.J. Gordon S 1/c. NARA 80G 331077.*

grated the plane as it was overhead. Commanding officer Lt. P.G. Beierl gave the command for flank speed and the plane's parts crashed astern.

Seeing the difficulties encountered by *Evans*, the *82* went to her aid. She tied up on the starboard forward side of the destroyer and began to help with firefighting. As the gunboat was being lashed to *Evans*, a Val dove on her bow with CAP aircraft in pursuit. The LCS(L)'s gunners followed the plane in, scoring numerous hits and splashing it 200 yards off *Evans'* port side. Fire from the gunboat put a few holes in the bow of the destroyer and started fires in the forecastle. Men on the gunboat immediately cut a hole in the forward deck of the destroyer and extinguished the fires. *LCS(L) 84* tied up to *Evan's* port quarter and began to pump her out.

With the *Evans* in trouble, *LCS(L) 84* had begun picking up survivors. While she was in the process of rescuing men from *Evans*, two Corsairs chased a Zeke over her fantail. She took it under fire and the enemy plane went down 400 yards off the ship. By 0945 she was again picking up survivors and then tied up to the *Evans* to assist in fire fighting and the transfer of wounded men. *Deliver ARS 23, LSM 167,* and the tugs *Cree* and *Arikara* arrived to assist, and *Arikara* began to tow the damaged destroyer back to Kerama Retto at 1345. *LCS(L) 82* had shot down three planes and assisted in splashing two. She was awarded the Navy Unit Commendation and her skipper, Lt. Peter Beierl, received the Silver Star.

Hugh W. Hadley had been separated from *Evans* during the melee. By 0900 the enemy had turned its attention to her. With so many planes attacking her, *Hadley* called for assistance from the combat air patrol. In her action report for the day, it was noted that:

> For 20 minutes, the Hadley fought off the enemy singlehanded being separated from the Evans, which was out of action, by three miles and the four small support ships by two miles. Finally, at 0920, ten enemy planes which had surrounded the Hadley, four on the starboard bow under fire by the main battery and machine guns, four on the port bow under fire by the forward machine guns, and two astern under fire by the after machine guns, attacked the ship simultaneously. All ten planes were destroyed in a remarkable fight and each plane was definitely accounted for. As a result of third attack, the Hadley was (1) Hit by a bomb aft (2) by a BAKA bomb seen to be released from a low flying BETTY (3) was struck by a suicide plane aft (4) Hit by a suicide plane in rigging.[40]

Although she suffered severe damage from the bomb and one of the planes that hit her, *Hadley* was finally put out of action by the *Oka*. She was approached from astern by a Betty which released the piloted bomb. It came in from about 600 feet altitude and hit the destroyer on the starboard side between the engine room and the forward fireroom. The explosion raised some of the decks twenty inches, breaking the knees and ankles of some of the crew. In spite of all this, the crew of the destroyer *Hadley* fought on and saved their ship.

Meanwhile, *Wadsworth, Harry E. Hubbard, Ringness, Barber* and *PCE(R) 852* had been sent toward the radar picket station to assist the stricken vessels. The high speed transport, *Barber,* had arrived at Okinawa on the previous day. Her initiation into the horrors of the radar picket stations was about to begin. She approached the station and spotted *Hadley, LSM(R) 193*, and *LCS(L) 83* about 1100. Oscar West, Jr., who served as a Gunners Mate on board *Barber* later recalled:

> ...The sea was calm and the Hadley was "dead in the water" and bleeding. No sounds, no wind, and no noise from our crew. I guess it was the stillness and our extreme alertness as to what had happened and that it may not be over. As we approached cautiously to come along side I could hear bells. The first reaction coming to mind was "Why bells?" Very soft bells with different tones. No one was speaking and no engine noises, just quiet. Then we could see the bells. The ocean seemed to be full of them around the Hadley. Empty brass 5 inch gun casings floating. The phenomenon was that heavy brass would float. Each casing had taken on a certain quantity of sea water as to change the pitch. The sound still remains with me today. I could imagine how many shell casings ejected into the sea that did not come back to the surface. And there were a lot of them still showing their tops. If the sea had not been as calm that day the lack of that sound would have made the silence deafening. ...[41]

Barber took a total of fifty of *Hadley's* wounded men from *LSM(R) 193* and *LCS(L) 83* for transport back to Hagushi. The fleet tug *Tawakoni* arrived and towed her back to Ie Shima.

Above the ships and for miles around the radar picket stations, the combat air patrol had been engaged in shooting down enemy planes. *Bunker Hill* had launched seven Corsairs from VMF-221 about 0700. After reporting to *Eldorado*, they were assigned to *Hadley*. At about 0800 they spotted a Frances near the station and a division led by Capt. J.E. Swett went after it. Swett damaged the plane and 1st Lt. W. Goeggel finished it off. At 0835 *Hadley* vectored them toward some incoming bogeys but could not find them. As they returned to their patrol they saw that the destroyer was under attack and firing on an incoming Jill. In the face of heavy anti-aircraft fire, Swett made two passes and shot the plane down before it could hit the ship. It was at this point that *Hadley* notified the CAP that they were on their own, since radio communications had broken down. Swett's division intercepted a Betty at 0855 and noted that it was carrying an *Oka*. Slowed by the

Damage to the *Hugh W. Hadley* after kamikaze attacks at Radar Picket Station # 15 on 11 May 1945. Photos courtesy of the *Hugh W. Hadley DD 774* Reunion Group.

LSM(R) 193 rescuing survivors from *Hugh W. Hadley DD 774* on 11 May at Radar Picket Station # 15. *Courtesy of the Hugh W. Hadley DD 774 Reunion Group.*

extra weight of the piloted bomb, the Betty was hit by fire from all four members of the division. The Betty began to burn at the wing-root and spun in. As it hit the water the *Oka* exploded. First Lt. R.O. Glendinning had scored the most hits and was given credit for the kill.

The VMF-221 planes headed back to their carrier not knowing that this was to be their last mission. They approached *Bunker Hill* just in time to see her hit by two kamikazes, effectively putting her out of the war. After circling survivors in the water and keeping a vigilant eye for other kamikazes, the planes landed on *Enterprise*.[42]

At 0915 1st Lts. R.J. Pinkerton and J.E. Webster of VMF-322 teamed up to shoot down a Val about twenty miles east of the station. At about the same time, twenty-five miles to the south of RP Station # 15, 1st Lt. Elliot F. Brown and 2d Lt. Creede Speake Jr. of VMF-441 had been vectored toward some incoming bogeys; each shot down a Zeke. Two other VMF-441 pilots were vectored in another direction. Second Lts. Raymond N. Wagner and Wendell M. Larson spotted a Hamp flying at a low altitude. Both pilots fired and Wagner hit it in the left wing and engine with his 20mm cannons. The plane exploded in a large ball of flame, probably from the bomb that it carried. The pilots headed back toward RP Station # 15. Wagner and Larson then spotted a Nate heading for the two

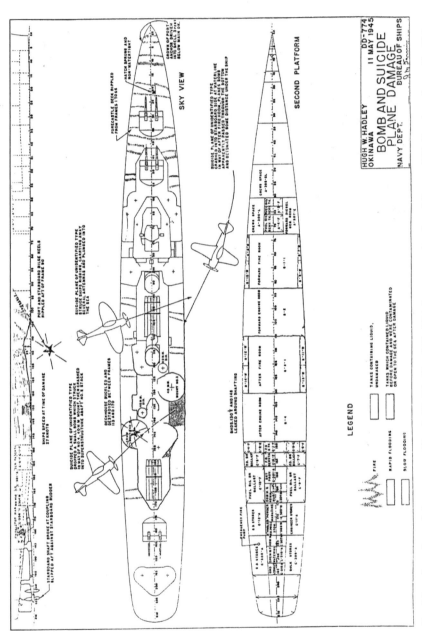

Buships drawing of damage to *Hugh W. Hadley DD 774* from attack of 11 May at RP Station # 15. *BuShips USS Hugh W. Hadley DD 774 Report of War Damage Okinawa Gunto 11 May 1945.*

· destroyers which at this point were dead in the water. Wagner
fired first but could not score. Larson managed to get on the Nate
at a seven o'clock position and hit the plane. He later reported that

> he stopped maneuvering immediately, and I kept firing until
> he began to flame and entered a moderate diving angle. I
> assumed he was either dead or incapacitated at that time, so I
> just followed him down until he hit the water about 250 yards
> from the *Evans*, aft and on the port side. A lone 40mm, located
> on the port side of the Evans, continued to fire on him even
> after he entered the water."[43]

Lt. J.M. Faddis, CO of the *LCS(L) 83*, commented: "I would
recommend that the destroyers make more use of the fire power of
the LCS's by staying closer. The 40MM guns of an LCS concentrated on a plane usually explode it in the air. This may be seen by
the one on our bow, the one over the 84 and the one over the 82."[44]

For her outstanding performance on 3 May and again on 11
May, *LCS(L) 83* was awarded the Navy Unit Commendation. *Hugh
W. Hadley*, which had shot down twenty-three planes and *Evans,*
which had downed fourteen, both received Presidential Unit
Citations.

Lowry, Henry A. Wiley, LCS(L)s 54, 55, 110, and *LSM(R) 191*
patrolled RP Station # 16A. During the morning hours the CAP
shot down a Kate near the station. First Lt. Francis Terrill and his
wingman,1st Lt. Glen Thacker, had been assigned radar picket
patrol. Flying their Corsairs out of Kadena, the VMF-323 pilots
had left their base about 1700 and headed out to cover the picket
ships at RP Station # 16A.

Late in the afternoon, at about 1917, they saw a Kate come
out of the clouds and make a run on *Lowry*. Terrill and Thacker
dropped down and got on the Kate's tail. About that time, *LCS(L)
55* opened fire with its forward single and twin 40mm guns, and
seconds later, *Henry A. Wiley* and *LSM(R) 191* took it under fire as
well. Terrill got in a few bursts before the enemy plane dropped its
torpedo. *Lowry* maneuvered to avoid the torpedo, which passed
fifty yards astern; it detonated soon after. Once it had dropped its
torpedo, the Kate banked and headed south with Terrill and
Thacker in hot pursuit. Within minutes they had completed their
job. The Kate had exploded and gone down in flames. It had been

an expensive day for the Japanese, they had lost a considerable number of planes and pilots.

Although the Japanese had suffered great losses, the effect of *Kikusui* raids 5 and 6 were deadly. On the radar picket stations, 540 men had been killed and 590 wounded. Once again the destroyer types took a beating. Three were sunk and seven damaged. Their support ships suffered greatly as well, with three LSM(R)s sunk and one damaged. LCS(L)s had fared marginally better; four were damaged in the air attacks.

In spite of increased radar picket and CAP proficiency, a number of Japanese planes had managed to slip through. Five other ships were hit in Okinawan waters, including two carriers. The escort carrier *Sangamon* and the carrier *Bunker Hill* were badly damaged and put out of the war. Losses were especially severe on *Bunker Hill* which had 396 men killed and 264 wounded. In all, 579 killed and 564 wounded were added to the losses on the picket stations.[45]

CHAPTER 6

A Hearty "Well-Done"

Additional fighter aircraft became available about the 14th of May as Army P-47N Thunderbolts of the 318th Fighter Group arrived at Okinawa. Based on Ie Shima, the "Jugs" had just flown in from Saipan and were ready for combat. From this point on the CAP would frequently consist of a combination of Hellcats, Wildcats, Corsairs and Thunderbolts. Other Thunderbolt squadrons would follow. The ground echelons for the 413th Fighter Group on board the *USAT Kota Inten* arrived at Ie Shima on 19 May and began preparations for the arrival of the flight echelons in mid-June. Since they were long-range fighters, their primary missions would involve attacks on Kyushu, Korea and China. They were also utilized in flying barrier CAPs to the north of Okinawa, as well as for coverage over the radar picket ships.

One of their important missions would be against the kamikaze home bases on Kyushu. Their continued sweeps of the bases hindered the Japanese efforts to send planes against the forces at Okinawa.

To the south of Okinawa, the airfields on Miyako Jima and Ishigaki Shima were hit frequently during the month by aircraft flying from the British carriers and the American escort carriers. In addition, diverse units of the Far East Air Force conducted continuous B-24 and B-25 raids against the fields on Taiwan.

Saturday, 12 May through Monday, 14 May 1945

The island of Tori Shima was occupied on 12 May and would serve as a new site for an air raid warning station. This would take some of the pressure off the ships serving on RP Stations # 15 and 16.

Radar Picket Station # 7 was patrolled by *Pritchett, Walke, LCS(L)s 14, 115, 118*, and *LSM(R) 192*. On the 13th at 1904 *Pritchett* vectored the CAP to intercept a bogey closing on the station. The division of VMF-312 Corsairs spotted a Dinah at 500 feet coming in from the west. Captain T.J. Cushman and Lieutenant Sterling scored the first hits as the plane turned away. It was then caught in the sights of 1st Lts. Al Thorne and Richard F. McKown who also fired on it. McKown followed the plane down and hit the engine, sending it flaming into the sea.

William D. Porter, Bache, LCS(L)s 23, 56, 87, and *LSM(R) 197* patrolled RP Station # 9 on 12 May. A single division of VMF-323 Corsairs had taken off from Kadena at 1730. Led by Capt. Joe McPhail, it included 1st Lt. John Rusham and his wingman, 1st Lt. Bob Wade. Seven special attack planes, two escort fighters and a guide plane from the Eighth Air Division fields on Taiwan were headed for them. At about 1930 the marine pilots spotted a Dinah closing on the picket station and gave chase. They followed it toward the station and Rusham caught it with several bursts before over-running it. Wade finished off the twin engine fighter and it splashed near the destroyers. The other planes did not attack the ships.

In the early evening, at 2014, an enemy plane came in on the station at a low altitude. *Bache* and *Porter* both fired and drove it off. *Cowell* relieved *William D. Porter* at 1745 on 13 May and took over duties as fighter director for the station. At about 1830, *Cowell* vectored four Corsairs from VMF-224 toward incoming bogeys. The Corsairs, piloted by 2d Lts. L.J. Michaels, H.S. Kovsky, L.R. Tucker, and Capt. E.F. Chase, encountered a combination of Willows, Petes, and Vals. Kovsky made the first kill. One of the Willows was cruising toward the ships only twenty feet off the water. Kovsky nosed his Corsair over and shot it down. Two Vals attacked from the northeast and one fell under the guns of the picket ships. Kovsky and Tucker teamed up and splashed the second. Chase picked up another Willow flying low and shot it down. A few minutes later, a Pete, about twenty feet off the water, fell under their guns.[1]

At about 1840, *Bache* detected more enemy planes on her radar but lost contact with them. Fearing that they might be flying at a low altitude to avoid radar, she vectored the two fighters under her control to intercept them. Corsairs from VMF-311, flown by

Capt. Scherer and Lieutenant Knight, found four Petes coming in at about 500 feet and splashed them.[2] Two Vals then approached the support vessels from starboard. *LSM(R) 197* and *Cowell* took them under fire and a 5-inch shell from the LSM(R) exploded one. At about the same time, three Vals were picked up coming in at a low altitude nine miles from the station. *Bache* fired on the first and shot it down when it was 7,000 yards to starboard. Another Val attacked simultaneously from port and fell victim to 40mm fire from the destroyer and *LCS(L)s 23* and *56*. The third Val, pursued by 1st Lt. F.E. Warren of VMF-322, made a dive on the ship.

Warren followed it right through the flak in an attempt to get the plane but, at 1850, the Val's wing hit the destroyer's number 2 stack and the plane spun around and careened down the center of the ship. Its 500 pound bomb exploded just above the deck, spraying it with shrapnel. The ship's electrical power and steam were knocked out.

Meanwhile Warren, who had pursued the Val to within 500 yards of *Cowell,* was hit in the right wing by AA fire from the ships. In spite of the damage, he almost made it back to Kadena but had to bail out just offshore. Personnel from a nearby anti-aircraft battery fished him out uninjured.[3]

At about the same time, Warren's squadron mate,1st Lt. Richard S. Wilcox, spotted a Zeke making a run on the destroyers and shot it down. Both Wilcox and Warren were awarded the Navy Cross for their heroism that day.

LSM(R) 197 spotted a Pete biplane coming in and took it under fire but ceased firing when a CAP plane was observed chasing it. *LCS(L) 87* placed herself between the stricken *Bache* and more incoming planes, hitting a Val as it closed on the destroyer. The CAP pilots chased the plane and finished the job. They shot down two more attackers before *Bache* caught a Dinah coming in on her and turned it away with 40mm fire. At about the same time, *Bache* vectored two Corsairs from VMF-311 to intercept four incoming Petes. Captain R.F. Scherer shot down three and 2d Lt. W.H. Knight got the other.

Bache was dead in the water and on fire. *LCS(L)s 56* and *87*, along with *LSM(R) 197,* went to her aid at 1900 and began to assist with the fires and in giving aid to the wounded. *LCS(L) 23* came along the lee side of the ship and was instrumental in helping fight the fires. *PCE(R) 855* arrived at the station and took nineteen of

Bache's casualties and one dead from the *197*. At 2128 *LCS(L) 56* began the task of towing *Bache* back to port. The destroyer had forty-one killed and thirty-two injured.

Two days later MAG-33 received the following communiqué from the *Bache*:

> THE F4U PILOTS ON RP 9 EVENING 13 MAY PERFORMED ADMIRABLE AND COURAGEOUS WORK IN SAVING THE BACHE FROM FURTHER INJURY X THESE PILOTS REPEATEDLY DOVE ON ATTACKING SUICIDERS IN THE FACE OF HEAVY ANTIAIRCRAFT FIRE X TWICE WHILE BACHE WAS DEAD IN THE WATER THESE SAME PILOTS SPLASHED SUICIDE PLANES ABOUT 4000 YARDS FROM SHIP X PLEASE CONVEY TO THESE PILOTS THE GRATI-TUDE OF THE OFFICERS AND MEN OF THE BACHE X FURTHER THE COMMANDING OFFICER WISHES TO MAKE KNOWN THAT ALL SMALL CRAFT ASSISTING RENDERED EXCELLENT HELP IN PARTICULAR THE LCS 23 WHICH CAME ALONG THE LEEWARD SIDE IN FACE OF HEAVY FLAMES AROUND NUMBER 1 TORPEDO TUBE TO SUPPLY WATER AND ELECTRIC POWER.[4]

American intelligence speculated that the carrier strikes on Kyushu had severely disrupted the attacks emanating from bases on the island. The limited attacks on the radar picket stations seemed to be coming from Taiwan.[5]

Tuesday, 15 May through Saturday, 19 May 1945

Intercepted messages from the Combined Naval Force brought news of changes in Japanese practices. Although the Japanese army had been using airfields in Korea as rear staging areas, for the first time there were indications that the navy was about to do so as well. Fuel allocations for Korean bases to be used by the navy were indicated in a message sent on 16 May. Other messages revealed that the Japanese were having difficulty in maintaining Zekes and Jacks.

The First Air Fleet on Taiwan was directed to send out recon-naissance planes on the 18th in order to locate American ships at Okinawa. An attack on the ships at Kerama Retto by eight planes from a training unit was scheduled for the night hours of the 18th.[6]

Kanoya Air Field on Kyushu was considered to be one of the most important air fields in Japan, making it a constant target for American planes. Here, two SB2C Helldivers and an F4U Corsair from Task Force 58 strike the field on 13 May 1945. *USS Bennington CV 20 Serial 0021 3 June 1945 Action Report of USS Bennington (CV-20) and Carrier Air Group Eighty-Two in Support of Military Operations at Okinawa 9 May-28 May (East Longitude Dates) Including Action Against Kyushu.*

The Ten Air Force and the Sixth Air Army scheduled new attacks for 19 May. Thirty fighters and two suicide units were to reach the Hagushi anchorage between 1630 and 1900. Part of an intercepted Japanese message on 17 May promised danger for the picket ships. According to the National Security Agency, it stated that: "The enemy takes to the air before we get close to our targets, making it difficult for us to attack. Choose a target which can most easily be attacked."[7] Many of the ships that were easiest to attack would be those closest to the bases on Taiwan and Kyushu and the radar picket ships would be seriously imperiled.

Bradford, Walke, LCS(L)s *12, 115, 117, 118,* and LSM(R) *192* patrolled RP Station # 7 on 17 May. *Bradford* picked up a bogey at sixteen miles and vectored the CAP to intercept it, but it missed the initial interception. After correcting its course, the CAP spotted a Willow with a 500 pound bomb heading toward the station from the west. Second Lt. C.E. Bacon of VMF-311 shot it down at 0625, fourteen miles from the station.

Patrolling RP Station # 9 on 15 May were *Cowell, Van Valkenburgh* and *LCS(L)s 65, 66, 67,* and *LSM(R) 197. LCS(L) 53* relieved *LSM(R) 197* at 1010. *Cowell* controlled the combat air patrol flying overhead. Toward the end of the day, enemy planes were reported near the station. Four Corsairs from VMF-323, led by 1st Lt. Charles Martin, were on patrol over the ships. A section under 2d Lt. H.P. Wells, with 2d Lt. Norman Miller as his wingman, spotted three Jills making for the station. According to Fighter Command Okinawa:

> Wells and Miller made stern runs from below, Wells firing at the wing roots and cockpit on the first kill and raking the entire plane on the second. Miller fired along the fuselage and wing roots until his adversary flamed. All attacks were initiated at 300 feet because of poor light and approaching darkness. Tail gunners, who fired on our aircraft, were observed on the trio of Jills. One enemy plane jettisoned a bomb while taking evasive action and all were apparently heading for shipping when attacked.[8]

When the action was over, Wells was credited with two kills and Miller with one. *Cowell* received news that the CAP had splashed the three planes southwest of her position. Within minutes, a Kate was observed heading for the picket ships at an altitude of one hundred feet.

The special two plane radar picket patrol was sent in pursuit and shot the Kate down about ten miles from the station. First Lt. E.F. Brown and 2d Lt. J.E. Croyle of VMF-224 shared the kill. At about the same time, a Jill torpedo bomber attacked *Cowell* and was downed by her gunners only fifty yards off its fantail. Still another bandit fell victim to the CAP at 1936.

Early in the morning of the 16th, at 0613, the ships went to general quarters with an enemy float biplane reported in the area. It soon fell under the guns of the CAP. Still another bogey was reported heading into the station at 0720, but it turned off twelve miles out. *Douglas H. Fox* relieved *Cowell* at 0851 and took control of the CAP. The CAP departed for its base that evening at about 1950. No sooner had they begun their journey back than bogeys appeared. Ordered back to the RP station, the CAP splashed two bandits, one at 2022 and another at 2029.

On 17 May, at 1900, the destroyers picked up incoming bogeys at seventy miles and vectored two VMF-323 Corsairs to intercept them. First Lt. James Feliton and his wingman, 2d Lt. Stuart Alley, found a Val and made two passes. On the second run, Alley's aim was true and the Val splashed. At 1912 the two were ordered back to base. At about the same time, another VMF-323 division, led by 1st Lt. Francis Terrill, was flying CAP near RP Station # 9. They were vectored toward a bogey and spotted a Val below them at 2,000 feet. All four planes made a run on the Japanese plane and overshot it. Terrill and 2d Lt. Keith Fountain turned and came in from the side. After many violent maneuvers, the Val was finally splashed and the division headed back to Kadena.[9]

Some of the potential air attacks were slowed by B-24 attacks on the fields at Nanseiho and Matsuyama on Taiwan. Units of the Far East Air Force conducted raids on them this day. Four Oscars from the 20th Air Regiment took off from Karenko South Airfield on Taiwan at 1730. Led by Lt. Takashige Sakamoto who flew guide, the other planes were piloted by 2d Lts. Shunsaku Tsuji, Shizuka Imano, Tadao Shiraishi, and Hisamitsu Inaba. Each of their fighters carried two 250 kg bombs mounted under their wings and their radios and cannons had been removed. For the initial part of their flight the fighter planes maintained high altitudes, but once past Ishigaki Shima, they dropped to sea level to avoid detection. They arrived over RP Station # 9 at about 1925, shortly after the CAP had departed.

Douglas H. Fox was first to spot the enemy aircraft at 1926 and took one under fire two minutes later. The plane went down in flames. Other bogeys were picked up at a range of four to five miles. Sakamoto watched as two of the Oscars were shot down by anti-aircraft fire from the ships. *Fox* splashed one off the starboard bow and another off the starboard quarter. Number four went into the sea at 1934 but, a minute later, Tsuji's Oscar got through the hail of fire and crashed into *Fox's* deck between 5"/38 mounts numbers 1 and 2. Just before crashing, it released a bomb which exploded on the deck as the plane impacted. Sakamoto saw the crash but was unable to determine the type of ship that had been hit. He radioed

Crewmen inspect damage to *Douglas H. Fox DD 779* at Kerama Retto on 18 May 1945. The ship was hit by a kamikaze while on Radar Picket Station # 9 the preceding day. *U.S.S. Douglas H. Fox (DD 779) Action Report of 24 May 1945.*

back to his base that they had hit a medium sized cruiser. He returned to his base, landing at Karenko at 2000.[10]

A Val came within range of the support ships and the LCS(L)s opened up with their twin 40mm guns. One of the ships, *LCS(L) 67,* was one of only twenty-five LCS(L)s assigned to radar picket duty that mounted a twin 40mm in the number one gun position and the only one at RP Station # 9 that day. The Val never had a chance and went down off the port quarter of *LCS(L) 53.* Still another plane was shot down on the port side of the *Fox's* fantail. As the attack on *Douglas H. Fox* was underway, *Van Valkenburgh* was also doing her best to drive off an attack. She splashed a Jill off her port side and a few minutes later downed an Oscar off her port quarter. A third plane went down under her guns 2,000 yards to starboard. By 1937 the main action was over and *Van Valkenburgh* went to the assistance of the *Douglas H. Fox.* Ten minutes later

Van Valkenburgh fired on another Japanese plane and drove it off. She then closed on *Fox* to render assistance but, at 2045, *Van Valkenburgh* fired on and drove off another plane. The RP ships had splashed nine of the enemy planes, with *Douglas H. Fox* claiming five, *Van Valkenburgh* three and one splashed by the combined firepower of the four LCS(L)s.

    William D. Porter and *Henry A. Wiley* relieved *Fox* and *Van Valkenburgh*. Daylight hours proved to be quiet, with the ships covered by sixteen Corsairs from VMF-441. At 1857 bogeys appeared on the radar screen and the Corsairs on CAP were sent to intercept them. They found enemy aircraft fifteen to twenty miles south of Point Able at 1,000 to 2,000 feet. Two Tonys were the first victims, hitting the water between 1910 and 1920. Major Hardy Hay got the first Tony after coming up behind the enemy plane from above and hitting the cockpit and engine; the plane burst into flame and crashed into the water. First Lt. John M. Mendinhall II got behind another Tony and his gunfire ignited the plane in the air. The Tony rolled over and crashed in the ocean. *LCS(L) 67* spotted a Tony making a run on her from one mile out. Followed by 2d Lt. Donald H. Edwards' Corsair, the plane fired at the gunboat which took it under fire with its twin 40mm guns and 20mm guns. Edwards' aim was true and he splashed it 800 yards to port of *LCS(L) 67*. The marine flyer did not realize that he was in danger. Smoke obscured the view of the forward 40mm gunners and they took his plane under fire, thinking it was an enemy plane. Fortunately he escaped unscathed.[11]

    First Lt. Raymond N. Holzwart fired on the fourth Tony on his second run, hitting it in the fuselage, wing and engine; it caught fire and crashed. The fifth plane, a Val, was hit by .50 caliber fire from 2d Lt. James R. Rector's Corsair. Two of Rector's guns jammed and his two remaining guns fired into the cockpit and engine of the bomber. The Val started smoking and disappeared into some low clouds, never to be seen again. Rector was credited with a probable. From that point through 19 May, enemy planes were reported in the area but there were no other attacks on the ships.

    Gainard, Drexler, LCS(L)s 22, 62, 81, and *PGM 9* patrolled RP Station # 15. Late in the evening of the 16th, several attackers closed on the station. The first, at 2145, orbited the ships at 10,000 yards and then made a run on *Gainard*. It turned away at 7,000 yards after the ships took it under fire. Unbeknownst to the ships, the plane had dropped a torpedo. Fortunately it missed, but exploded at the end of its run, giving them notice that they had a close call. *LCS(L) 81* was shaken by the explosion but not damaged. At 2242 *Gainard* fired on another incoming plane and knocked its tail off. *Drexler* joined in the shoot and the twin engine plane went down 3,800 yards from *Gainard*.

Following their standard attack procedure, two more enemy planes positioned themselves for a suicide run. After orbiting out of gun range and dropping window to confuse the ships' radar, they came in on the destroyers from opposite sides. *Drexler* fired on the plane coming in from the northeast and *Gainard* fired on the attacker coming in from the south. *Gainard's* target turned away but *Drexler* had better luck, splashing the plane 200 yards out. Still another bogey headed for the *Gainard* at 2350. Hit by the ship's 5" guns at 6,000 yards, it turned away and flew over the support gunboats. The gunboats reported that the enemy plane went down in flames 12,000 yards from the formation.

Six marine night fighters had taken off from Yontan at 1915 and headed out over the ocean. First Lt. Robert M. Wilhide came in contact with two enemy bombers heading for Ie Shima and closed in on them.

In spite of warnings from his ground control that he was getting too close to the ships and might be taken under fire, he continued his pursuit. He was last heard from at 2011, about the same time that *Gainard* reported an unidentified plane splashed two miles from the station. Only two days before Wilhide had become the first VMF(N)-533 pilot to score at Okinawa when he shot down a Betty. *Gainard* headed out to investigate the crash, but found no survivors.

Still another Hellcat, piloted by 1st Lt. Maynard C. Kelley, was in hot pursuit of a bogey when he was hit by anti-aircraft fire as well. The ships finally received the word that he was a friendly and held back their fire. Kelley was not able to make it back to Yontan but managed to get to Ie Shima.[12] He was lucky that night but not so fortunate a week later. He was shot and killed by a Japanese commando in the Giretsu Raid at Yontan on 24 May. Other Hellcats in the flight continued to chase bogeys without success. After extending their patrols, the remainder were also forced to land at Ie Shima when Yontan was covered by smoke.

On the 18th, *LCS(L) 121* relieved the *22* at 1025 and at 1245 *LCS(L) 85* relieved *LCS(L) 81*. That evening, at 2203, another plane made a run on the station and was turned away by the ships' gunfire. At 2324 *Gainard* and *Drexler* both opened fire on an incoming plane and splashed it nearby. The VMF(N)-533 night fighters were again in peril. After shooting down two Bettys, 1st Lt. R.E. Wellwood's plane was hit by friendly anti-aircraft fire. In spite of the damage to his plane, he shot down a third Betty before heading back to base with his badly shot up Hellcat. First Lt. E.N. LeFaivre splashed a Hamp and a Betty on the same mission.

On 15 May, RP Station # 16A was patrolled by *Ammen*, *Boyd*, *LCS(L)s 64*, *90*, *94*, and *LSM(R) 189*. Daylight hours on the 15th were quiet until 1912 when a bogey was detected at a range of eighteen miles. First Lt. R. Brown, of VMF-322, spotted a Paul at 2,000 feet and went in pursuit. He scored hits on the top of the fuselage and the empennage, flaming the plane which subsequently crashed into the sea. Within minutes the planes were vectored toward another bogey which turned away. The CAP retired at 1954.

The first half of May had been difficult. A summation of the picket ships' activities until 17 May was given by the Commander of Task Force 51 Vice Adm. Richmond K. Turner:

> These ships and their supporting craft absorbed the brunt of 560 raids from 2228 enemy planes during the period from 1 April to 0900 17 May. Attrition was severe. Of the original 19 ships in which Fighter Director equipment was installed, HALLIGAN was sunk by an enemy mine; BUSH, COLHOUN, M. L. ABELE and LUCE were sunk by the enemy "Sure Hit, Sure Death" corps; 8 others were seriously damaged and 3 received minor damage from suicide attacks. As replacements, fourteen other ships were equipped in the combat area for fighter direction during the course of this operation, and Fighter Director teams from previously damaged ships were placed aboard. Of these 14 additional ships, MORRISON was sunk, 5 were seriously damaged and 2 others received minor damage, all from enemy suicide crashes.[13]

These words would be Turner's last as CTF 51. On 17 May he turned over his command to Vice Adm. Harry W. Hill. Turner would spend the remaining days of the war planning the invasion of Japan.

Vice Admiral Harry W. Hill on 26 July 1944. *Official US Navy Photo. NARA 208-PU-92QQ-2.*

The Japanese, in preparing for the coming assault, found themselves in a difficult position. One of the units slated to attack the American ships at Okinawa, the Territorial Naval Air Force, reported that they were in need of reinforcements. The only planes they had in usable condition were seaplanes and *Shiragiku* trainers.[14] By 25 May, the Fifth Air Fleet would report that "The strength of our air force is so low that at present, we are unable to cooperate with the Army."[15]

American intelligence noted that the Japanese navy had drawn aircraft and pilots from its training units and that the army might have done so also. Indications were that the Japanese army was forming suicide units at their training bases, particularly Tachikawa and Kagamigahara on Honshu. Still another air depot at Mukden, Manchuria had been identified as forming such units as well. According to the National Security Agency the training command at Nanyuan (Peking) was preparing to transfer their To units to the Sixth Air Army on the 10th.[16]

Sunday, 20 May through Tuesday, 22 May 1945

From 20 to 22 May some changes in the radar picket stations took place. On 21 May, RP Station # 7 was closed and a new station, RP Station # 11A was manned. Most of the ships that had been assigned to RP Station # 7 were reassigned to RP Station # 11A. RP Station # 15 was also closed and ships shifted over to a new station, RP Station # 15A, which was located five miles to the west.

Wednesday, 23 May through Friday, 25 May 1945

The continuing efficiency of the marine fighter squadrons prompted the Japanese to take further action against them. Yontan and Kadena, the major bases on Okinawa, had to be neutralized. At the beginning of May, the Japanese Sixth Air Army began to prepare an attack. Referred to as the G-I Operation, it would involve a commando raid on the two airstrips by the Giretsu Airborne Raiding Unit. Early in May this unit, under the command of Captain Okuyama, was transferred from Nishitsukuba to Kumamoto to prepare for the assault. Providing aircraft for the commando attack would be the Third Independent Air Unit at Hamamatsu. The assault would include a command section and five flights, each carrying twenty men and officers. Twelve heavy bombers were assigned to deliver the raiders to the objective. Weaponry carried by the assault troops would include light machine guns, short rifles and machine guns, revolvers and grenade launchers. Each man would also carry hand grenades and explosive charges. Upon landing on the airstrip, they were to destroy as many of the American planes as they could.

Preparations for the assault included stripping twelve Mitsubishi Ki-21-II (Sally) bombers of their guns and adding front and top exits. These planes would be flown by skilled pilots specially trained for the mission. The base at Kumamoto would need some improvement so that the mission could be launched from there. Additional planes from the Eighth Air Division on Taiwan and navy planes would also support the attack.

Tokyo Headquarters issued orders on 18 May to commence the operation. Army planners decided that it should be executed on the 23rd. The original plan was to bomb Ie Shima Airfield and shipping around Okinawa. It also included a preliminary bombing attack on the airfields at Kadena and Yontan. Thirty minutes later, the Giretsu Raiding Unit would land on the airfields at Yontan and Kadena and destroy as many planes as possible. Four planes were to land at Kadena and eight at Yontan. With the marine squadrons damaged, *Kikusui # 7* would be launched the following day.

Unfortunately for the Japanese, the plan did not go well. After six planes from the 60th Air Regiment and eight from the 110th took off for the initial bombing run on the fields, reports filtered back to Kumamoto about poor weather conditions at the fields and the mission was aborted until the following day. Confusion over the postponement prevented the navy from supporting the operation. The following day, on the 24th, the army units set out on the mission. After the heavy bomber units had attacked Yontan and Kadena, planes from the Fifth Air Army bombed Ie Shima. Of the Giretsu planes heading for the marine bases, only four reached one of the targets, the field at Yontan. Three had turned back after getting lost and one had engine trouble. Others were shot down.[17] Once again the Japanese belief in the ten *To Shi Bi* days, was reaffirmed.[18]

At Yontan, 1st Lt. Maynard C. Kelley and Staff Sgt. Robert N. Dietrich, were on duty in the field control tower. As they watched, four Sallys appeared from the northeast at about 2225. Anti-aircraft fire hit three of the planes and they crashed in flames. One of the planes came in low and made a wheels-up landing on the field. Kelley got out his field glasses and observed a small party of

Japanese troops exit the plane. Armed with only a .38 revolver, Kelley left the tower. At its foot was a jeep and driver and they set out in the direction of the plane.

As they approached, the Giretsu raiders took them under fire and began blowing up aircraft on the flight line. Kelley headed back to the tower to phone in a warning to the squadron. He killed one attacker near the tower, but as he climbed it to turn on the searchlight, he was hit in the chest and killed. The men at the tower held their ground as other marines engaged the raiders in battle.[19]

The firefight disrupted field operations for the remainder of the night. Planes returning to Yontan were redirected and landed at about Kadena about midnight. Giretsu raiders managed to do a great deal of damage to the MAG-31 planes.

Tactical Air Force reported the destruction of three transports, three Corsairs, an R4D and a PB4Y-2. In addition, twenty-four fighters and a Liberator were damaged, with at least three of the fighters probable losses. Personnel losses included 1st Lt. Kelley and Tech Sgt. Roderick J. Wogan. Eighteen other men had been wounded in the fighting.[20] The following day would see the launch of *Kikusui # 7*. The marines had been slowed but other fighters were available to cover the ships.

Kikusui # 7 had originally been scheduled to begin on 14 May. American carrier strikes on 13-14 May caused the operation to be postponed. It was rescheduled for the 22nd, but was again postponed, this time by foul weather.

Operational Instructions for the attack were as follows:

1). At night of x-1 day, the Night Assault Unit of the Territorial Naval Air Force will attack enemy ships in the vicinity of OKINAWA and KAIRAKAN, and the Night Bomber Unit of the Territorial Naval Air Force will attack enemy airfields on IEKO ISLAND.

2). The GI Air Unit of the 6th Air Fleet will patrol the area around OKINAWA during the night of x-1 day and a large number of the planes stationed in the western district will attack enemy ships in the vicinity of OKINAWA.

3). If air superiority should be attained, training planes will be utilized in this operation.

4). The Territorial naval Air Force will wait for a favorable opportunity to attack an enemy task force.

The Sally bomber that carried the *Giretsu* raiding party lays on the field at Yontan. *NARA 208-AA-264S.*

> 5). The 5th Air Unit will, at an opportune moment attack enemy ships with the assistance of the Territorial naval Air Force and the 6th Air Fleet.[21]

In spite of their plans to attack, the Japanese were feeling the effects of the continuing raids on the Kyushu airfields. Air Group 203, operating from Kanoya and Kagoshima, found themselves too vulnerable to attack and they requested that any new Zekes sent to their units "be ferried to IZUMI until [the] end of May and thereafter to IWAKUNI."[22]

The brief respite for the RP ships would end with the launch of the next *Kikusui* attack. *Kikusui* # 7 would include 165 special attack planes, sixty-five from the navy and one hundred from the Japanese army. As they had done before, they would take their toll.

Many of the suicide planes were trainers. Vice Admiral Ugaki wrote:

> Planes to be employed in *tokko* attacks are gradually getting scarce, and it has become necessary to employ some trainers. Apart from their use at night, they couldn't stand even one second against enemy fighter attacks. Therefore, when they have to be used, we should provide them with thorough command of

The body of one of the Japanese *Giretsu* commandos lies on the field at Yontan the morning after the raid of 24 May 1945. *NARA 208-AA-41923-FMC.*

the air. Though they are many in number, we can't expect much from them.[23]

Shiragiku training planes, based at Kanoya and Kushira, would be sent out on special attack missions for the next few days. On the 24th, twenty would fly from Kanoya and on the 25th, another twenty from Kanoya and Kushira. On the 27th, twenty more would scramble from Kanoya and on the 28th, eleven from Kushira. Of the seventy-one sent on the missions during this time period, only thirty-three made it back to their bases without having attacked or fallen prey to the American fighters and the picket ships.

The National Security Agency reported:

. . . that "Kikusui # 7 is the first operation in which trainer aircraft are scheduled to participate in substantial numbers. . . . TAIC estimates that Shiragiku can carry a 500-pound bomb 600 miles at 100 mph, and that their maximum diving speed is less than 200 mph.[24]

Kyushu K11w1 Shiragiku trainer. These planes were increasingly used as kamikazes during the later stages of the Okinawan campaign. The plane pictured here is shown at Sasebo Air Base on Kyushu in September 1945. It is painted white with green crosses by American direction. Planes painted in the manner were used for courier service from mid-September to mid-October 1945. *NARA USMC 138377.*

The Sixth Air Army was to supply about sixty fighters and 120 suicide planes for *Kikusui* # 7. Original plans called for both army and navy planes to look for the American task force east of Okinawa. If they were not located, the attack would center on the Okinawa anchorage in mid-morning. Val dive bombers and Bettys with *Okas* were to attack allied shipping around Okinawa between 0830 and 0930. The navy would make additional attacks on the fields at Ie Shima and the ships at Kerama Retto would be hit by advanced navy trainers flying kamikaze missions. In the afternoon, the First Air Fleet planes from Taiwan would strike American ships near Okinawa as well as Ie Shima.[25]

Although *Kikusui* # 7 originally might have included as many as eight hundred Japanese planes, further American attacks on the Kyushu fields by carrier aircraft and long range P-47Ns from Ie Shima forced many of them to fly away to avoid destruction. This limited the sorties to an estimated 250 aircraft, most of which staged their attacks on the 25th of May.[26]

Bennion, Anthony, and *LCS(L)s 13, 82, 86,* and *123* patrolled RP Station # 5 on 25 May. At 0100 the ships went to general quarters with incoming planes. *Bennion* picked up a Betty on her radar at a range of twenty miles and took it under fire at 6,300 yards. The plane dropped a torpedo before being hit by gunfire from *Bennion* and *Anthony* and crashed into the water 1,700 yards aft of *Bennion.* Its torpedo exploded at the end of its run without damaging the ships. At 0139 a single engine float plane from Ibusuki came in astern of the support ships. The destroyers shot it down 4,300 yards to port of *Bennion. LCS(L) 123* also fired on the plane as it passed only fifty feet over its bow. No further incidents were reported that day.

Patrolling RP Station # 11A on 24 May were *Gainard, Fullam, Walke,* and *LCS(L)s 12, 83, 84,* and *115.* At 1915 *Gainard* detected enemy planes on radar and then spotted five Vals over Kume Shima. The two plane radar picket patrol from VMF-311 was sent to intercept them and shortly thereafter the four plane CAP from VMF-312 was vectored toward them as well. When the dogfight was over, the enemy had lost five Vals, two Zekes, a Tony and an Oscar with no American losses. High scorers during the melee were Second Lieutenants Dorell and Soreide of VMF-311. Dorell shot down two Vals and a Zeke, and Soreide accounted for three Vals.[27]

Radar Picket Station # 15A was patrolled by *Bradford, Massey, Foote, Watts,* and *LCS(L)s 52, 61, 85,* and *121* on 23 May. Bogeys began to appear on the radar screens at 0007 and continued for the next hour. Their flight patterns made it clear that they were conducting a search of the area. A comparison of radar plots indicated that the planes seemed to be covering a specific area and might be trying to locate the picket ships.[28] A raid at 0106 was taken under fire and turned away.

The ships saw no action during the daylight hours but in early evening the raids began. At 2017 bogeys appeared on the radar screens. *LCS(L) 121* went to GQ at 2020 with enemy planes reported to her port side. Suddenly at 2027, a Rufe from the Seaplane Reconnaissance Unit of the 12th Fighter Group, based at Ibusuki, appeared out of the clouds on the starboard side. It dropped a bomb estimated to be 250 lbs., which exploded above the surface of the water twenty-five yards off the gunboat's starboard side. Shrapnel from the bomb's blast showered the ship killing two men and wounding four. The plane was taken under fire by one of the ship's

LCS(L) 121 on patrol off Okinawa. *NARA 80G 325109.*

20mm guns but it did not appear to have been hit. Because of its sudden appearance, the other gunboats did not have a chance to open fire on it. Damage to the ship included several holes in the hull and gun tubs and damage to the mast, fire hoses, ship's boat and a 20mm gun.

Other raids appeared from the east and *Watts* opened fire at 2031, splashing another of the Ibusuki Rufes off her port beam. *Bradford* took another plane under fire at 2039 and it also turned away. For the next hour planes skirted the formation, but none came close enough to fire upon until 2345, when one of them changed course and made a run on the ships from astern. *Massey* was last in line and turned to starboard to bring maximum firepower to bear on the plane. Her gunners found the mark and it was splashed at 7,000 yards.

The 23rd of May soon became the 24th, and with the new day came new raids. *Bradford* and *Massey* took a plane under fire at 0033 turning it away. All four destroyers fired on a second plane at

0041, with reports that it splashed a few minutes later seven miles from the station. *Foote* spotted two planes coming in on the formation and took them under fire, splashing one at 3,500 yards at 0106; the other turned off. Two minutes later *Bradford, Foote* and *Watts* were confronted by a Jake making a run on them from the port bow and took it under fire. *Massey* had a better angle of fire and hit the plane, splashing it at 2,000 yards. Credit for the kill was shared with *Bradford*, which also scored some hits on the plane.

Foote reported that a total of fourteen to sixteen planes had attacked the station that night. The raids usually consisted of one or two planes. Six of them had been shot down, with *LCS(L) 121, Watts, Foote* and *Massey* credited with one each, *Massey* and *Bradford* sharing credit for another and all four destroyers sharing credit for a sixth.[29]

Early in the morning of the 25th, other bogeys began to appear. *LCS(L) 52* took planes under fire at 0215 and again at 0305 but scored no hits. CAP aircraft splashed an incoming Oscar at 0825, but at 0930 missed another contact which came in from the south. *Stormes* spotted a Zeke at 0904, but the close proximity of two CAP fighters made her hold her fire. It had been chased by 2d Lts. D.E. Ruyle and J.P. McAlister of VMF-224. Both pilots hit the plane with short bursts and the cockpit smoked as small pieces flew off it. The Zeke disappeared into the overcast sky and then reappeared astern *Stormes,* heading for *Ammen*. Both destroyers took the plane under fire. By this time, the kamikaze pilots were using a new tactic. They approached the target ship from astern, flying parallel to its course. As they drew abeam of the vessel, they executed a wing over. Using this maneuver, the Zeke crashed into the after torpedo mount of *Stormes*. Just prior to the crash, it released a bomb which penetrated the superstructure deck and exploded in the number three magazine.[30] The blast tore holes in the deck and the bottom of the ship and it began to flood. Fires on deck were soon under control and the below decks flooding was contained. Twenty-one men had been killed and six wounded. With the aft end of her keel blown off and severe damage to her hull, *Stormes* was out of the war but not out of danger.

Radar Picket Station # 16A was patrolled by *Cowell, Ingersoll, Wren*, and *LCS(L)s 14, 17, 18,* and *90* on 24 May. Late in the evening, at about 2030, *Wren* picked up about fifteen small surface

A *Type 1 Model 1 Shinyo* suicide boat shown at Nagasaki in the fall of 1945. This particular type was used by the Japanese Navy. Within the bow as an explosive charge that was designed to detonate upon impact with the target. *NARA 127-GW-1523-140563.*

targets moving toward the formation at twenty knots. Assuming that they were suicide boats attempting to crash the picket ships, she took them under fire. One was seen to burn and others disappeared from the radar screens. *Wren* claimed one sunk and most of the others damaged, although some of the targets may have been reflectors placed in the water to mask the movement of the boats.

Early in the morning of the 25th, at 0130, *Wren* picked up an incoming bogey and took it under fire at 3,500 yards. It went down in flames near *Cowell*. Fifteen minutes later another bogey approached the formation and *Wren* fired on it as well. The enemy plane disappeared from the radar screen, leaving observers to believe that it had been splashed. The closest call for the ships came at 0845, when a Betty made a run on them. *Cowell, Ingersoll* and *Wren* opened up with their five-inch guns at a range of 9,980 yards. The Betty splashed between *Wren* and *Ingersoll*. It was one of twelve that had taken off from Kanoya laden with *Okas*. Fortunately for the picket ships, nine of them had to turn back after encountering bad weather. Another bogey was picked up at 0919 closing on the formation from fifteen miles out. Taken under fire by *Ingersoll*, the Tony made a suicide dive on the ship. Shells from the 20mm guns hit the pilot, killing him just as he began his dive. His plane passed over the ship and crashed fifteen feet off the starboard side. At 0945 1st Lt. D.R. Mahlberg of VMF-224 shot down a Jill to the south of the station.

Saturday, 26 May through Thursday, 31 May 1945

Damage to the picket ships had been severe. Part of the problem lay in the delayed establishment of land based radar installations that would eliminate many of the radar picket stations. At a meeting with Admiral Raymond Spruance on 26 May, Admiral Halsey was made aware of the problem. Later in the day he met with Lt. Gen. Simon B. Buckner and voiced the Navy's concerns over the problem. Buckner indicated that he would take immediate action to rectify the situation.[31] As a result, Iheya Shima was captured on 3 June and Aguni Shima on 9 June. Marine Air Warning Squadron 1 began operation on Iheya Shima on 9 July and on Aguni Shima on 29 June. On 3 July, Air Warning Squadron 8 began operating on Aguni Shima as well. Had they been established sooner, the installation at Iheya Shima would have provided relief for the ships at RP Stations # 1 and # 2 and the radar at Aguni might have taken the pressure off ships at RP Stations # 11A and # 16.

Commodore Moosbrugger moved his command to *Panamint*. *Biscayne* was needed by Rear Adm. L.F. Reifsnider for the attacks on Iheya Shima and Aguni Shima.

Kikusui # 8 was scheduled for 27 to 29 May and involved a total of 110 Japanese special attack aircraft, sixty from the navy and fifty from the army. Vice Admiral Ugaki wrote:

> In concert with the ninth general offensive against Okinawa by the Sixth Air Army, *Kikusui* No. 8 was ordered carried out. In addition to twenty medium-class trainers which will sortie at dusk as the spearhead, fifteen seaplanes will be sent as special attack aircraft. Besides them, six *Gingas* [Frances], eleven

heavy bombers, four *Tenzans* [Jills], and four land-based bombers will attack enemy vessels while six land bombers and eleven night fighters will be used to take command of the air over the north [Yontan] airfield.[32]

Patrolling on RP Station # 5 were *Braine*, *Anthony*, and *LCS(L)s 13*, *82*, *86*, and *123*. In the early daylight hours of 26 May, at 0830, *Braine* vectored the CAP towards incoming bogeys. They splashed two Tojos. Seven minutes elapsed before the next raid appeared, and both destroyers took the enemy plane under fire. It was a Betty with an *Oka* but the destroyers splashed it before the pilot could release its missile. No further action occurred on the 26th.

During the early daylight hours on 27 May, the fighter director in *Braine* received a request from the eight Thunderbolts flying CAP over the station. Foul weather was making it difficult for them to operate, and they asked for permission to return to their base on Ie Shima.[33] Shortly thereafter, at 0737, the ships at RP Station # 5 went to general quarters. *LCS(L) 123* sighted a Val closing on her from dead ahead. Taken under fire by the gunboat's twin 40mm guns, the Val turned off at 2,000 yards and headed for *Anthony*.

Fortunately the damage from *LCS(L) 123*'s guns was severe, and the enemy plane splashed astern the destroyer at 0750. Just prior to that time, at 0743, lookouts on *Braine* spotted another Val that ducked in and out of the clouds. A moment later it picked up the Val with two companions at a range of seven miles. One of them headed for *Anthony* and *Braine* took it under fire. In flames, the plane seemed to be out of control and *Braine* shifted its guns to a second Val, but the first plane passed over *Anthony* at an altitude of fifty feet, regained control and headed for *Braine*, she crashed her from dead ahead in the number 2 handling room.

A minute later, a second Val, hit by gunfire and aflame, crashed into *Braine* at frame 100. The plane's bomb penetrated the deck and exploded in the ship's sick bay. The blast destroyed a number of interior compartments and seriously damaged the bridge structure. Communications throughout the ship went down and fires started in a number of areas, effectively dividing the ship into three sections and making communications impossible. A third plane headed for *LCS(L) 86* but it was turned away by the ship's gunfire at 1,200 yards. It headed for *Anthony* instead. Hit repeatedly by fire from *LCS(L)s 86, 82,* and *123,* the plane wavered erratically and splashed 500 yards to starboard of the destroyer at 0808. *Braine* was out of control. With her steering damaged and on fire, she moved along at about ten knots. She almost ran down *LCS(L) 123* which was coming to her aid. Backing his ship's engines at full power, the gunboat's commanding officer, Lt. D.A. Oliver, Jr., watched as the destroyer crossed her bow ten yards away. Separated by the fires and explosions, men began to jump off *Braine.* This proved to be as hazardous as remaining on ship, as the waters were shark infested.

As Paul Conway, a Yeoman on *Braine,* was being rescued by one of the gunboats, he was confused as to why they were firing rifles. He soon found out that sharks were closing in on him and his crew mates. Others in the crew were not so lucky and the sharks took some of them. Frank Szymanek, a cook on *Braine,* watched in horror as one of his shipmates jumped into the waiting jaws of a shark.[34] *LCS(L) 82* gunners took their toll on the sharks with machine gun fire while other men on the gunboats blasted away with rifles. After the war John Rooney, a radioman on the *LCS(L) 82,* recalled: "We recovered one who had not made it, hanging pale and lifeless in his Mae West, a leg torn away, the other arm gone, gutted by the sharks . . .We machine-gunned the sharks. In their mindless savagery they started tearing each other apart, this time turning the ocean crimson with their own blood."[35] The LCS(L)s and *Anthony* undertook the task of picking up survivors and assisting the stricken ship. *Anthony,* which had come alongside *Braine,* began to assist with fire fighting. *LCS(L) 86* and *LCS(L) 82* tied up to the destroyer and put its firefighting equipment to work. By 0957 *LCS(L) 123* had put a boarding party aboard the destroyer to assist with fire fighting.

Many men from *Braine* had gone into the water and were quickly rescued by the support ships. With the confusion at the battle scene, not all were so lucky. Drifting away from *Braine* in the shark infested water were Steve Johnson RM 3/c, Earl F. Viens TM 1/c, Thomas J. Burke, S 1/c; Arthur L. Quinn, S 1/c; Thurman Lord, S 1/c; Lawrence B. Armor, Coxswain; Ernest Y. Thomason, RM 1/c; Homer L. Schutz, S 1/c; Robert J. Cornelius, RM 3/c, and Walter E. Teetsel, Coxswain. As they watched the battle they realized that they were too far from the ships to be seen.

Braine DD 630 underway. *NARA 80G 335070.*

Shortly after *Braine* had been hit, word spread back to the seaplane base at Kerama Retto. The seaplane tender *Hamlin AV 15* sent out three PBM-5 Mariners to search the area. They took off at 0837. One Mariner, piloted by Lt. M.W. Kouns, arrived over the station at 0917 and quickly spotted the men in the water. He set his Dumbo down about 1,000 feet away. Within fifteen minutes, the plane had picked up all the men and taken off for its base. Teetsel, who had sustained burns and other wounds, died as he was being transferred to the hospital ship.[36]

Anthony had to cast off about noon with enemy planes in the area. Fortunately none attacked the ships. *Anthony* had also suffered some damage from the near miss by the suicide plane. She began the job of towing *Braine* back to Kerama Retto and was met by the fleet tug *Ute* which completed the task. It had been a terrible day for the picket ships. *Braine* suffered sixty-seven killed and 103 wounded. The wounded picked up by the gunboats were transferred to *Anthony* for transport back to the anchorage.

Replacing the two destroyers at RP Station # 5 on 27 May were *William D. Porter* and *Massey*. *Massey* reported in at 1120 and *William D. Porter* at 1300. *Dyson*, which had arrived on the station with *Massey*, escorted *Braine* back to the anchorage.

The following day, 28 May, the station was approached by two bogeys at 0103. After *Porter* fired on one, they both turned away. At 0730 an incoming Tojo was picked up on radar. A division of VMF-323 Corsairs was sent to intercept it. First Lt. D.L. Davis and 2d Lt. R.J. Woods teamed up and shot it down eight miles east of the ships.

Pritchett, Aulick, and *LCS(L)s 11, 20, 92* and *122* patrolled RP Station # 9. Early on 28 May, at 0050, *Aulick* picked up an incoming Betty at eight miles. *Aulick* and *Pritchett* took it under fire at 0105 without scoring any hits. The bomber went to a low altitude of about thirty feet to avoid the ships' gunfire, placing it on a course directly at *LCS(L) 122*. *LCS(L) 122* opened fire at a range of 800 yards, scoring hits with 20mm rounds. *LCS(L) 20* got in a few shots as well until the destroyers got in the line of fire. Unfortunately this was not sufficient to down the aircraft, and it disappeared into the overcast sky dropping window as it retreated.

Patrolling the station on the 29th were *Dyson, Aulick, Pritchett, LCS(L)s 11, 20, 92*, and *122*. At 1915, the ships again

Damage to *Braine DD 630* after a kamikaze hit on Radar Picket Station # 5 on 27 May 1945. *U.S.S. Braine DD 630 Action Report of 8 June 1945.*

went to GQ with three Zekes attacking the formation. *LCS(L)s 20* and *92* spotted the first coming in at an altitude of seventy-five feet heading for the destroyers. They opened fire with their guns and hit the lead plane, sending it crashing into the ocean in flames. The second Zeke, about a quarter mile behind the other, was also taken under fire by *LCS(L)s 20, 92,* and *122,* all of which scored hits.

The destroyers also got a piece of the action. The Zeke, hit by fire from several ships went out of control. It nearly hit the water but then gained altitude. Passing close over the stacks of *Pritchett,* the enemy plane went out of control again. According to *Pritchett's* action report, the plane: "hooked a wing in the water about 200 yards from the ships, bounced, and finally crashed and sank about 500 yards to port, nearly in line with USS AULICK. In the meantime, the third ZEKE had come in on the starboard quarter and had been taken under fire by the after 40mm, 20mm, and .50 caliber guns"[37] of *Pritchett* and also by other ships. The Zeke went into the water 800 yards behind *Pritchett.* With the action over, the ships resumed patrol. Later, at 2035, bogeys were again reported in the area but none closed on the station. *Bennion* reported in at 2135 and relieved *Pritchett* of fighter director duties.

May 30 was uneventful. Early in the morning of the 31st, at 0358, *Dyson* fired on a bogey and turned it away. *Willard Keith* relieved *Aulick* at 0847. The daylight hours were non-threatening, but at 1449 bogeys were again in the area. Spotting one on radar at a range of twenty-five miles, the ships awaited the next attack. They did not have long to wait. A Frances made a run on the station. Four Corsairs chased it into the guns of the ships and it was hit by fire from all three destroyers. It went down in flames 200 yards off *LCS(L) 20's* starboard quarter. The ships soon secured from general quarters and awaited the arrival of 1 June.

Patrolling RP Station # 11A on 27 May were *Wadsworth,* *Sproston* and *LCS(L)s 54, 83, 84,* and *115.* The daylight hours were quiet, but the evening of the 27th to the 28th was much different. Between 2229 and 2328 several enemy planes made runs on the ships but were driven off by gunfire. *Wadsworth* directed a night fighter toward the last plane and it reported shooting down a Hamp nine miles from the station. *LCS(L) 83* reported firing on two or three planes to her east.[38] At 0016 on the 28th· general quarters was sounded with several bogeys approaching the station. Coming in from over Kume Shima was a twin engine plane believed to be a Betty. The gunboats took it under fire first at 0040 but were unable to score. After the Betty passed astern the LCS(L) formation, the destroyers opened fire and *Wadsworth* reported splashing it. At about the same time the destroyers reported that they had shot down a Kate at 0045 that was closing on the formation. About an hour later, at 0135, four Kates approached the LCS(L) formation from astern. *LCS(L) 115* shot down one enemy plane, and a few minutes later, assisted the *84* in shooting a second. Other aircraft were in the vicinity for the remainder of the night, giving the crews no respite from their ordeal.

Near the end of the day at 2357 *Bradford,* which had relieved *Wadsworth* at 1746, picked up bogeys at thirteen miles. *Shubrick,* which was heading for a new RP Station, # 16A, was called for a confirmation. Unable to reach *Shubrick*, *Bradford* watched the raid split into two, with one plane coming toward her and the other heading for *Shubrick*. Meanwhile, *Shubrick* had spotted the plane herself, and watched as the ships at RP Station # 11A took it under fire without hitting it. She slowed to ten knots in an attempt to keep the plane from noticing her wake. This trick did not work and, within minutes, it was obvious that the plane was making a suicide run on her. At 0010 *Shubrick* went to twenty-five knots and took the enemy plane under fire, splashing it at 3,500 yards. A second plane then attacked the destroyer, striking her in the starboard quarter. The plane carried a 500 pound bomb which blew a thirty foot hole in the main deck. It also blew open the starboard side of the ship, and the after engine room and fire rooms began to flood. Ammunition from the 40mm and 20mm gun tubs that had been hit began to explode and shrapnel sprayed over the deck. At 0029 a depth charge that was heated by the fires went off, causing additional damage and killing one man. The force of the blast extinguished most of the fires in the area, but *Shubrick* was already down by the stern and listing three degrees to port. Topside gear was jettisoned to improve her stability. At 0013 *Van Valkenburgh,* which had been patrolling on RP Station # 16A, came alongside and began to take off the wounded.

By 0130 the destroyer's fantail was awash and the ship was in danger of sinking. Handy-billies supplied by *Van Valkenburgh* slowly brought the flooding under control and, with the arrival of more pumps on the high speed transport *Pavlic,* the situation began to improve. The fleet tug *Menominee* arrived at 0400 and prepared to tow *Shubrick* back to Kerama Retto. It was not an easy trip back to the harbor. The wind increased to eighteen knots and put some of the pumps out of commission, increasing the flooding once again. *Shubrick* was finally able to anchor in Kerama Retto at 1339. Her first task was to build a cofferdam to allow the rescue of three men who had been trapped in the handling room for over twenty hours. Her casualties for the day were eleven dead, one officer and twenty men missing and one officer and twenty-seven men wounded in action. *Shubrick* was out of the war. She headed back to the States on 15 July and was decommissioned on 16 November.

About the same time that *Shubrick* was under attack, *Bradford* was attacked by a plane from the same raid. At 0007 she splashed the enemy plane 200 yards astern. Accompanied by *Sproston,* she headed for *Shubrick* to render assistance. They rescued several survivors and transferred them to *Pavlic.* The radar picket patrol arrived at 0530 and was directed to search the area for survivors. The search turned out negative.

At RP Station # 15A on 27 May were *Ammen, Boyd, LCS(L)s 52, 55, 56,* and *61.* The low ceiling remained over the station but it cleared in the afternoon. At 1739 *Ammen* picked up four incoming enemy aircraft and vectored the CAP to intercept them. They turned away, thwarting the CAP's efforts.

The sun set at 1918 and the CAP headed back to base a few minutes later. The coast was clear for the Japanese attackers. At 2028 the destroyers turned away an incoming plane with their gunfire after it had closed to 3,000 yards. Still another plane approached the station and was driven off at 2047. Destroyer men would be safe that night, but not so those on the gunboats. At 2221 the destroyers picked up a Zeke at four miles and they, along with the LCS(L)s, took it under fire.

The Zeke turned away from the destroyers, came in from astern the gunboats, passing over *LCS(L) 61*, which scored numerous hits on it. As the enemy plane continued on, heading for a crash into *LCS(L) 52,* the combined gunfire of the two ships knocked it off course, but both the plane and its bomb exploded only 20 yards off the ship's starboard quarter.

It had been a close call for *LCS(L) 52* and it was costly. One officer was killed and another wounded, along with nine enlisted men. *LCS(L) 61* moved in to assist the stricken gunboat as another plane made a run on them. The gunboats drove it away.

LCS(L) 52 was ordered back to port for repairs and transfer of dead and wounded. LCS(L) 61 was assigned to escort her back, but the gunboats would not have an easy journey. Shortly after they left the station, four bogeys appeared near the two LCS(L)s and one made a run on the ships. The plane, a twin engine Betty bomber, came in from astern and LCS(L) 52 took it under fire at 2,000 yards. Firing from the 52 was sporadic and the Betty passed over her and headed for LCS(L) 61, which also took her under fire. The commanding officer of LCS(L) 61, Jim Kelley, watched from his position on the conn as the Betty headed right for his ship. Under fire from the aft twin 40mm guns, the plane appeared headed directly for the conning tower. At the last moment, Kelley gave the order for hard left rudder and Quartermaster Bob Rielly turned the wheel sharply. The gunboat made a radical turn to port and the Betty passed close over the ship, crashing into the water only twenty feet off the starboard bow.[39] The crash of the plane, coupled with the extreme heel of the ship caused by the sharp turn, led crewmen to believe that they had been hit. Gasoline and debris showered the ship, but it quickly righted itself and continued on. The impact with the water broke the Betty apart and a section of the tail bounced back onto the bow of the ship where it knocked out Boatswain Joe Columbus. The pilot's parachute was found on the foredeck. The ships continued back to the anchorage without further incident.

At 0410 on the 28th, Drexler and Lowry relieved Ammen and Boyd. The departure of LCS(L)s 52 and 61 left only two destroyers and two gunboats on the station. It was a clear day with a calm sea, the type that sailors preferred and kamikazes did not. At 0643 incoming bogeys were picked up by the Drexler's SC-Radar. The CAP planes reported that it was a PBM, but it soon became obvious that they were mistaken. Twin engine Japanese planes, identified as either Franceses or Nicks, were seen at a high altitude and the destroyers maneuvered to bring them abeam. At about the same time, 1st Lt. R. Brown and 2d Lt. J.B. Seaman, of VMF-322, spotted the planes and began their attack. By the time it was over, Brown and Seaman had shot down two and damaged two others. Unfortunately, one of the enemy planes dropped altitude and made a run on the destroyers. Drexler and Lowry opened fire as it aimed for Lowry. Drexler's action report indicated that the plane, hit by numerous shells, passed over Lowry and hit her. Serious damage to the starboard side of the ship had occurred. The after fire room was put out of action and two of the 40mm guns were knocked out. Gasoline from the plane started fires but they were quickly extinguished.

Lowry came under attack next, with another of the twin engine planes heading straight for her. The enemy plane was hit by fire from both destroyers and crashed into the sea astern of the *Lowry*. At 0703 a third enemy plane came in from starboard. *Drexler's* guns fired on it but could not keep on target. The plane circled and made a run on the ship from dead ahead. The two VMF-322 Corsairs, piloted by Brown and Seaman, braved the antiaircraft fire from the ship and followed her in. Caught between the fire of the CAP and the ship, the bomber appeared ready to splash but it managed to right itself, circle again and crash into the superstructure deck amidships.

Estimates were that the plane carried a two thousand pound bomb load. Their detonation blew the sides of the ship out and *Drexler* began to list rapidly to starboard. In less than a minute after the second crash, *Drexler* turned on her side and slid beneath the waves stern first.[40] The rapidity of the sinking left many men trapped below.

Lowry, under attack again, intercepted enemy planes at 0718 and 0838, and the CAP splashed a Val at 0842. During this time, a division of VMF-323 Corsairs from Kadena, led by 1st Lt. Del Davis, was cruising in the area. *Lowry* vectored the four planes forty miles to the east of Point Bolo and they soon spotted a Tojo headed for the picket ships. Davis and his wingman, 2d Lt. Robert Woods, dove to an altitude of only 300 feet and spotted the enemy plane on a course toward RP Station # 15A. They took it under fire. The Tojo dove for the deck with the two Corsairs on its tail. Alternating bursts from Davis and Woods flamed the plane and it exploded.[41]

LCS(L) 114, which had arrived in the midst of the melee, assisted the *55* and *56* in picking up survivors. *Watts* and *Wren* joined the formation for support at 0915. After collecting all the survivors, *Watts* headed back to the anchorage. *Drexler* suffered 158 killed and fifty-one wounded. *Lowry's* action report indicated that the toll for the day was "Two planes destroyed by A/A, 5 planes destroyed by CAP, 2 planes suicided USS DREXLER."[42]

Commander R.L. Wilson, the CO of *Drexler* reported:

Crewmen begin repair work on *Shubrick DD 639* at Kerama Retto on 30 May 1945. She was hit by a kamikaze the day before while she was on her way to Radar Picket Station # 16A. *NARA 80G 331221.*

This attack was well coordinated and determined. There is no doubt that the objective on that morning was the destroyers in Radar Picket Station 15. It was not a surprise attack; however, it is interesting to note that the Japs were down a little earlier in the morning than usual. The pilots were not amateurs or hurriedly graduated students; they were good pilots and knew how to handle their planes.[43]

Radar Picket Station # 16A was patrolled by *Robert H. Smith*, *Shannon*, and *LCS(L)s 14*, *17*, *18*, and *21*. Daylight hours on the 27th were quiet, with some activity reported on nearby stations. However, in the evening hours the ships saw some action. Between 1949 and 2235 bogeys were reported but did not close the station. At 2232 an incoming bogey caused the ships to change course and speed and *Shannon* and *Robert H. Smith* took it under fire. It was splashed by fire from *Shannon* on her starboard beam at 2308.

Early the next morning, at 0026, a raid of four to six planes came toward the station. *Smith* and *Shannon* fired on them and turned them away. *Robert H. Smith* then spotted two planes coming at her from her starboard beam and her starboard quarter. Both were splashed at 0127. Within the next half hour several more bogeys approached the ships and were driven off by their fire.

May had been a deadly month for the radar picket ships. *Little, Luce, Morrison, Drexler,* and *LSM(R)s 190, 194,* and *195* had been sunk by kamikazes. *Aaron Ward, Anthony, Macomb, Gwin, Ingraham, Shea, Hugh W. Hadley, Lowry, Evans, Bache, Douglas H. Fox, Stormes, Braine, Shubrick, LSM(R) 192,* and *LCS(L)s 25, 31, 52, 88,* and *121* had been damaged. Of the damaged ships, *Aaron Ward, Hugh W. Hadley,* and *Evans* were finished. They would eventually be decommissioned and scrapped. *LCS(L) 88, Ingraham, Shea, Bache,* and *Douglas H. Fox* were out of the war; their repairs would not be completed until it was over. Naval personnel losses on the radar picket stations were 870 killed and 834 wounded.

Elsewhere around Okinawa, the kamikazes had taken their toll. From 13 May through 31 May, three ships had been sunk and fourteen damaged. The carrier *Enterprise* was put out of the war and suffered thirteen dead and sixty-eight wounded. Total casualties for the other ships during the period were 139 killed and 366 wounded.[44]

The great sacrifice of the picket ships was recognized. On 29 May, CTF 31 sent the following message:

DURING THE RECENT ATTACKS THIS FORCE HAS AGAIN DEMONSTRATED ITS ALERTNESS AND EFFICIENCY BY KNOCKING OUT THE MAJORITY OF JAP PLANES SENT AGAINST IT X THE TOTAL FOR THE PAST TWO DAYS IS NOT MORE THAN 115 X AGAIN THE PICKETS, MIGHTY MIDGETS [nickname for LCS(L) ships] AND SCREEN HAVE BORN THE BRUNT OF THE ATTACK AND BY THEIR SHARPSHOOTING AND INTESTINAL FORTITUDE HAVE ADDED TO THE ALREADY GLORIOUS TRADITIONS OF THE OKINAWA CAMPAIGN X ALSO TO THE COMBAT AIR PATROL AND SALVAGE GROUPS WE TIP OUR HATS FOR THEIR SPLENDID PERFORMANCE UNDER THE MOST DIFFICULT CONDITIONS X YOU ARE LICKING THE JAPS AND THEY KNOW IT X A HEARTY WELL DONE TO ALL HANDS.[45]

CHAPTER 7

"For conspicuous gallantry . . ."

The month of June would see an end to the campaign for Okinawa, but not an end to the kamikaze missions. Although *Kikusuis # 9* and *# 10* would occupy the radar picket ships for several days, the numbers of special attack planes had dwindled. Where once the Japanese sent hundreds of planes against the American ships, they now began to hold back. In the two *Kikusui* raids in June, only ninety-five special attack planes were sent out. Air raids continued, but the Japanese realized that the battle for Okinawa was lost and that the home islands would be the next target. Consequently, they began to conserve their air power for what would be the final battle, the invasion of Japan.

Friday, 1 June and Saturday, 2 June 1945

Robert H. Smith, Thomas E. Fraser, Cassin Young, and *LCS(L)s 16, 54, 83*, and *84*, patrolled RP Station # 11A on 1 June. In the early evening, at 1917, the ships went to general quarters. Unfortunately, the CAP was sent back to its base shortly thereafter at 1932. Within minutes an enemy plane came in from astern and made a torpedo run on *Robert H. Smith*. The light minelayer maneuvered to dodge the torpedo and took the aircraft under fire. The LCS(L)s saw the plane as it passed about 3,000 yards off their port beam and took it under fire without hitting it. A second plane came in from starboard and dropped another torpedo and *Robert H. Smith* again turned to avoid being hit. Gunfire forced the second plane to turn away. At 1953 a third plane appeared dead ahead of the *Smith* and was fired on as well, but it was heading away from the ships. It had been a close call for the minelayer. She had successfully dodged two torpedoes. The ships secured from general quarters at 0058 the next morning.

Sunday, 3 June through Thursday, 7 June 1945

American intelligence reported that the "Japanese Navy has formed two new fighter commands. Air Flotilla 71 comprises all Naval fighter units in the Tokyo and Nagoya areas; Air Flotilla 72, commanding Naval fighter units in Kyushu, is responsible for (i) interception over Kyushu and western Honshu and (ii) participation in operations in the Ryukyus."[1] The reports further noted that Omura, Fukuoka, and Saitozaki fields on Kyushu would be used as fueling bases.

Kikusui # 9 ran from 3 to 7 June and included a total of fifty special attack planes, thirty from the army and twenty from the navy. It was planned to coincide with the army's 10th General Attack plan. June would also prove to be a dangerous month for the picket ships.

Patrolling RP Station # 5 on 3 June were *Ammen, Guest, Fullam,* and *LCS(L)s 67, 87, 93,* and *94.* June 3 dawned with a cloudy sky, intermittent showers and a calm sea. At 0915 and again at 1316, enemy aircraft were reported in the area and the ships went to general quarters.

A raid was detected thirty-four miles north of the station and *Ammen* directed the CAP to intercept it. Three VMF-323 Corsairs led by 1st Lt. C.E. Spangler were vectored to intercept the Japanese planes. They caught up with them near the picket station and the battle was on.

The enemy group consisted of six Vals and one Nate. Spangler shot down a Val and 1st Lt. S.C. Alley shot down three. Second Lt. Dewey Durnford shot down a Val and the Nate. Two Corsairs from VMF-441 were flying radar picket patrol over the ships. They had been vectored to the area to assist in the interception. One was piloted by 1st Lt. M.M. FiField who splashed a Val during the action. Second Lt. James R. Rector spotted a Val heading toward the picket ships at an altitude of 200 feet. He dove for the attack and splashed it. When it was over, *Ammen* reported that the CAP had shot down six Vals with bombs as well as one Nate and one Tojo. The group of six Vals had flown from Kokubu #2 field on Kyushu bent on attacking the ships at Okinawa.

A division of army air force P-47N Thunderbolts from the 333rd Fighter Squadron was also flying CAP in the area. At about 1345 Capt. Art Bowen and his wingman, Lt. Albert, were cruising at 500 feet when Albert spotted two Nates and went after them; one of the planes ducked into a cloud and the other dove. In his eagerness to get the Japanese plane, Albert crashed into the sea as one of the Nates made a sharp turn to avoid his fire. Lieutenants Sadler and Ellis gave chase and the Nate was splashed by Sadler. Bowen, after seeing his wingman crash, went up after another Nate and scored some hits but lost sight of the plane in the clouds. He observed another Nate in the area being shot down by the tail gunner of a PB2Y. It was one of the two Nates first spotted by the fliers which had escaped by taking cover in the clouds.

Another VMF-441 Corsair, piloted by 2d Lt. Robert L. Gibson, had also been assigned radar picket patrol over the ships. He joined with 1st Lt. Malcolm M. Fifield. At 1350 they were vectored north to the battle scene. They spotted two Nates and a Val heading south at an altitude of 500 feet and dove to attack. Fifield hit the Nate in the cockpit and then hit the Val in the engine and left wing. Both crashed into the sea. They observed the second Nate shot down by the other Corsairs in the area.

Reports of a typhoon circulated throughout the American fleet. *Lowry* and *Rowe* relieved *Fullam* and *Ammen* at about 1700, but the ships were soon ordered back to port to ride out the storm. At 0845 the next morning the ships were back on radar picket duty.

Patrolling RP Station # 5 on 6 June were *Wren, Lowry, Rowe,* and *LCS(L)s 17, 67, 87,* and *93.* Later in the afternoon of the 6th, at 1710, incoming bogeys appeared on the radar screens. The CAP, which had taken off from Ie Shima at 1504, was from VMF-422. It was led by 1st Lt. R.A. Wrisley and included 1st Lts. E.H. Spinas, E.C. Harper, and D.A. Weston. At 1700 the radar picket ships picked up bogeys south of the station and *Rowe* vectored the CAP to investigate. Within a few minutes they spotted a Val at a low altitude and the chase was on. Wrisley got off a single burst but Corsairs from another squadron beat him to the plane and shot it down. Wrisley's division climbed to 4,000 feet and headed back toward the Chimu Peninsula.

At 1900 on the 7th, bogeys were detected at a range of twenty-four miles and then disappeared from the screen. This was a common occurrence, as planes approaching the station frequently

P-47N Thunderbolts of the 507th Fighter Group line the field at Ie Shima in mid-July 1945. *NARA 58185 AC.*

dropped to a low altitude of fifty to one hundred feet off the water in order to escape detection. In this case, the tactic allowed the enemy planes to get within 13,000 yards of the ships before they were spotted. Two Vals were making a run on the destroyers from their starboard side. All three of the destroyers opened fire and the first Val splashed between *Rowe* and *Lowry* and the second astern the three ships. *Kikusui # 9* was underway but the ships at RP Station # 5 had been spared.

In the early evening of 6 June, RP Station #9 came under attack. Patrolling there were *Stoddard, Massey, Claxton*, and *LCS(L)s 12, 85, 117*, and *123*. At 1627 *Claxton* picked up an incoming raid at fifteen miles and vectored the combat air patrol in its direction. Two Tonys flying close to the water were shot down at a distance of eleven and eight miles from the station.

At about the same time, four Thunderbolts from the 19th Fighter Squadron were on combat air patrol just to the north near Kume Shima. Led by Maj. Charles W. Tennant, the flight included Lt. Col. Harry E. McAfee and 1st Lts. Charles S. Marcinko and

Cuneo. They spotted a Judy at 3,000 feet heading towards the station and McAfee flamed it.[2] More incoming bogeys were picked up by *Massey* at 1854. *Massey* relayed the word to the other destroyers which were not able to detect them until they had closed to seven miles. Four planes were in the raid, one Val, and three Zekes. Soon two Zekes were observed making a run on *Massey's* port beam. She took them under fire but had to stop when two Corsairs got in the way. Resuming fire at a range of 7,000 yards, *Massey's* 20mm and 40mm guns scored hits. The first plane passed astern *Massey* and was taken under fire by *Stoddard* and *LCS(L) 117*; it crashed into the water at 1902. The second plane also passed astern *Massey* and crashed forty yards off her starboard quarter. The Val attempted to come in from behind the formation but *Stoddard* and *Claxton* caught it in a crossfire and splashed it. The fourth plane, a Zeke, made a dive on *Massey,* which maneuvered to bring its guns to bear. It was chased by a Corsair which was nearly hit by fire from the destroyer. *Massey* splashed the Zeke 1,500 yards off its starboard quarter.

The intense anti-aircraft fire from the ships made it impossible for at least one division of VMF-314 Corsairs to approach the station and they took off for Amami O Shima. Two divisions remained and 1st Lt. E.F. Wall of VMF-314 splashed a Sonia ten miles west of Yokoate Shima. *LCS 85* splashed one Dinah and, assisted by other LCSs, got another Tony. *LCS(L) 12* was attacked from astern. Her gunfire caused the plane to miss her and it splashed only fifty feet off her bow. It was a close call.

With the danger over and night closing in, the VMF-314 planes headed back to base about 1925. Other Corsair divisions from VMF-113 and VMF-422 remained overhead. At about the same time that the VMF-314 planes were leaving, the VMF-113 Corsairs were vectored west toward a bogey. Corsairs from VMF-422 remained with the picket ships.

Reports came back that in the diminishing daylight, the VMF-113 planes had missed the bogey and those from VMF-422 were sent intercept the enemy plane. The reports proved to be inaccurate. Five miles from the ships they spotted a twin engine Frances with a flaming starboard engine.

The Frances jettisoned its bombs and dropped to an altitude of fifty feet. Hot on its tail were two VMF-113 Corsairs. The four planes from VMF-422 attacked from a front angle and hit it with several bursts. However, VMF-113 got credit for shooting down the Frances.[3]

About the same time a new group of bogeys, first reported as Vals, was picked up closing on the station at 1933. The destroyers maneuvered as five planes approached the formation at a low altitude. At nine miles out the raid split, with two enemy planes coming directly at the ships, two circling north and the fifth remaining out of range. *Massey* and *Claxton* went to thirty knots and took the planes to the north under fire.

Claxton had a close call as a Dinah made a dive on her. The Dinah sustained a number of hits from the 40mm, 20mm and 5" guns and splashed only ten yards off *Claxton's* starboard quarter. Her crew felt their luck was holding since the plane's bombs failed to explode. If they had exploded, the damage to the destroyer would have been severe.

With the attacks escalating, the CAP was called back to protect the ships and they arrived at about 1945. *Massey* spotted two more bandits at four and seven miles and took them under fire; both went down in flames. Another enemy plane escaped to the west and night fighters were sent after it. *LCS(L) 12* was firing on these planes when she spotted another enemy plane at 4,000 yards making a dive on her from dead ahead. She took it under fire with her twin 40mm and 20mm guns and the plane passed over her by about ten feet, crashing twenty-five feet astern. June 6 had been a dangerous day for the ships at RP Station # 9 but they had managed to come through unscathed.

Wadsworth relieved *Claxton* at 1417 on the 7th. The ships went to general quarters several times in the early morning and daylight hours without encountering the enemy. At 1820 *Massey* reported a bogey closing on the station, and *Wadsworth* vectored a division of VMF-113 Corsairs to intercept the twin engine Nick. The division, led by 1st Lt. W.F. Bland, included 1st Lts. B.N. Tuttle and R.F. Scott and 2d Lt. H.L. Mixon. They spotted the Nick at 2,500 feet and climbed to attack it. Scott's burst missed the plane but Bland and Tuttle hit it in the fuselage and knocked out the port engine. The Japanese pilot jettisoned his bombs and tried to evade further damage. He turned toward the picket station in an obvious attempt to make a run on *Wadsworth*, but the Corsair shot it down. Bland was credited with the kill. The day passed without further enemy action.

Radar Picket Station # 11A was patrolled by *Robert H. Smith*, *Thomas E. Fraser*, *Cassin Young*, and *LCS(L)s 16, 54, 83*, and *84* on 3 June. During the early morning hours, between 0215 and 0358, several bogeys appeared on the screens but turned away from the ships and did not engage them. The remainder of the morning hours held no action.

While the destroyers were busy looking for enemy planes, the LCS(L)s found them. The four LCS(L)s were steaming in a diamond formation three miles to the east. At 1330 *LCS(L) 16*, in the lead, spotted a Zeke dodging in and out of the clouds. The enemy plane reappeared a couple of minutes later and did a wing over, heading for *LCS(L) 54* in a crash dive. Under fire from *LCS(L)s 16* and *54*, it veered away from *54* and headed for *16*, crashing into the water fifty feet to port of the gunboat. *LCS(L) 16* got credit for the kill with *54* getting an assist. A moment later, another enemy plane appeared and the gunboats turned it away with their fire. Within a few minutes, observers on the gunboats saw two Corsairs shoot down an enemy plane dead ahead of the formation. Two other enemy planes were reported splashed by the CAP near the station but, due to the clouds, they were not seen by the ship's crews. As frequently happened during the heat of combat, confusion reigned over the type of plane, with ships reporting the aircraft as either a Zeke or an Oscar. By 1450 the ships had secured from general quarters but were soon back on alert. At 1802 a raid was reported at seventy-five miles and the CAP was sent to intercept it. They reported splashing two Bettys. At 1915 the ships headed for their night patrol location.

On 5 June RP Station # 11A was patrolled by *Cassin Young*, *Smalley*, *Van Valkenburgh*, and *LCS(L)s 13, 14, 16*, and *21*. At 1950 two enemy planes dove on the destroyers and were taken under fire. At 2012 three more enemy planes attacked the station and *Smalley* fired on one. All of the enemy planes escaped unharmed.

Ingersoll joined the station at 1740 on the 7th. At 1852 a low flying plane approached the ships and was splashed by the CAP a few minutes later. Another bogey was spotted over Kume Shima and the CAP was vectored to intercept it. The enemy plane was shot down at 1908. The seven ships continued their patrol through 9 June when *Smalley* was relieved by *Harry E. Hubbard,* and *Pritchett* relieved *Cassin Young* at 0927. The ships went to general quarters at 1919 with the approach of two enemy planes. During the next twenty minutes the CAP shot down both of them seven to eight miles from the ships.

The invasion of Iheya Shima that took place on 3 June required extra radar picket protection for the invading ships. A special station was set up five miles to the north of the island. It was approximately twenty miles due east of RP Station # 15A and about ten miles south of a position about halfway between RP Stations # 1 and 2. Beginning at 1000 on 3 June, *Gainard*, along with the destroyer escort *Edmonds*, began to patrol it. *Gainard* had a fighter director team on board and was assigned a CAP of eight planes with an additional two to fly radar picket patrol. Many bogeys were picked up at 1215 but were intercepted and shot down by CAP aircraft controlled by the ships at RP Station # 15A. At various times additional aircraft were sent to the area and at the peak of the action, *Gainard* controlled twenty-eight planes. A total of forty-five enemy planes went down during the fray, with twelve Zekes shot down by the two divisions originally assigned to *Gainard* and a Val shot down by their radar picket patrol aircraft.

One of the divisions from VMF-113 at Ie Shima was vectored to the north at about 1330. The division, led by Capt. Robert Dailey, included 1st Lt. K. Flynn and 2d Lts. J.L. Scott and R.J. Munro. They encountered about twenty Zekes at 16,000 feet. As they climbed to meet them, seven of the planes were chased downward by other Corsairs and got into a dogfight with them. The division passed by the first two and fired upon them with undetermined results. Immediately, two more appeared in front of them. Scott followed one down to 10,000 feet and shot it down. Daily and Munro were on the tail of another Zeke. Through evasive maneuvers it managed to escape Dailey's fire, but Munro hit it with a burst. As the Zeke made a dive to the water and pulled up, Flynn hit the enemy plane with a full deflection burst and then hit it again from head on. The plane began to smoke. Daily and Munro once again fired into the plane and its engine went out. The Zeke made a water landing and the pilot tried to exit the plane only to be killed by fire from Dailey's guns. Flynn was credited with the kill. With the securing of Iheya Shima, the special radar picket station was closed late in the day on 7 June.

On 3 June Radar Picket Station # 15A was patrolled by *Wadsworth*, *Cogswell*, *Caperton*, and *LCS(L)s 55, 56, 66,* and *114.*

The ships went to general quarters at 0215 as numerous planes appeared on their radar screens. Night fighters in the area were alerted and within minutes they had splashed three enemy planes. Morning came and the ships had a brief respite before the enemy approached again. At 1235 *Wadsworth* picked up an incoming raid consisting of six planes. She vectored the CAP Corsairs to the north and they reported splashing one Kate and one Val. This broke up the group and they began to approach the station on individual courses. At 1235 one of the planes appeared heading for the ships from the south. Two Corsairs from VMF-441 at Yontan were assigned to fly radar picket patrol over the station. *Wadsworth* vectored them to pick the incoming Val. First Lt. Robert C. Bennett got in a few hits on the plane before overrunning it. His wingman, 2d Lt. James R. Rector, followed up the attack, scoring 20mm hits on the cockpit and engine. *LCS(L) 55* took it under fire and the Val went out of control and crashed.

One division of VMF-323 Corsairs was flying in company with a division from MAG-22 on Ie Shima when they were vectored to intercept an incoming raid. Within minutes, the Corsairs ran into a flight of twenty-five Zekes heading for the landing beaches at Iheya Shima. The VMF-323 division, led by 1st Lt. Cy Dolezel, also included 1st Lt. Al Wells and Bill Drake and 2d Lt. Jerry Connors. They soon got into a dogfight with twelve of the Zekes. Outnumbered three to one, the four pilots were on their own as the enemy swirled about them. In a raging battle, the Corsairs knocked down nine of the enemy planes, with Drake getting four kills and one probable, Connors and Wells two each and Dolezel one. Drake's instruments were knocked out in the melee and he called for help, but his squadron could not locate him. Fortunately the army air force did. After dropping his altitude in an attempt to find his way, Drake was spotted by a division of P-47N Thunderbolts, which promptly dove on him. Drake maneuvered his Corsair so that they could identify him and they broke off their attack. The Thunderbolts escorted him back to Kadena.[4] Dolezel's plane was also hit by a 20mm shell which struck the armor plate behind the cockpit. The shot stunned Dolezel but he quickly recovered, grateful to the plane's designers for the armor plating.

At 1310 a large group of bogeys was picked up at a range of sixty miles and the CAP was vectored to meet them. At 1315 a division of VMF-314 Corsairs, led by 1st Lt. Charles W. Egan, intercepted a Hamp at 3,000 feet. As the Corsairs went after it, the Hamp dropped its wheels in an attempt to slow down. The result was that all four Corsairs overran it. Egan peeled off to the left and got on its tail again. After he hit it in the wings and cowling it went down. Other CAP planes splashed a Kate, a Zeke and a Val. Twelve minutes later, two Vals appeared headed for the ships at a range of 7,000 yards. The CAP splashed one, but the other began a strafing run on *LCS(L) 114*, which promptly opened fire. With the CAP chasing the plane, *114* had to cease fire but resumed it after the CAP had made a pass. Gunfire from *114* drove it off, but only briefly. The Val circled and made a suicide run on *LCS(L) 56*. Both *56* and *114* scored hits, but *56* had a deadlier aim and splashed the Val 200 feet off her port bow.

Still another enemy plane was shot down by the CAP at 1330 just to the north of the gunboats. First Lt. Elbert E. Rutledge's VMF-314 division had taken off from Ie Shima at 0920. They spotted a Jill at 800 feet and all four planes went after it. Its rear gunner fired back, hitting 1st Lt. Maxwell M. Westover's plane. After many maneuvers by the Jill and bursts fired by all of the Corsairs, it finally went down in flames. It had been hit so many times that it was impossible to determine who should get the kill. In typical American fashion, the pilots flipped a coin. Rutledge won the toss and was given credit.[5] A few minutes later, a Val came at *Caperton* from dead ahead, strafing as it made its suicide run. The attack occurred so suddenly that the only guns able to open fire were .50 caliber machine guns. Fortunately their aim was true and the Val missed the destroyer, crashing only twenty yards astern. A second Val, cruising overhead made a steep dive on *Caperton*, which opened fire, hitting it with her 5"/38 and 40mm guns. *Wadsworth* also hit the plane and the Val splashed close aboard *Caperton's* port beam. A few minutes later the combined fire of both destroyers shot down an Oscar.

Meanwhile, the combat air patrol was still busy. At 1345, VMF-314 1st Lts. Charles W. Egan and Bruce J. Thomas intercepted another Val at 7,000 feet heading for the picket ships. As they started their run, the Val turned and passed them head on, not affording them a chance to shoot. The enemy plane came up behind Thomas. Meanwhile, 1st Lt. James A. Klein, the division leader, had followed the action. Klein hit the Val's fuselage and wing roots with his 20mm cannons. The kamikaze turned into a ball of fire and exploded in mid-air. A half hour later, at 1415, the VMF-314 pilots claimed their last kill for the day. They intercepted another Val at 7,000 feet. All four Corsairs came in from behind and fired on the plane but they had to peel off as F4Us from another squadron dove in front of them in an attempt to get in on the action. Their intrusion was no help as the Val was already considered destroyed. Its pilot was apparently dead and the rear gunner bailed out.

As the Val splashed in the ocean, the VMF-314 pilots checked out the gunner as he floated down. They reported that he appeared to be dead.[6] In the middle of all the action, another Val had also dropped a parachute mine and *LCS(L) 56* sank it with gunfire. With the immediate threat passed, the ships resumed their patrol.

A few hours later, at 1803, a new raid was reported coming in from the north. Second Lt. James H. Taylor and 1st Lt. Joseph A. Ross of VMF-441 were vectored to intercept it and discovered a Hamp and a Tojo heading south. Ross got on the tail of the Hamp but found that it was capable of turning inside his Corsair. He finally got in a seven o'clock position above the plane and his 20mm cannons exploded the plane in mid-air. Meanwhile, Taylor's cannons had hit the Tojo, which also exploded from the impact.

June 6 would prove to be different with the ships seeing good deal of action again. They were at battle stations between 1117 and 1125 and again from 1240 to 1250. Later in the afternoon, at about 1555, more bogeys began to appear. One division of F4U-1C Corsairs from VF-9 on *Shangri La* was vectored to intercept the enemy planes. At 1606 the Corsairs tallyhoed the intruders, shooting down three Tonys and one Jack. Overhead, the two planes on radar picket patrol shot down two more Tonys that had evaded the other aircraft.

Anthony spotted an Oscar directly overhead and took it under fire with its machine guns just as one of the radar picket Corsairs fired on it. The Oscar began to go down and the pilot bailed out at 500 feet. His chute failed to open and he hit the water. His plane went in 1,500 yards off *Walke's* bow.

A division of F6F-5 Hellcats, led by Lt. J.P. Snyder of *Yorktown's* VF-9, appeared over the station. The naval aviators were looking for a fight and got one. Snyder spotted a Tony at 2,000 feet, dove on the enemy plane and fired into its engine. The plane flamed, rolled over, and crashed into the sea.

More enemy planes were reported in the area and *Bradford* spotted another Tony to port, diving on her at 1607. She took it under fire with her 40mm battery and splashed it 1,000 yards off her port bow. Realizing that he was going down in flames and too far away to crash the ship, the Japanese pilot jumped, but his parachute failed to open completely and he died on impact with the water.

Between the ships and planes at RP Station # 15A, seven Japanese aircraft had gone down. An enemy plane appeared overhead at 2125 and attempted to bomb the ships but missed. The destroyers drove it off with gunfire. At 2150 the ships headed to their night patrol at RP Station # 1.

On 7 June the ships were at general quarters from 1427 to 1505, during which time the CAP successfully intercepted and shot down three enemy planes. Shortly thereafter, at 1856, *Bradford* spotted two Vals coming in from the northeast.

Flying low over the water, the two enemy planes split up and came at the formation from different sides; both made suicide runs on the *Anthony*. The first was splashed at a distance of 2,000 yards from the destroyer after being hit by its 40mm guns and by fire from the *Bradford*. The second Val circled the *Anthony*, crossed astern of her and came in on the port side. In spite of being hit numerous times, the plane narrowly missed *Bradford,* splashing just to port of the ship.

The crash created a small hole in the ship, dished in the side, and covered the nearby deck with burning gasoline. The fire was quickly extinguished. The crash of the plane and waves generated by the maneuvers washed five men overboard. They were recovered by *LCS(L)s 66* and *86*. Three of the men suffered second degree burns and the other two were only shaken up. It had been a close call for *Anthony*.

Radar Picket Station # 16A was patrolled by *Pritchett, Knapp, Harry E. Hubbard*, and *LCS(L)s 63, 64, 118*, and *121* on 3 June. The first contact with the enemy came at 0205 when two bogeys were picked up at eleven and seventeen miles. The four LCS(L)s were patrolling near the destroyers in a diamond formation. At 0205 they spotted a Kate at 800 yards heading for the DDs. Both the *118* and the *121* opened fire, hitting the plane, which splashed 1,000 yards to port of the gunboats. The second plane began its run on the three destroyers and was taken under fire at 0236. A bright blue flame appeared in the distance leaving the lookouts to believe that it had been shot down, but radar reported the plane climbing and turning away.

Daylight hours saw the radar picket patrols and the combat air patrols overhead. The CAP splashed two planes around 0810 about twelve miles from the station. Two Vals approached the picket ships at 1301 and *Pritchett* sent the CAP after them. Both were shot down about fourteen miles from the station. Another raid, consisting of two more Vals, was picked up on radar at 1352. Five minutes later the CAP had downed both. The remainder of the day was uneventful.

On 6 June, *Cowell, Watts, Aulick* and *LCS(L)s 63, 64, 118,* and *121* patrolled the station. In the afternoon, at about 1600, the ships went to general quarters with a bogey spotted at fifteen miles. When it had closed to 8,000 yards, *Cowell* and *Watts* took it under fire. VF-88 Hellcats from *Yorktown* made their appearance and the ships ceased firing. The CAP splashed the enemy plane. Immediately thereafter, the F6F-5s led by Lt. H.R. Hudson and Lieutenant Ball, spotted four Tonys heading for the destroyers. Two were at 2000' and the other two skimmed the waves as they headed for their targets. Hudson and McLaurin, his wingman attacked the Tonys at 2,000 feet and shot them down. Two other Hellcat flyers, Champion and Hudspeth, teamed up to shoot down the other two.

As the division reformed and headed back toward the radar picket ships, they spotted a Tony with a Hellcat and a Corsair on its tail. Both planes overran the Tony giving Hudson his opening. He fired and hit the Tony in the wings and fuselage; it rolled over and splashed in the ocean.

Meanwhile, the division led by Ball had spotted the Tonys, but thought they were P-51s. Hesitant to attack until he could verify the type of plane, Ball gave two Hellcats their opening. They got credit for the kill. Meanwhile, the gunboats were patrolling in a diamond formation with *LCS(L) 118* closest to the destroyers. She spotted an Oscar over the destroyers at 1606. As the crew watched, the plane began a nearly vertical dive on *Watts*.

Opening fire with all her guns, *LCS(L) 118* hit the plane repeatedly, driving it off course. The Oscar splashed fifty yards off the port beam of the destroyer. With the immediate action over, the ships returned to their patrol.

Kikusui # 9 had ended, and although there had been some close calls, the ships had managed to escape any damage. Many aircraft had been shot down by the picket ships and their CAP.

Friday, 8 June through Tuesday, 12 June 1945

Additional protection for the picket stations arrived on Ie Shima on 8 June. Black Widows of the 548th Night Fighter Squadron landed and would soon begin to accompany the Hellcats in patrolling the night skies. They would be over the picket ships in a week. During this time, command of the Tactical Air Force passed from Maj. Gen. Francis Mulcahy to Maj. Gen. Louis E. Woods. Commodore Moosbrugger departed from *Panamint* and returned his command to *Biscayne.*

Changes for the night radar picket stations were deemed necessary and made official at 1400 on 9 June. According to the report of Commander Fifth Amphibious Force CTF 51 and CTF 31:

> RP 5 moves to position bearing 080 distance 50 miles from ZAMPA MISAKI; RP 15 moves to RP 1; RP 16A moves to position bearing 320 distance 30 miles from ZAMPA MISAKI; RP 11A moves to RP 11; RP 9 moves to position bearing 225 distance 50 miles from ZAMPA MISAKI; pickets leave day stations one hour after sunset and return at sunrise.[7]

Radar Picket Station # 11A was patrolled by *Van Valkenburgh, Cassin Young, Smalley, Ingersoll,* and *LCS(L)s 13, 14, 16,* and *21* on the 8th. At 0230 night fighters splashed enemy aircraft near the station.

At 0733 a flight of P-47s from the 333rd Fighter Squadron took off from Ie Shima. Led by 1st Lt. Harry Vaughan, the flight also included 1st Lts. Swanberg, S. Davis, and Otis W. Bennett. The Thunderbolts were soon in action. The flight had been orbiting near RP Station # 11A at 2,000 feet without seeing the enemy. While his squadron mates monitored the ground control station, Bennett switched his frequency to the navy channel and soon heard welcome news. The fighter director ship had picked up incoming bogeys near the Thunderbolts. A quick check revealed that there were two Zekes heading south a few hundred feet above them. Vaughan and Swanberg went after the first of the Zekes and both scored hits on the plane. Meanwhile the second Zeke had turned toward the Thunderbolts and came at Swanberg's plane in a head-on attack. Swanberg dove to the left, but the Zeke managed to put a few rounds into his plane, causing it to smoke and putting him out of action. Swanberg had to return to base where he landed safely at 0835. Meanwhile, Vaughan was still engaged in a dogfight with the first Zeke. He followed the Zeke through a number of evasive maneuvers, split-Ss, chandelles and loops, and finally caught the Zeke at the top of a loop. A long burst to the plane's wing root sent it into the water.

Meanwhile, Bennett had taken off after the second Zeke. After seeing it score hits on Swanberg's plane, he engaged in a wild dogfight with the enemy plane. During the ten minute battle, it became obvious to Bennett that he was up against a good pilot, since the Zeke made a number of violent maneuvers to avoid him. Bennett made two passes on the enemy plane, scoring hits on each pass. Finally on the third pass, as the Zeke was attacking Swanberg, Bennett went after it. According to Bennett, the Japanese plane tried to ram him and missed him by only two feet. Bennett ducked under the plane, came up from behind and shot it down, hitting the Zeke in the wing root, fuselage and cockpit. The Thunderbolt pilots reported that both Zekes carried a pair of 500 pound bombs, which they jettisoned as the dogfight began. They also reported that both pilots appeared to be very experienced, as judged by their flying skills.[8]

Shortly after the Thunderbolts had taken off from Ie Shima, VMF-314 sent its planes toward RP Station # 11A. At 0800 1st Lts. Burrus and C.B. Carroll took off from Ie Shima, assigned to radar picket patrol. As the VMF-314 pilots were heading to RP Station # 11A, they spotted a Zeke with three of the 333rd's Thunderbolts pursuing it and watched as Vaughan splashed it. Another Zeke appeared at 12 o'clock only one hundred feet off the water. Carroll and Burrus dove on it and Carroll got in a quick burst before the Zeke passed him by. He turned and came up from behind the plane, which tried to avoid his fire by banking left. Dropping his wheels to slow his Corsair, Caroll hit the Zeke in the wing root and cockpit with his 20mm cannons, killing the pilot. The plane peeled off and splashed. *Ingersoll* and *Smalley* took other enemy planes under fire later at 2038 and 2109 and turned them away. About the same time, night fighters also shot down enemy aircraft.

Pritchett and *Harry E. Hubbard* relieved *Cassin Young* and *Smalley* on 9 June at 0920. The daylight hours were uneventful, but an incoming bogey was picked up at 1919. Flying overhead were four VMF-113 Corsairs from Ie Shima. Captain W.A. Baldwin was the division leader and his wingman was 2d Lt. B.N. Tuttle. The second section was led by 2d Lt. D.C. Hallquist with 2d Lt. H.L. Jungi flying wing. At 1940 the division, flying at 1,200 feet, made contact with a Judy flying directly toward *Pritchett* at an altitude of only twenty-five to fifty feet. They turned and dove to meet the Judy and all four Corsairs spread out behind it. Baldwin closed to 150 feet and was fired on by the plane's rear gunner. He fired a short burst which flamed the left wing and then overran the Judy. Hallquist hit it with another burst just as its left wing hit the water. The enemy plane bounced off the water twice and exploded.

Back on RP Station # 15A, at 0639 on the 10th, the ships continued on their patrol. On station were *William D. Porter* as fighter director, with *Aulick* and *Cogswell* in support. Along with the destroyers were four gunboats, *LCS(L)s 18, 86, 94,* and *122.* Cruising overhead were two CAP divisions from VMF-212 at Awase and VMF-314 on Ie Shima. Two additional planes on radar picket patrol also covered the ships directly. Lieutenant Klein of VMF-314 spotted a Val a mile and a half from him. His division turned to intercept it but had to turn away at 800 feet in the face of anti-aircraft fire from the ships. *Aulick* and *William D. Porter* had spotted the incoming suicide plane about 0823, and *Aulick* managed to get off a half dozen rounds from her main battery before the Val crashed close astern *Porter.* The action report of the *William D. Porter* describes the attack that led to her sinking:

> At this time (0815) AULICK, who was about 1000 yards astern, reported by TBXS "Possible bogey, bearing 100, 7000 yards." Immediately thereafter, our lookouts reported "A Val is diving at us." The plane had come out of the overcast at a range of about 5000 yards making a tight turn to port and approached the ship from dead ahead in a 301 power glide, on a course the reverse of the ship's course and very slightly to port of the ship's track. Two corsairs were seen close behind that apparently following the enemy plane. Immediately upon receiving the report from lookouts the Officer of the Deck had sounded the General Alarm. The plane struck the water close aboard to port, abreast the after engine room. There was a single violent,

but almost silent explosion, which seemed to lift the ship bodily and drop it again in a quick movement. The Commanding Officer who had been asleep in the sea cabin was awakened by the explosion, and coming out on the bridge was informed by the Officer of the Deck that the ship had been struck by a Val. It is not known whether the explosive was carried within the plane or in a bomb which might have been released, but it is believed that the explosion occurred nearly directly under the ship, under the after engine room or slightly aft of it. All the events of this paragraph occurred within a space of seconds. Pertinent to the failure of any ship in company to make radar contact on this plane until it had closed to 7000 yards, and to the failure of this ship to make radar contact at all was a later report from one of the LCS's which had recovered parts of the plane, that paper and wood appeared to have been used extensively in its construction.[9]

Action reports from the LCS(L)s indicated that a major problem in detecting this kamikaze was caused by the many American aircraft in the area that were not properly showing IFF. As a result, the CAP was constantly vectored to intercept aircraft that turned out to be friendly.[10]

The gunboats immediately came to the aid of the destroyer, tying up to her sides in an attempt to help pump out the ship which was quickly developing a list to starboard and was down by the stern. *Aulick* and *Cogswell* circled the stricken destroyer to provide AA protection. Men serving on the ships had their own way of gauging the danger. Tom Spargo, a radioman on the *Cogswell*, described the feeling. "As the plane came closer, I heard the 40 mm's go off, and then after, what seemed like an eternity, the 20mm's started. But when the 50 Cal's started, I thought the end could be near."[11]

At about 1910, the destroyer began to jettison its depth charges. One, not properly disarmed, went off under *LCS(L) 86*, but fortunately did not damage it. Casualties from the *Porter* were transferred to *LCS(L) 86* and given aid. The gunboats attempted to take the destroyer in tow, but it was too far gone. Commander C.M. Keyes, the commanding officer of *Porter,* gave the word to abandon ship. At 1113 he stepped off his ship and onto *LCS(L) 86*. As it pulled away, he watched the destroyer point her bow skyward and slip below the waves. *William D. Porter* was gone. She had suffered

LCS(L)s 86 and *122* rescue men from the sinking *U.S.S. William D. Porter DD 579* after it was hit by a Val on 10 June 1945 while on patrol at Radar Picket Station # 15A. *NARA 80G 490024.*

The *U.S.S. William D. Porter DD 579* settles by the stern after kamikaze hit. *LCS(L) 18* stands by to assist in pumping and rescuing crew. This photo was taken from *LCS(L) 122, courtesy of Richard K. Bruns.*

The U.S.S. William D. Porter DD 579 with decks awash after being hit by kamikaze on 10 June 1945. Unidentified LCS(L) behind ship aids in pumping. This photo was taken from *LCS(L) 122* in foreground. *Photo courtesy of Richard K. Bruns.*

U.S.S. William D. Porter DD 579 goes to the bottom as gunboats pull clear with survivors. *NARA 80G 490028.*

sixty-one wounded but no one had been killed. *Frament, Tekesta, Smalley*, and *LCS(L) 18* left the area for Okinawa at 1340 carrying the dead and wounded.

On 11 June *Aulick, Ammen*, and *LCS(L)s 19, 86, 94*, and *122* were back at RP Station # 15A at 0730. About twenty minutes later a bogey was reported to the north and the CAP shot it down. Most of the day passed without incident but, at 1845, a group of Vals was reported forty miles to the north and closing on the station. The CAP splashed two but three others got through to the ships. At

Aulick DD 569 was one of the supporting destroyers on Radar Picket Station # 15A when the *William D. Porter* was sunk. *NARA 80G 450224.*

LCS(L) 122 was hit by a Val on Radar Picket Station # 15A on 11 June 1945. The plane struck the base of the conning tower, killing eleven men and wounding twenty-nine, but the ship survived. Commanding Officer Lieutenant Richard M. McCool received the Congressional Medal of Honor for his efforts in saving his men and his ship. *Official U.S. Navy Photograph, courtesy of Captain Richard M. McCool USN (Ret.).*

A Japanese Navy Aichi D3A, code named Val. *NARA 80G 345604.*

1901 the gunboats spotted the Vals and, as the first dove at the ships, they all took it under fire. The enemy plane splashed to port of *LCS(L) 86* and astern of *122*. A second Val managed to survive hits from the LCS(L)s and *Aulick* and crashed into the base of the conning tower on the *122*. Moments later a third made a run on *86* and was shot down 1,000 yards from the ship by fire from the gunboat and *Cogswell*.

On *LCS(L) 122*, the situation was serious. Eleven men had been killed and twenty-nine wounded including the skipper, Lt. Richard M. McCool. McCool would later write:

For the second plane, I had ordered "hard right rudder" to make the pilot have to try to adjust his run after it had begun, but I doubt that it had time to be effective. This plane, I believe a so-called VAL bomber with fixed landing gear, hit us at the base of the conning tower with the closest part of the plane about 6-8 feet from me. I believe that I actually made out the face of the pilot before he hit, but that may be my imagination. The bomb (or naval projectile) apparently exploded a split second after impact, having gone through the radio shack and the passageway, exiting on the port side. Probably, the cylindrical structure of the pilot house is what saved my life.[12]

Raging fires from the impact burned a number of men and twenty-three jumped overboard. McCool, knocked unconscious and badly wounded by the impact, came to and took charge of the operation. His leadership rallied the crew and they began the task of saving their ship. Wounded men were transferred to *LCS(L) 86* and the other LCS(L)s in the group helped extinguish the fires. With his ship in safe hands, McCool was transferred off *122* and his executive officer took command. For McCool the war was over. By 2110 the LCS(L)s were on their way back to Hagushi with *122* in tow.

Unique situations call for unique men. Of the 440 Medals of Honor awarded to military men in World War II, only fifty-seven went to the navy. Of these fifty-seven, only five of the medals were awarded for actions at Okinawa. Four were won by navy corpsmen serving with marine ground units on Okinawa proper. Only one was awarded to a navy man serving on board a ship, and that went to the CO of *LCS(L) 122*, Lt. Richard M. McCool for his work in saving his men and his ship. McCool's Medal of Honor Citation reads:

For conspicuous gallantry and intrepidity at the risk of his life above and beyond the call of duty as commanding officer of the U.S.S. LCS(L) 3 122 during operations against enemy Japanese forces in the Ryukyu chain, 10 and 11 June 1945. Sharply vigilant during hostile air raids against Allied ships on radar picket duty off Okinawa on 10 June, Lt. McCool aided materially in evacuating all survivors from a sinking destroyer which had sustained mortal damage under the devastating attacks. When his own craft was attacked simultaneously by 2 of the enemy's suicide squadron early in the evening of 11 June, he instantly hurled the full power of his gun batteries against the plunging aircraft, shooting down the first and dam-

Lieutenant Richard M. McCool, Commanding Officer of *LCS(L) 122*, receives the Congressional Medal of Honor from President Harry S. Truman. *Official U.S. Navy Photograph, courtesy of Captain Richard M. McCool USN (Ret.).*

aging the second before it crashed his station in the conning tower and engulfed the immediate area in a mass of flames. Although suffering from shrapnel wounds and painful burns, he rallied his concussion-shocked crew and initiated vigorous firefighting measures and then proceeded to the rescue of several trapped in a blazing compartment, subsequently carrying 1 man to safety despite the excruciating pain of additional severe burns. Unmindful of all personal danger, he continued his efforts without respite until aid arrived from other ships and he was evacuated. By his staunch leadership, capable direction, and indomitable determination throughout the crisis, Lt. McCool saved the lives of many who otherwise might have perished and contributed materially to the saving of his ship for further combat service. His valiant spirit of self-sacrifice in the face of extreme peril sustains and enhances the highest traditions of the U.S. Naval Service.[13]

The following day a repair crew from *LCS(L) 118* boarded the *122* to clean up the debris. They found pieces of the Japanese pilot's body scattered about the ship. After collecting the parts in a mail sack, they weighted it down with an old typewriter and dropped it over the side. The working party found that the guns were still loaded and set to fire, indicating that the gunners had continued firing on the kamikaze until it hit them.[14]

Ammen controlled a flight of P-47s from the 73rd Fighter Squadron led by Captain Kane. At 1935, about a half hour after the *122* was hit, she picked up incoming bogeys and sent the Thunderbolts after them. Five minutes later, 1st Lt. J.T. Spivey, who was flying one of the four P-47s, spotted two Oscars heading for the station and sent one of them flaming into the ocean. His wingman Lieutenant Campbell went after the other, chasing it toward the radar picket ships. Campbell followed the Oscar until it came within range of the ships' guns and *Ammen* shot it down. With a typhoon warning issued, the destroyers left for shelter.

Patrolling RP Station # 16A on 8 June were *Cowell*, *Watts*, *Aulick*, and *LCS(L)s 63*, *64*, *118*, and *121*. At 0804 *Aulick* made radar contact with an enemy plane at a range of sixteen miles and, within minutes, the CAP had splashed a Val. A few minutes later the destroyers opened fire on a Tojo coming in from port on a suicide run. Fire from both ships managed to knock the plane off course; it passed across the bow of *Cowell* and splashed five yards to starboard of the ship. Other enemy planes were in the area and 1st Lt. C.B. Carroll of VMF-314 who was flying radar picket patrol, shot down a Zeke. Three other Zekes were caught ten miles to the south of the station by Thunderbolts from the 19th Fighter Squadron. A flight of the P-47s took off from Ie Shima at 0715 and were on patrol just to the south of the station. They spotted the three Zekes heading south and the flight leader, Capt. Michael Slepecky Jr., caught the first Zeke with a burst to the fuselage and sent it down. Second Lt. Donald E. Kennedy caught the second as Slepecky splashed the third. Still another CAP fighter shot down a Tony fifteen miles from the ships at 0845. *Willard Keith* joined the station at 1318 as relief for *Aulick* and, at 1330, *LCS(L) 53* reported as relief for *LCS(L) 118*. The ships went to general quarters for the evening hours but encountered no enemy aircraft.

At 0200 on 13 June, an enemy plane was picked up closing the station. The plane alternately approached and turned away as the ships took it under fire. Finally, at 0036, the gunners on *Cowell* and *Willard Keith* found the mark and the plane went down in flames about 7,000 yards to starboard of the destroyers. Enemy planes continued to cruise the area for the remainder of the night but no others came within range.

Wednesday, 13 June through Sunday, 17 June 1945

Additional fighters arrived at Ie Shima on the 14th, bolstering the number available for various missions including the CAP. Thirty-four Thunderbolts of the 34th Fighter Squadron, 413th Fighter Group arrived on that date after a long over water flight from Saipan; they would fly their first CAP mission on 17 June. According to the *413th Fighter Group Combat History*:

> The 413th started on its first mission from Ie Shima, a combat air patrol flight, briefed to the saturation point. On the previous day Tactical Air Forces had sent over a Major from Okinawa to instruct the pilots on the importance of knowing the location of picket boats which were actually seaborn radar stations. The picket boat crews were on constant edge, he reported, because so many bogies were in the area their crews would shoot any aircraft that looked suspicious.[15]

Intercepted enemy messages indicated that the Japanese were moving additional *Shiragiku* trainers to Kanoya and Kushira Air Bases. More float planes were scheduled to move to Ibusuki sea plane base as well. The plan was to have them carry out night attacks starting on 17 June. In addition, the First Air Fleet was to be dissolved effective 15 June.[16] The Willow, a biplane trainer, was to be preserved for use as a suicide plane in future attacks. Japanese air depots were advised to take all necessary measures to prevent damage to them.[17]

Monday, 18 June through Friday, 22 June 1945

During this period the Japanese launched the tenth and last of their *Kikusui* raids. The actual attack, which lasted from 21-22 June, included a total of forty-five special attack planes, including thirty from the navy and fifteen from the army. Japanese air power was on the decline. According to Japanese reports:

Approx. 50 fighters and 50 KAMIKAZE planes constitute the entire strength of our Army Air force [Sixth Air Army] at present.

The strength of our Naval Air Force which is scheduled to attack the enemy anchorage near OKINAWA has been almost reduced to nothing. Because of the shortage of planes in our Army and Navy Air Forces, the main body of our attack force will consist of OKA bombers . . . The OKA bomber will be used in operations of the following categories:

    a. Continuous day and night attacks.

    b. Daylight attacks

    c. Attacks utilizing craft other than the OKA bombers will be carried out only during the day.[18]

American air raids on the fields continued to slow down the Japanese effort. From 18-19 June, the XXI Bomber Command sent 480 B-29s to bomb Toyohashi, Fukuoka and Shizuoka. At the same time, P-47s from Ie Shima attacked the air field on Tokuno Shima.

Concurrent with the launch of *Kikusui # 10* came the announcement from Gen. Roy Geiger, at 1830 on June 21, that the island of Okinawa had been secured. Geiger had taken over command of the Tenth Army after Lt. Gen. Simon Bolivar Buckner was killed by an artillery shell on 18 June. If the announcement reached Japanese ears, it did not deter the kamikazes. On 12 June, the Ten Air Force put forth the order for *Kikusui # 10*. It stated:

(1) Objectives of the Operation: We anticipate the success of Cherry Blossom [Oka] operations through the use of our entire operational strength.

(2) Plan of operations:

    (a) Attacks on bases and surface craft will be increased beginning on X-minus-1. The entire fighter strength and a part of the Cherry Blossoms and fighter-bombers will take off at dawn on X-Day and carry out daylight [word missing] attacks.

    (b) Type Zero [Zeke] fighters participating in the above attacks on X-Day will carry out radar deception and will verify battle results.

    (c) Beginning on X-minus-1, we will engage in dummy communications with Minami Daito [225 m. E of Naha] and [decoy] the enemy striking force.

(3) Army strength will consist of about 50 fighters and about 50 suicide units.[19]

The operation had originally been scheduled to start on 14 June, but had been delayed. Military intelligence reported that it had been postponed until the night of the 21st. Inclement weather caused the cancellation of some attacks that were scheduled late on the 22nd. Intercepted reports indicated that the Japanese were having problems with communications devices. Continuous B-29 raids at Tokyo and Kawasaki in April and May had damaged the Oriental Communications Equipment Company and the Oki Electric Company. Both were major producers of radio transmitters. "On 18 June Air Flotilla 12 (Kyushu) informed its subordinate units that it 'will not be able to supply radio transmitters for suicide attack plane units [during] the middle of the month'"[20] because of the raids.

Van Valkenburgh, *Walke*, *Gainard*, and *LCS(L)s 34, 62, 81,* and *118* patrolled RP Station # 7 on the 22nd. The ships came under attack early in the morning. The gunboats were steaming about 5,000 yards north of the destroyers in a box formation when *Claxton* reported two bogeys heading for the station at fifteen miles out. At 0055 the gunboats made radar contact with a Betty only two miles from the ships and heading in at 150 knots. *LCS(L) 62* was closest and opened fire with her 40mm guns as the Betty flew down the port side of the formation, circled behind the ships and came up the starboard side. *LCS(L) 81* got in a few hits with one of its 20mm guns, but *LCS(L) 62*'s gunners had hit the plane's port engine and it went down in the center of the formation. *LCS(L) 62* was given credit for the kill. No further encounters with the enemy occurred for the remainder of the day.

Pritchett, *Picking*, *Willard Keith*, and *LCS(L)s 11, 18, 36,* and *63* were patrolling RP Station # 15A on 18 June. During the night hours, from about 2200 to daybreak, the ships shifted their patrol to RP Station # 1. *Pritchett* was in control of the CAP and RPP.

VMF(N)-533 pilots 1st Lt. K.B. Witte, Capt. Robert Baird, and 1st Lts. J.H. Mahoney and R.S. Hempstead had taken their F6F-5N Hellcats off from Charlie Strip at Ie Shima just after midnight on 22 June. They were flying just to the north of the radar picket station when they intercepted and splashed four twin-engine Japanese bombers headed for the ships. Baird was high scorer, shooting down a Frances at 0045 and a Betty at 0233. Witte shot down a Sally at 0057. At 0150, 1st Lt. R.S. Hemstead, of VMF(N) 533, chased a Betty toward the picket ships. Expecting the ships to open fire, Hemstead avoided the area and then picked up the plane as it was leaving. After following it for several minutes he was able to get into position. He fired into the bomber's right engine and wing root. It caught fire and splashed near *Picking* at 0157. Mahoney accounted for another Betty at 0230. Six of these medium bombers had taken off from Kanoya late in the evening of the 21st and four had fallen victim to the sharpshooting night fighters of VMF(N)-533.

Although the ships at RP Station # 15A had seen no action, they had been well protected. Their own CAP consisted of sixteen Corsairs, with an additional two acting as direct cover for the ships. When the action started on 22 June, at about 0749, *Massey* and *Dyson* divided the sixteen CAP planes between them and directed the Corsairs toward the incoming enemy planes, estimated to be about forty in number. The CAP reported splashing twenty-nine planes during the action. At about 0815, a division of VMF-224 Corsairs led by Capt. J.E. Montagne, was flying CAP near RP Station # 15A when the pilots spotted a Betty and four Zekes. Second Lt. H.L. Triece and his wingman, 2d Lt. George Tregay, went after them. When the Betty saw them it dropped an *Oka*, which missed the picket ships and splashed in the ocean. Triece's plane was hit by machine gun fire from the bomber but he was uninjured; Tregay was not so lucky. His plane was reported missing and he was presumed dead. Meanwhile, Montagne and his wingman, 2d Lt. P.R. Rezen, went after the Zekes. They shared a kill on one and Rezen shot down another.

The heavy action during this period took place at RP Station # 16A. On patrol there were *Wickes, Cogswell, Brown*, and *LCS(L)s 35, 82, 86,* and *124.* Early in the morning of the 19th, at 0146, the ships went to general quarters with an approaching bogey. The enemy plane got no closer than sixteen miles from the ships before one of the night fighters splashed it. *LCS(L) 124* joined the station at 0844. *Wickes, Cogswell,* and *Brown* were relieved by *Converse, Ammen,* and *Ingersoll* at 0800 on the 20th. *Converse* took over duties as the fighter director ship.

Late in the day on the 21st, enemy air activity began at the station as described by the action report of *Ammen:*

> This evening most of the Japs were using some type of plane which was capable of flying at very slow speeds. The average

speed was in the vicinity of 100 mph. The bandits maneuvered peculiarly, doing many sharp turns, making erratic, wandering tracks. It was most apparent that they had no radar. There appeared to be a lack of coordination between planes, so apparently they had no radios either. Their altitudes were usually very low but the SG could not pick them up satisfactorily.[21]

These enemy aircraft were *Shiragiku* training planes. Six of them had flown out of Kanoya on Southern Kyushu. With a top speed of 143 m.p.h., they were frequently used for kamikaze attacks in the latter part of the war. Although earlier models were of metal construction, the later models were all wood, making it difficult to pick up on radar. When fitted for kamikaze missions, the planes carried a 550 lb. bomb.[22] Their slow speed and lack of armament made them easy pickings for the CAP Corsairs and Hellcats, so the Japanese only used them at night or when they had sufficient escort fighters.

Between 2245 on the 21st and 0230 on the 22nd, bogeys were near the formation on several occasions but gunfire from the ships drove them away. It was impossible to determine if any had been hit. Night turned to day and, in the early morning, the attacks began anew. At 0741 *Ammen* reported a raid of five or six planes approaching at seventy-five miles and requested additional CAP support. The CAP located about nineteen planes closing on the station, ten were Bettys, accompanied by nine Zekes. The CAP shot down sixteen enemy planes and lost three of their own. Some of the Bettys carried *Okas* and exploded when they were hit. A flight of six Bettys with *Okas* was reported to have taken off from Kanoya at 0543. Japanese sources claim to have lost four.[23] Among the *Oka* pilots was Tomitaro Horie who was one of the last of his unit left at the Kanoya base. Domei News Agency in Japan reported that he had been lost in that attack.[24]

Aggressive marine flyers made short work of the intruders; none were able to successfully attack the ships. Taking off from Ie Shima at 0720, were two divisions of VMF-314 Corsairs led by Capts. J.D. Constantine and L.H. Smith. Constantine's division spotted a Betty at 16,000 feet. As they looked around they saw more than twenty Zekes, Jacks and Oscars surrounding the Betty. First Lts. R.F. Webb and C.W. Glunk got on the Betty's tail, bracketing it with their fire. Both pilots scored .50 caliber hits on the bomber and then ran into problems with their guns. Seeing this, the Japanese fighters began to attack them. Webb and Glunk broke off and headed back to Ie Shima. Meanwhile, Constantine had a Jack on his tail. His wingman, Lt. J.B. Brown, told him to dive as he went after the Jack. Constantine lost the Jack in cloud cover and came out too close to *Ammen*. Not being able to identify the Corsair at first, the destroyer opened fire. Constantine dove and evaded the ship's fire. Apparently the G force from his dive switched off his radio. Thinking it was out, he headed back to base. Brown caught up with him and they made it safely to the field.

Meanwhile, Smith's division was going after another Betty at 7,000 feet. Smith's guns failed because of an electrical problem. Between 0800 and 0830, 1st Lt. John W. Leaper and his wingman, 1st Lt. W.L. Milne, each accounted for downing a Betty and a Zeke. Low on ammunition after engaging a number of enemy planes, Leaper spotted a Zeke coming at him from dead ahead. He did a split-S maneuver and came out behind and below the enemy. After firing his last ten rounds and missing, he attempted to chew the Zeke's tail off with his propellor. Below, crewmen on *LCS(L) 35* watched the duel overhead as Leaper overshot his mark, came down from above, and crashed into the enemy plane between the propellor and cockpit. The Zeke went down but so did the Corsair. The collision caused the Corsair's right pylon tank to explode, blowing its starboard wing off and putting it into a spin.[25] On board *LCS(L) 35*, crewman Charlie Thomas watched. He later wrote:

> The Corsair has also been struck a mortal blow - - his left wing is knocked off. Pieces of the broken wing flutter in the sky while the stricken Corsair goes into a flat spin, then falls end-over-end. On the ships, we all hold our breaths waiting for the Corsair pilot to escape from his aircraft which is now falling completely out of control. To our relief, a white parachute appears and begins a slow descent while the Corsair crashes into the sea.[26]

Leaper managed to bail out but his chute was damaged. As he drifted down he spotted a Zeke making a run on him. He collapsed his chute and dropped rapidly downward, opening it again near the water and avoiding the attack. He was later picked up uninjured by *Ammen* at 1010.[27]

At 0530 on 22 June, a division of VMF-113 Corsairs had taken off from Ie Shima. Led by 1st Lt. E.G. Dick, it included 1st Lt. S.R. Crowell and 2d Lts. John J. Kissell and M.W. Harke. After orbiting about ten miles northwest of their base, they were directed to report to *Ammen* at RP Station # 16A.

As they approached the station at about 0830, they could hear the sounds of an air battle over the picket ships. *Ammen* reported a bogey in their vicinity and they soon spotted a Betty being chased by two Corsairs. It dove into a cloud layer and, anticipating its exit, the four Corsairs were waiting. Dick fired on the plane just as it was turning toward *Ammen* and hit the starboard engine, setting it on fire. His second burst cut the end off the starboard wing and the enemy plane plummeted to the sea where it exploded.

After reforming, the division patrolled just to the west of the station. They soon spotted a Zeke being chased by a Corsair which it evaded by a diving turn. Crowell and Harke got behind the enemy plane and bracketed it. Bursts from both Corsairs hit the Zeke and it dove smoking into the water and exploded. As the battle raged, gunfire was heard in the clouds over the station. At 0910 *Ammen* maneuvered radically at the last moment to avoid a Corsair in its death dive. It had fallen victim to a Tojo and splashed ten yards to starboard of the destroyer, showering her with debris. In this battle, the marines lost three Corsairs and two pilots, the Japanese lost ten Bettys, two Zekes and four other aircraft.

Later in the evening, at 2201, the ships again went to general quarters. During the following hour several planes made runs on the ships and were turned away by gunfire. Lieutenant Col. M.M. Magruder of VMF(N)-533 was flying his F6F-5N Hellcat near the station when ground control vectored him toward two bogeys flying below him at 15,000 feet. He made contact with the two planes, but one turned away, leaving him with only one target. Magruder dropped his wheels in order to slow his Hellcat down as the Betty was doing only 130 knots. It turned right and he hit it with several bursts, flaming both engines. The Betty turned toward him in an attempt to ram him, but he pulled away and then hit it with another burst in the fuselage, sending the enemy plane down to crash in the ocean.

The picket ships reported seeing the splash at 2242 and were relieved as they had not been able to hit the plane. By 2327 the enemy left the area and the ships continued on patrol.

Kikusui # 10 had been a failure for the Japanese. None of the picket ships had been hit and the CAP had taken a heavy toll of their aircraft. The only casualties were *LSM 213* and *LST 534*, both of which sustained heavy damage. Japanese estimates were much higher and they deemed the operation a success.[28] They reported that the morning action on the 22nd had resulted in the loss of one ship by the Americans, with one other damaged. Air Flotilla 12, using *Shiragiku* trainers and other planes, was ordered to continue their attacks through the 27th before retiring for repair and maintenance.[29]

The ending of the campaign for Okinawa caused some commanding officers pause to reflect on the experience. Commander R.D. Fusselman, CO of the destroyer *Wadsworth*, identified one of the many problems caused by the duty. According the action report of *Wadsworth*:

> Any extended operation which brings a ship in contact with the enemy 24 hours a day is sure to produce fatigue and mental strain for all hands. Radar Picket duty imposes the additional considerations of isolated position and greater incidence of enemy attack. The impact of the operation varied with the psychological make-up of the individual, some men being able to stand the extended strain well but excitable when actually under attack, and the reverse. There is no substitute for personal courage, and one was needed. The problem was fatigue and mental strain. . .[30]

With the ending of the campaign to capture Okinawa, many commands submitted an action report for the period. In his action report Commander Fifth Fleet, Adm. Raymond A. Spruance, noted the role of the radar picket ships:

> The effectiveness of radar pickets in protecting an amphibious operation against enemy air attack was demonstrated. They provided air warning service, shot down many planes by AA fire and, by controlling their own CAP's, contributed to the destruction of many more. Although the radar picket ships suffered heavy losses from these attacks, it is believed that the enemy committed a serious error in concentrating upon them instead of avoiding or ignoring them in favor of the transports. As it became apparent that the enemy was concentrating his attacks on outlying stations it was evident that radar picket

stations must be strengthened. A unit of two destroyer types with a fighter director team and four LCS types gave good results. A board of officers experienced in picket duty was convened by CTF 51 to determine the best tactics for radar pickets. . . .

Earlier installations of radar and GCI facilities on outlying islands near OKINAWA would have been advisable. These would have replaced radar picket and fighter director ships and reduced the damage received by these vessels.[31]

Sunday, 24 June 1945

Patrolling RP Station # 16A on 24 June were *Moale*, *Charles Ausburne*, *Ingersoll*, and *LCS(L)s 35*, *82*, *86*, and *124*. At 0235 the ships went on alert with a bogey approaching at fourteen miles. Overhead, 1st Lt. R.S. Hemstead of VMF(N)-533 was flying his F6F-5N Hellcat night fighter on patrol. Hemstead had taken off from his base on Ie Shima at 0020. An hour later, ground control vectored him to intercept an incoming bogey near RP Station # 16A which was flying at 20,000 feet. Hemstead picked up the bogey when it was about forty miles from Ie Shima. It dropped window in an attempt to escape, but the marine pilot was soon on its tail. He closed to within fifty yards and identified it as a Sally. A short burst from his guns flamed the bomber's right engine. He fired again, hitting the wing root and fuselage. After pulling to the right to observe, he noticed that the plane was turning in an apparent attempt to ram him. Hemstead fired again, hitting the Sally's cockpit; it went into a dive and splashed near the picket ships. *Ingersoll* spotted the action and reported the crash. A few minutes later, *Ingersoll* mistook Hemstead's Hellcat for a bandit and fired a few rounds at it. Fortunately none hit the American plane.

Monday, 25 June 1945

With the island of Okinawa considered secured, the Office of War Information took time to evaluate the status of the Japanese air forces. They reported:

> The enemy now has about 4,000 combat planes and is maintaining a production of 1,250 to 1,500 planes a month. Current losses are more than 1,000 a month. Significantly, there is a greater increase in production of fighters than in other types.

The Japanese have shown some improvement in the quality of their planes it was said, and have also developed some proficiency in the defensive tactics which they have been forced to adopt, particularly in night combat tactics. Pilot ability on the other hand has steadily declined.[32]

The war production figures were interesting but they gave little relief to the picket ships. American intelligence picked up Japanese radio messages indicating that approximately forty planes of various types would attack the ships and the airfields at Okinawa.[33]

Patrolling RP Station # 15A were *Boyd*, *Caperton*, *Lowry*, and *LCS(L)s 63, 97, 98,* and *99.* The daylight hours were uneventful but, at 2215, the ships went to general quarters with an incoming bogey picked up on radar twenty-five miles northeast of the station. *Boyd* was the first of the ships to open fire, picking up a single plane at four and one-half miles.

For the next five hours, a series of approximately twenty-five raids approached the station, with some turning away and several hit by the combined fire of the ships. *Caperton* and the LCS(L)s fired on another bogey and the destroyer reported it splashed. In the midst of the five hour ordeal, the ships had a lucky turn of fate. What began as a bright, moonlit night turned into black, with an almost total eclipse of the moon. By the end of the action, at about 0309 on the 26th, two Betty bombers had been splashed and several other planes damaged. The ships escaped unscathed.

American intelligence intercepted reports from the Ten Air Force that indicated the extent of its involvement. According to the reports, "during the night of 25-26 June a total of 58 planes, including 14 suicide *Shiragiku* utility trainers, took off for attacks on Okinawa. Three bombers and seven *Shiragiku* tuned back 'because of mechanical difficulties.' Three bombers failed to return, and two others were seriously damaged; presumably the other seven *Shiragiku* also failed to return."[34] Task Force 51 reported shooting down twelve of the sixteen planes they encountered near Okinawa.

Saturday, 30 June 1945

By the end of June, the major air battles of the Okinawa area were over. With the invasion of the homeland imminent, the Japanese held back their fighter strength. A running tally had been kept by the Headquarters of the Tactical Air Force showing that by 30 June, the Tactical Air Force planes alone had shot down 602 aircraft.[35] Numerous others had gone down under the guns of the carrier squadrons and the picket ships.

Ground personnel at the airfields on Okinawa and Ie Shima no longer lived under the threat of Japanese aircraft attacks. The combination of radar picket ships, their combat air patrols, and shore based radar had considerably diminished them. Captain Parker R. Tyler, Jr. of the 413th Fighter Group on Ie Shima, wrote that the "Jap was effectively cleared from the heavens, we never looked up during the daylight hours when we heard aircraft overhead, except from curiosity."[36]

The events of June encompassing the loss of Okinawa had changed Japanese strategy toward the American ships at the island. Air units that had been used to attack American ships in the Ryukyus were now withdrawn to various bases in preparation for the defense of the homeland. Numerous new fields were constructed on the main islands of Japan, each capable of handling small groups of kamikaze aircraft. Many of these were converted training planes, which were in good supply.

Air bases in the southern areas of Kyushu were now open to continued attack from Okinawan based aircraft, as well as the planes of the carrier task forces and those flying from Iwo Jima and the Marianas. To preserve as many aircraft as possible, the Japanese transferred many air units to bases in North Kyushu, Honshu and Shikoku. Aircraft that had previously operated in southern areas of China were moved to the border of China and Korea, in preparation for staging south to defend the homeland. A Japanese communication intercepted by the Military Intelligence Service stated that "Air Flotilla 12, with over 900 suicide planes (mostly trainers), is to be concentrated in Kyushu."[37] Other suicide trainers would be centered around Tokyo.

Monday, 1 July 1945

The months of July and August saw a marked decline in the number of attacks on the radar picket stations. This was the result of a change in Japanese strategy after the fall of Okinawa, as well as material shortages. In an attempt to better coordinate activities, the navy air forces on Taiwan were placed under the command of the army 8th Air Division. Serviceability rates among the various air units also fell. According to Capt. Minoru Genda who commanded Air Group 343 based at Kokubu, their serviceability rate was "About 70% at first, but after the heavy and continuous B-24 raids beginning in July, our serviceability rate went down continuously. At the end, I estimate that it was somewhere around 50%."[38] The change directly affected the ships on the radar picket stations. At about the same time, the Fifth Air Fleet reported: "All air units were instructed to cease hostile activities against small enemy planes because of a severe fuel shortage."[39]

From 2 July until 16 July, only RP Stations # 9A and 15A would be manned. Beginning on 17 July, RP Station # 9A would be the remaining station. Ships on radar picket duty at various times from 1 July through 13 August were *Alfred A. Cunningham, Aulick, Callaghan, Cassin Young, Charles Ausburne, Claxton, Compton, Converse, Dyson, Foote, Frank E. Evans, Gainard, Harry E. Hubbard, Heywood L. Edwards, Irwin, John A. Bole, Laws, Preston, Pritchett, Richard P. Leary,* and *LCS(L)s 61, 64, 74, 76, 78, 82, 84, 85, 86, 96, 97, 98, 99, 100, 101, 102, 103, 104, 105, 107, 120, 121, 123, 124, 125, 128, 129,* and *130.*

Tuesday, 2 July through Saturday, 13 July 1945

From 2 through 13 July the picket ships had a peaceful respite. Occasional bogeys appeared on the screens but usually turned out to be friendlies. The CAP fliers patrolled a broad expanse of blue water and blue sky in boring flights. American military intelligence reported the relocation of Japanese air units:

> On 6 July, however, the Sixth Air Army (Hq Fukuoka), NW Kyushu) reported that the Hqs of two flying brigades, previously located in Honshu, had been transferred on 4 July to Chiran (SW Kyushu) and Miyakanojo West (S Kyushu), respectively. . . . One of the brigades has controlled a twin-engine bomber regiment, and the other has controlled three fighter regiments. . . .In the same report the Sixth Air Army stated that "partially trained" suicide units organized "in the central sector" began moving on 1 July and that 14 such units had moved to "the Kyushu sector" by 6 July. The deployment of suicide units was to be completed by about 10 July. <u>Note:</u> Japanese messages have indicated that the average strength of the JAAF suicide units is about 10 planes.[40]

It was further noted that Japanese Navy Air Group 721, the primary Betty/*Oka* tactical unit, was preparing to leave Kanoya for Komatsu and would eventually be stationed in Korea. Air Group 762 was directed to form another *Oka* unit at Komatsu. This unit would be different in that the mother planes were to be Frances bombers.[41] Another intercepted message from the Bureau of Aeronautics directed that *Shiragiku* and Willow trainers used as kamikazes would no longer be fitted with formation lights. They would have to rely on guide planes to get them to their target.[42]

By 10 July, shortages of fuel, spare parts and other maintenance units had forced the Japanese to abandon their pilot training program. There was a surplus of air crews, with American estimates of the situation indicating that there were "58 per cent more crews than aircraft."[43]

The Tenth Army Tactical Air Force, which by this time had grown to include four marine air groups, three army air force fighter groups and four army air force bomber groups, as well as their supporting elements, had outlived its usefulness. It was originally designed to support and protect the forces engaged in the conquest of Okinawa but increasingly became involved in missions against Japanese targets in the homeland. As of midnight on 13 July, the TAF was dissolved.

The marine air groups once again became part of the Second Marine Air Wing and, along with the army air force groups, were placed under the operational control of the Far East Air Force. The marine air groups would have as their primary responsibility the defense of Okinawa. They would fly additional attack and escort missions against distant Japanese bases. The army air force fighter and bomber groups would fly attack and escort missions against the Japanese islands as well as targets in Korea, China and the surrounding waters.

In one of his last reports, Maj. Gen. Louis E. Woods revealed that fighters from the Tactical Air Force had shot down 625 enemy aircraft. The marine squadrons had accounted for 496 and the army squadrons 129. There were an additional twenty-nine planes listed as probables. Other duties for the Tactical Air Force had included 38,192 sorties against ground targets at Okinawa, as well as continued attacks on Japanese shipping and land targets in Japan. Under the control of the Tactical Air Force at the end were 378 Corsairs, 259 Thunderbolts, 30 Hellcat night fighters, 12 Black

Widow night fighters, 48 TBM Avengers, 91 B-24 Liberators, 68 B-25s and 17 F5B Lightning Reconnaissance planes.[44]

Sunday, 14 July 1945

Patrolling RP Station # 15A on 14 July were *Aulick*, *Foote*, *Converse*, and *LCS(L)s 97, 102, 103,* and *104*. At 0402 *Aulick's* radar picked up an incoming bogey at a distance of forty-eight miles. The ships went to general quarters at 0411. Unfortunately for the enemy plane, American night fighters were in the vicinity. Captain Robert Baird of VMF(N)-533 was flying his F6F-5N Hellcat near the station when he was notified that a bomber was headed in his direction after it had attacked Ie Shima. It had evaded another night fighter in the area after completing its mission. Baird was vectored toward the plane and found it at 21,000 feet. After identifying it as a Betty, he hit it with a burst from his 20mm and .50 caliber guns and the plane went down in flames at 0441.

This aerial victory demonstrated that a problem for the Hellcat fliers had been solved. Previously, they had a difficult time shooting down Bettys with their machine guns, but the addition of the 20mm cannon made a significant difference. For Baird it was a double victory. He was the only marine to become an ace while flying a Hellcat, and the marine's only night fighter ace, since the Betty was his sixth kill. For the Japanese pilot it was a poor day for a mission. He had flown from his base on one of the six *Jippogure* days of 1945. The *Jippogure* days occurred "when the ten signs of the Element Zodiac and the twelve signs of the Animal Zodiac clash and become dangerous for mankind."[45] Bad luck was sure to accompany anyone beginning a journey that day.

Monday, 29 July 1945

The last serious attack on the radar picket ships came on 29 and 30 July. With only a few weeks left in the war, men were still at grave risk on the radar picket stations. Patrolling RP Station # 9A were *Callaghan*, *Pritchett*, *Cassin Young*, and *LCS(L)s 125, 129,* and *130*. At 0030 the ships picked up an incoming raid at a distance of about thirteen miles, and *Callaghan* tracked a single bogey in to about 10,000 yards before she and *Pritchett* took it under fire. The destroyers maneuvered to bring their guns to bear and it appeared

Major General Louis E. Woods, Commanding General of the Second Marine Air Wing, congratulates Captain Robert Baird after a sixth enemy plane fell victim to his night fighter. *NARA 127GW-528-128785.*

that the plane would pass astern *Callaghan* but, at the last moment, it turned into her and crashed the main deck near the starboard forward corner of the number 3 5" gun mount. A 250 pound bomb penetrated her deck and exploded in the aft engine room, disabling the ship. Fires started by the explosion knocked out a number of pumps and the fire fighting apparatus, making it impossible to stop the fires. Many men were killed and wounded. Within two minutes the upper handling room of the number 3 mount exploded and tore a hole in the ship that would prove fatal. *Callaghan* quickly listed fifteen degrees to starboard and began to go down by the stern. Lieutenant Howell C. Cobb, CO of *LCS(L) 125*, moored his ship to her port side and began to pour water on the fires. On the port side, Lt. William H. File, Jr., CO of *LCS(L) 130*, brought his ship close in to fight the fires. Other enemy planes appeared in the area and the *130* had to back off. *LCS(L) 129*, under the command of Lt. Louis A. Brennan, circled the area picking up survivors. Captain A.E. Jarrell, Commander of Destroyer Squadron 55, reported:

> At about 0155 CALLAGHAN'S fires had been almost extinguished. At this time, however, the ships automatic ammunition began exploding. It continued with increasing intensity. LCS 125 was retained for a few minutes with his bow touching CALLAGHAN'S port bow, and LCS 130 was directed to get clear. Explosions continued with increasing intensity, endangering LCS 125 and the personnel remaining in CALLAGHAN. I recommended to the commanding officer [Commander C.M. Bertholf] that he complete abandoning ship immediately. This was done approximately between 0200 and 0205.[46]

LCS(L) 130, just having stood clear of *Callaghan*, spotted an enemy plane closing on the ships from starboard. She took the enemy plane under fire and splashed it close to *Pritchett*. Salvage operations were still being considered when *Callaghan* pointed her bow skyward at 0234 and went to the bottom in 600 fathoms. As she slid below the waves, her boilers blew in a gigantic explosion and she disappeared. *Callaghan* had suffered forty-seven dead and seventy-three wounded. She had the dubious distinction of being the last ship sunk at Okinawa.

As it developed, there was not a single plane in the attack; later estimates placed the number of planes at eight to twelve. Shortly after *Callaghan* was hit, a second plane dove on *Pritchett* at 0148 and struck her, but the damage was minor. *Cassin Young* spotted other planes near the station and fired on them, shooting

Yokosuka K5Y biplane takes off as Japanese ground crewman watches. Code named "Willow," the plane was a trainer, but became increasingly useful as a kamikaze plane toward the end of the Okinawa campaign. Constructed of wood and fabric, it was hard to pick up on radar. *NARA 80G 193114A.*

one down and driving the others off. A biplane made a run on her and she took it under fire, splashing it one hundred feet off her starboard bow. She had escaped the attacks at the radar picket station but was not so lucky the following day. After transporting survivors back to Hagushi with *LCS 129*, she was reassigned to screen the entrance to Nakagusuku Wan and was hit by a another biplane there, causing heavy damage. Twenty-two men were killed and forty-five wounded. *Cassin Young* was out of the war.

The success of the attacks at RP Station # 9A were credited to the type of plane used. Wreckage retrieved by the ships and descriptions from Japanese sources indicate that the biplanes were

Willow (*Yokosuka K5Y*) intermediate trainers. Constructed mainly of wood and fabric, they were difficult to detect with radar, and the proximity fuses on the shells fired at them did not detonate. *Pritchett* reported:

> The ability of these old bi-planes to absorb punishment is surprising; numerous machine gun hits (40mm, 20mm, .50 Cal.) were observed on the plane which attacked at 0148, at ranges of 200-400 yards, but the bullets caused little apparent damage. Although a number of VT bursts were evident in the planes' vicinity on both runs, competent observers say that the bursts were on the other side of the target . . . these bursts causing no apparent damage.[47]

The Willow trainer had a top speed of about 123 miles per hour and a cruising speed of about 86 miles per hour. The planes made good kamikazes since they were hard to pick up on radar and very maneuverable. Known to the Japanese as the *Akatonbo* or Red Dragonfly, they were flown only from the bases on Taiwan. These were navy planes from the 29th Air Wing of the First Air Fleet which was stationed there.[48] The pilots flying the Willows were not raw recruits, but experienced fighter pilots who had been transferred from the Southwest Area to Taiwan in May and June.

On 24 July, eight of the Willows, under the command of Lt. Comdr. Nobuo Fuji, had taken off from Taiwan and made it to Miyako Jima Island. At 9 p.m on the 28th, the eight biplanes took off on their special attack mission but soon returned with engine problems. After another abortive attempt the next day, four of the planes finally left the field headed for the radar picket ships. Another one returned with engine trouble, but the others made it to RP Station # 9A where they joined in the attack on the ships.[49]

Frank E. Evans approached the station to render aid and accounted for a Betty at 0207. Overhead marine night fighters from VMF(N)-543 at Awase were busy chasing bogeys. Second Lt. T.H. Danaher splashed one at 0145 and 2d Lt. P. Moser, Jr. got another at 0245. Danaher found another Betty near the station at about the same time as Moser. He emptied his guns into the plane and damaged it, but it did not go down. The action had not gone unnoticed. Nearby *Hanger Lil,* a P-61 from the 548th Night Fighter Squadron on Ie Shima, was on patrol. First Lt. Robert O. Bertram maneuvered the plane to intercept the Betty and the P-61 shot it down.

P-61 Black Widow of the 548th Night Fighter Squadron flying over Ie Shima in mid-1945. *Courtesy of Colonel David B. Weisman USAF (Ret.).*

Alfred A. Cunningham, Frank E. Evans, and *Laws* reported to the station at 0638 on the 29th to relieve the beleaguered destroyers. For their work in supporting the destroyers that day, the commanding officers of *LCS(L)s 130, 125,* and *129.* were recognized. Lieutenant File (*130*) was awarded the Silver Star and Lieutenants Cobb (*125*) and Brennan (*129*) the Bronze Star.

Tuesday, 30 July and Wednesday, 31 July 1945

Early in the morning of 30 July, the ships again came under attack. *Alfred A. Cunningham* picked up several incoming bogeys at 0120. Second Lt. Irving B. Hardy of VMF(N)-533 had been loaned to VFM(N)-542 and was flying one of their F6F-5N Hellcats on combat air patrol near the station. He was vectored to intercept a bogey by ground control and found a Betty at 19,000 feet.

For the next half hour, Hardy stalked the Betty. In spite of numerous evasive maneuvers, the marine flier kept on its tail and finally hit it with several bursts.

With both engines in flames and heading down, the Betty was in position for the *coup de grace*. Hardy delivered it from behind, hitting the fuselage and wing roots. The bomber splashed into the sea in flames thirteen miles from RP Station # 9A. *Evans* opened fire on another bogey at 0237 that had closed to within 3,000 yards of the ships. The enemy aircraft passed overhead and then flew off. Still another unidentified plane approached the ships at 0325 and *Evans* fired on it with its main battery without result.

Thursday, 1 August through Tuesday, 6 August 1945

American attacks on the Kyushu airfields had taken their toll. In the closing days of July, Tachiarai, Ibusuki, Chiran, Izumi, and Omura were hit by P-47s, A-26s and B-25s. Kanoya received special attention, suffering attacks on three days. The constant bombings and strafing at Kanoya forced Ugaki to withdraw his headquarters to Oita in North Kyushu. His move was to be effective 1 August, but poor weather slowed his arrival until 3 August. Headquartered at Oita from this date on would be the Fifth Air Fleet, Air Flotilla 72 and Air Flotilla 12. Air Flotilla 72 was comprised of fighters and Air Flotilla 12 of suicide training planes. Additional American air attacks hit Miyakonojo, Tsuiki, Chiran and Izumi during the first week of August. The largest strike was against Miyakonojo on the 6th, which was comprised of 150 P-47s and A-26s.

The first four days of August were uneventful as RP# 9A was unmanned due to foul weather most of the time.

Wednesday, 7 August and Thursday, 8 August 1945

Overnight, between 7 and 8 August, as RP Station # 9A was patrolled by *Frank E. Evans, Alfred E. Cunningham, Irwin*, and *LCS(L)s 97, 98, 99*, and *101*, the night skies were under close watch by the Black Widows of the 548th Night Fighter Squadron.

While other P-61s patrolled to the north of Ie Shima, pilot 2d Lt. Paul M. Herron, radar observer Lieutenant Puttick and gunner observer Cpl. Victor Harris, Jr. flew their Black Widow near RP

Station # 9A. At 0245 they made contact with a bogey at nine miles. After they closed to 500 feet the enemy plane spotted them and took violent evasive actions. On three more occasions the P-61 closed to 500 feet, but each time the plane banked, turned and dove away. Finally the Japanese plane escaped.

This was typical for the night fighter patrols. For the next several nights they spent their time chasing bogeys through the night skies without any luck. Offensive action against the Kyushu airfields continued, with strikes against numerous targets by the FEAF on 8 August. Attacking Usa and Tsuiki airfields were B-24s, B-25s, A-26s, P-51s and P-47s.

Friday, 9 August through Tuesday, 13 August 1945

Patrols at RP Station # 9A continued through 9 August. No enemy planes approached the formation until the 10th. Late that evening, at about 2235, *Irwin*, *Frank E. Evans*, *Alfred A. Cunningham*, and *LCS(L)s 97*, *98*, *99*, and *101* went to general quarters with enemy planes reported in the area. None approached the station. Night fighters from the Black Widow squadrons on Ie Shima chased occasional bogeys but were unable to bring any down.

During the four and one half months of radar picket duty, 206 ships and over 39,000 men served on the radar picket stations. At 0040 on 13 August, *Foote*, *Charles Ausburne*, *John A. Bole*, and the support gunboats *LCS(L)s 76* and *78*, patrolling at RP Station # 9A, received orders to head back to Hagushi. With only one day left in the war, the radar picket ordeal was over.

Although *Kikusui* raids 9 and 10 had far fewer aircraft, they had still caused much damage on the radar picket stations. From 1 June through 13 August 1945 two destroyers had been sunk, while two others and an LCS(L) were damaged. On the radar picket stations fifty-eight men had died and 166 were wounded. The few kamikazes that did slip through the pickets took their toll in the waters around Okinawa.

The destroyer *Twiggs* went down off southern Okinawa, losing 126 men with an additional thirty-four wounded. Three destroyer types, a destroyer escort and five other ships sustained damage in air raids and kamikaze attacks. Added to the casualties on the radar picket stations were a total of 211 dead and 218 wounded.[50]

Post Script

Thursday, 15 August 1945

The radar picket ships' ordeal had ended, but the kamikaze threat had not. Individual diehards among the Japanese military still desired to continue the fight against the Americans and a few would fly kamikaze missions during the next week. Vice Adm. Matome Ugaki, in a last show of samurai spirit, decided to make a final attack on the American forces at Okinawa. Although the Naval High Command had ordered the fleet to cease offensive operations against the Americans, Ugaki was in disagreement and determined to continue the fight. In his last diary entries, he noted that he felt responsible in large part for Japan's defeat and would follow in the footsteps of the men he had sent to crash their planes into the American fleet at Okinawa.[51]

Ugaki ordered three planes of the 701st Air Group at Oita to be prepared. When he arrived at the field he found eleven planes and twenty-two airmen ready for their last mission. Many had been inspired by his heroism and were determined to accompany him. After a brief farewell ceremony Ugaki, his uniform shorn of all rank, climbed into the rear seat of a *Yokosuka D4Y4 Suisei* (Judy) dive bomber piloted by Lt. Tatsuo Nakatsuru. The plane's observer, Warrant Officer Akiyoshi Endo, joined him in the rear seat, refusing to be left behind. Ugaki carried with him a pair of binoculars and a short sword that had been presented to him by Admiral Isoroku Yamamoto. In a short time, the planes were airborne and heading for Okinawa. Four of the planes developed engine problems and had to return to the base, leaving seven heading for a suicide mission at Okinawa. Somewhere in the vicinity of Okinawa, Ugaki radioed back his last thoughts. He accepted responsibility for all of his decisions and vowed to join the other kamikaze pilots in the spirit of *Bushido*. His transmission, and those of the other planes, ended about 1924 with an indication that his plane was about to crash into an enemy ship.[52] No attacks on American ships are recorded for that date, so it is not clear if Ugaki was over a ship or thought that he soon would be.

Meanwhile, night fighters on the fields at Okinawa had been put on alert. VMF(N)-533, flying out of Chimu Airfield on Okinawa, reported that they were "assigned to fly second and fourth period patrols. A Red Alert during the first period caused some anticipation of action among the pilots, but no bogeys were encountered in either patrol."[53] Marine night fighter pilots from VMF(N)-543 at Awase reported flying "a total of nine sorties (22 plane hours) with negative results."[54]

The *War Diary of the 2nd Marine Aircraft Wing*, indicates the crash of two kamikaze planes on Ie Shima in the closing hours of the war.[55] Did some or all of Ugaki's flight get lost or run out of fuel and go down in the Pacific's waters or did some of them make it to Okinawa before they crashed? His exact fate may never be known.

New night fighters arrived too late to assist in the victory. Marine night fighter squadrons had patrolled the skies over Okinawa in their F6F-5N Hellcats during the campaign. The eagerly awaited twin engine F7F-2N Tigercat night fighters arrived on 18 August at VMF(N)-533, too late to be of any use. They would patrol the night skies in vain searching for the ghosts of the Special Attack Corps.

CHAPTER 8

"The losses seem quite reasonable . . ."

The losses at the radar picket stations had been great, but the navy felt that they were acceptable. Rear Admiral Allan E. Smith CTF 54 reported:

> But the cordon of destroyer radar pickets around the island have given advance information of enemy planes approaching. This timely information has been a most important factor in the security of the entire operation. A number of destroyers on picket duty have been sunk but the number of planes shot down by them has been very high. In view of the security given by the radar pickets, the losses seem quite reasonable and the general situation from a naval view point very satisfactory indeed.[1]

In closing this study of the radar pickets' ordeal at Okinawa, one must try to assess the factors that led to the losses on the radar picket stations. It must be concluded that the great losses suffered by the radar picket ships came not from one factor but a combination of several. Among the factors that weighed heavily in the equation of these losses were: (1) the nature of the kamikaze attacks, (2) improper use of support gunboats, (3) assignment of ships ill-suited for the task, (4) failure to establish land-based radar at the earliest possible times and (5) crew fatigue. The impact of each of these factors is addressed below.

Kamikaze Attacks

The nature of the kamikaze attacks were not initially apparent in the Okinawa campaign. The planners of Operation Iceberg had no doubt in their minds that the Japanese would use suicide tactics similar to those used in the Philippines. Both suicide planes and boats had successfully attacked American ships during that campaign. Many ships had been hit by enemy aircraft and were either damaged or sunk during the battle for the Philippines. In addition, the sinking of *LCS(L)s 7, 26,* and *49* by suicide boats at Mariveles Harbor was a precursor of things to come. Vice Adm. H.W. Hill CTF-51 and CTF 31 later stated:

> Continual concern was felt from the outset of the operation for the safety of radar picket vessels, which were taking the brunt of Japanese air effort. Antiaircraft firepower of these stations was augmented as practicable, and finally standardized at three destroyers and four LCS's on each station. Destroyer types on picket station were further increased when air attack was expected. This policy, combined with heavy combat air patrols in the vicinity of the pickets, eventually resulted in a decrease in the concentration of Japanese effort on picket ships.[2]

During the battle for the Philippines small groups of kamikazes attacked the ships. At that time, the Japanese thought that small formations of from three to five planes would have the best chance of approaching American ships without being detected. No one could have foreseen the size of the first *Kikusui* raid at Okinawa which included 355 suicide planes along with 344 attacks by conventional aircraft.[3] Vice Adm. Richmond K. Turner CTF-51 reported:

> For the first time the enemy employed mass suicide plane attacks against our naval forces, with as many as 51 planes attacking a single ship. These attacks were anticipated and the early intelligence gained from vessels stationed in advanced picket stations regarding them was excellent. In spite of the many raids on enemy airfields and the high toll taken by the CAP, many enemy planes made determined attacks on ships in all areas, but especially on the screens. The brilliant firing of the DD's and LCS's and the fighting spirit of these and other ships dealt effectively with this most formidable threat of the enemy.[4]

The sheer numbers of Japanese aircraft flying toward the picket stations was in excess of what the combat air patrols could handle.

In addition to the kamikazes and their escorts there were also regular attack aircraft. One of the factors that saved the picket ships from even greater loss was the relative inexperience of the Japanese pilots. Numerous Japanese planes were shot down easily after American pilots intercepted them. In many cases the Japanese ignored the American fighters in an attempt to get to the picket ships and crash them. In fact, some of the planes had been stripped of their guns in order to allow them to carry a heavier bomb load. Unaware of this tactic, some picket ship commanding officers wondered why the planes did not strafe on their final approach.

Shooting down an airplane that does little to evade shipboard antiaircraft fire would seem to be a simple matter, but kamikaze tactics called for attacks from a variety of altitudes and directions in order to confuse the gunners on the ships. If enough of the enemy planes were in the attack and too few American fighters on the scene, it was inevitable that some would evade the CAP. Studies conducted by the Division of Naval Intelligence after the end of the Okinawa campaign revealed that although the CAP had shot down many enemy planes, a great number got through. They found that

> . . .the average [enemy planes shot down] achieved by the forces supporting the Okinawa Campaign was probably somewhat less, with 60% as an upper limit, and 40% a lower limit. These percentages are assumed to apply to suicide and non-suicide aircraft alike.
>
> (c) That of the suicide sorties penetrating to the target area, 47% scored hits or damaging near misses. This percentage is derived in reference (c) on the basis of a study of the Philippines Campaign, October 1944 - January 1945.[5]

Improper Use of Support Gunboats

The initial assignments to the radar picket stations in early April usually included the designation "R" or "L" for the station. In most instances this meant using a configuration where the destroyer type patrolled on the station and that the support gunboat patrolled to the right or left of the station approximately one-third of the way to the adjoining station. With this configuration, the support gunboats were of little use in assisting the fighter director destroyer in fighting off kamikazes. In the early phase of the Okinawa campaign the use of this configuration was a necessity, as many of the LCS(L)s were engaged in coastal patrols against Japanese suicide boats and other small craft. Lieutenant Harry L. Smith, commanding officer of *LCS(L) 57* noted: "It is felt that better opposition to attack by suicide planes would be provided if ships were closer together while on this type of duty. At no time was a ship closer than 4 miles from this ship while under attack. Consequently there was no supporting fire power."[6]

After the first of the *Kikusui* raids it became obvious that additional firepower would be needed to protect the fighter director destroyer. Gunboats, along with another destroyer type or two, became the constant companions of the fighter director ship on the radar picket station. The manner in which these support gunboats were used frequently determined the amount of protection available to the fighter director ship. Many of the LCS(L) skippers complained that the Officer in Tactical Command of the station positioned their ships miles away from the destroyers, thus negating their effectiveness. When used properly, the LCS(L)s were a valuable asset. *Luce DD 522*, sunk at RP Station # 12 on 4 May, 1945, was unable to gain the help of her gunboats. In her action report of 8 May 1945 the commanding officer of *LCS(L) 118*, Lt. P.F. Gilmore Jr., noted: "Had our station been one of close support, all the close support vessels that day might have rendered better assistance to the DD-522."[7] And Lt. John L. Cronk, commanding officer of *LCS(L) 94* wrote:

> . . . mistakes made by destroyers on Radar Picket duty are worthy of mention. . . . On every picket patrol we have been on, almost all the time the destroyers on patrol with the LCS's have been deployed 3 or 4 miles away from our formation, thereby losing any support we might give them and also any support they might give us. Destroyers should remember that on a clear day nine chances out of ten a suicider will pick the larger ship if he sees both.[8]

Many of the destroyer commanding officers did realize how important the support gunboats could be. In his action report of 1 June 1945, Lt. Comdr. W.R. Hunnicutt, Jr., CO of *Aulick*, asserted that "The small support craft should be kept near the destroyers, within 4,000 yards if possible, in order to give the destroyers the best protection."[9] Although some of the destroyer commanding officers wanted to utilize the firepower of the LCS(L)S, in some cases it was not possible. *Douglas H. Fox*, hit on RP Station # 9 on 17 May, endeavored to keep the gunboats close but found that it was not possible in the heat of the battle. In *Douglas H. Fox's* action report of 24 May 1945, her fighter director officer Lt. B.M. Demarest reported:

> At one time, and one time only, an order to the helm was given for the purpose of closing the support craft who were being maneuvered by Commander, LCS Group 12. This order was quickly countermanded for the more important and immediate consideration of unmasking batteries. Had a lull occurred, DOUGLAS H. FOX would have maneuvered to close the small boys, but it was not until after the coordinated attack had passed that this could be considered.[10]

Most destroyer commanding officers felt that speed was their greatest ally. Destroyer types at high speed could maneuver quickly and bring their guns to bear on kamikazes, but this high speed left the LCS(L)s far behind as the destroyer types were capable of more than double their speed.

Ill-suited Ships

Seven ship types were assigned to the radar picket stations: destroyers (DD), light mine layers (DM), high speed minesweepers (DMS), destroyer escorts (DE), LCS(L)s, PGMs, and LSM(R)s. The destroyer-types had a high turn of speed but many were lacking sufficient anti-aircraft capabilities. The two DEs assigned, *Bowers DE 637* and *Edmonds DE 406*, also were lacking in anti-aircraft capability. The LCS(L)s were capable of defending themselves because they possessed two or three twin 40mm guns in their armament and were small targets. PGMs had more speed, but fewer 40mm guns. The ship least capable of fighting off air attacks was the LSM(R).

LSM(R)s were specialty ships designed to attack shore targets with multiple rocket launchers and a single 5"/38 DP gun. The 5"/38 was of little use against kamikazes. Also included in their armament were two 40mm singles and three 20mm single guns. None of these weapons were found to be ideal to combat suicide

planes. Of the eleven LSM(R)s assigned to the duty, three were
sunk and two damaged, one so badly it was not repaired until the
war was over. Given the limited duration of their service on the
radar picket stations, this compares quite unfavorably to the losses among the 101 destroyer types and 88 LCS(L)s.

That the LSM(R)s were unsuited to the task was noted early
on in the campaign for Okinawa. On 21 April 1945, Comdr. Dennis
L. Francis, the CO of LSM Flotilla Nine, reported:

> . . . It is believed that these ships are not particularly suited
> for this duty. Since their primary function is to deliver rockets
> during invasion operations, it seems feasible that subjecting
> them to continual enemy air attack will allow a secondary duty
> to seriously effect their ability to perform their primary func-
> tion due to mechanical damage. They have no great value in
> combating enemy air craft due to the absence of air search
> radar, adequate director control for the 5"38 main battery, and
> director control for the 40mm single guns. The fact that they
> carry a considerable quantity of explosive rockets in their mag-
> azines presents another hazard. In general it is believed that
> assigning them to this duty should be avoided . . .[11]

An additional problem for the LSM(R) was its size and slow
speed. With a maximum speed of 13.2 knots, the 203' rocket ship
was a large, slow and relatively defenseless target. On the picket
stations, thirty-four LSM(R) men died and sixty-two were wounded. In his report of 7 July 1945, Vice Adm. Richmond K. Turner
explained their assignment to the radar picket stations. "LSM(R)s
have been assigned to radar picket duty despite their large silhou-
ette and inadequate armament. This was necessary because the
LCSs were too small for rescue and towing work."[12]

Early assignments to radar picket duty consisted of lone
destroyer types with the support of one or two LCS(L)s. After the
first *Kikusui* raid of 6-7 April, additional ships were quickly added
to the duty. A total of nineteen destroyer-type ships and LCS(L)
gunboats faced the Japanese planes of *Kikusui # 1*. By 10 April, the
number of ships assigned to the duty quickly jumped to thirty-
seven. This was possible since the initial landings that required the
use of LCS(L)s and LSM(R)s were over and the ships could be used
for other duties. LSM(R)s served on radar picket duty from 7 April
until 22 May 1945. By that time, more LCS(L)s had arrived from

the states and additional destroyer types were freed from other duties and could patrol the stations.

Although the other ship types mentioned above were better suited than the LSM(R) for radar picket duty, they were still ships designed for a variety of tasks and not specifically as anti-aircraft vessels. LCS(L)s, which were primarily created to support amphibious landings and intercept inter-island barge traffic, found themselves supporting destroyers on the picket lines. Of the eighty-eight assigned to the duty, two were sunk and twelve damaged as a result of enemy air attacks which caused the deaths of sixty men and the wounding of 123 on the LCS(L) ships. Vice Admiral Turner indicated that the LCS(L) ships were hard to hit and this is probably an accurate assessment. The LCS(L)s were the smallest target on the RP station and could maneuver well. *LCS(L) 61* avoided a crash by a Betty bomber on 27 May by a last minute hard turn which caused the Betty to splash twenty feet off her bow. None of the support vessels had the speed of the destroyer types. They had to rely solely on slow speed maneuvers and firepower to escape being hit; this placed them at a disadvantage.

The destroyer-types suffered the most damage when compared numerically with the other ships. Since so many of them (101) were assigned the duty and they were continuously on radar picket patrols, it is logical that they suffered the greatest losses. On the destroyer-types, 1,254 men were killed and 1,404 wounded while serving on radar picket duty. Destroyer-types had varying abilities when it came to combating kamikazes, with the newer classes mounting more twin and quad 40mm guns than the earlier ones.

PGMs, possessing a good turn of speed and a twin 40mm mount among their armament, spent considerably less time on the radar picket stations and suffered no hits or casualties.

The data in the chart below must be weighed against the duration and frequency of the radar picket assignments. Throughout the ordeal, destroyer types and LCS(L)s were continually on patrol, whereas PGMs and LSM(R)s only served a small percentage of the actual days on radar picket duty. The percentage of LSM(R)s hit while on the duty would seem to indicate that of the ships assigned to the duty, they were most vulnerable to attack. This seems particularly true since they were not in continual use as were the destroyer types and the LCS(L)s.

Percentage of Ships Suffering Kamikaze Hits on Radar Picket Duty			
Ship Types	Number Assigned to RP Duty	Number Sunk or Damaged by Kamikzes	Percentage
DD, DM, DMS*	101	42	.42
LCS(L)	88	13	.15
PGM	4	0	0
LSM(R)	11	5	.45

* Two DEs, *Bowers DE 37* and *Edmonds DE 406* each served only one day on radar picket duty and are not included in this chart. Neither was struck by a kamikaze during that assignment.

A comparison of the data shown in the two charts above can lead to some conclusions about the relative danger to the ships assigned to the duty. LSM(R)s, which were on the radar picket stations only one-third of the days possible, suffered the most from kamikazes with 45 percent of them hit. Destroyer types, which were on the picket stations 100 percent of the time suffered only slightly lower percentages of hits at 42 percent. LCS(L)s, which were present on the stations 95 percent of the days suffered only 15 percent hits.

These figures may be misleading since they do not take into account target choice by the Japanese kamikazes. If given the choice, the kamikaze would pick the larger ship, a destroyer-type or LSM(R) over an LCS(L). In all, the radar picket experience was extremely dangerous. Of the 206 ships which served on the duty, sixty were damaged or sunk, which means that 29 percent of the ships serving on radar picket duty at Okinawa became casualties.

The experience of the destroyers on radar picket duty was similar to their experience throughout the entire Okinawa campaign. On 23 July 1945, the Division of Naval Intelligence released a study entitled "Statistical Analysis of Japanese Suicide Effort Against Allied Shipping During Okinawa Campaign." The finding of the study verified that destroyers were among the ships most heavily damaged in kamikaze attacks. It indicated:

Comparative Time on Radar Picket Duty by Ship Type			
Ship Types	Number of Days this type was Assigned To RP Duty	Total Radar Picket Days 26 March - 13 August, 1945	Percentage of total days each type served on a RP station
DD, DM, DMS*	141	141	100
LCS(L)	134	141	.95
LSM(R)	46	141	.33
PGM	27	141	.19

* Two DEs, *Bowers DE 37* and *Edmonds DE 406* each served only one day on radar picket duty and are not included in this chart. Neither was struck by a kamikaze during that assignment.

It will be noticed that ships belonging to the CV, DD, DE, and BB types were significantly overhit in relation to their percentage contribution to the force as a whole. Perhaps the most striking case is that of the destroyers which made up only 10.7% of the force, but comprised 30.6% of the total ships hit.[13]

Rear Adm. Allan E. Smith, CTF 54, gave further consideration to the types of ships assigned to the radar picket stations. Based on the experiences at Okinawa, he felt that the stations did not have adequate strength. He identified the ideal unit as a fast carrier task group, indicating that this configuration of ships would be able to handle any situation. Since such carrier groups were not available, he suggested that one light cruiser and four destroyers on each station would have the requisite firepower to handle the kamikaze threat. Unfortunately, enough cruisers were not available to do the job. Without the cruiser addition to the group, he further recommended that five destroyers might be assigned to each station, but this would require a great number of this class of vessel, perhaps to the detriment of other operations. It would also require that the number of radar picket stations be reduced, which might have worked if the land-based radar stations had been completed earlier. Each of the stations would require a daylight CAP with one or two night fighters covering them after the day CAP had retired. To bolster the defenses of the radar picket ships, a submarine radar screen might be placed fifty miles from the station between it and the source of incoming raids.[14] Vice Admiral Turner's views were different. According to him, "The ideal composition is 4 - 6 DD and 6 support craft of similar speed and maneuvering characteristics."[15]

Failure to Establish Land-based Radar at the Earliest Possible Times

There was no doubt of the necessity of establishing a ring of early warning radar sites around Okinawa in order to protect the transport area and the troops ashore from Japanese air attacks.

What the planners of Operation Iceberg did not recognize, however, was that the Japanese would commit such large numbers of kamikazes to the *Kikusui* attacks. They also failed to realize that the picket ships, serving as the eyes and ears of the invasion fleet, would come under heavy attack as soon as the Japanese located them.

In his *Report on the Okinawa Gunto Operation from 17 February to 17 May, 1945*, Vice Admiral Turner stated.

> It is recommended that in planning all future operations much greater emphasis be placed on securing outlying land areas or islands at the earliest practicable date and installing adequate land-based radars and fighter director units thereon in order that vulnerable shipping will have to remain on exposed stations no longer than is absolutely necessary.[16]

Vice Adm. H.W. Hill concurred: " . . .the paramount importance of the earliest possible installation of land based Radar cannot be overemphasized. Cruelly prolonged exposure of Radar Picket vessels to enemy attack is the price paid when any unnecessary delay occurs in the establishment of land Radar stations."[17]

Crew Fatigue Affecting Gunnery Skills, Observation and Judgement

Still another factor, difficult to assess qualitatively, was crew fatigue. Although ships were rotated continually, after a day or two of resupply they usually found themselves back on the radar picket stations. Destroyer types and LCS(L)s in particular suffered greatly. Vice Adm. H.W. Hill noted that "Personnel fatigue, particularly in ships on radar picket stations, became marked . . . ." [18]

In his action report of 17 April 1945, Comdr. J.N. McDonald, CO of the destroyer *Bennett*, reported that "The entire crew was beginning to show signs of extreme fatigue by the morning of 7 April . . ." [19] On that day, *Bennett* suffered a crash which killed two men and injured eighteen during a kamikaze raid. Normal rotation of duty gave some occasional rest, but each sailor could never be sure when incoming bogeys would cause the general quarters horn to sound, summoning them to battle stations.

Not even the anchorages were safe. Kamikazes could slip by the CAP and picket ships to find targets at Hagushi or Kerama Retto. In many cases there were false alarms, with bogeys turning off some distance from the ships. Numerous bogeys turned out to be American planes on patrol or rescue missions, and still others might be night fighters assigned to patrol near the ships.

Commander G.K. Carmichael, the commanding officer of *Caperton*, complained about constant calls to general quarters when unidentified American aircraft were in the vicinity and how it impacted crew fatigue.[20] Additionally, Lt. Comdr. W.R. Hunnicutt Jr., CO of the destroyer *Aulick*, in his action report of 9 July 1945, added that unidentified friendly planes had caused his ship to go to general quarters twenty times between 28 May and 21 June, stating how "This decreased the efficiency of the ship in that it was tiring to the crew and detracted attention from actual enemy reports."[21]

Long hours at battle stations and the knowledge that a suicide attack could occur at any time left men in a continuous state of nervous tension which could not be overcome. Another destroyer CO, Comdr. C.J. Van Arsdall, Jr. of *Anthony*, wrote in his action report of 26 June 1945:

> . . .that anyone never having been regularly assigned to such duty can fully realize the effect which this duty has upon the officers and crew, particularly of vessels which have witnessed successful suicide crashes on other ships and have themselves been under direct attack. A tension builds up which is evident in many ways, and which is not relaxed by the periods for logis-

tics between tours of duty on picket stations, largely because of the knowledge that coming assignments are "more of the same." Cases of active hysteria, requiring transfer, were few on this ship. How long others, still on board, could have held out, is subject to question. After a certain time, the best efforts to "boost morale" are futile. The boys know what they are in for, and you can't fool them.[22]

Lieutenant H.D. Chickering, commanding officer of *LCS(L) 51* added his description of the picket sailors' plight:

The raids seemed ceaseless, our guns were always manned and the gunners literally slept at them. As Captain, I seldom left the bridge. Food was coffee, hard boiled eggs and occasionally sandwiches. Sanitary facilities were a bucket. Once in a while I caught a catnap in my seat. For a week, we fired on, or reported, dozens of raids, and lost count very quickly. The strain became almost intolerable. We were gaunt and filthy, red-eyed and stinking. The ship was a mess, with empty shell casings everywhere. My face was pocked with particles of burned gunpowder, since one Oerlikon anti-aircraft gun fired as close as three yards from my battle station. We prayed for bad weather, which was about the only thing that slowed down the stream of Japanese planes.[23]

Men posted on watch frequently fell asleep, sometimes with their eyes open. At times no amount of terror could overcome the extreme fatigue felt by the sailors on the picket line. Commander R.R. Pratt, commanding officer of *Hudson*, in his action report of 13 May 1945, stated:

Due to the rigorous operating schedule, nervous tension ran extremely high throughout the ship's company. This was manifest in inability of many men to sleep even though they had very little. Some complained of loss of appetite and a smaller number complained that nausea accompanied this. About six men required sedation so that they were able to eat and sleep . . . Starting about 15 April, it was noted that the sick list carried about three men daily as compared with a normal of a rare admission to the sick list.[24]

Pratt concluded that the higher than average rate of sick crew members was directly linked to the tension of being on the picket line and its resultant lack of sleep. How this translated into additional casualties among the ships is hard to determine, but it is probable that more than one kamikaze managed to slip by exhausted lookouts. Commanding officers, in some cases, might have made different decisions if they were not so tired. That they managed to do so well against a determined and relentless enemy is a credit to the officers and crews of the ships which underwent this terrible ordeal.

After the war, Robert Wisner, who served as communications officer on board *LCS(L) 37* noted the particular plight of the support gunboats.

> We had been on picket duty for days and days and the men, of course, looked forward to going in to get some rest and relaxation, changing clothes at least and we'd have to make smoke all night long. This is the story of every LCS that was on picket duty, we always had to make smoke when we went in. Some never got any rest, never changed clothes, never took a shower, we all stank like crazy, and then we got hit.[25]

Vice Admiral Turner suggested that "While not on duty crews of radar picket ships should be afforded an opportunity for rest and recreation. Athletic fields ashore should be established at the first opportunity. This will have an important effect on morale."[26]

Not only were the crews in danger from kamikazes, fatigue sometimes caused accidents that were of their own making. At RP Station # 7 on 16 May, *LCS(L) 118* was fired upon by her sister ship, *LCS(L) 12*. The pointer on the forward twin 40mm gun fell asleep and accidentally set off the gun which sent eight 40mm shells toward *LCS(L) 118*. Fortunately they missed, but it was a close call.[27]

Crewmen on board the radar picket ships lived under a strain so constant that it seemed unendurable. In recalling the ordeal after the war, Sonarman 1/c Jack Gebhardt, on *Pringle* when she was sunk by a kamikaze on 16 April 1945, recalled:

> Once the airfield on Okinawa was secured, our Marine pilots began using it, but had a difficult time because everybody was so trigger happy from the constant Japanese attacks. The air raids were endless and our nerves became frayed and stomach churned at the thought of being killed in a horrible blast or gasoline fire.[28]

In his *Action Report – Capture of Okinawa Gunto, Phase II 5 May to 28 May 1945*, the commander of Task Force 54, Rear Adm. Allan E. Smith noted: ". . . it can be stated that the personnel of a fire support ship which maintains fire for 45 to 65 days and half the nights with about every fifth day for a hard job of replenishment, are not as mentally alert as the best suicider defense requires."[29] Smith also felt that the amount of drill and exercise for combating the kamikazes was insufficient. He attributed this to the lack of time needed to complete the training due to the constant combat use of the destroyers. Additionally, he noted that the command organization was exceedingly complex, making it difficult for individual ship commanders to accomplish the task.

The radar picket ships had suffered greatly during the campaign for Okinawa. Throughout the ordeal, they had displayed the fighting courage traditional in the United States Navy. A fitting tribute to them was paid by Vice Admiral Turner:

> The gallant ships in these stations were at all times, and in a very literal sense, in the first line of defense at OKINAWA. Their expert raid reporting and efficient fighter direction made possible the timely interception of enemy aircraft which would otherwise have been able successfully to attack our transport and supply ships in force. The enemy pressed his attacks with fanatical determination and still failed to disrupt our progress, largely because the Radar Pickets were an obstacle he could not overcome. By their steadfast courage and magnificent performance of duty in a nerve wracking job under morale shattering conditions, the crews of the ships and craft on the Radar Picket stations have emblazoned a glorious new chapter in naval tradition.[30]

Further accolades by Vice Adm. H.W. Hill indicated the stature of the radar picket ships. "The outstanding work of the RADAR PICKET continued to be the highlight of the campaign. The importance of their work is evidenced by the attention they received from enemy aircraft, as well as the amount of damage they directly or indirectly inflicted."[31]

In a significant way, the radar picket ships saved many other ships from damage. In a speech at the Air War College at Maxwell Air Force Base in 1947, Vice Admiral Turner asserted:

One of the things that was very fortunate for the transports and the troops was that the Japanese suicide airplanes, as soon as they began to be attacked by our outlying fighters, would themselves deliver attacks on our pickets instead of trying to penetrate our screen to attack the transports. It was tough on the pickets, but the Japanese themselves thus contributed to the successful defense of the vulnerable elements of the Amphibious Force.[32]

How can the performance of any group of combatants be assessed against the greater panorama of a world war? Surely throughout the vast battlefields of the world many men fought bravely and suffered greatly. In the air, on land and on the sea, soldiers, sailors and marines answered the call of their country and put their lives on the line. Wherever the brave and courageous are thought of, the men who served on the radar picket ships and the pilots who flew over them at Okinawa earned their place.

Appendix I

SHIPS DAMAGED OR SUNK ON
RADAR PICKET DUTY

Ship	Location	Date	Sunk	Damaged	Killed	Wounded
Kimberly DD 521	RP # 9	26 Mar		X	4	57
Pritchett DD 561	RP # 15	2 April		X	0	0
Pritchett DD 561	RP # 1	3 April		X	0	0
Bush DD 529	RP # 1	6 April	X		94	32
Colhoun DD 801	RP # 1	6 April	X		35	21
Bennett DD 473	RP # 1	7 April		X	3	18
Gregory DD 802	RP # 3	8 April		X	0	2
Sterrett DD 407	RP # 4	9 April		X	0	9
Stanly DD 478	RP # 1	12 April		X	0	3
LCS(L) 115	RP # 1	12 April		X	0	2
Purdy DD 734	RP # 1	12 April		X	13	27
Cassin Young DD 793	RP # 1	12 April		X	1	59
LCS(L) 33	RP # 1	12 April	X		4	29
LCS(L) 57	RP # 1	12 April		X	2	6
Jeffers DMS 27	RP # 12	12 April		X	0	0
Mannert L. Abele DD 733	RP # 14	12 April	X		79	35
LSM(R) 189	RP # 14	12 April		X	0	4
LCS(L) 51	RP # 1	16 April		X	0	0
LCS(L) 116	RP # 1	16 April		X	12	12

APPENDIX I, Continued
SHIPS DAMAGED OR SUNK ON RADAR PICKET DUTY

Ship	Location	Date	Sunk	Damaged	Killed	Wounded
Laffey DD 724	RP # 1	16 April		X	31	72
Bryant DD 665	RP # 2	16 April		X	34	33
Pringle DD 477	RP # 14	16 April	X		65	110
Hobson DMS 26	RP # 14	16 April		X	4	8
Harding DMS 28	en route RP # 14	16 April		X	22	10
Macomb DMS 23	RP # 3	17 April		X	0	0
Ammen DD 527	RP # 2	20 April		X	0	8
Wadsworth DD 516	RP # 10	22 April		X	0	1
LCS(L) 15	RP # 14	22 April	X		15	11
Bennion DD 662	RP # 1	28 April		X	0	0
Twiggs DD 591	RP # 2	28 April		X	0	2
Daly DD 519	RP # 2	28 April		X	2	15
Wadsworth DD 516	RP # 12	28 April		X	0	0
Macomb DMS 23	RP # 9	3 May		X	7	14
Little DD 803	RP # 10	3 May	X		30	79
Aaron Ward DM 34	RP # 10	3 May		X	45	49
LSM(R) 195	RP # 10	3 May	X		8	16
LCS(L) 31	RP # 1	4 May		X	5	2
Ingraham DD 694	RP # 1	4 May		X	14	37
Morrison DD 560	RP # 1	4 May	X		159	102
LSM(R) 194	RP # 1	4 May	X		13	23
Lowry DD 770	RP # 2	4 May		X	2	23
LCS(L) 25	RP # 10	4 May		X	1	8
Gwin DM 33	RP # 10	4 May		X	2	9
LSM(R) 192	RP # 10	4 May		X	0	1
Luce DD 522	RP # 12	4 May	X		149	94
LSM(R) 190	RP # 12	4 May	X		13	18
Shea DM 30	RP # 14	4 May		X	27	9
Evans DD 552	RP # 15	11 May		X	30	29
LCS(L) 84	RP # 15	11 May		X	0	1
LCS(L) 88	RP # 5	11 May		X	7	9

APPENDIX I, Continued
SHIPS DAMAGED OR SUNK ON RADAR PICKET DUTY

Ship	Location	Date	Sunk	Damaged	Killed	Wounded
Hugh W. Hadley DD 774	RP # 15	11 May		X	28	67
Bache DD 470	RP # 9	13 May		X	41	32
Douglas H. Fox DD 779	RP # 9	17 May		X	9	35
LCS(L) 121	RP # 15A	23 May		X	2	4
Stormes DD 780	RP # 15A	25 May		X	21	6
Braine DD 630	RP # 5	27 May		X	66	78
Anthony DD 515	RP # 5	27 May		X	0	0
LCS(L) 52	RP # 15A	27 May		X	1	10
Drexler DD 741	RP # 15A	28 May	X		158	51
Shubrick DD 639	RP # 16A	29 May		X	32	28
Anthony DD 515	RP # 15A	7 June		X	0	3
William D. Porter DD 579	RP # 15A	10 June	X		0	61
LCS(L) 122	RP # 15A	11 June		X	11	29
Callaghan DD 792	RP # 9A	29 July	X		47	73
Pritchett DD 561	RP # 9A	29 July		X	0	0
Totals			**15**	**50**	**1,348**	**1,586**

Sunk: DD–10, LCS(L)–2, LSM(R)–3
Damaged: DD–25*, DM–3, DMS–4*, LCS(L)–11, LSM(R)–2

Macomb DMS 23 was damaged twice, once by a near miss. *Pritchett DD 561* was hit and damaged three times. *Anthony DD 515* and *Wadsworth DD 516* were hit and damaged two times.

Damage to the above ships was varied, with some severely damaged and others sustaining minor damage after the attack. In some cases, the damage was caused by bombs carried by conventional attack aircraft that were not on kamikaze missions.

Appendix II

SHIPS SERVING ON RADAR PICKET DUTY AT OKINAWA

DESTROYER TYPES BY CLASS

BENHAM CLASS
Lang DD 399
Sterett DD 407

SIMS CLASS
Mustin DD 413
Russell DD 414

LIVERMORE CLASS
Nicholson DD 442
Shubrick DD 639
Wilkes DD 441

FLETCHER CLASS
Ammen DD 527
Anthony DD 515
Aulick DD 569
Bache DD 470
Beale DD 471
Bennett DD 473
Bennion DD 662

Boyd DD 544
Bradford DD 545
Braine DD 630
Brown DD 546
Bryant DD 665
Bush DD 529
Callaghan DD 792
Caperton DD 650
Cassin Young DD 793
Charles Ausburne DD 570
Claxton DD 571
Cogswell DD 651
Colhoun DD 801
Converse DD 509
Cowell DD 547
Daly DD 519
Dyson DD 572
Evans DD 552
Foote DD 511
Fullam DD 474
Gregory DD 802

Guest DD 472
Heywood L. Edwards DD 663
Hudson DD 475
Ingersoll DD 652
Irwin DD 794
Isherwood DD 520
Kimberly DD 521
Knapp DD 653
Laws DD 558
Little DD 803
Luce DD 522
Morrison DD 560
Picking DD 685
Preston DD 795
Pringle DD 477
Pritchett DD 561
Richard P. Leary DD 664
Rowe DD 564
Smalley DD 565
Sproston DD 577
Stanly DD 478

Stoddard DD 566
Twiggs DD 591
Van Valkenburgh
 DD 656
Wadsworth DD 516
Watts DD 567
Wickes DD 578
William D. Porter
 DD 579
Wren DD 568

**ALLEN M.
SUMNER CLASS**
Alfred A.
Cunningham
 DD 752
Barton DD 722
Compton DD 705
Douglas H. Fox
 DD 779
Drexler DD 741
Frank E. Evans
 DD 754
Gainard DD 706
Harry E. Hubbard
 DD 748

Hugh W. Hadley
 DD 774
Ingraham DD 694
John A. Bole
 DD 755
James C. Owens
 DD 776
Laffey DD 724
Lowry DD 770
Mannert L. Abele
 DD 733
Massey DD 778
Moale DD 693
Purdy DD 734
Putnam DD 757
Stormes DD 780
Walke DD 723
Willard Keith
 DD 775

**LIGHT
MINELAYERS**
Aaron Ward DM 34
Gwin DM 33
Harry F. Bauer
 DM 26

Henry A. Wiley
 DM 29
J. William Ditter
 DM 31
Robert H. Smith
 DM 23
Shannon DM 25
Shea DM 30
Thomas E. Fraser
 DM 24

**HIGH SPEED
MINESWEEPERS**
Ellyson DMS 19
Emmons DMS 22
Harding DMS 28
Hobson DMS 26
Jeffers DMS 27
Macomb DMS 23

**DESTROYER
ESCORTS**
Bowers DE 637
Edmonds DE 406

SUPPORT SHIPS
BY CLASS

LCS(L)			
11	52	90	121
12	53	91	122
13	54	92	123
14	55	93	124
15	56	94	125
16	57	95	128
17	61	96	129
18	62	97	130
19	63	98	
20	64	99	**PGM**
21	65	100	9
22	66	101	10
23	67	102	17
24	70	103	20
25	71	104	
31	74	105	**LSM(R)**
32	76	107	189
33	78	109	190
34	81	110	191
35	82	111	192
36	83	114	193
37	84	115	194
38	85	116	195
39	86	117	196
40	87	118	197
51	88	119	198
	89	120	199

Appendix III

JAPANESE AIRCRAFT
TYPES OF PLANES USED TO ATTACK THE RADAR PICKET STATIONS
Japanese Army Air Force

Code Name	Type	Japanese Designation
Babs	Reconnaissance	Mitsubishi Ki-15 Army Type 97
Dinah	Reconnaissance	Mitsubishi Ki-46, Army Type 100
Frank	Fighter	Nakajima Ki-84, Army Type 4
Ida	Advanced Trainer	Tachikawa Ki-55, Army Type 99
Lily	Light bomber	Kawasaki Ki-48, Army Type 99
Nate	Fighter	Nakajima Ki-27, Army Type 97
Nick	Fighter	Kawasaki Ki-45 KAI, Army Type 2
Oscar	Fighter	Nakajima Ki-43, Army Type 1
Peggy	Heavy Bomber	Mitsubishi Ki-67, Army Type 4
Sally	Heavy Bomber	Mitsubishi Ki-21, Army Type 97
Sonia	Assault	Mitsubishi Ki-51, Army Type 99
Tojo	Fighter	Nakajima Ki-44, Army Type 2
Tony	Fighter	Kawasaki Ki-61, Army Type 3

Imperial Japanese Navy Air Force

Code Name	Type	Japanese Designation
Alf	Reconnaissance Seaplane	Kawanishi E7K Navy Type 94
Ann	Light Bomber	Mitsubishi Ki-30 Type 97
Babs	Reconnaissance	Mitsubishi C5M, Navy Type 98

Code Name	Type	Japanese Designation
Baka	Piloted Bomb	Yokosuka MXY7, Navy Special Attack Oka
Betty	Attack Bomber	Mitsubishi G4m1/G4M3, Navy Type 1
Dave	Reconnaissance Seaplane	Nakajima E8N, Navy Type 95
Frances	Night Fighter	Yokosuka P1Y1-S, P1Y2-S
George	Fighter/Interceptor	Kawanishi N1K1-J/N1K5-J
Grace	Carrier Borne Attack Bomber	Aichi B7A
Hamp	Fighter	Mitsubishi A6M3, Type 0 Carrier Fighter model 32 (Also Zeke 32)
Irving	Night Fighter	Nakajima J1N1-S
	Reconnaissance	Nakajima J1N1-C, R, Type 2
Jack	Fighter/Interceptor	Mitsubishi J2M
Jake	Reconnaissance Seaplane	Aichi E13A, Type 0
Jill	Carrier Borne Attack Bomber	Nakajima B6N
Judy	Carrier Borne Attack Bomber	Yokosuka D4Y
Kate	Carrier Borne Attack Bomber	Nakajima B5N, Navy Type 97
Myrt	Reconnaissance	Nakajima C6N
Paul	Reconnaissance Seaplane	Aichi E16A
Pete	Observation Seaplane	Mitsubishi F1M, Navy Type 0
Rufe	Fighter Seaplane	Nakajima A6M2-N, Navy Type 2
Shiragiku	Operations Trainer	Kyushu K11W1 (no code name)
Val	Carrier Bomber	Aichi D3A, Navy Type 99
Willow	Intermediate Trainer	Yokosuka K5Y, Navy Type 95
Zeke	Fighter	Mitsubishi A6M, Navy Type 0 (also Zero)

The code names assigned above were used by the Allied powers. The Japanese used numerical designations for their aircraft until 1943. At that time they began to assign names to their aircraft.

Some of the aircraft listed above are represented by photos within the text; however, many are not. To aid the reader in identifying and comparing various models of Japanese aircraft, the following pages contain a reproduction of an aircraft identification manual put out by the Division of Naval Intelligence. This manual is dated 15 April 1945 and would have been in use during the campaign for Okinawa.

RESTRICTED

SUPPLEMENT NO. 2

PHOTOGRAPHIC INTERPRETATION HANDBOOK—UNITED STATES FORCES

AIRCRAFT IDENTIFICATION

15 APRIL, 1945

PHOTOGRAPHIC INTELLIGENCE CENTER,
DIVISION OF NAVAL INTELLIGENCE, NAVY DEPARTMENT

RESTRICTED

Operational Japanese Aircraft have been given short Allied Code Names for purposes of simplicity in reporting. These code names take the form of male and female names, such as "TONY" and "SALLY". Male designations are given to Army and Navy fighter planes and to Navy reconnaissance float planes. All other planes receive female designations. At the present time the sole authority for the issuance of future code names is vested in the Technical Air Intelligence Center, NAS, Anacostia, D.C. Photographs and pertinent data on suspected new aircraft types should be forwarded immediately to the above activity. Tentative code names should not be assigned in the field or by other agencies.

In addition to a code name each aircraft has a model designation. Formerly, arbitrarily chosen "Mark Numbers" were used to indicate the various modifications of an aircraft type. These proved confusing, however, and inadequate to handle the numerous modifications being encountered. As a result the Mark System has been abandoned and, instead, the nomenclature applied to the planes by the Japanese themselves has been adopted. This consists of a system of separate Navy and Army model numbers.

Japanese Navy model numbers are composed of two digits and the first version of a Navy plane is always known as Model 11. As modifications are made to this original version the first digit of the model number is increased if the change is structural and the second digit is increased if the engine is changed. Thus, a ZEKE 11 becomes a ZEKE 21 if the wing shape is altered, a ZEKE 12 if only the engine is changed and a ZEKE 22 if both changes are made. With further changes the digits increase in progression.

Japanese Army model numbers are composed of only one digit and the first version of an Army plane is always known as Model 1. This model number may be increased if either an engine or a structural change is made in the original version.

Training aircraft are now being assigned Allied Code Names as well. These designations will be in the form of tree names, such as "CEDAR" and "OAK", in order to avoid confusion with code names of combat aircraft.

Photo Interpretation reports should list the aircraft by code names and by model numbers whenever possible. Older forms of nomenclature listing the aircraft by manufacturer, year of adoption and purpose, such as "Kawanishi 97 Flying Boat", are awkward as well as unnecessary.

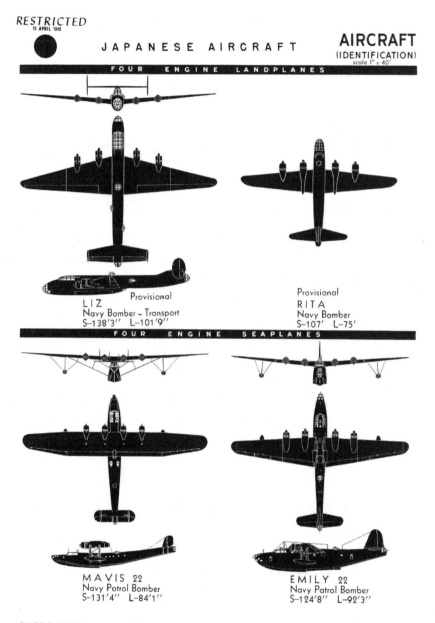

JAPANESE AIRCRAFT

AIRCRAFT
(IDENTIFICATION)
scale 1" = 40'

FOUR ENGINE LANDPLANES

Provisional
LIZ
Navy Bomber – Transport
S–138'3'' L–101'9''

Provisional
RITA
Navy Bomber
S–107' L–75'

FOUR ENGINE SEAPLANES

MAVIS 22
Navy Patrol Bomber
S–131'4'' L–84'1''

EMILY 22
Navy Patrol Bomber
S–124'8'' L–92'3''

13.01

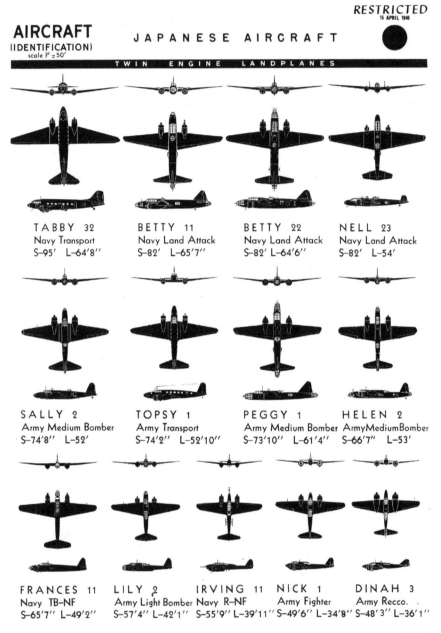

RESTRICTED
15 APRIL 1945

AIRCRAFT
(IDENTIFICATION)
scale 1″ = 50′

JAPANESE AIRCRAFT

TWIN   ENGINE   LANDPLANES

TABBY 32
Navy Transport
S–95′ L–64′8″

BETTY 11
Navy Land Attack
S–82′ L–65′7″

BETTY 22
Navy Land Attack
S–82′ L–64′6″

NELL 23
Navy Land Attack
S–82′ L–54′

SALLY 2
Army Medium Bomber
S–74′8″ L–52′

TOPSY 1
Army Transport
S–74′2″ L–52′10″

PEGGY 1
Army Medium Bomber
S–73′10″ L–61′4″

HELEN 2
Army Medium Bomber
S–66′7″ L–53′

FRANCES 11
Navy TB–NF
S–65′7″ L–49′2″

LILY 2
Army Light Bomber
S–57′4″ L–42′1″

IRVING 11
Navy R–NF
S–55′9″ L–39′11″

NICK 1
Army Fighter
S–49′6″ L–34′8″

DINAH 3
Army Recco.
S–48′3″ L–36′1″

13.02

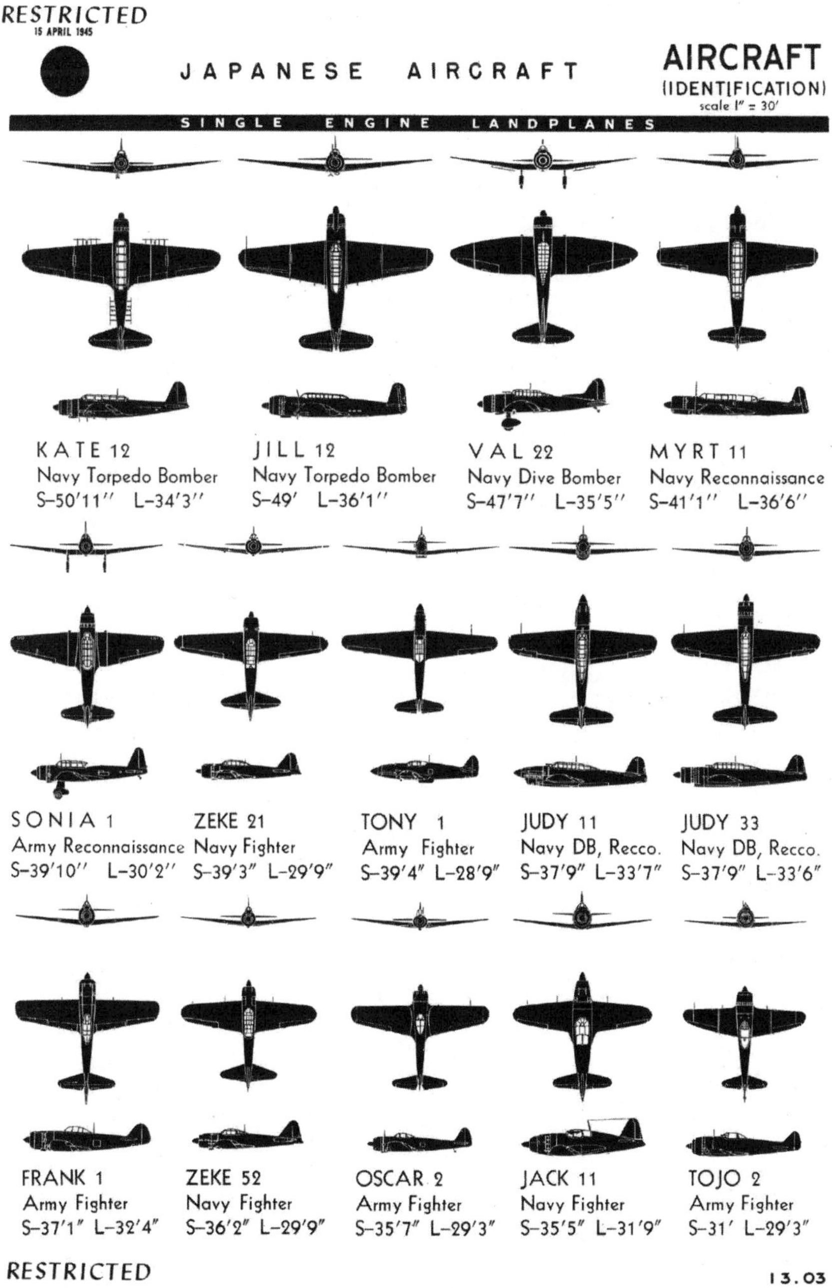

RESTRICTED
15 APRIL 1945
JAPANESE AIRCRAFT
AIRCRAFT
(IDENTIFICATION)
scale 1" = 30'
SINGLE ENGINE LANDPLANES
KATE 12
Navy Torpedo Bomber
S-50'11" L-34'3"
JILL 12
Navy Torpedo Bomber
S-49' L-36'1"
VAL 22
Navy Dive Bomber
S-47'7" L-35'5"
MYRT 11
Navy Reconnaissance
S-41'1" L-36'6"
SONIA 1
Army Reconnaissance
S-39'10" L-30'2"
ZEKE 21
Navy Fighter
S-39'3" L-29'9"
TONY 1
Army Fighter
S-39'4" L-28'9"
JUDY 11
Navy DB, Recco.
S-37'9" L-33'7"
JUDY 33
Navy DB, Recco.
S-37'9" L-33'6"
FRANK 1
Army Fighter
S-37'1" L-32'4"
ZEKE 52
Navy Fighter
S-36'2" L-29'9"
OSCAR 2
Army Fighter
S-35'7" L-29'3"
JACK 11
Navy Fighter
S-35'5" L-31'9"
TOJO 2
Army Fighter
S-31' L-29'3"
RESTRICTED
13.03

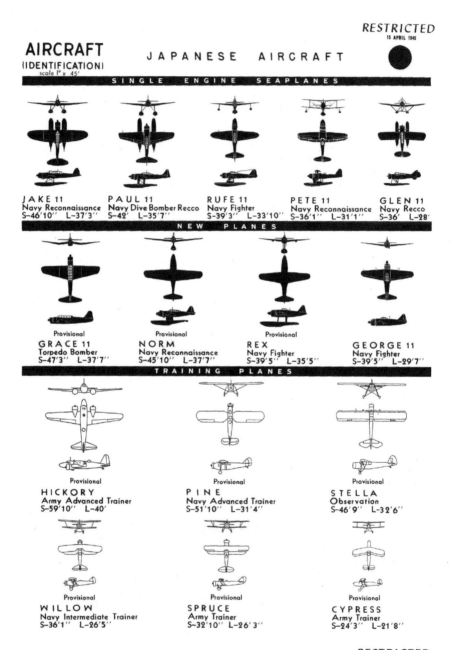

RESTRICTED
15 APRIL 1945

AIRCRAFT
(IDENTIFICATION)
scale 1" ≡ 45'

JAPANESE AIRCRAFT

SINGLE ENGINE SEAPLANES

JAKE 11
Navy Reconnaissance
S–46'10'' L–37'3''

PAUL 11
Navy Dive Bomber Recco
S–42' L–35'7''

RUFE 11
Navy Fighter
S–39'3'' L–33'10''

PETE 11
Navy Reconnaissance
S–36'1'' L–31'1''

GLEN 11
Navy Recco
S–36' L–28'

NEW PLANES

Provisional
GRACE 11
Torpedo Bomber
S–47'3'' L–37'7''

Provisional
NORM
Navy Reconnaissance
S–45'10'' L–37'7''

Provisional
REX
Navy Fighter
S–39'5'' L–35'5''

GEORGE 11
Navy Fighter
S–39'5'' L–29'7''

TRAINING PLANES

Provisional
HICKORY
Army Advanced Trainer
S–59'10'' L–40'

Provisional
PINE
Navy Advanced Trainer
S–51'10'' L–31'4''

Provisional
STELLA
Observation
S–46'9'' L–32'6''

Provisional
WILLOW
Navy Intermediate Trainer
S–36'1'' L–26'5''

Provisional
SPRUCE
Army Trainer
S–32'10'' L–26'3''

Provisional
CYPRESS
Army Trainer
S–24'3'' L–21'8''

13.04

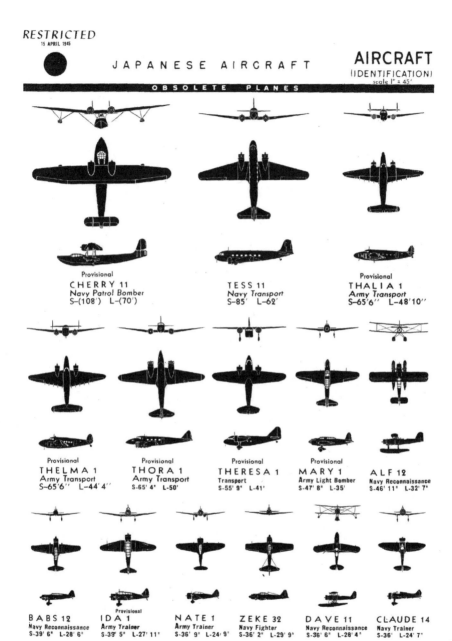

JAPANESE AIRCRAFT

AIRCRAFT
(IDENTIFICATION)
scale 1" = 45'

OBSOLETE PLANES

Provisional
CHERRY 11
Navy Patrol Bomber
S–(108') L–(70')

TESS 11
Navy Transport
S–85' L–62'

Provisional
THALIA 1
Army Transport
S–65'6" L–48'10"

Provisional
THELMA 1
Army Transport
S–65'6" L–44'4"

Provisional
THORA 1
Army Transport
S–65' 4" L–50'

Provisional
THERESA 1
Transport
S–55' 9" L–41'

Provisional
MARY 1
Army Light Bomber
S–47' 8" L–35'

ALF 12
Navy Reconnaissance
S–46' 11" L–32' 7"

BABS 12
Navy Reconnaissance
S–39' 6" L–28' 6"

Provisional
IDA 1
Army Trainer
S–39' 5" L–27' 11"

NATE 1
Army Trainer
S–36' 9" L–24' 9"

ZEKE 32
Navy Fighter
S–36' 2" L–29' 9"

DAVE 11
Navy Reconnaissance
S–36' 6" L–28' 4"

CLAUDE 14
Navy Trainer
S–36' L–24' 7"

Appendix IV

JAPANESE AIR FIELDS AND PRINCIPLE USES

ARMY

Kyushu

Chiran	Army reconnaissance and suicide planes
Fukuoka	Headquarters Sixth Air Army
Karesahara	Transports and Army airborne training base
Kumamoto	Alternate field for twin-engine bombers
Kumanosho	Alternate field for twin-engine bombers
Miyakanojo	Principal Army fighter base
Nittagahara	Alternate field for twin-engine bombers
Tachiarai	Major base for twin-engine bombers

Taiwan

Ensui	Training base
Giran	Fighters
Kagi	Medium Bombers
Taichu (Toyohara)	Fighters
Taihoku (Matsuyama)	Headquarters Eighth Air Division, twin-engine bomb-ers and reconnaissance planes
Tansui	Reconnaissance planes

Korea

Gunzan	Fighters, training center
Keijo	Headquarters Fifth Air Army, fighters

369

NAVY
Kyushu

Amakusa (Goryo)	Rear base for suicide seaplanes
Hakata	Important rear base for seaplanes such as Paul bombers, suicide Jakes, and Alfs normally stationed at Ibusuki
Ibusuki	Seaplanes such as Paul bombers, suicide Jakes, and Alfs
Izuki	Alternate field for fighters
Izumi	Alternate field for fighters
Kagoshima	Alternate field for fighters
Kanoya	Headquarters Fifth Air Fleet, fighters, interceptors, Zeke fighter-bombers employed to attack US task forces, twin-engine bombers in tactical units including Betty/Oka
Kisaratsu	Headquarters Third Air Fleet
Kasanohara	Fighters
Kasumigaura	Headquarters Tenth Air Fleet
Kokubu # 1	Fighters, Tenth Air Fleet suicide Zekes and Vals
Kokubu # 2 (Ronchi)	Tenth Air Fleet suicide Zekes and Vals (satellite base)
Komatsu	Rear base for twin-engine bombers in tactical units including Betty/Oka
Kushira	Single engine torpedo bombers in tactical units and also Tenth Air Fleet training units
Miho	Rear base for twin-engine bombers in tactical units including Betty/Oka
Miyazaki	Twin-engine bombers in tactical units including Betty/Oka
Oita	Airfield and seaplane base
Omura	Interceptors, patrol planes, suicide planes
Saeki	Rear base for Kushira units, training and maintenance base for Fifth Air Fleet
Takuma	Important rear base for seaplanes such as Paul bombers, suicide Jakes, Alfs normally stationed at Ibusuki

Tomitaka	Zeke fighter-bombers employed to attack US Task force, earlier use as base for twin-engine bombers in tactical units including Betty/Okas
Usa	Rear base for Kushira units, rear base for twin-engine bombers in tactical units including Betty/Oka. Rear base for Betty/Oka Units at Kanoya and

Taiwan

Karenko	Primary fighter base
Shinchiku	Headquarters First Air Fleet from mid-April 1945, fighters
Taichu (Toyohara)	Fighters
Matsuyama (Taihoku)	Reconnaissance planes
Takao (Shozokan)	Headquarters First Air Fleet until mid- April 1945, medium bombers
Tansui	Reconnaissance planes

Korea

Genzan	Zeke fighters and trainers

Notes

Preface and Acknowledgements

1. Lt. Gen. Masakazu Kawabe. *USSBS Interrogation # 277.* 2 November 1945. p. 5.

Introduction

1. Commander Task Force Fifty-One. Commander Amphibious Forces U.S. Pacific Fleet. Report on Okinawa Gunto Operations from 17 February to 17 May, 1945, p. (V)(E)–18.
2. *USS Dyson (DD 572) Report of Capture of Okinawa Gunto–Phases 1 and 2.* 27 June 1945, Enclosure (H) I. "Present strength" at the time of the report usually included four destroyer types along with four support gunboats, primarily LCS(L)s.
3. *Amphibious Forces Pacific Fleet (TF 52) Serial 000166 16 March 1945 Operation Order A6- 45, Annex A-2.*
4. *Commander Task Force Fifty-One. Commander Amphibious Forces U.S. Pacific Fleet. Report on Okinawa Gunto Operation from 17 February to 17 May, 1945,* (V) (D)–6-7.
5. *U.S.S. Pritchett (DD 561) Serial 037 Action Report 10 July 1945,* p. 10.
6. *USS Dyson (DD 572) Report of Capture of Okinawa Gunto–Phases 1 and 2.* 27 June 1945, Enclosure (H) II.
7. Charles Thomas, *Dolly Five: A Memoir of the Pacific War.* (Chester, VA: Harrowgate Press, 1996), p. 191.
8. James W. Vernon, *The Hostile Sky A Hellcat Flier in World War II.* (Annapolis: Naval Institute Press, 2003), p. 146.
9. United States Strategic Bombing Survey (Pacific) Naval Analysis Division, *The Campaigns of the Pacific War.* (Washington: United States Government Printing Office), p. 325.
10. It should be noted that of the sixty ships serving on radar picket duty, four were hit on more than one occasion, with *Pritchett* hit three times and *Macomb, Anthony* and *Wadsworth* each hit twice.

CHAPTER 1

1. *USS Eldorado AGC 11 Serial 034 Action Report of the U.S.SS. Eldorado (AGC-11) Report of the Capture of Okinawa Gunto, Phases One and Two–12 March 1945 to 18 May 1945. 7 June 1945,* VI-D(1)–p. 5.
2. *CTF 5 Action Report 20 July 1945,* p. 17.
3. Commandant, Navy Shipyard, S.C. letter to Bureau Of Ships/ Bureau of Ordnance. 1 Dec. 1944.
4. *U.S.S. LSM(R) 194 Action Report 6 May 1945,* pp. 1-2.
5. Nicolai Timines, *An Analytical History of Kamikaze Attacks against Ships of the United States Navy During World War II.* Arlington, VA: Center for Naval Analyses, Operations Evaluation Group, 1970, p. 67.
6. Air Intelligence Group Division of Naval Intelligence. *Observed Suicide Attacks by Japanese Aircraft Against Allied Ships.* OpNav-16-V #A106. 23 May 1945, p. 11.
7. *Secret Information Bulletin, No. 24.*
8. *U.S.S. Mustin (DD413) Serial 068 Action Report, Okinawa Gunto Operation –0930 (Item), 17 April to 0815 (Item) 2 May 1945* dated 3 May 1945, pp. 5-7.
9. *USS Shubrick DD 639 Serial 003 Action Report 16 June 1945,* p.6.
10. *USS Laffey DD 724 Serial 023 Action Report 29 April 1945.* p. 44.
11. *USS Hobson DMS 26 Serial 014-45 1 May 1945 Report of Action, Invasion of Okinawa, 19 March 1945 to 28 April 1945,* p. 27.
12. John Rooney, "Sailor."
13. Philip M. Morse and George E. Kimball, *Methods of Operations Research* (Cambridge: The M.I.T. Press, 1970), pp. 82-84.
14. Headquarters of the Commander in Chief Navy Department. *Anti-Suicide Action Summary CominCh P-0011.* 31 August 1945, p.16.
15. *U.S.S. Bennion (DD 662) Serial 00120 9 May 1945 Tactical Plans for Radar Picket Groups,* Enclosure (C), p. 1.
16. *USS LCS(L)(3) 118 Serial 02 Action Report 8 May 1945.*
17. Morse and Kimball, pp. 89-92.
18. *USS Caperton (DD 650) Serial 096-43 Action Report 12 July 1945.*
19. *USS LCS(L) (3) 114 Serial 6 Action Report 14 April 1945.*
20. *Commander Task Force Fifty-One. Commander Amphibious Forces U.S. Pacific Fleet. Report on Okinawa Gunto Operation from 17 February to 17 May 1945* page (V) (D)–p. 6.
21. As noted previously, this included three ships that were struck on two or three occasions. See endnote 10 in my Introduction.
22. *USS Douglas H. Fox DD 779 Serial 002 Action Report 18 May 1945,* p. 5.
23. *Commander Destroyer Squadron 55 Serial 0023 of 7 August 1945,* Enclosure (A) pp. 9-10.5

CHAPTER 2

1. *Air Defense Command (Fighter Command) Operation Plan 1-45,* p. 3.
2. *CTF 51 CAFUSPAC Fleet, Report on Okinawa Gunto* (V)(E)–p. 15.
3. *USS Lowry DD 770 Serial 021 Action Report 30 June 1945,* p. 10.
4. *USS Ingraham (DD 694) Serial 004 Action Report 8 May, 1945,* p. 21.

5. Don Ball, First Lieutenant *LCS(L) 85*. Interview of 10 August 2002.

6. According to Commander Ryosuke Nomura IJN. See USSBS *Interrogations of Japanese Officials Vol II.* (Washington: United States Government Printing Office, 1945), p. 532.

7. Captain Minoru Genda IJN in USSBS *Interrogations of Japanese Officials Volume II.* p. 495. Genda commanded Air Group 343 of the Fifth Air Fleet which was based on Kyushu during the Okinawa campaign.

8. Military History Section–General Headquarters Far East Command Military Intelligence Section General Staff. *Japanese Monograph No. 86. War History of the 5th Air Fleet (The "Ten" Air Unit) Operational Record from 10 February 1946 to 19 August 1945,* pp. 41-42.

9. Military History Section–General Headquarters Far East Command Military Intelligence Section General Staff. *Japanese Monograph No. 141 (Navy) "Okinawa Area Naval Operations" Supplement Statistics on Naval Air Strength.* August, 1949.

10. Military History Section–General Headquarters Far East Command Military Intelligence Section General Staff. *Japanese Monograph No. 51 Air Operations on Iwo Jima and the Ryukyus,* p. 33. Hereafter *JM 51.*

11. Axtel quoted in William Wolf. *Death Rattlers Marine Squadron VMF-323 over Okinawa.* (Atglen, PA: Schiffer Military History, 1999), p. 124.

12. *History of the 318th Fighter Group,* p. 10.

13. *Headquarters 318th Fighter Group Operations Memorandum.* 16 May 1945.

14. Durwood B. Williams, pilot 333rd Fighter Squadron, 318th Fighter Group, 7th AF, E-mail of 11 August 2001.

15. *Headquarters 318th Fighter Group Operations Memorandum.* 15 May 1945.

16. *VC-85 Aircraft Action Report 6 April 1945.*

17. *USS Robert H. Smith (DM 23) Serial034 Action Report 26 June1945,* p. 47.

18. *VF 10 Aircraft Action Report 11 May 1945.*

19. *VF 84 Aircraft Action Report 17 April, 1945.*

20. John Pomeroy Condon, *Corsairs and Flattops* (Annapolis: Naval Institute Press, 1998), p. 55.

21. Eric Hammel, *Aces Against Japan The American Aces Speak. Volume I* (Pacifica, CA: Pacifica Press, 1992), p. 276.

22. Wolf, p. 102.

23. *VMF 314 Aircraft Action Report 3 June 1945.*

24. Division of Naval Intelligence, *Technical Air Intelligence Center Report # 17 Combat Evaluation of Zeke 52 with F4U-1D, F6F-5, and FM-2* (Anacostia, DC: Technical Air Intelligence Center, November 1944), p. 2. Hereafter *TAIC Report # 17.*

25. ibid., pp. 3-4.

26. Second Lieutenant Willis A. "Bud" Dworzak, VMF-441. Interview of 21 July 2003.

27. Saburo Sakai with Martin Caidin and Fred Saito, *Samurai!* (New York: ibooks, Inc. 2001), p. 317.

28. CPO Takeo Tanimizu quoted in Henry Sakaida, *Imperial Japanese Navy Aces 1937-45.* (Oxford: Osprey Publishing Limited, 1999), pp. 81-82.

29. *TAIC Report # 17,* p. 3.

30. ibid., pp. 3-4.

31. *VF 23 Aircraft Action Report 11 April.*
32. Masatake Okumiya, Jiro Horikoshi with Martin Caidin, *Zero! The Air War in the Pacific During World War II from The Japanese Viewpoint* (Washington, D.C.: Zenger Publishing Co., Inc., 1956), p. 222.
33. Division of Naval Intelligence, *Technical Air Intelligence Center Report # 38 Comparative Performance Between Zeke 52 and the P-38, P-51, P-47* (Anacostia, DC: Technical Air Intelligence Center, April, 1945), pp. 6-7. Hereafter *TAIC Report # 38.*
34. Commander Ryosuke Nomura IJN. USSBS *Interrogations of Japanese Officials Vol. II*, p. 532.
35. Superior Petty Officer Ichiro Tanaka. *ADVATIS Interrogation Report No. 11*, p. 13.
36. *TAIC Report # 38*, p. 7.
37. Far Eastern Bureau, British Ministry of Information. Japanese Translation, Series No. 163, 31st January, 1944. Jiro Takeda. "The Present State of Aircraft Production." *Fuji Magazine* November 1943.
38. Col. Ichiji Sugita. Doc. No. 58512 in General Headquarters Far East Command Military Intelligence Section, General Staff. *Statements of Japanese Officials on World War II. (English Translations) Volume 3.* 1949-1950, p. 342.
39. Capt. Toshikazu Omae. Doc. No. 50572 in General Headquarters Far East Command Military Intelligence Section, General Staff. *Statements of Japanese Officials on World War II. (English Translations) Volume 4.* 1949-1950, p. 319.
40. Comdr. Yoshimori Terai. Doc. No. 50572 in General Headquarters Far East Command Military Intelligence Section, General Staff. *Statements of Japanese Officials on World War II. (English Translations) Volume 4.* 1949-1950, p. 321.
41. Comdr. Yoshimori Terai, Rear Adm. Sadatoshi Tomioka, and Capt. Mitsuo Fuchida. Doc. No. 50572 in General Headquarters Far East Command Military Intelligence Section, General Staff. *Statements of Japanese Officials on World War II. (English Translations) Volume 4.* 1949-1950, p. 317.
42. Headquarters Far East Command Military History Section, *Imperial General Headquarters Navy Directives Volume II. Directives No. 316- No 540 (15 Jan 44-26 Aug 45) Special Directives No. 1–No. 3 (2 Sep 45-12 Sep 45),* p. 143. Hereafter *Navy Directives Vol II.*
43. ibid., pp. 161-162.
44. *Navy Directives Vol II.* p. 164.
45. Rear Adm. Sadatoshi Tomioka. Doc. No. 50572 in General Headquarters Far East Command Military Intelligence Section, General Staff. *Statements of Japanese Officials on World War II. (English Translations) Volume 4.* 1949-1950, p. 326.
46. United States Strategic Bombing Survey (Pacific), *The Campaigns of the Pacific War* (Washington: United States Government Printing Office, 1947), p. 328.
47. *Headquarters XXI Bomber Command Tactical Mission Report, Missions No. 46 and 50, 27 and 31 March 1945.* 30 April 1945, p. 2.
48. The last *kanji* in General Sugawara's name may be read as either "*wara*" or "*hara*." Some authors have used the second reading and his name sometimes

appears in print as "Sugahara." I have based my romanization on post-war interrogations of Japanese officials conducted by various branches of the U.S. military. During their conversations it is apparent that his name was pronounced as Sugawara.

49. National Security Agency. *"Magic" Far East Summary Number 400.* 24 April 1945, pp. 1-2.

50. Based on *Japanese Monograph # 135 Okinawa Operations Record (8th Air Division),* p. 249, CinCPacCinCPOA Bulletin No. 102-45. *Translations Interrogations Number 26 Airfields in Formosa and Hainan.* 25 April 1945, p. 6 and *CINCPAC PEARL Dispatch AI88009.* 18 June 1945.

51. Maj. Gen. Ryosuke Nakanishi. USSBS Interrogation # 312. 4 November 1945.

52. *JM 51*, p. 24.

53. *Japanese Monograph No.51* claims a large warship, two smaller warships and a transport hit. Morison indicates that no American shipping was hit that day near Okinawa. See *JM # 51*, p. 27 and Morison *Victory in the Pacific*, p. 390.

54. Director Air Intelligence Group, *Statistical Analysis of Japanese Suicide Effort Against Allied Shipping During OKINAWA Campaign.* 23 July, 1945, p. 4.

CHAPTER 3

1. National Security Agency. *"Magic" Far East Summary # 377.* 1 April 1945, pp. 1-2.

2. *Headquarters XXI Bomber Command Tactical Mission Report, Missions No. 46 and 50*, 30 April 1945.

3. National Security Agency. *"Magic" Far East Summary # 394.* 1 April 1945, pp. 1-2.

4. ibid., pp. 12-13.

5. Military History Section–General Headquarters Far East Command Military Intelligence Section General Staff. *Japanese Monograph No. 51 Air Operations on Iwo Jima and the Ryukyus*, p. 32. Hereafter *JM 51.*

6. *JM 86*, p. 41

7. ibid., p. 42.

8. *JM 51*, p. 34.

9. *VF-33 Aircraft Action Report No. 8, 5 April 1945.*

10. Records of the Naval Security Group Central Depository, Crane, Indiana. *Explanatory Notes on the KAMIKAZE Attacks at Okinawa, April-June 1945.* 6 May 1945.

11. *VF-82 Aircraft Action Report No. 62, 6 April 1945.*

12. *War Diary VMF (CV) 112 and 123 1-30 April 1945.*

13. *USS Colhoun DD 801 Serial None Action Report 27 April 1945*, p. 7.

14. *VF-30 Aircraft Action Report No. 35-45, 6-7 April 1945.*

15. *VF-45 Aircraft Action Report No. 87, 6 April 1945.*

16. *VF-82 Aircraft Action Report No. 62, 6 April 1945.*

17. Aircraft Action Reports frequently credit a pilot with a fractional kill. This means that credit for the destruction of the enemy airplane was shared with another pilot.

18. *VF-82 Aircraft Action Report No. 62, 6 April 1945.*

19. *VF-17-VBF-17 Aircraft Action Report No. 90, 6 April 1945.*
20. *The History of Fighting Squadron Seventeen 18 April 1944-30 June 1945* pp. 10-11.
21. ibid., p. 13.
22. Air Intelligence Group Division of Naval Intelligence. *Air Operations Memorandum No. 83.* OPNAV-16-V- #S243. 1 June 1945, p. 16.
23. Robert J. Wisner, Communications Officer, *LCS(L) 37.* Interview, 10 August 2002.
24. Gordon H. Wiram, *LCS(L) 64,* Letter to Ray Baumler, 13 April 1991.
25. Air Intelligence Group Division of Naval Intelligence. *Air Operations Memorandum No. 83.* OPNAV-16-V- #S243. 1 June 1945, p. 16.
26. *Commander Task Force Fifty-One. Commander Amphibious Forces U.S. Pacific Fleet. Report on Okinawa Gunto Operation from 17 February to 17 May, 1945.* Page (II)–p. 17.
27. H.D. Chickering, Lieutenant. CO *LCS(L) 51. World War II.* Typescript–undated, p. 32.
28. *VF-82 Aircraft Action Report No. 65, 7 April 1945.*
29. *VF-29 Aircraft Action Report No. VF-108, 7 April 1945.*
30. *VF-84 Aircraft Action Report No. 41, 7 April, 1945.*
31. National Security Agency. *"Magic" Far East Summary # 397.* 21 April 1945, pp. 1–2.
32. *LCS(L) 33* [Serial not available] *Action Report 15 April 1945.*
33. *VMF-224 Aircraft Action Report No. 125, 8 April 1945.*
34. *ATIS Research Report No. 76, Prominent Factors in Japanese Military Psychology.* Part IV. 7 February 1945, pp. 6-7.
35. Vice Adm. Matome Ugaki, *Fading Victory The Diary of Admiral Matome Ugaki 1941-1945.* Chihaya, Masataka, Translator (Pittsburgh: University of Pittsburgh Press, 1991), pp. 575-579.
36. ibid., p. 578.
37. ibid., p. 581.
38. Air Defense Command Intelligence Section. *Chronological Account of Air Action During Morning of 12 April, 1945, At Yontan and Kadena Air Fields.* 12 April 1945, p. 2.
39. National Security Agency. *"Magic" Far East Summary # 385.* 9 April 1945, A pp.1-2.
40. *War Diary VMF (CV) 112 and 123 1-30 April 1945.*
41. National Security Agency. *"Magic" Far East Summary # 383.* 7 April 1945, B–p. 2.
42. *VC-93 Aircraft Action Report No. 37, 12 April 1945.*
43. *The History of Fighting Squadron Ten,* p. 17.
44. *USS Purdy DD 734 Serial 024 Action Report 20 April 1945,* pp. 7-10.
45. ibid., p. 28.
46. *USS LCS(L)(3) 57* [Serial Not Available] *Action Report, Battle of Okinawa at RP Station # 1, 1945. 15 April, 1945.*
47. Lt. Comdr. Frank C. Osterland, *Dolly Three.* Typescript 28 August 1993, pp. 10-11.
48. *USS Purdy DD 734 Serial 024 Action Report 20 April 1945,* p. 10.
49. *USS LCS(L) 114 Serial 6 Action Report 16 April 1945.*

50. *VMF-221 Aircraft Action Report No. 39, 12 April 1945.*
51. *USS Stanly (DD748) Serial 087 Action Report Occupation of Okinawa Gunto 25 March-13 April 1945.*
52. *VF-30 Aircraft Action Report No. 37-45, 12 April 1945.*
53. Hatsuho Naito, *Thunder Gods The Kamikaze Pilots Tell Their Story* (Tokyo: Kodansha International 1989), pp. 153-155.
54. *U.S.S. Mannert L. Abele (DD 733) Serial A-12 Action Report 14 April 1945.*
55. James M. Stewart, CO *LSM(R) 189 Autobiography.* Typescript. Undated, p. 5.
56. Ugaki, p. 584.
57. Lt. Col. William Trabue, G.S.C., *Observer's Report: The Okinawa Operation (Period Covered: 8 February 1945 to 2 June 1945).* 15 June 1945.
58. *VF-40 Aircraft Action Report No. 5, 13 April 1945.*
59. Casualty figures are based on Samuel Eliot Morison. *History of United States Naval Operations in World War II. Volume XIV Victory in the Pacific 1945.* (Boston: Little, Brown and Company, 1960), pp. 390-392.

CHAPTER 4

1. Military History Section–General Far East Command Military Intelligence Section General Staff. *Japanese Monograph No. 86. War History of the 5th Air Fleet (The "Ten"Air Unit) Operational Record from 10 February 1945 to - 19 August 1945*, p.53. Hereafter *JM 86.*
2. ibid., p. 53.
3. National Security Agency. *"Magic" Far East Summary # 391.* 15 April 1945, A pp.1-2.
4. Samuel Eliot Morison. *Victory in the Pacific 1945.* (Boston: Little, Brown and Company, 1968), p. 248.
5. William Wolf. *Death Rattlers Marine Squadron VMF-323 over Okinawa.* (Atglen, PA: Schiffer Military History, 1999), pp. 181-182.
6. *USS Laffey DD 724 Serial 023 Action Report 29 April 1945*, p. 23.
7. ibid., p. 25.
8. *VMF-441 War Diary for 1 April, 1945 to 30 April, 1945.*
9. *USS Laffey DD 724 Serial 023 Action Report 29 April 1945*, p. 26-A.
10. Julian F. Becton. *The Ship That Would Not Die* (Missoula, Montana: Pictorial Histories Publishing Company, 1980), pp. 258-259.
11. John R. Henry. "Out Stares Jap Pilot After Ammo Runs Out." *Honolulu Advertiser*, 27 April 1945.
12. *VMF-451 Aircraft Action Report No. 39, 16 April 1945.*
13. *VMF-323 Action Report No. 10, 16 April 1945.*
14. Jack Gebhardt Sonarman 1st Class. *USS Pringle DD 477.* Naval Historical Foundation Oral History Program. *Recollections of Sonarman 1st Class Jack Gebhardt USN.* 7 November 2000.
15. Matome Ugaki, Vice Adm. *Fading Victory: The Diary of Admiral Matome Ugaki 1941-1945.* Masataka Chihaya, trans., (Pittsburgh: University of Pittsburgh Press, 1991), pp. 587-588.
16. *CTF 51 to TF 51 16 April 1945.*
17. *JM 51*, pp. 39.
18. Wesley Frank Craven and James Lea Cate. *The Army Air Forces in World War*

II. Volume Five: The Pacific: Matterhorn to Nagasaki June 1944 to August 1945. Chicago: The University of Chicago Press, 1953, p. 633.

19. *VF-84 Aircraft Action Report No. 55, 17 April 1945.*
20. *Air Group 47 Aircraft Action Report No. AG-47 # 47, 17 April 1945.*
21. *CTU 52.9.1 OUTGOING MESSAGE OF 17 APRIL 1945.*
22. Powell Pierpoint, Lt. (jg) XO *LCS(L) 61. The War History of the LCS(L) 61*, p. 4.
23. National Security Agency. *"Magic" Far East Summary # 395.* 19 April 1945, pp. 4-5.
24. *VMF-441 War Diary 1 April 1945 to 30 April 1945.*
25. Harold J. Kaup, RM 3/c *LCS(L) 15. The Death of a Ship*, (Typescript. Undated).
26. *VF-12 Aircraft Action Report No. VF-12-32, 22 April 1945.*
27. Wolf, pp. 134-137.
28. *ATIS Research Report No. 76 Prominent Factors in Japanese Military Psychology.* Part IV, pp. 6-7.
29. *War Diary MAG 31 1 April to 30 April 1945*, Annex A.
30. Headquarters of the Commander in Chief Navy Department, Washington, D.C. *Effects of B-29 Operations in Support of the Okinawa Campaign From 18 March to 22 June 1945.* 3 August 1945. 3, App. B–p. 4.
31. National Security Agency. *"Magic" Far East Summary # 400.* 24 April 1945, pp. 1-2.
32. *JM 51*, p. 43.
33. National Security Agency. *"Magic" Far East Summary # 403.* 27 April 1945, pp. 6-7.
34. *Headquarters XXI Bomber Command Tactical Mission Report, Missions No. 97 through 125,* 6 June 1945.
35. Headquarters of the Commander in Chief Navy Department, Washington, D.C. *Effects of B-29 Operations in Support of the Okinawa Campaign From 18 March to 22 June 1945.* 3 August 1945. 3, App. B pp. 4-5.
36. National Security Agency. *"Magic" Far East Summary # 404.* 28 April 1945, p. 12.
37. United States Pacific Fleet and Pacific Ocean Areas. *Japanese Air Forces Current Employment, Area Distribution and Unit Locations 23 April 1945*, p. 9.
38. National Security Agency. *"Magic" Far East Summary # 400.* 24 April 1945, pp. 6-7. Many of the pilots flying special attack missions probably fell into the Class D category.
39. Wolf, pp. 140-142.
40. Pierpoint, p. 5.
41. *USS Bennion DD 662 Serial 153 9 June 1945 Aircraft Action Report of 28 April 1945.*
42. Ugaki, p. 599.
43. Wolf, pp. 141-142.
44. *U.S.S. Robert H. Smith (DM 23) Serial 034-cpd Action Report 26 June 1945*, p.16.
45. *MAG 31 War Diary 1 April to 30 April 1945*, Annex A.
46. *USS Ammen DD 527 Serial 038 Action Report 7 July 1945*, p. 5.
47. Military History Section – General Headquarters Far East Command Military

Intelligence Section General Staff. *Japanese Monograph No. 141 (Navy) "Okinawa Area Naval Operations" Supplement Statistics on Naval Air Strength.* August 1949. Hereafter *JM # 141.*

48. *USS Van Valkenburgh DD 656 Serial 007 Action Report 11 June 1945,* pp.11-12.
49. Ichishima in Nihon Senbotsu Gakusei Kinen-Kai (Japan Memorial Society for the Students Killed in the War-Wadatsumi Society). *Listen to the Voices from the Sea (Kike Wadatsumi no Koe).* Trans. By Midori Yamanouchi and Joseph L. Quinn, (Scranton: The University of Scranton Press, 2000), p. 226.
50. *JM # 141.*
51. Casualty figures are based on Samuel Eliot Morison. *History of United States Naval Operations in World War II. Volume XIV Victory in the Pacific 1945.* (Boston: Little, Brown and Company, 1960), pp. 390-392.
52. National Security Agency. *"Magic" Far East Summary # 421.* 15 May 1945, pp. 1-2.
53. Earl Blanton, GM 3/c *LCS(L) 118.* Interview of 19 September 2002.

CHAPTER 5

1. *VMF 311 War Diary 1 May - 31 May 1945,* pp. 9-10.
2. Military History Section–General Headquarters Far East Command Military Intelligence Section General Staff. *Japanese Monograph No. 51 Air Operations on Iwo Jima and the Ryukyus,* pp. 43-44. Hereafter *JM 51.*
3. ibid., p. 44.
4. *Headquarters XXI Bomber Command Tactical Mission Report, Missions No. 127 through 138, 140 through 145, 147 through 149.* 14 June 1945.
5. Records of the Naval Security Group Central Depository, Crane, Indiana. *Explanatory Notes on the KAMIKAZE Attacks at Okinawa, April-June 1945.* 3 May 1945.
6. *VF-9 Aircraft Action Report Nos. 96-45, 98-45, 4 May 1945.*
7. *Marine Air Group 33 War Diary 1 May - 31 May 1945,* p. 5.
8. W.H. Stanley, *Kamikaze: The Battle for Okinawa Big War of the Little Ships.* (By the author, 1988), p. 14.
9. *USS Ingraham DD 694 Serial 004 Action Report 8 May 1945,* p. 20.
10. *The History of Fighting Squadron Twenty Three 1 January 1945 through 10 June 1945,* p. 66.
11. *USS Drexler Serial 0109-45 Action Report 12 May 1945.* Enclosure (A) p. (2).
12. DD475 Dispatch 5 June, 1945.
13. *Melvin Fenoglio, Y3C "This I Remember."* circa 2000, http://skyways.lib. ks.us/history/dd803/crew/fenoglio1.html
14. *Doyle Kennedy, "The World War II Sinking of the Destroyer USS Little (DD803) May 3, 1945."* circa 2000, http://skyways.lib.ks.us/ history/dd803/crew/doyle1.html.
15. Ray Baumler, *LCS(L) 14.* Letter to the author of 4 March 2003.
16. *U.S.S. LCS(L) 83 Serial 02-45 Anti Aircraft Action Report of 3 May, 1945.*
17. Robert W. Landis, SK 1/c *LSM(R) 192.* Interview of 14 February, 2002.
18. Ron Surels, *DD 522: Diary of a Destroyer. The action saga of the USS Luce from the Aleutian and Philippine Campaigns to her sinking off Okinawa.*

(Plymouth, NH: Valley Graphics, Inc., 1996), pp. 119-123.

19. ibid., pp. 114-161.

20. *U.S.S. Henry A. Wiley (DM-29) Serial 031 Action Report 5 May 1945*, p. 7.

21. *U.S.S. LCS(L) 81 Serial 03-45 Action Report 1 August 1945*, pp. 2-3.

22. Earl Blanton, *Boston–to Jacksonville (41,000 Miles by Sea)*. (Seaford, VA: Goose Creek Publications, 1991), p. 88.

23. This is unusual, since American intelligence had not considered the Dinah as a possible carrier of the *Oka*. It was a much smaller plane than any of the other probable carriers. Given this knowledge, the pilots were questioned extensively, but maintained that the plane was definitely a Dinah. See *Aircraft Action Report CompRon Ninety 4 May 1945.*

24. *Aircraft Action Report CompRon Ninety 4 May 1945.*

25. Military History Section – General Headquarters Far East Command Military Intelligence Section General Staff. *Japanese Monograph No. 141 (Navy) "Okinawa Area Naval Operations" Supplement Statistics on Naval Air Strength.* August, 1949.

26. National Security Agency. *"Magic" Far East Summary # 416.* 10 May 1945, p. 5.

27. Military History Section–General Headquarters Far East Command Military Intelligence Section General Staff. *Japanese Monograph No. 86. War History of the 5th Air Fleet (The "Ten" Air Unit) Operational Record from 10 February 1945 to 19 August 1945*, p. 74. Hereafter *JM 86.*

28. *JM 86*, pp. 77-78.

29. Masataka Okumiya and Jiro Horikoshi with Martin Caiden. *Zero! The Air War in the Pacific During World War II from the Japanese Viewpoint.* (Washington, DC: Zenger Publishing Co., Inc., 1956), pp. 354.

30. National Security Agency. *"Magic" Far East Summary No. 416.* 10 May 1945, p. 6.

31. ibid., p. 8.

32. Matome Ugaki, Vice Admiral, *Fading Victory: The Diary of Admiral Matome Ugaki 1941-1945.* Masataka Chihaya, trans. (Pittsburgh: University of Pittsburgh Press, 1991), p. 610.

33. Willis A. "Bud" Dworzak, Second Lieutenant VMF-441. Interview of 21 July 2003.

34. *USS Harry F. Bauer DM 26 Serial 006 Action Report 12 June 1945*, p. 38.

35. *USS Hugh W. Hadley DD 774 Serial 066 Action Report 15 May 1945*, p. 2.

36. Eric Hammel, *Aces Against Japan The American Aces Speak. Volume I.* (Pacifica, CA: Pacifica Press, 1992), pp. 276-278.

37. *USS Hugh W. Hadley DD 774 Serial 066 Action Report 15 May 1945*, p. 2.

38. ibid., p. 6.

39. *Lynda Howell letter to Ray Baumler March 27, 1992*, p. 9.

40. *USS Hugh W. Hadley DD 774 Serial 066 Action Report 15 May 1945*, p. 3.

41. Oscar West Jr. Letter to Thomas English dated 18 August 1992. L. Richard Rhame Papers, Navy Historical Center.

42. *VMF-221 Aircraft Action Report No.63, 11 May 1945.*

43. Wendell M. Larson, 2d Lt. Letter of 2 September 2003.

44. *U.S.S. LCS(L)(3) 83 Serial 03-45 A.A. Action Report. 12 May 1945.*

45. Casualty figures are based on Samuel Eliot Morison. *History of United States*

Naval Operations in World War II. Volume XIV Victory in the Pacific 1945. (Boston: Little, Brown and Company, 1960), pp. 390-392 and individual ship action reports.

CHAPTER 6

1. *Fighter Command Okinawa Intelligence Section Daily Intelligence Summary 14 May, 1945,* pp. 3-4.
2. *VMF 311 War Diary 1 May-31 May 1945,* p. 75.
3. *MAG 33 War Diary 1 May-31 May, 1945.*
4. Marine Aircraft Group Thirty Three Communique, 15 May 1945.
5. National Security Agency. *"Magic" Far East Summary No. 423.* 17 May 1945, p. 4.
6. ibid., pp. 5-6.
7. ibid., pp. 6-7.
8. *Fighter Command Okinawa Intelligence Section Daily Intelligence Summary 16 May, 1945,* p. 1.
9. William Wolf, *Death Rattlers Marine Squadron VMF-323 over Okinawa.* (Atglen, PA: Schiffer Military History, 1999), pp. 165-166.
10. Albert Axell and Hideaki Kase. *Kamikaze Japan's Suicide Gods.* (London: Pearson Education Limited, 2002), pp. 158-161.
11. *U.S.S. LCS(L)(3) 67 Ship's History and Records,* p. 4.
12. *VMF(N) 533 War Diary 1 May through 31 May 1945.*
13. *Commander Task Force Fifty-One. Commander Amphibious Forces U.S. Pacific Fleet. Report on Okinawa Gunto Operation from 17 February to 17 May, 1945* p. (II) – p. 17.
14. Military History Section - General Headquarters Far East Command Military Intelligence Section General Staff. *Japanese Monograph No. 86. War History of the 5th Air Fleet (The "Ten" Air Unit) Operational Record from 10 February 1945 to 19 August 1945,* p. 90. Hereafter *JM 86.*
15. *JM 86,* p. 94.
16. National Security Agency. *"Magic" Far East Summary No. 425.* 19 May 1945, p. 5.
17. Military History Section–General Headquarters Far East Command Military Intelligence Section General Staff. *Japanese Monograph No. 51 Air Operations on Iwo Jima and the Ryukyus.,* pp. 45-50.
18. *ATIS Research Report No.76 Prominent Factors in Japanese Military Psychology.* Part IV. 7 February 1945, pp. 6-7.
19. *War Diary VMF(N) 533,* 24 May.
20. *War Diary Hdqtrs. TAF 10th Army 1 May-31 May 1945,* p. 11.
21. *JM 86,* pp. 89-90.
22. Headquarters of the Commander in Chief Navy Department, Washington, D.C. *Effects of B-29 Operations in Support of the Okinawa Campaign From 18 March to 22 June 1945.* 3 August 1945. App. A – p.4.
23. Ugaki, p. 617.
24. National Security Agency. *"Magic" Far East Summary No. 430.* 24 May 1945, p. 10.
25. National Security Agency. *"Magic" Far East Summary No. 428.* 22 May 1945,

pp. 5-6.

26. National Security Agency. *"Magic" Far East Summary No. 437.* 31 May 1945, p. 6.

27. *VMF 311 War Diary 1 May - 31 May 1945,* pp. 79.

28. *U.S.S. Bradford (DD 545) Serial 028 Action Report 5 July 1945,* p. 9.

29. *U.S.S. Foote (DD 511) Serial 0-35 Action Report 28 May 1945,* p. 1.

30. *USS Stormes (DD-780) Serial 072 Action Report 2 June 1945,* p. 5.

31. William F. Halsey, Fleet Adm. and Lt. Comdr. J. Bryan III. *Admiral Halsey's Story.* (New York: McGraw-Hill Book Company, Inc. 1947), pp. 251-253.

32. Ugaki, p. 619.

33. Samuel Eliot Morison, *Victory in the Pacific 1945.* (Boston: Little, Brown and Company, 1968), p. 260.

34. Fred Szymanek, "Eyewitness to Carnage." http://www.ussbraine dd630.com/witness.htm.

35. John Rooney, *Mighty Midget U.S.S. LCS 82* (PA: Self-Published 1990), p. 140.

36. Donald H. Sweet, with Lee Roy Way and William Bonvillian, Jr. *The Forgotten Heroes.* (Ridgewood, NJ: DoGo Publishing, 2000), pp. 130-131.

37. *U.S.S. Pritchett (DD 561) Serial 037 Action Report 10 July 1945,* p. 3.

38. *USS LCS (L) (3) 83 Serial 04-45 Action Report 28 May 1945.*

39. Robert F. Rielly, QM 2/c *LCS(L) 61.* Interview of 20 May 2001.

40. *U.S.S. Drexler (DD 741) Serial 01 Action Report 26 June 1945,* p. 6.

41. Wolf, pp. 171-172.

42. *U.S.S. Lowry (DD 770) Serial 021 Action Report 30 June 1945,* p. 3.

43. *U.S.S. Drexler (DD 741) Serial 01 Action Report 26 June 1945,* p. 7.

44. Casualty figures are based on Samuel Eliot Morison. *History of United States Naval Operations in World War II. Volume XIV Victory in the Pacific 1945.* (Boston: Little, Brown and Company, 1960), pp. 390-392 and individual ship action reports.

45. *CTF 31 Action to TF 31, TG 99.3, 29 May 1945.*

CHAPTER 7

1. National Security Agency. *"Magic" Far East Summary # 444.* 7 June 1945, p. 5.

2. *19th Fighter Squadron Mission Report No. 6-7,* 6 June 1945.

3. *VMF-422 Aircraft Action Report No. 85, June 7, 1945.*

4. William Wolf, *Death Rattlers Marine Squadron VMF-323 over Okinawa.* (Atglen, PA: Schiffer Military History, 1999), pp. 176-179.

5. *VMF 314 Aircraft Action Report No. 2, 3 June 1945.*

6. ibid.

7. Commander Fifth Amphibious Force CTF-51 and CTF-31. *Report of Capture of Okinawa Gunto Phases I and II.* 17 May 1945 - 21 June 1945, (III)–p. 65.

8. *333rd Fighter Squadron Mission Report No. 6-10, 8 June 1945.*

9. *U.S.S. William D. Porter (DD 579) Serial 00236 Action Report 18 June 1945,* pp. 2-3.

10. *USS LCS(L) (3) 86 Serial 04 Action Report 10 June 1945.*

11. Tom Spargo, *USS Cogswell DD 651.* E-mails to the author, 21 May 2001.

12. Richard M. McCool, Capt. (Ret.). CO *USS LCS(L) 122.* Letter to the author with narrative, 23 May 1997.

13. *Committee on Veteran's Affairs, U.S. Senate, Medal of Honor Recipients: 1863-1973.* (Washington, D.C.: Government Printing Office), 1973.
14. Earl Blanton, *Boston–to Jacksonville (41,000 Miles by Sea).* (Seaford, VA: Goose Creek Publications, 1991), pp. 120-121.
15. *413th Fighter Group Combat History*, p. 4.
16. National Security Agency. *"Magic" Far East Summary No. 451.* 14 June 1945, p. 5.
17. *CINCPAC PEARL Dispatch AI 88009.* 18 June 1945.
18. *JM 86*, pp. 104-105.
19. National Security Agency. *"Magic" Far East Summary No. 449.* 12 June 1945, pp. 4-5.
20. National Security Agency. *"Magic" Far East Summary No. 460.* 23 June 1945, pp. 1-2.
21. *U.S.S. Ammen (DD 527) Serial 038 Action Report 7 July 1945*, p. 15.
22. Rene J. Francillon. *Japanese Aircraft of the Pacific War.* (Annapolis: Naval Institute Press, 1979), pp. 330-332.
23. *JM 86*, p. 109.
24. Andrew Adams, Ed. *The Cherry Blossom Squadrons: Born to Die.* By the Hagoromo Society of Kamikaze Divine Thunderbolt Corps Survivors. Intro. By Andrew Adams. Edited and supplemented by Andrew Adams. Translation by Nobuo Asahi and the Japan Technical Company. (Los Angles: Ohara Publications, 1973), p. 162.
25. *VMF 314 War Diary 1-30 June 1945*, p. 3
26. Charles Thomas, *Dolly Five: A Memoir of the Pacific War.* (Chester, VA: Harrowgate Press, 1996), p. 248.
27. *VMF 314 Tactical and Operational Data on Combat Air Patrol, 22 June 1945.*
28. Matome Ugaki, Vice Admiral. *Fading Victory: The Diary of Admiral Matome Ugaki 1941-1945.* Masataka Chihaya, Translator. (Pittsburgh: University of Pittsburgh Press, 1991), p. 636.
29. National Security Agency. *"Magic" Far East Summary No. 463.* 26 June 1945, p. 4.
30. *USS Wadsworth DD 516 Serial 028 Action Report for Invasion of Okinawa Jima, 24 June 1945*, p. 80.
31. *Commander Fifth Fleet Serial 0333 Action Report, RYUKYUS Operation through 27 May 1945.* 21 June 1945, VI-A-2.
32. *Headquarters MAG 31 Daily Intelligence Summary, 25 June 1945.*
33. National Security Agency. *"Magic" Far East Summary No. 462.* 25 June 1945, p. 6.
34. National Security Agency. *"Magic" Far East Summary No. 464.* 27 June 1945, pp. 1-2.
35. *Commanding General Tactical Air Force Tenth Army No Serial Action Report–Phase 1–Nansei Shoto, 12 July 1945.* p. 8-I-1.
36. Parker R. Tyler, Jr., Captain USAAF. *From Seattle to Ie Shima with the 413rd Fighter Group.* (New York: Parker R. Tyler, Jr. 1945), p. 25.
37. National Security Agency. *"Magic" Far East Summary No. 472.* 5 July 1945, p. 3.
38. Minoru Genda, Captain. *USSBS Interrogation No. 479.* 28 November 1945, p. 16.

39. *JM 86*, p. 114.
40. National Security Agency. *"Magic" Far East Summary No. 476.* 9 July 1945, p. 7.
41. National Security Agency. *"Magic" Far East Summary No. 477.* 10 July 1945, p. 2.
42. National Security Agency. *"Magic" Far East Summary No. 479.* 12 July 1945, p. 8.
43. National Security Agency. *"Magic" Far East Summary No. 487.* 20 July 1945, pp. 1-2.
44. Commanding General, Tactical Air Force, *TAF G-2 Daily Summary.* 14 July 1945, p. 2.
45. *ATIS Research Report No. 76 Prominent Factors in Japanese Military Psychology.* Part. IV. 7 February 1945, pp. 6-7.
46. *Commander Destroyer Squadron 55 Action Report 7 August 1945.* Enclosure (A) p. 4.
47. *U.S.S. Pritchett (DD 561) Serial 045 Action Report 6 August 1945.*
48. According to Captain Rikehei Inoguchi, Willows only flew from Taiwan–see The United States Strategic Bombing Survey Naval Analysis Division. *Interrogations of Japanese Officials Volume I.* 1945, p. 63.
49. Albert Axell and Hideaki Kase. *Kamikaze Japan's Suicide Gods.* (London: Pearson Education, 2002), pp. 172-173.
50. Casualty figures are based on Samuel Eliot Morison. *History of United States Naval Operations in World War II. Volume XIV Victory in the Pacific 1945.* (Boston: Little, Brown and Company, 1960), pp. 390-392 and individual ship action reports.
51. Ugaki, pp. 664-665.
52. Rikihei Inoguchi, *The Divine Wind: Japan's Kamikaze Force in World War II.* (New York: Bantam Books, 1958), pp.157-159.
53. *VMF(N) 533 War Diary, 1 August through 31 August, 1945.*
54. *VMF(N) 543 War Diary, 1 August 1945 to 31 August 1945,* p. 5.
55. *War Diary 2nd Marine Aircraft Wing 1 August–30 August 1945,* p. 8.

CHAPTER 8

1. *CTF 54 Serial 0022 Action Report 4 June 1945.* Appx. II, p. 15.
2. Commander Fifth Amphibious Force CTF-51 and CTF-31. *Serial 0268 Report of Capture of Okinawa Gunto Phases I and II. 17 May 1945-21 June 1945.* (II)–p. 1. Hereafter *CTF-51 and CTF-31. Serial 0268*
3. See Samuel Eliot Morison, *Victory in the Pacific 1945.* (Boston: Little, Brown and Company, 1968), p. 181. This is suggested, the exact number is not known.
4. *Commander Task Force Fifty-One. Commander Amphibious Forces U.S. Pacific Fleet. Serial 01400 Report on Okinawa Gunto Operation from 17 February to 17 May, 1945* (V) (K) (1). Hereafter *CTF Serial 01400.*
5. Director, Air Intelligence Group, Division of Naval Intelligence. *Statistical Analysis of Japanese Suicide Effort Against Allied Shipping During Okinawa Campaign.* 23 July 1945, p. 7.
6. *USS LCS(L)(3) 57 Action Report 15 April 1945,* p. 7.

7. *USS LCS(L)(3) 118 Serial 02 Action Report 8 May, 1945.*
8. *LCS(L)(3) 94 Radar Picket Patrol, Tactical Plans for. 20 June 1945*, p. 12.
9. *U.S.S. Aulick (DD 569) Serial 0300 Action Report. 1 June 1945*, p. 4.
10. *USS Douglas H. Fox DD 779 Serial 004 Action Report 24 May 1945*, p. 7.
11. *LSM Flotilla Nine Serial C010 Action Report–Ie Shima and Southeastern Okinawa 2 April through 20 April 1945.* p. 7.
12. *Office of the Commander Amphibious Forces, U.S. Pacific Fleet. Serial 00470. 7 July 1945. Suicide Plane Attacks.* Enclosure (A) p. 6.
13. Director, Air Intelligence Group, *Statistical Analysis . . .* , p. 3
14. *CTF 54 Serial Serial 0022 Action Report 4 June 1945.* Appx. II p.16.
15. *Office of the Commander Amphibious Forces, U.S. Pacific Fleet. Serial 00470. 7 July 1945. Suicide Plane Attacks,* Enclosure (A) p. 6.
16. *CTF Serial 01400.,* (V) (E)-p. 37.
17. *CTF-51 and CTF-31. Serial 0268* (VII)–p. 8.
18. ibid. (II)–p. 2.
19. *U.S.S. Bennett (DD 473) Action Report Serial 015 17 April 1945*, p. 13.
20. *U.S.S. Caperton DD 650 Action Report Serial 096-45 12 July 1945*, p. 15.
21. *U.S S. Aulick (DD 569) Serial 0318 Action Report 9 July 1945*, p. 10.
22. *U.S.S. Anthony (DD 515) Serial 0168 Action Report.* 26 June 1945, p. 6.
23. H.D. Chickering, Lt. *World War II.* Typescript–undated, pp. 32-33.
24. *U.S.S. Hudson (DD 475) Serial 003 Action Report. 13 May 1945*, p. 5.
25. Robert Wisner, communications officer *LCS(L) 37.* Interview, 10 August 2002.
26. *Office of the Commander Amphibious Forces, U.S. Pacific Fleet. Serial 00470. 7 July 1945. Suicide Plane Attacks.* Enclosure (A) p. 8.
27. Earl Blanton, *Boston–to Jacksonville (41,000 Miles by Sea).* Seaford, VA: Goose Creek Publications, 1991), p. 97.
28. Jack Gebhardt Sonarman 1st Class. *USS Pringle DD 477.* Naval Historical Foundation Oral History Program. *Recollections of Sonarman 1st Class Jack Gebhardt USN.* 7 November 2000.
29. *Action Report–Capture of Okinawa Gunto, Phase II 5 May to 28 May 1945,* Appx. II, p. 13.
30. *CTF 51 Serial, 01400,* (II)–p. 18.
31. *CTF-51 and CTF-31. Serial 0268,* (VII)–p. 8.
32. Richmond Kelley Turner, Admiral, *Problems of Unified Command in the Marianas, Okinawa, and (Projected) Kyushu Operations.* An address given to the students of the Air War College, Maxwell Field, Alabama. 11 February 1947, pp. 31-32.

Bibliography

A bibliography of this sort encompasses a broad spectrum of materials, both primary and secondary in nature. Secondary sources are quite simple to list, however, in the case of primary materials it becomes necessary to improvise a bit. I have done this so that others may save time in the course of research.

Primary source materials for this book were found in a number of locations. As an aid I am listing them here not only by title, but by the facility in which I found them. The bulk of the primary materials came from the National Archives and Records Administration in College Park, Maryland. The record groups of particular use were:

RG 18 WWII USAAF Mission Record Index-Fighter Groups and Squadrons,
RG 19 Records of the Bureau of Ships,
RG 24 List of Logbooks of U.S. Navy Ships, Stations and Miscellaneous Units, 1801-1947,
RG 38 Records of the Chief of Naval Operations,
RG 127 Records of the United States Marine Corps–Aviation Records Relating to World War II,
RG 165 War Department General and Special Staffs,
RG 243 Records of the United States Strategic Bombing Survey,
RG 457 Records of the National Security Agency.

A second repository, also in the Washington, DC area, is the Navy Historical Center at the Washington Navy Yard. The Operational Archives Branch there houses the L. Richard Rhame Papers, a large collection of unique material encompassing the activities of the LCS(L) ships during World War II. Included in the collection are personal reminiscences, as well as photos and official documents. The library at the Navy Historical Center also contains many valuable materials in both their general and special collections. The United States Army Military History Institute at Carlisle, Pennsylvania was also an important source, with materials found there that were not in other collections. Selected records of the United States Army Air Forces in World War II were obtained from the Air Force Historical Research Agency at Maxwell Air Force Base in Alabama. Other materials relating to my topic were found in the Library of Congress in Washington, DC, the archives of the Tailhook Association in San Diego, California, the History

Department and the Alexander Library, Rutgers University, New Brunswick, New Jersey and the Firestone Library of Princeton University in Princeton, New Jersey.

Primary source materials and their locations are listed in the following bibliography which is organized by facility. Specific reports in each category are listed in my end notes for each chapter. It should be noted that there is an inconsistency in the way in which many of the official reports are listed, particularly in the end notes.

I have entered each of the reports exactly as the original is written. Navy action reports, for instance, may show the ship's number written as USS or U.S.S. The ship's number may or may not be in parentheses and the date of a report sometimes contains a comma between the month and year. Many variations in style appear in the different types of official ship and aircraft squadron reports. Inconsistencies in the end note and bibliographic entries contained in the text are found in the originals, I have not made changes for the sake of consistency.

PRIMARY SOURCES

Air Force Historical Research Agency, Maxwell Air Force Base

Records of the 318th Fighter Group Microfilm Publication BO522–2309
Records of the 318th Fighter Group Narrative Microfilm Publication BO239–2078

Library of Congress

Archival Manuscript Collection. Deyo, Morton L. Papers of Vice Admiral M.L. Deyo USN 1911-1981. Call Number 0535S
Deyo, M.L. Vice Admiral. *Kamikaze.* Typescript, Circa 1955.

National Archives and Records Administration, College Park, MD

RG 18 WWII USAAF Mission Record Index–Fighter Groups and Squadrons

USAAF Squadron and Groups Mission reports and Squadron and Group Histories for the: 1st, 19th, 21st, 34th, 333rd, 418th (N) and 548th (N) Fighter Squadrons and the 318th and 413th Fighter Groups.

RG 19 Records of the Bureau of Ships

BuShips General Correspondence 1940-1945 LSM(R)/L 11–3 to C-LSM(R)/S 29-2.
BuShips General Correspondence 1940-1945 LSM(R)/S87 to LSM(R) 188-189/S 17.

BuShips General Correspondence 1940-1945 LSM(R)/S87 to LSM(R) 188-189/S 17.

BuShips General Correspondence 1940-1945 C-DD 552 to DD 553

BuShips General Correspondence 1940-1945 C-DD 734/L 11–1 (350-C-44LIL).

BuShips General Correspondence 1940-1945 DD 741–C-DD 742

RG 24 List of Logbooks of U.S. Navy Ships, Stations, and Miscellaneous Units, 1801-1947

Ship Logs

For the amphibious command ships *Ancon AGC 4*, *Biscayne AGC 18*, *Eldorado AGC 11*, *Panamint AGC 13*,

for the carriers *Belleau Wood CVL 24*, *Bennington CV 20*, *Block Island CVE 106*, *Cape Gloucester CVE 109*, *Chenango CVE 28*, *Essex CV 9*, *Franklin CV 13*, *Gilbert Islands CVE 107*, *Hancock CV 19*, *Hornet CV 12*, *San Jacinto CVL 30*, *Vella Gulf CVE 111*, *Wasp CV 18*, *Yorktown CV 10*,

for the destroyers *Alfred A. Cunningham DD 752*, *Ammen DD 527*, *Anthony DD 515*, *Aulick DD 569*, *Bache DD 470*, *Barton DD 722*, *Beale DD 471*, *Bennett DD 473*, *Bennion DD 662*, *Boyd DD 544*, *Bradford DD 545*, *Braine DD 630*, *Brown DD 546*, *Bryant DD 665*, *Bush DD 529*, *Callaghan DD 792*, *Caperton DD 650*, *Cassin Young DD 793*, *Charles Ausburne DD 570*, *Claxton DD 571*, *Cogswell DD 651*, *Colhoun DD 801*, *Compton DD 705*, *Converse DD 509*, *Cowell DD 547*, *Daly DD 519*, *Douglas H. Fox DD 779*, *Drexler DD 741*, *Dyson DD 572*, *Evans DD 552*, *Foote DD 511*, *Frank E. Evans DD 754*, *Fullam DD 474*, *Gainard DD 706*, *Gregory DD 802*, *Guest DD 472*, *Harry E. Hubbard DD 748*, *Heywood L. Edwards DD 663*, *Hudson DD 475*, *Hugh W. Hadley DD 774*, *Ingersoll DD 652*, *Ingraham DD 694*, *Irwin DD 794*, *Isherwood DD 520*, *James C. Owens DD 776*, *John A. Bole DD 755*, *Kimberly DD 521*, *Knapp DD 653*, *Laffey DD 724*, *Lang DD 399*, *Laws DD 558*, *Little DD 803*, *Lowry DD 770*, *Luce DD 522*, *Mannert L. Abele DD 733*, *Massey DD 778*, *Moale DD 693*, *Morrison DD 560*, *Mustin DD 413*, *Nicholson DD 442*, *Picking DD 685*, *Preston DD 795*, *Pringle DD 477*, *Pritchett DD 561*, *Purdy DD 734*, *Putnam DD 757*, *Richard P. Leary DD 664*, *Rowe DD 564*, *Russell DD 414*, *Shubrick DD 639*, *Smalley DD 565*, *Sproston DD 577*, *Stanly DD 478*, *Sterett DD 407*, *Stoddard DD 566*, *Stormes DD 780*, *Van Valkenburgh DD 656*, *Wadsworth DD 516*, *Walke DD 723*, *Watts DD 567*, *Wickes DD 578*, *Wilkes DD 441*, *Willard Keith DD 775*, *William D. Porter DD 579*, and *Wren DD 568*,

for the fleet tugs *Arikara ATF 98*, *Cree ATF 84*, *Lipan, ATF 85*, *Menominee ATF 73*, *Pakana ATF 108*, *Tekesta ATF 93*, and *Ute ATF 76*,

for the light mine layers *Aaron Ward DM 34*, *Gwin DM 33*, *Harry F. Bauer DM 26*, *Henry A. Wiley DM 29*, *J. William Ditter DM 31*, *Lindsey DM 32*, *Robert H. Smith DM 23*, *Shannon DM 25*, *Shea DM 30*, and *Thomas E. Fraser DM 24*,

for the high speed minesweepers *Butler DMS 29*, *Ellyson DMS 19*, *Emmons DMS 22*, *Forrest DMS 24*, *Gherardi DMS 30*, *Hambleton DMS 20*, *Harding DMS 28*, *Hobson DMS 26*, *Jeffers DMS 27*, *Macomb DMS 23*, and *Rodman*

DMS 21,
for the destroyer escorts *Bowers DE 637* and *Edmonds DE 406,*
for the patrol motor gunboats *PGM 9, PGM 10, PGM 17,* and *PGM 20,*
for the landing crafts support (large) *11* through *22, 31, 32, 34* through *40, 51* through *57, 61* through *67, 68, 70, 71, 74, 76, 81* through *90, 92* through *94, 97* through *105, 107, 109, 110, 111, 114* through *125,* and *128* through *130,*
for the landing ships medium *14, 82, 167, 222, 228, 279,*
for the landing ships medium (rockets) *189, 191, 192, 193, 196, 197, 198,* and *199,*
for the high speed transports *Barber APD 57, Clemson APD 31, Frament APD 77,* and *Ringness APD 100,*
for the patrol crafts rescue *PCE(R)s 851, 852, 853, 854, 855,* and *856.*
Specific log references are listed in my chapter end notes.

RG 38 Records of the Chief of Naval Operations - Records Relating to Naval Activity During World War II

Japanese Suicide Effort Against Allied Shipping During OKINAWA Campaign, Statistical Analysis of. OP-16-VA-MvR. Serial 001481916. 26 July 1945.

CINC-CINCPOA BULLETINS

Airfields in Kyushu. Bulletin No. 166–45, 15 August 1945.
Airways Data Taiwan Chiho Special Translation No. 36, 1 June 1945.
Daito Shoto Bulletin No. 77–45, 20 March 1945.
Digest of Japanese Air Bases Special Translation No. 65, 12 May 1945.
Suicide Force Combat Methods Bulletin No. 129–45, 27 May 1945.
Suicide Weapons and Tactics "Know Your Enemy!" Bulletin No. 126–45, 28 May 1945.
Translations Interrogations Number 26. Bulletin No. 102–45, 25 April 1945.
Translations Interrogations Number 35. Bulletin No. 170–45, 7 July 1945.

Action Reports

For the amphibious command ships *Ancon AGC 4, Biscayne AGC 18, Eldorado AGC 11, Panamint AGC 13,*
for the carriers *Belleau Wood CVL 24 , Bennington CV 20, Chenango CVE 28, Essex CV 9, Franklin CV 13, Hancock CV 19, Hornet CV 12, San Jacinto CVL 30, Wasp CV 18, Yorktown CV 10,*
for the destroyers *Ammen DD 527, Anthony DD 515, Aulick DD 569, Bache DD 470, Beale DD 471,Bennett DD 473, Bennion DD 662, Boyd DD 544, Bradford DD 545, Braine DD 630, Brown DD 546, Bryant DD 665, Bush DD 529, Callaghan DD 792, Caperton DD 650, Cassin Young DD 793, Claxton DD 571, Cogswell DD 651, Colhoun DD 801, Converse DD 509, Cowell DD 547, Daly DD 519, Douglas H. Fox DD 779, Drexler DD 741, Dyson DD 572, Evans DD 552, Foote DD 511, Frank E. Evans DD 754, Fullam DD 474, Gainard DD 706, Gregory DD 802, Guest DD 472, Harry E. Hubbard DD*

748, Heywood L. Edwards DD 663, Hudson DD 475, Hugh W. Hadley DD 774, Ingersoll DD 652, Ingraham DD 694, Irwin DD 794, Isherwood DD 520, John A. Bole DD 755, Kimberly DD 521, Knapp DD 653, Lang DD 399, Laffey DD 724, Laws DD 558, Little DD 803, Lowry DD 770, Luce DD 522, Mannert L. Abele DD 733, Massey DD 778, Morrison DD 560, Mustin DD 413, Preston DD 795, Pringle DD 477, Pritchett DD 561, Purdy DD 734, Putnam DD 757, Rowe DD 564, Russell DD 414, Sampson DD 394, Shubrick DD 639, Smalley DD 565, Sproston DD 577, Stanly DD 478, Sterett DD 407, Stoddard DD 566, Stormes DD 780, Taussig DD 746, Twiggs DD 591, Van Valkenburgh DD 656, Wadsworth DD 516, Walke DD 723, Watts DD 567, Wickes DD 578, Wilkes DD 441, William D. Porter DD 579, and *Wren DD 568,*
for the fleet tugs *Arikira ATF 98, Cree ATF 84, Lipan ATF 85, Menominee ATF 73, Pakana ATF 108, Tawakoni ATF 114, Tekesta ATF 93,* and *Ute ATF 76,*
for the light mine layers *Aaron Ward DM 34, Gwin DM 33, Harry F. Bauer DM 26, Henry A. Wiley DM 29, J. William Ditter DM 31, Robert H. Smith DM 23, Shannon DM 25, Shea DM 30,* and *Thomas E. Fraser DM 24,*
for the high speed minesweepers *Ellyson DMS 19, Harding DMS 28, Hobson DMS 26, Jeffers DMS 27,* and *Macomb DMS 23,*
for the patrol motor gunboats *PGM 10* and *PGM 20,* for the landing crafts support (large) *11* through *21, 31, 32, 34* through *40, 51* through *57,* 61 through *67, 68, 81* through *90, 94,* through *109, 110, 111, 114* through *117, 119* through *125, 129, 130,*
for the landing ships medium *14, 82, 167, 222, 228, 279,*
for the landing ships medium (rockets) *189, 190, 192, 193, 194, 195,* and *197,*
for the high speed transports *Barber APD 57, Clemson APD 31,* and *Ringness APD 100,*
for the patrol crafts rescue *PCE(R)s 851, 852, 853,*
for the seaplane tender *Hamlin AV 15,* and
for the sub chaser *SC 699.*
Various serials and dates were used for each ship. Specific reports are listed in my chapter end notes.

War Diaries

For the amphibious command ships *Ancon AGC 4, Biscayne AGC 18, Eldorado AGC 11, Panamint AGC 13,*
for the destroyers *Anthony DD 515, Bryant DD 665, Lowry DD 770, Wadsworth DD 516* and *Wickes DD 578,*
for the fleet tug *Arikara ATF 98,*
for the high speed minesweeper *Macomb DMS 23,* and for the landing ships medium *14, 82, 167, 222, 228,* and *279.*

Destroyer Division, Mine Division, LSM, LCS Flotilla, Group, Division Reports, War Diaries, and Histories

Commander Destroyer Division 92 Serial 0192 Action Report. 23 July 1945.
Commander Destroyer Division 112 Serial 030 Action Report Amphibious

Assault on Okinawa Gunto. 18 April 1945.

Commander Destroyer Division 120 Serial 002 Action Report–Okinawa Gunto Operation, for Period from 29 April through 4 May 1945. 6 May 1945.

Commander Destroyer Division 126 Serial 08 Action Report, Attack by Japanese Aircraft off Okinawa Gunto on Hyman–6 April, 1945, and on Purdy, Cassin Young, Mannert L. Abele and Supporting Gunboats on 12 April 1945. 15 April 1945.

Commander Destroyer Squadron 2 Serial 00551 Action Report, Okinawa Gunto Operation 1 March to 17 May 1945. 1 June 1945.

Commander Destroyer Squadron 24 Serial 0118 Iceberg Operation, 23-27 May 1945. 29 May 1945.

Commander Destroyer Squadron 24 Serial 0155 Invasion of Okinawa Jima, 19 April–28 May 1945. 18 June 1945.

Commander Destroyer Squadron 24 Serial 0166 Invasion of Okinawa Jima, 28 May to 27 June 1945. 28 June 1945.

Commander Destroyer Squadron 45 Serial 00138 Report of Capture of Okinawa Gunto Phases 1 and 2, Commander, Destroyer Squadron Forty-Five for the Period 27 March to 21 June 1945. 27 June 1945.

Commander Destroyer Squadron Forty-Nine. Serial 0011 Action Report–OKINAWA CAMPAIGN–9 March 1945 to 23 June 1945. 28 June 1945.

Commander Destroyer Squadron 55 Action Report 7 August 1945.

Commander Destroyer Squadron Sixty-Four. Serial 032 Report of Capture of Okinawa Gunto, Phases 1 and 2. 25 June 1945.

Commander LCS(L) Flotilla THREE Serial 621 LCS(L) Flotilla THREE Staff–Factual History of. 21 November 1945.

Commander LCS(L) Flotilla FOUR Serial 25–46 War History, Commander LCS(L) Flotilla FOUR. 6 January 1946.

Commander LCS(L)(3) Group 11 Serial 0138 Action Report Capture and Occupation of Okinawa Gunto Phases I and II. 30 July 1945.

Commander LSM Flotilla Nine Serial 006 War Diary for the Month of March 1945.

Commander LSM Flotilla Nine Serial 021 War Diary for the Month of April 1945.

Commander LSM Flotilla Nine Serial C010 Action Report–Ie Shima and Southeastern Okinawa, 2 April through 20 April 1945. 21 April 1945.

Commander Mine Division 58 War Diary. April 1945.

Commander Mine Division 58 War Diary. May 1945.

Commander Mine Squadron Three Serial 078 Action Report, Capture of Okinawa Gunto, Phase I and II, 9 March to 24 June 1945. 5 July 1945.

Commander Mine Squadron Twenty Serial 0106 Action Report. 3 July 1945.

Commander Task Flotilla 5 Serial 0894 Action Report, Capture of Okinawa Gunto 26 March to 21 June 1945. 20 July 1945.

DD-475 Dispatch 5 June, 1945.

LCS(L)(3) Flotilla Five Confidential Memorandum No. 5-45, 10 July 1945.

LCS Group Nine Operation Order No. 1-45 Annex "Dog" Fighting Instructions.

LCS Group Eleven Serial 0138 Composite Action Report Okinawa Gunto 1 April 1945-21 June 1945.

CinCPac, 5th Fleet, Task Force, Task Group and Task Unit Records, Reports, Communiques

Amphibious Forces Pacific Fleet (TF 52) Serial 000166 16 March 1945 Operation Order A6-45.

CinCPac Adv. Hdqtrs. 17 April 1945.

CinCPac United States Pacific Fleet Serial 0005608 *War Diary for the Period 1 March through 31 March 1945.* 11 April 1945.

- - -. *0005643 War Diary for the Period 1 April through 30 April 1945.* 13 May 1945.

- - -. *0005685 War Diary for the Period 1 May through 31 May 1945.* 13 June 1945.

- - -. *0005748 War Diary for the Period 1 June through 30 June 1945.* 15 July 1945.

- - -. *0005801 War Diary for the Period 1 July through 31 July 1945.* 9 August 1945.

- - -. *0005849 War Diary for the Period 1 August through 31 August 1945.* 9 September 1945.

Commander Fifth Amphibious Force CTF-51 and CTF-31 *Serial 0268 Report of Capture of Okinawa Gunto Phases I and II. 17 May 1945–21 June 1945. 4 July 1945.*

Commander Fifth Amphibious Force letter of 11 June 1945. *Translation of a Japanese Letter.*

Commander Fifth Fleet. *Serial 0333 Action Report, RYUKYUS Operation through 27 May 1945.* 21 June 1945.

Commander Task Force Fifty-One. Commander Amphibious Forces U.S. Pacific Fleet. *Serial 01400 Report on Okinawa Gunto Operation from 17 February to 17 May, 1945.*

Commander Task Force 54. *Serial 0022 Action Report–Capture of Okinawa Gunto, Phase II 5 May to 28 May 1945.* 4 June 1945.

CTF 31 to TF 31, TG 99.3, 29 May 1945.

CTF 51 to TF 51 16 April 1945.

CTF 51 to TF 51 24 April 1945.

CTU 52.9.1 OUTGOING MESSAGE OF 17 APRIL 1945.

Task Force 51 Communication and Organization Digest, 1945.

Navy Carrier Air Group and Individual Squadron Histories, War Diaries and Aircraft Action Reports

For CAG 40, 46, 47, 82, VBF-17, VC 8, 83, 85, 90, 93, 96, VF 9, 10, 12, 17, 23, 24, 29, 30, 31, 33, 40, 45, 82, 84, 85, 86, 87, and 90(N). Various dates.

Record Group 38 Records of the Chief of Naval Operations–Office of Naval Intelligence

Monograph Files–Japan 1939-1946 1001-1015

Air Branch, Office of Naval Intelligence. *Naval Aviation Combat Statistics*

World War II. OPNAV-P-23V No. A 129. Washington, DC: Office of the Chief of Naval Operations Navy Department, 17 June 1946.

Air Intelligence Group, Division of Naval Intelligence. *Air Operations Memorandum No. 81.* 18 May 1945.

Air Operations Memorandum No. 82. 25 May 1945.

Air Operations Memorandum No. 83. OpNav-16-V # S234. 1 June 1945.

Air Operations Memorandum No. 88. 6 July 1945.

Brunetti. Col. N. *The Japanese Air Force.* (undated).

Chain of Command of Naval Air Forces Attached to the Combined Fleet (as of August 15th 1945).

Data Table - Japanese Combat Aircraft.

NAVAER 1335A (Rev. 1-49) *Standard Aircraft Characteristics F6F-5 "Hellcat."*

NAVAER (no number given) *Standard Aircraft Characteristics F4U-4 "Corsair."*

Observed Suicide Attacks by Japanese Aircraft Against Allied Ships. OpNav-16-V # A106. 23 May 1945.

Photographic Interpretation Handbook - United States Forces. Supplement No. 2. Aircraft Identification. 15 April, 1945.

Secret Information Bulletin, No. 24.

Technical Air Intelligence Center. *Report # 17 Combat Evaluation of Zeke 52 with F4U-1D, F6F-5 and FM-2.* OpNav - 16-V # T 217. November 1944.

- - -. *Report # 38 Comparative Performance Between Zeke 52 and the P-38, P-51, P-47.* OpNav - 16-V # T 238. April 1945.

- - -. *Summary # 31 Baka.* OpNav - 16-V # T 131. June 1945.

U. S. Naval Technical Mission to Japan. Index No. *S-O2 Ships and Related Targets Japanese Suicide Craft.*

Record Group 38 Records of the Naval Security Group, Crane, Indiana

Kamikaze Attacks at Okinawa, April - June 1945. 6 May 1946.

Record Group 127 Records of the United States Marine Corps–Aviation Records Relating to World War II

US Marine Corps Unit War Diaries, Daily Intelligence Summaries, Aircraft Action Reports and Unit Histories 1941-1949

For 2nd MAW, MAG 14, 22, 31, 33, VMF 112, 113, 123, 212, 221, 222, 223, 224, 311, 312, 314, 322, 323, 351, 422, 441, 451, 511, 512, 513, 533(N), 542(N), 543 (N), and VMTB 232. Various dates.

Tenth Army Tactical Air Force Records

Air Defense Command (Fighter Command) Operation Plan 1-45.

Air Defense Command Intelligence Logs #s 1 through 5, 7 April to 27

November 1945 inclusive.
Air Defense Command Intelligence Section–Daily Intelligence Summaries for 12, 15, 16, 17, 22, 23, 24, 29 April, 1,4, 5, 7, 10, 11, 12 May 1945.
Commanding General Tactical Air Force Tenth Army No Serial 12 July 1945 Action Report–Phase 1–Nansei Shoto. Covers Period 1 April–30 June 1945.
Fighter Command Okinawa Intelligence Section–Daily Intelligence Summary for 12, 13, 14, 16, 18, 26, 27, 28, 29 May, 4, 12, 23 June, 1945.
Tactical Air Force Score Board 7 April–12 July 1945.
Tactical Air Force, Tenth Army Action Report, Phase I Nansei Shoto Period 8 December 1944 to 30 June 1945 Inc..
Tactical Air Force Tenth Army Operation Plan No. 1-45.
Tactical Air Force Tenth Army Periodic Reports Periodic Reports April-June 1945.
Tactical Air Force, Tenth Army War Diary for 1 May to 31 May 1945.
Tactical Air Force, Tenth Army War Diary for 1 June to 30 June 1945.

Record Group 165 War Department General and Special Staffs

Captured Personnel and Material Reports

Reports–(Air) 20-22 Japanese Interrogations 1945 through A (Air) 186-192 Japanese Interrogations + (A) 193-204 Japanese Interrogations through AL 1-39 German, French and Dutch Interrogations, 1944.
Report from Captured Personnel and Material Branch, Military Intelligence Service, U.S. War Department. Reports A(Air) 22 of 10 March 1945, A-220 of 20 July 1945, A (Air) - 32 11 August 1945.
Japanese Translations–British Ministry of Information No. 9-28, 146-169.

RG 243 Records of the United States Strategic Bombing Survey

243.4.2 Records of the Intelligence Branch–Microfilm Publication M-1654 Transcripts of Interrogations of Japanese Leaders and Responses to Questionnaires, 1945-46. (9 rolls)
Interrogations of: Lt. Gen. Saburo Endo, Lt. Col. Kazumi Fuji, Col. Heikichi Fukami, Comdr. Fukamizu, Capt. Minoru Genda, Maj. Gen. Hideharu Habu, Lt. Col. Maseo Hamatani, Col. Hiroshi Hara, Col. Junji Hayashi, Capt. Gengo Hojo, Maj. Gen. Asahi Horiuchi, Capt. Rikibei Inoguchi, Lt. Kunie Iwashita, Lt. Col. Naomichi Jin, Col. Katsuo Kaimoto, Rear Adm. Seizo Katsumata, Lt. Gen. Masakazu Kawabe, Maj. Toshio Kinugasa, Lt. Gen. Kumao Kitajima, Comdr. Mitsugi Kofukuda, Col. M. Matsumae, Col. Kyohei Matsuzawa, Capt. Takeshi Mieno, Gen. Miyoshi, Lt. Gen. Ryosuke Nakanishi, Lt. Comdr. Ohira, Capt. Toshikazu Ohmae, Comdr. Masatake Okumiya, Capt. Tonosuke Otani, Maj. Iori Sakai, Maj. Hideo Sakamoto, Lt. Comdr. Takeda Shigeki, Lt. Gen. Michio Sugawara, Maj. O. Takahashi, Maj. O. Takauchi, Capt. T. Takeuchi, Col. Shushiro Tanabe, Col. Isekichi Tanaka, Rear Adm. Toshitanea Takata, Comdr. Oshimori Terai, Superior

Pvt. Guy Toko, Maj. Gen. Sadao Yui.

JANIS 87 Change No. 1. Joint Intelligence Study Publishing Board, August, 1944. Microfilm Publication 1169, Roll 14.

JANIS 84-2. *Air Facilities Supplement to JANIS 84. Southwest Japan (Kyushu Island, Shikoku Island, Southwestern Honshu Island).* Joint Intelligence Study publishing Board. June 1945. Microfilm Publication 1169, Roll 10.

Supplemental Report of Certain Phases of the War Against Japan Derived From Interrogations of Senior Naval Commanders at Truk. Naval and Naval Air Field Team No. 3, USSBS. Microfilm Publication M1655, Roll 311.

Tactical Mission Reports of the 20th and 21st Bomber Commands, 1945. Microfilm Publication M1159, Rolls 2, 3.

Record Group 457 Records of the National Security Agency

Explanatory Notes on the KAMIKAZE Attacks at Okinawa, April-June 1945. 6 May 1946.

Intelligence Reports from U.S. Joint Services and other Government Agencies, December 1941 to October 1948.

SRMD–007 *JICPOA Summary of ULTRA Traffic, 1 April-30 June 1945, 1 July-31 August 1945.*

SRMD–011 *JICPOA Estimate of Japanese Army and Navy Fighter Deployment 8 August 1944–23 April 1945.*

SRMD–015 *Reports and Memoranda on a Variety of Intelligence Subjects January 1943–August 1945.*

Magic Far East Summaries 1945–1945

SRS341 (24-2-45)–SRS 410 (4-5-45).

SRS411 (5-5-45)–SRS 490 (23-7-45).

SRS491 (24-7-45)–SRS547 (2-10-45).

Special Research Histories (SRHS)

SRH-52 Estimated Japanese Aircraft Locations 15 July 1943–9 August 1945.

SRH-53 Estimates of the Japanese Air Situation 23 June 1945.

SRH-54 Effects of B29 Operations in Support of the Okinawa Campaign 18 March–22 June 1945.

SRH-55 Estimated Unit Locations of Japanese Navy and Army Air Forces 20 July 1945.

SRH-103 Suicide Attack Squadron Organizations July 1945.

SRH 183 Location of Japanese Military Installations.

SRH-257 Analysis of Japanese Air Operations During Okinawa Campaign.

SRH-258 Japanese Army Air Forces Order-Of-Battle 1945.

SRH-259 OP-20G File of Reports on Japanese Naval Air Order of Battle.

United States Navy Records Relating to Cryptology 1918 to 1950

SRMN 013 *CINCPAC Dispatches* May–June 1945

Princeton University–Firestone Library

Wartime Translations of Seized Japanese Documents. Allied Translator and Interpreter Section Reports, 1942-1946. Bethesda, MD: Congressional Information Service, Inc., 1988. (Microfilm)
    ADVATIS Bulletins 405, 656
    ADVATIS Interrogation Reports
        1. 601. Ens. Sadao Nakamuara
        11. Superior Petty Officer Ichiro Tanaka
        13. 1st Class Petty Officer Hirokazu Maruo
        15. 1st Class Petty Officer Takao Musashi
        17, 694. 1st Class Petty Officer Tadayoshi Ishimoto
        603. Lt (jg) Takahiko Hanada
        650. Leading Pvt. Masakiyo Kato
        727. Sgt. Jyuro Saito
        749. Cpl. Nobuo Hayashi
        775. Probational Officer Toshio Taniguchi
    Enemy Publications
        No. 8. Mimeographed Identification Sketches of Japanese Aircraft
        No. 152. References on Piloting Type 1 Fighter, Model 2
        No. 184. KI-61 (Type 3F Tony) Piloting Procedure
        No. 391. Data on Navy Airplanes and Bombs
    Research Reports
        No. 76. Self-Immolation as a Factor in Japanese Military Psychology
        No. 125. Liaison Boat Units.

Rutgers University–New Brunswick History Department

Oral History Archives of WW-II - Interview with Alfred Nisonoff, Executive Officer *LCS(L) 130.*

The Tailhook Association

Allowances and Location of Naval Aircraft 1943-1945.
Ship's History of the U.S.S. Cabot (CVL-23) 26 September, 1945.
U.S.S. Bennington CV-20 Cruise Book 1944-1945.

Navy Individual Squadron Histories

For VF-9, 10, 17, 23, and 90(N).

United States Navy Historical Center

Operational Archives Branch–L. Richard Rhame Collection– Papers of the National Association of USS LCS(L)(3) 1-130, 1940s–, Individual Ship Histories for LCS(L)s, Assorted documents and personal memoirs.
Naval Foundation Oral History Program.–War in the Pacific: Actions in the

Philippines including Leyte Gulf, as well as the battles of Iwo Jima and
Okinawa, 1943-45. Recollections of Sonarman 1st Class Jack Gebhardt,
USS Pringle DD 477 ed. By Senior Chief Yeoman (YNCS) George Tusa - 7
Nov. 2000.

United States Army Military History
Institute–Carlisle, PA

Allied Translator and Interpreter Section South West Pacific Area A.T.I.S.
Publication. *Japanese Military Conventional Signs and Abbreviations.* 4
March 1943.
CinCPac-CinCPOA Bulletin 120-45. *Symbols and Abbreviations for Army Air
Units.* 21 May 1945.
Commander in Chief Navy Department. *CominCh P-0011 Anti-Suicide Action
Summary.* 31 August 1945.
Commander in Chief United States Fleet. *Antiaircraft Action Summary
Suicide Attacks.* April 1945.
General Headquarters, Far East Command Military Intelligence Section,
Historical Division. *Interrogations of Japanese Officials on World War II
(English Translations) Vol. I & II.* 1949.
General Headquarters, Far East Command Military Intelligence Section,
Historical Division. *Statements of Japanese Officials on World War II
(English Translations).* 1949-1950.
The Gerald Astor Papers. Letter from Maj. Gen. Yoshihiro Minamoto to
Gerald Astor. 10- August 1994.
Headquarters Far East Command Military History Section. *Imperial General
Headquarters Navy Directives.* Volume II, Directives No. 316–No. 540 (15
Jan 44–26 Aug 45) Special Directives No. 1–No. 3 (2 Sep 45 - 12 Sep 45).
Headquarters Far East Command Military History Section. *Imperial General
Headquarters Navy Orders.* Orders No. 1–No. 57 (5 Nov. 41–2 Sep 45).
Joint Intelligence Study Publishing Board. *Air Facilities Supplement to
JANIS 86 Nansei Shoto (Ryukyu Islands).* May 1945.
Trabue, William Lt. Col. G.S.C. *Observer's Report The Okinawa Operation (8
February 1945 to 2 June 1945).* Headquarters United States Army Forces
Pacific Ocean Areas G-5. 15 June 1945.

Unpublished Histories

Brader, Charles. Pharmacist's Mate *LCS(L) 65. LCS Men in a Spectacular
Part of Okinawa Campaign.* Typescript, undated.
Causemaker, Richard. GM 3/c *LCS 84. Duty with the LCS(L)(3) 84.*
Typescript, undated.
Chickering, H.D. Lt. CO *LCS(L) 51. World War II.* Typescript, undated.
Conway, Paul L. *A Fiery Sunday Morning.* Warren, PA: Paul L. Conway.
Typescript, 2000.
Glasser, Robin, *Wings of Gold.* Typescript, 6 June 2002.
History of the U.S.S. LCS(L) (3) 53.
Ie Shima Diary. (318th Fighter Group) Unpublished typescript. Circa 1945.

Contributed by Lt. John W. Cook, 73rd Fighter Squadron.

Kaup, Harold J. RM3/c *LCS(L) 15. The Death of a Ship.* Typescript, Undated.

Martin, Arthur R. Signalman. *History of the U.S.S. LCS 88.* Typescript, Undated.

MacGlashing, John. Yeoman VF(N) 90. *Biography of Night Air Group Ninety its Contribution to WW II and Naval Warfare.* Typescript, Undated.

Osterland, Frank C. Lt. Cmdr. *Dolly Three.* Typescript, August 28, 1993.

Pierpoint, Powell. Lt. (jg) XO *LCS(L) 61. The War History of the LCS(L) 61.* Typescript, 1945-1946.

Prunty, Jonathan G. GM 1/c. *My Days in the U.S. Navy 1944 to 1946.* Typescript, December, 1998.

Schneider, Philip J. *The Diary of Philip J. Schneider.* Typescript, Undated.

Scott, Eugene Winfield. *Experiences of a Sailor in World War Two and the Korean War.* Typescript, Undated.

Stewart, James M.. CO *LSM(R) 189 Autobiography.* Typescript, Undated.

Tyler, Parker R. Jr. *Captain USAAF. From Seattle to Ie Shima with the 413rd Fighter Group.* New York: Parker R. Tyler, Jr. Typescript, 1945.

Interviews, Correspondence, Personal Papers, Diaries

Ball, Donald L. *LCS(L) 85.* Interview. 18 September 2002.

Barkley, John. L. YN2 *USS Rowe DD 564* E-Mails 25, 26 November 2002.

Barnby, Frank. *LCS(L) 13.* Collected papers and photographs.

Baumler, Raymond. *LCS 14.* Letter of 4 March 2003.

Blanton, Earl. *LCS(L) 118.* Interview. 19 September 2002.

Bennett, Otis Wayne. 1st. Lt. 333rd Fighter Squadron. Interview. 8 October 2002.

Blyth, Robert. *LCS(L) 61.* Interview. 25 August 1995.

Burgess, Harold H. *LCS(L) 61.* Interview. 25 August 1995.

Cardwell, John H. *LCS(L) 61.* Collected papers.

Christman, William R. *LCS(L) 95.* Letter of 9 April 2003.

Davis, George E. EM 1/c *USS Pakana ATF 108.* E-mail of 6 April 2003

Davis, Franklin M., Sr. *LCS(L) 61.* Interview. 25 August 1995.

Diary of Philip J. Schneider Signalman 1st Class USS Boyd.

Dworzak, W. A. "Bud". 1st Lieutenant VMF-441. Interview. 21 July 2003.

Fenoglio, Melvin. *USS Little* Interview. 3 September 2003.

Gauthier, David. TM3/c *USS Knapp.* E-mails to the author, 22 December 2000, 16, 19 March 2001.

Glasser, Paul. Lieutenant (jg) VF 12. Interview. 4 August 2003.

Hoffman, Edwin Jr. QM 3/c *USS Emmons* e-mails 23, 24 December 2003, 30 January 2004.

Howell, Linda. Letter to Ray Baumler March 27, 1992.

Huber, John. Sonar Man 2nd Class *USS Cogswell DD 651.* Personal Diary. 1944-45.

Hudson, Hugh. RM 2/c LSM-49, LSM 467. Collected papers and Photographs.

International News Service Press Release 153.

Irwin, Curtis J. 333rd Fighter Squadron. Interview. 18 June 2001.

Katz, Lawrence S. *LCS(L) 61.* Diary, Interview. 25 August 1995.

Kaup, Harold. *LCS(L) 15.* Interview. 29 September 1996.

Kelley, James. W. Commanding Officer *LCS(L) 61.* Interview. 18 December 1995.

Kendall, Lee (Formerly Capt. Solie Solomon). USAAF 548th NFS. E-mails, 9, 10 December 2001.

Kennedy, Doyle. *USS Little.* Interview. 3 September 2003.

Landis, Robert W. SK/1c *LSM(R) 192.* Interview. 14 February 2002.

Larson, Wendell. Letter of 2 September 2003.

Logan, Stanley E. 1st Lieutenant 418th NFS. Letter of 24 March 2002.

McCool, Richard M. Capt. USN (Ret). CO *USS LCS(L) 122.* Interview 21 May 1997, Letter to the author with narrative of 23 May 1997.

Moulton, Franklin. *LCS(L) 25.* Collected papers and photographs.

Okazaki, Teruyuki. Interview. 6 September 2003.

Pederson, Marvin letter to the editor of LCS Assn. newsletter undated.

Peterson, Phillip E. *LCS(L) 23.* Collected papers and photographs.

Robinson, Ed. Letter to Lester O. Willard. 10 January 1991.

Rielly, Robert F. *LCS(L) 61.* Interview of 20 September 2001.

Rooney, John. *Sailor.* (Interview with Julian Becton, CO of *Laffey.*)

Russell, L. R. Lt. (jg) *LSM(R) 191.* Letters of 18 July, 22 July 2003.

Selfridge, Allen. *LCS(L) 67.* Collected papers and photographs.

Sellis, Mark. Executive Officer *LCS(L) 61.* Interview. 25 August 1995.

Spargo, Tom. *USS Cogswell DD 651.* E-mails to the author, 15 April, 21 May 2001.

Sprague, Robert. *LCS(L) 38.* Letter of 29 September 2002.

Staigar, Joseph. *LCS(L) 61.* Interview. 14 July, 1995.

Sweet, Donald H. VH-3 Interview. 29 June, 2002.

Tolmas, Harold. RM 2/c *LCS 54.* Letter of 5 December 2002.

Towner, Doug. 19th Fighter Squadron, 318th Fighter Group. E-mails of 4, 9 October 2002.

Tyldesley, Robert H. Col. USAF (Ret.) Interview. 12 March 2002.

Vaughan, Harry B. Lt. Col. USAF (Ret.) Formerly of 333/318 Letter of 26 August 2002.

Weisman, David B. Col.USAF (Ret.) Historian 548th Night Fighter Squadron. Letter of 22 February 2002, Interview. 12 January 2002.

West, Oscar Jr. Gunners Mate *U.S.S. Barber APD 57.* Letter to Thomas English dated 18 August 1992.

Williams, Durwood B. Col. USAF (Ret.), formerly of 333/318 e-mail of 11 August 2001.

Wiram, Gordon H. *LCS(L) 64* letter to Ray Baumler, 13 April 1991.

Wisner, Robert. *LCS 37* Interview 15 August 2001.

Official Histories

Carter, Kit C. and Robert Mueller. *The Army Air Forces in World War II Combat Chronology 1941-1945.* Washington, DC: U.S. Government Printing Office, 1974.

Committee on Veteran's Affairs, U.S. Senate, Medal of Honor Recipients: 1863-

1973. Washington, D.C.: Government Printing Office, 1973.

Craven, Wesley Frank and James Lea Cate, eds. U.S. Air Force, USAF Historical Division, *The Army Air Forces in World War II Vol. 5, The Pacific: Matterhorn to Nagasaki, June 1944 to August 1945*. Chicago, U of C Press, 1953.

Dictionary of American Naval Fighting Ships (Nine Volumes). Office of the Chief of Naval Operations. Naval History Division, Washington, DC, 1959-1991.

Dyer, George C. *The Amphibians Came to Conquer: The Story of Admiral Richmond Kelly Turner Vol. I & II*. Washington D.C.: Department of the Navy, 1969.

Frank, Benis M. and Henry I. Shaw, Jr. *Victory and Occupation History of U.S. Marine Corps Operations in World War II Vol. V*. Historical Branch, G-3 Division, Headquarters, U.S. Marine Corps. Washington: U.S. Government Printing Office, 1968.

General Staff, Supreme Commander for the Allied Powers. *Reports of General MacArthur. Japanese Operations in the Southwest Pacific Area Vol. II–Part II*. Facsimile Reprint, 1994.

- - -. *Reports of General MacArthur. MacArthur in Japan: The Occupation: Military Phase Volume I Supplement*. Facsimile Reprint, 1994.

- - -. *Reports of General MacArthur. The Campaigns of MacArthur in the Pacific Volume I*. Facsimile Reprint, 1994.

Handbook on Japanese Military Forces U.S. War Department. Baton Rouge: Louisiana State University Press, 1995.

King, Ernest J. *U.S. Navy at War 1941-1945*. Washington: United States Navy Department, 1946.

Kreis, John F. Gen. Ed. *Piercing the Fog Intelligence and Army Air Force Operations in World War II*. Air Force History and Museums Program, Bolling Air Force Basse. Washington, D.C., 1996.

Military History Section–General Headquarters Far East Command Military Intelligence Section General Staff. *Japanese Monograph No. 51 Air Operations on Iwo Jima and the Ryukyus*.

- - -. *Japanese Monograph No. 53 3rd Army Operations in Okinawa March-June, 1945. Army Defense Operations*.

- - -. *Japanese Monograph No. 86. War History of the 5th Air Fleet (The "Ten" Air Unit) Operational Record from 10 February 1946 to - 19 August 1945*.

- - -. *Japanese Monograph No. 135 Okinawa Operations Record*.

- - -. *Japanese Monograph No. 141 (Navy) "Okinawa Area Naval Operations" Supplement Statistics on Naval Air Strength*. August, 1949.

Mission Accomplished Interrogations of Japanese Industrial, Military, and Civil Leaders of World War II. Washington, D.C.: Government Printing Office, 1946.

Morison, Samuel Eliot. *History of United States Naval Operations in World War II. Volume VI Breaking the Bismarcks Barrier 22 July 1942–1 May 1944*. Boston: Little, Brown and Company, 1950.

- - -. *History of United States Naval Operations in World War II. Volume VII Aleutians, Gilberts and Marshalls June 1942–April 1944*. Boston: Little, Brown and Company, 1951.

- - -. *History of United States Naval Operations in World War II. Volume VIII New Guinea and the Marianas March 1944–August 1944*. Boston: Little, Brown and Company, 1984.

- - -. *History of United States Naval Operations in World War II. Volume XII Leyte June 1944–January 1945*. Boston: Little, Brown and Company, 1958.

- - -. *History of United States Naval Operations in World War II. Volume XIII The Liberation of the Philippines Luzon, Mindanao, the Visayas 1944–1945*. Boston: Little, Brown and Company, 1968.

- - -. *History of United States Naval Operations in World War II. Volume XIV Victory in the Pacific 1945*. Boston: Little, Brown and Company, 1968.

Navy Department Communiques 601-624 May 25, 1945 to August 30, 1945 and Pacific Fleet Communiques 373 to 471. Washington: United States Government Printing Office, 1946.

Timenes, Nicolai. *An Analytical History of Kamikaze Attacks against Ships of the United States Navy During World War II*. Arlington, VA: Center for Naval Analyses, Operations Evaluation Group, 1970.

The United States Strategic Bombing Survey Naval Analysis Division. Washington, D.C.: U.S. Government Printing Office.

Air Campaigns of the Pacific War. 1947.

The Campaigns of the Pacific War. 1946.

The Fifth Air Force in the War Against Japan. 1947.

Interrogations of Japanese Officials Volume I. 1945.

Interrogations of Japanese Officials Volume II. 1945.

Japanese Air Power. 1946.

The Seventh and Eleventh Air Forces in the War Against Japan. 1947.

Summary Report (Pacific War). 1946.

SECONDARY SOURCES

Books

Abrams, Richard. *F4U Corsair at War*. New York: Charles Scribner's Son's, undated.

Adams, Andrew. Ed. *The Cherry Blossom Squadrons: Born to Die*. By the Hagoromo Society of Kamikaze Divine Thunderbolt Corps Survivors. Intro. by Andrew Adams. Edited and supplemented by Andrew Adams. Translation by Nobuo Asahi and the Japan Technical Company. Los Angles: Ohara Publications, 1973.

Astor, Gerald. *Operation Iceberg The Invasion and Conquest of Okinawa in World War II*. New York: Donald I. Fine, Inc., 1995.

Axell, Albert and Hideaki Kase. *Kamikaze Japan's Suicide Gods*. London: Pearson Education, 2002.

Baker, A.D. III. *Allied Landing Craft of World War Two*. Annapolis: Naval Institute Press, 1985.

Ball, Donald L. *Fighting Amphibs The LCS(L) in World War II*. Williamsburg, VA: Mill Neck Publications, 1997.

Becton, F. Julian. *The Ship That Would Not Die*. Missoula, Montana: Pictorial Histories Publishing Company, 1980.

Bergerud, Eric M. *Fire in the Sky The Air War in the South Pacific*. Boulder, CO: Westview Press, 2000.

Billingsley, Edward Baxter Rear Admiral USN (Ret.) *The Emmons Saga*. Winston-Salem, NC: USS Emmons Association, 1989.

Bunce, William K. *Religions in Japan Buddhism, Shinto, Christianity*. Tokyo: Charles E. Tuttle Company, 1955.

Calhoun, C. Raymond. *Tin Can Sailor Life Aboard the USS Sterett, 1939-1945*. Annapolis: United States Naval Institute, 1993.

Condon, John Pomeroy. *Corsairs and Flattops*. Annapolis: Naval Institute Press, 1998.

Cook, Haruko Taya and Theodore F. Cook. *Japan at War An Oral History*. New York: The New Press, 1992.

Costello, John. *The Pacific War 1941-1945*. New York: Atlantic Communications, Inc., 1981.

Craig, William. *The Fall of Japan*. New York: The Dial Press, 1967.

Bruce, Roy W. and Charles R. Leonard. *Crommelin's Thunderbirds Air Group 12 Strikes the Heart of Japan*. Annapolis: Naval Institute Press, 1994.

DeChant, John A. *Devilbirds The Story of United States Marine Corps Aviation in World War II*. New York: Harper & Brothers Publishers, 1947.

Doll, Thomas E., Berkley R. Jackson and William A. Riley. *Navy Air Colors United States Navy, Marine Corps, and Coast Guard Aircraft Camouflage and Markings Vol. 1 1911-1945*. Carrolton, TX: Squadron/Signal Publications, 1983.

Drea, Edward J. *In the Service of the Emperor: Essays on the Imperial Japanese Army*. Lincoln: University of Nebraska Press, 2003.

- - -*MacArthur's Ultra Codebreaking and the War Against Japan, 1942-1945*. Lawrence, Kansas: University Press of Kansas, 1992.

Dresser, James. *Escort Carriers and Their Air Unit Markings During W.W. II in the Pacific*. Ames, Iowa: James Dresser, 1980.

Edgerton, Robert B. *Warriors of the Rising Sun A History of the Japanese Military*. New York: W.W. Norton & Company, 1997.

Erickson, Roy D. Lt. (jg). *Tail End Charlies I Navy Combat Fighter Pilots at War's End*. Paducah, KY: Turner Publishing Company, 1995.

Fahey, James C. *The Ships and Aircraft of the United States Fleet Victory Edition*. Annapolis: Naval Institute Press, 1977.

Fairbank, John K., Edwin O. Reischauer and Albert M. Craig. *East Asia The Modern Transformation*. Boston: Houghton Mifflin Company, 1965.

Foster, Simon. *Okinawa 1945 Final Assault on the Empire*. London: Arms and Armour Press, 1994.

Francillon, Rene J. *Japanese Aircraft of the Pacific War*. Annapolis: Naval Institute Press, 1979.

Frank, Benis M. *Okinawa: The Great Island Battle*. New York: Talisman/Parrish Books, Inc., 1978.

Frank, Richard B. *Downfall The End of the Imperial Japanese Empire*. New York: Penguin Books, 2001.

Gibney, Frank B. ed. *The Japanese Remember the Pacific War*. Armonk, New

York: An Eastgate Book, 1995.

Griffith, Thomas E. Jr. *MacArthur's Airman: General George C. Kenney and the War in the Southwest Pacific.* Lawrence, Kansas: University of Kansas, 1998.

Halsey, William F. Fleet Admiral and Lieutenant Commander J. Bryan III. *Admiral Halsey's Story.* New York: McGraw-Hill Book Company, Inc., 1947.

Hammel, Eric. *Aces Against Japan The American Aces Speak. Volume I.* Pacifica, CA: Pacifica Press, 1992.

Hammel, Eric. *Aces Against Japan II. The American Aces Speak. Volume III.* Pacifica, CA: Pacifica Press, 1996.

Harries, Meirion and Susie Meirion. *Sheathing the Sword The Demilitarisation of Japan.* New York: Macmillan Publishing Company, 1987.

Hata, Ikuhiko and Yasuho Izawa. *Japanese Naval Aces and Fighter Units in World War II.* Trans. By Don Cyril Gorham. Annapolis: Naval Institute Press, 1989.

Hata, Ikuhiko, Yasuho Izawa and Christopher Shores. *Japanese Army Air Force Fighter Units and Their Aces 1931-1945.* London: Grub Street, 2002.

Haughland, Vern. *The AAF against Japan.* New York: Harper & Brothers Publishers, 1948.

Havens, Thomas R. H. *Nishi Amane and Modern Japanese Thought.* Princeton: Princeton University Press, 1970.

Hickey, Lawrence J. *Warpath Across the Pacific. Eagles Over the Pacific Vol. 1.* Boulder, Colorado: International Research and Publishing Corporation, 1996.

Horiyoshi, Jiro. *Eagles of Mitsubishi The Story of the Zero Fighter.* Trans. by Shojiro Shindo and Harold N. Wantiez. Seattle: University of Washington Press, 1981.

Hoyt, Edwin P. *The Kamikazes.* New York: Arbor House, 1983.

- - -*The Last Kamikaze The Story of Admiral Matome Ugaki.* Westport, Ct.: Praeger, 1993.

Hurst, Cameron G. III. *Armed Martial Arts of Japan.* New Haven: Yale University Press, 1998.

Hynes, Samuel. *Flights of Passage: Reflections of a World War II Aviator.* Annapolis: Naval Institute Press, 1988.

Ienaga, Saburo. *The Pacific War, 1931-1945 A Critical Perspective on Japan's Role in World War II.* New York: Pantheon Books, 1978.

Ike, Nobutaka. "War and Modernization," in *Political Development in Modern Japan.* Robert E. Ward, ed. Princeton: Princeton University Press, 1968. pp. 189-211.

Inoguchi, Rikihei. *The Divine Wind: Japan's Kamikaze Force in World War II.* New York: Bantam Books, 1958.

Iritani, Toshio. *Group Psychology of the Japanese in Wartime.* New York: Kegan Paul International, 1991.

The Japanese Air Forces in World War II: The Organization of the Japanese Army & Naval Air Forces, 1945. New York: Hippocrene Books, Inc., 1979.

Kaigo, Tokiomi. *Japanese Education; Its Past and Present.* Tokyo: Kokusai

Bunka Shinkokai, 1968.

Keenleyside, Hugh L. *History of Japanese Education and Present Educational System*. Ann Arbor: Michigan University Press, 1970.

Knight, Rex A. *Riding on Luck: The Saga of the USS Lang (DD-399)*. Central Point, OR: Hellgate Press, 2001.

Kuwahara, Yasuo and Gordon T. Allred. *Kamikaze*. New York: Ballantine Books, 1957.

Larteguy, Jean. Ed. *The Sun Goes Down Last Letters from Japanese Suicide-Pilots and Soldiers*. London: William Kimber, 1956.

Logan, Stanley E. and David O. and Millie Sullivan, Eds. *History of the 418th Night Fighter Squadron: from New Guinea to Japan in World War II*. Santa Fe: S.E. Logan Books, 2001.

Lorelli, John. *To Foreign Shores U. S. Amphibious Operations in World War II*. Annapolis: Naval Institute Press, 1995.

Lory, Hillis. *Japan's Military Masters The Army in Japanese Life*. New York: The Viking Press, 1943.

Mason, William. *U.S.S. LCS(L)(3) 86 "The Mighty Midget."* San Francisco: By the author, 1993.

McBride, William M. ed. *Good Night Officially The Pacific War Letters of a Destroyer Sailor The Letters of Yeoman James Orvill Raines*. Boulder, CO: Westview Press, Inc., 1994.

Mersky, Peter. *The Grim Reapers Fighting Squadron Ten in WW II*. Mesa, AZ: Champlin Museum Press, 1986.

Mikesh, Robert C. *Broken Wings of the Samurai The Destruction of the Japanese Airforce*. Annapolis: Naval Institute Press, 1993.

Millot, Bernard. *Divine Thunder The Life & Death of the Kamikazes*. Trans. By Lowell Bair. New York: The McCall Publishing Company, 1971.

Monsarrat, John. *Angel on the Yardarm: The Beginnings of Fleet Radar Defense and the Kamikaze Threat*. Newport, RI: Naval War College Press, 1985.

Morison, Samuel Loring. *United States Naval Vessels*. Atglen, PA: Schiffer Military History, 1996.

Morris, John. *Traveller from Tokyo*. London: The Book Club, 1945.

Morse, Philip M. and George E. Kimball. *Methods of Operations Research*. First Edition Revised. Cambridge, MA: The M.I.T. Press, 1970.

Moskin, J. Robert. *The U.S. Marine Corps Story*. New York: McGraw-Hill Book Company, 1982.

Nagatsuka, Ryuji. *I was a Kamikaze: The Knights of the Divine Wind*. Trans. From the French by Nina Rootes. New York: Macmillan Publishing Co., Inc. 1973.

Naito, Hatsusho. *Thunder Gods The Kamikaze Pilots Tell Their Story*. Tokyo: Kodansha International, 1989.

Nihon Senbotsu Gakusei Kinen-Kai (Japan Memorial Society for the Students Killed in the War-Wadatsumi Society). *Listen to the Voices from the Sea (Kike Wadatsumi no Koe)*. Trans. By Midori Yamanouchi and Joseph L. Quinn. Scranton: The University of Scranton Press, 2000.

Nitobe, Inazo. *Bushido: The Soul of Japan*. Tokyo: Charles E. Tuttle Company, 1969.

Norman, E. Herbert. *Soldier and Peasant in Japan The Origins of Conscription.* Vancouver: University of British Columbia, 1965.

Ohnuki-Tierney, Emiko. *Kamikaze, Cherry Blossoms, and Nationalisms: The Militarization of Aesthetics in Japanese History.* Chicago: University of Chicago Press, 2002.

- - -*Kamikaze Diaries Reflections of Japanese Student Soldiers.* Chicago: University of Chicago Press, 2006.

Okumiya, Masatake, Jiro Horikoshi with Martin Caidin. *Zero! The Air War in the Pacific During World War II from The Japanese Viewpoint.* Washington, D.C.: Zenger Publishing Co., Inc., 1956.

Peattie, Mark R. *Ishiwara Kanji and Japan's Confrontation with the West.* Princeton: Princeton University Press, 1975.

Porter, R. Bruce, Colonel with Eric Hammel. *Ace! A Marine Night-Fighter Pilot in World War II.* Pacifica, CA: Pacifica Press, 1985.

Prados, John. *Combined Fleet Decoded The Secret History of American Intelligence and the Japanese Navy in World War II.* Annapolis: Naval Institute Press, 1995.

Pyle, Kenneth B. *The Making of Modern Japan.* Lexington, Massachusetts, D.C. Heath and Company, 1978.

Rearden, Jim. *Cracking the Zero Mystery.* Harrisburg, PA: Stackpole Books, 1990.

Rielly, Robin L. *Mighty Midgets at War: The Saga of the LCS(L) Ships from Iwo Jima to Vietnam.* Central Point, OR: Hellgate Press, 2000.

Rogers, David H., Alvin L. Sigler and Charley F. Wilcox, eds. *494th Bombardment Group (H) History WWII.* Annandale, MN: 494th Bombardment Group (H) Association, Inc., 1996.

Rooney, John. *Mighty Midget U.S.S. LCS 82.* PA: By the author, 1990.

Roscoe, Theodore. *United States Destroyer Operations in WWII.* Annapolis: Naval Institute Press, 1953.

Rottman, Gordon L. *U.S. Marine Corps World War II Order of Battle.* Westport, CT: Greenwood Press, 2002.

Rutter, Joseph W. *Wreaking Havoc: A Year in an A-20.* College Station, Texas: Texas A & M University, 2004.

Sakae, Shioya. *Chushingura An Exposition.* Tokyo: The Hokuseido Press, 1949.

Sakai, Saburo with Martin Caidin and Fred Saito. *Samurai!* New York: ibooks, Inc. 2001.

Sakaida, Henry and Koji Tanaka. *Genda's Blade Japan's Squadron of Aces 343 Kokutai.* Surrey, England: Classic Publications, 2003.

Sakaida, Henry. *Imperial Japanese Army Air Force Aces 1937-45.* Oxford: Osprey Publishing Limited, 1997.

- - -. *Imperial Japanese Navy Aces 1937-45.* Oxford: Osprey Publishing Limited, 1999.

Sherrod, Robert. *History of Marine Corps Aviation in World War II.* Washington: Combat Forces Press, 1952.

Sims, Edward H. *Greatest Fighter Missions of the Top Navy and Marine Aces of World War II.* New York: Harper & Brothers, 1962.

Smethurst, Richard J. *A Social Basis for Prewar Japanese Militarism The*

Army and the Rural Community. Berkeley: The University of California Press, 1974.

Stanley, W.H. *Kamikaze The Battle for Okinawa Big War of the Little Ships*. By the author, 1988.

Staton, Michael. *The Fighting Bob: A Wartime History of the USS Robley D. Evans (DD-552)*. Bennington, VT: Merriam Press, 2001.

Stone, Robert P. *USS LCS(L)(3) 20 A Mighty Midget*. By the author, 2002.

Styling, Mark. *Corsair Aces of World War 2*. Oxford: Osprey Publishing, 1995.

Sumrall, Robert F. *Sumner-Gearing Class Destroyers Their Design, Weapons, and Equipment*. Annapolis: Naval Institute Press, 1995.

Surels, Ron. *DD 522: Diary of a Destroyer*. Plymouth, NH: Valley Graphics, Inc., 1996.

Sweet, Donald H. with Lee Roy Way and William Bonvillian, Jr. *The Forgotten Heroes*. Ridgewood, NJ: DoGo Publishing, 2000.

Tagaya, Osamu. *Imperial Japanese Naval Aviator 1937-45*. Oxford: Osprey Publishing, 1988.

   Mitsubishi Type 1 Rikko: Betty' Units of World War 2. Oxford: Osprey Publishing, 2001.

Thomas, Charles. *Dolly Five: A Memoir of the Pacific War*. Chester, VA: Harrowgate Press, 1996.

Thompson, Warren. *P-61 Black Widow Units of World War 2*. Oxford: Osprey Publishing Ltd., 1998.

Thorpe, Donald W. *Japanese Army Air Force Camouflage and Markings World War II*. Fallbrook, CA: Aero Publishers, Inc., 1968.

- - -. *Japanese Naval Air Force Camouflage and Markings World War II*. Fallbrook, CA: Aero Publishers, Inc., 1977.

Tillman, Barrett. *Hellcat Aces of World War 2*. Oxford: Osprey Publishing, 1996.

- - -. *Hellcat: The F6F in World War II*. Annapolis: Naval Institute Press, 1979.

- - -. *U.S. Navy Fighter Squadrons in World War II*. North Branch, MN: Speciality Press Publishers and Wholesalers, 1997.

- - -. *Wildcat: The F4F in WW II*. Annapolis: Naval Institute Press, 1990.

Toliver, Raymond F. & Trevor J. Constable. *Fighter Aces of the U.S.A.* Atglen, PA: Schiffer Military History, 1997.

Ugaki, Matome, Vice Admiral. *Fading Victory The Diary of Admiral Matome Ugaki 1941-1945*. Chihaya, Masataka, Translator. Pittsburgh: University of Pittsburgh Press, 1991.

Vernon, James W. *The Hostile Sky A Hellcat Flier in World War II*. Annapolis: Naval Institute Press, 2003.

Veigele, William J. *PC Patrol Craft of World War II*. Santa Barbara, CA: Astral Publishing Co., 1998.

Warner, Denis and Peggy Warner with Commander Sadao Seno. *The Sacred Warriors Japan's Suicide Legions*. New York: Van Nostrand Reinhold Company, 1982.

Wilson, William Scott, translator. *Budoshoshinshu The Warrior's Primer of Daidoji Yuzan*. Burbank, California: Ohara Publications, Inc., 1984.

- - -. *The Ideals of the Samurai Writings of Japanese Warriors*. Burbank,

California: Ohara Publications, Inc., 1982.

Winton, John. *Ultra in the Pacific: How Breaking Japanese Codes & Cyphers Affected Naval Operations Against Japan 1941-45.* Annapolis: Naval Institute Press, 1993.

Wolf, William. *Death Rattlers Marine Squadron VMF-323 over Okinawa.* Atglen, PA: Schiffer Military History, 1999.

Yamamoto, Tsunetomo. *Hagakure The Book of the Samurai.* Translated by William Scott Wilson. Tokyo: Kodansha International Ltd., 1979.

Y'Blood, William T. *The Little Giants U.S. Escort Carriers Against Japan.* Annapolis: U.S. Naval Institute Press, 1987.

Yoshimura, Akira. *Zero Fighter.* Trans. By Retsu Kaiho and Michael Gregson. Westport, CT: Praeger Publishers, 1996.

Articles

Andrews, Harold. "F4U Corsair." *Naval Aviation News.* May-June, 1986: 28-29.

- - -. "F6F Hellcat." *Naval Aviation News.* September-October 1988: 16-17.

Coox, Alvin D. "The Rise and Fall of the Imperial Japanese Air Forces." *Air Power and Warfare Proceedings of the Eighth History Symposium USAF Academy 1978*: 84-97.

Dore, R. P. "Education–Japan." In *Political Modernization in Japan and Turkey,* edited by Robert E. Ward, and Dankwart A. Rustow, 176-204. Princeton: Princeton University Press, 1964.

Friedman, Norman. "Amphibious Fire Support" *Warship Vol. IV.* London: Conway Maritime Press, 1980: 199-205.

Guyton, Boone T. "Riding a Thoroughbred A Test Pilot's View of the Corsair." *The Hook.* Volume 28 Number 4 Winter 2000: 23-30.

Hackett, Roger F. "The Military–Japan." In *Political Modernization in Japan and Turkey,* edited by Robert E. Ward, and Dankwart A. Rustow, 328-351. Princeton: Princeton University Press, 1964.

Hattori, Shogo. "Kamikaze Japan's Glorious Failure." *Air Power History.* Spring 1996, Volume 43 Number 1: 14-27.

Henry, John R. "Out Stares Jap Pilot After Ammo Runs Out." *Honolulu Advertiser.* April 27, 1945.

Ike, Nobutaka. "War and Modernization." In *Political Development in Modern Japan,* edited by Robert E. Ward, 189-211. Princeton: Princeton University Press, 1968.

Inoguchi, Rikihei, Captain and Commander Tadashi Nakajima. "The Kamikaze Attack Corps." in *United States Naval Institute Proceedings.* Annapolis, MD: United States Naval Institute, September, 1953: 993-945.

Kawai, Masahiro Lieutenant Colonel. *The Operations of the Suicide-Boat Regiment in Okinawa Their Battle Result and the Countermeasures Taken by the U. S. Forces.* National Institute for Defense Studies. (Undated)

Kendall, Major Lee (ex Solie Solomon). "The Final Kill WW II's last victory as told by the P-61 pilot who made it." *Pacific Fighters Air Combat Stories.* Winter 2003: 90-96.

Martin, Paul W. "Kamikaze!" *United States Naval Institute Proceedings.*

Annapolis: United States Naval Institute, August, 1946: 1055-1057.

Mersky, Peter B. Cdr. USN (Ret.). "The Kamikazes: Japanese Suicide Units." *Naval Aviation News*, July-August 1994: 30-35.

Nagai, Michio. "Westernization and Japanization: The Early Meiji Transformation of Education." In *Tradition and Modernization in Japanese Culture*, edited by Donald H. Shively, 35-76. Princeton: Princeton University Press, 1971.

Rooney, John. "Sailor" *Naval Institute Proceedings* (Unpublished Article). Rooney's interview of Rear Admiral F. Julian Becton, conducted in Wynewood, PA, Fall 1992.

Scott, J. Davis. "No Hiding Place–Off Okinawa," *US Naval Institute Proceedings*, Nov. 1957: 208-13.

Suzuki, Yukihisa. "Autobiography of a Kamikaze Pilot." *Blue Book Magazine,* Vol. 94, No. 2 December, 1951: 92-107, Vol. 93, No. 3 January, 1952: 88-100. Vol. 93, No. 4 February, 1952.

Trefalt, Beatrice. "War, commemoration and national identity in modern Japan, 1868-1975." in *Nation and Nationalism in Japan*, edited by Sandra Wilson, 115-134. London: RoutledgeCurzon, 2002.

Turner, Admiral Richmond K. "Kamikaze." *United States Naval Institute Proceedings*. Annapolis: United States Naval Institute, March, 1947: 329-331.

Vogel, Bertram. "Who Were the Kamikaze?" *United States Naval Institute Proceedings*. Annapolis: United States Naval Institute, July, 1947: 833-837.

Wehrmeister, R.L. Lt (J.G.). "Divine Wind Over Okinawa." *United States Naval Institute Proceedings*. Annapolis: United States Naval Institute, June, 1957: 632-641.

Yokoi, Rear Admiral Toshiyuki. "Kamikazes and the Okinawa Campaign." *United States Naval Institute Proceedings*. Annapolis: United States Naval Institute, May, 1954: 504-513.

Web Sites

Haze Gray and Underway: http://www.hazegray.org

National Association of Fleet Tug Sailors: http://www.nafts.com

NavSource: http://www.NavSource.org

Tin Can Sailors: http://www.destroyers.org

USS Aaron Ward DM 34: http://www.ussaaronward.com/

USS Alfred A. Cunningham DD 752:
http://home.infini.net/~eeg3413/index.htm

USS Arikara ATF: http://ussarikara.com

USS Boyd DD 544:
http://www.destroyers.org/DD544-Site/DD544.htm

USS Braine DD 630:
http://www.ussbrainedd630.com/witnes.htm

USS Bush DD: http://www.ussbush.com

USS Callaghan DD 792:
http://www.destroyers.org/DD792-Site/index.htm

USS Cogswell DD 651: USS-Cogswell@destroyers.org

USS Evans DD 552:
  http://www.ussevans.org
USS Little DD 803:
  http://skyways.lib.ks.us/history.dd803/info/picket.html
USS Macomb DMS 23:
  http://www.destroyers.org/bensonlivermore/ussmacomb.html
USS Purdy DD 734: http://www.destroyers.org/uss-purdy/

Photo Sources

Kyodo News Agency, New York Branch
National Archives and Records Administration
        RG 19 Records of the Bureau of Ships RG 19 Series Z
        RG 80G General Records of the Department of the Navy 1941-1945
        RG 111-SC Records of the Army Signal Corps 1941-1945
        RG 127 MC Records of the US Marine Corps
        United States Information Agency–New York Times Paris Bureau
        Collection
Navy Historical Center
Tailhook Association
United States Naval Institute

Index